PRAISE FOR *DEVIL'S KNOT*

"*Devil's Knot* becomes the best horror novel you've ever read, one of those that leaves you wondering what new sick dread might be lying in wait on the next page. . . . The monster Leveritt reveals in the end, however, is more terrifying than even the fork-tailed bogeymen conjured by West Memphis police and prosecutors to fit their crime. What Leveritt reveals to us is the most horrible fiend a rational person can imagine when matters of life and death are at stake: the Specter of Doubt."

—*Arkansas Times*

"An affecting account of a controversial trial. . . . Leveritt's carefully researched book offers a riveting portrait of a down-at-the-heels, socially conservative rural town with more than its share of corruption and violence."

—*Publishers Weekly*

"Well written in descriptive language, [*Devil's Knot*] is an indictment of a culture and legal system that failed to protect children as defendants or victims. Highly recommended."

—*Library Journal*

"The chronology [of *Devil's Knot*] is the first time all elements of the case have been assembled in one narrative, which offers surprises, even for those familiar with the events. As such, it is a true public service."

—*Arkansas Democrat Gazette*

ALSO BY MARA LEVERITT

The Boys on the Tracks

DEVIL'S KNOT

THE TRUE STORY OF
THE WEST MEMPHIS THREE

MARA LEVERITT

ATRIA BOOKS

NEW YORK LONDON TORONTO SYDNEY SINGAPORE

ATRIA BOOKS

1230 Avenue of the Americas
New York, NY 10020

ISBN: 0-7434-1759-3
      0-7434-1760-7 (Pbk)

First Atria Books trade paperback edition October 2003

10   9   8   7   6   5   4   3   2   1

ATRIA BOOKS is a trademark of Simon & Schuster, Inc.

Manufactured in the United States of America

For information regarding special discounts for bulk purchases,
please contact Simon & Schuster Special Sales at 1-800-456-6798
or business@simonandschuster.com.

To LSB,
with love and gratitude

ACKNOWLEDGMENTS

I thank my beloved family; my many generous friends; the filmmakers, musicians, and other artists who have recognized this story's importance; the reporters whose accounts have contributed to this book; the public officials who provided information and access to records; the lawyers who explained aspects of the case; and everyone who granted me interviews. I thank, in particular, Sandra Dijkstra, Wendy Walker, Tracy Behar, Judith Curr, Ron Lax, Dan Stidham, Burk Sauls, Grove Pashley, Kathy Bakken, Stan Mitchell—and, of course, the inmates whose story this is.

AUTHOR'S NOTE

Many of the figures in this book were juveniles when the key events took place. Others were on the cusp of adulthood. One or two had recently reached their majority. It is customary in reporting events involving children to refer to them by their first names. I have tried, in general, to do this. The ages of two of the accused, as well as many of the witnesses, were factors in the events related here. I felt that it would distort the story to refer to the children in it as though they were adults, though most were treated as adults by the legal system.

Three teenagers figure at the center of this book. Although one of them had recently observed his eighteenth birthday at the time this book begins, I opted to refer to all three consistently by their first names.

Because of the attention this case has received—and the further scrutiny I believe it deserves—I have written it on two levels. The text tells the story. The endnotes deepen it.

Occult. 1. Hidden (from sight); concealed (by something interposed); not exposed to view. 2. Not disclosed or divulged, privy, secret; kept secret; communicated only to the initiated. 3. Not apprehended, or not apprehensible, by the mind; beyond the range of understanding or of ordinary knowledge; recondite, mysterious. 4. Of the nature of or pertaining to those ancient and medieval reputed sciences (or their modern representatives) held to involve the knowledge or use of agencies of a secret and mysterious nature (as magic, alchemy, astrology, theosophy, and the like); also treating of or versed in these; magical, mystical.

Oxford English Dictionary

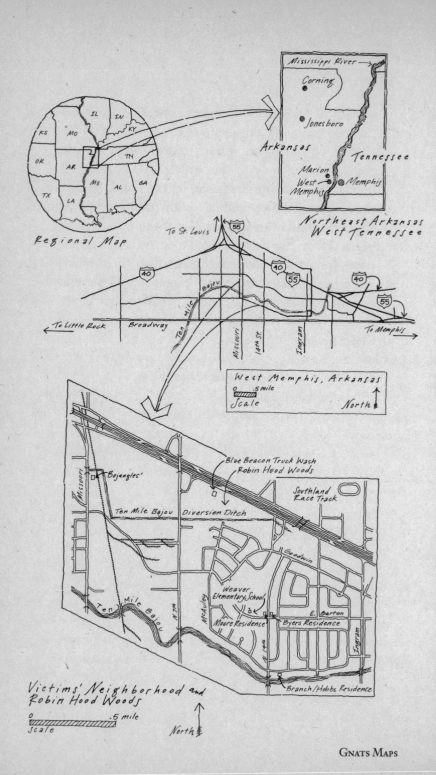

Regional Map

Northeast Arkansas
West Tennessee

West Memphis, Arkansas
0   .5 mile
Scale   North

Victims' Neighborhood and
Robin Hood Woods
0   .5 mile
scale   North

GNATS MAPS

PROLOGUE

WERE THE WEST MEMPHIS trials witch trials?

Had a jury sentenced someone to death based on nothing more than children's accusations, confessions made under pressure, and prosecutors' arguments linking the defendants to Satan?

Were the 1994 trials in Arkansas like those in Salem three centuries ago?

These were the questions that gave rise to this book. These, and a couple more:

If talk of demons had diverted reason, *how* had things gone so awry—in the United States of America, at the end of the twentieth century—before not just one jury but two, in trials where lives were at stake? And if something so terrible had happened, *why?*

Modern readers might think it impossible that prosecutors in a murder case, facing a dearth of factual evidence, would build their argument for execution on claims that the accused had links to "the occult." Educated readers might recoil from the idea that prosecutors would cite a defendant's tastes in literature, music, and clothing to support such an archaic theory. Even fans of lurid fiction might find it a stretch to believe that a prosecutor in this day and age would point to a defendant and say, "There's not a soul in there."

Yet in the spring of 1994, that is what *seemed* to have happened. A teenager was sentenced to death. His two younger codefendants were dispatched to prison for life.

Impossible.

And yet the police insisted that their case was strong. The judge who presided at the trials said that they had been fair. And in two separate opinions, the justices on the Arkansas Supreme Court agreed. Unanimously.

Outside the state, however, news of the unusual trials began to attract attention. A documentary released in 1996 raised widespread concern. A Web site was dedicated to the case, and its founders unfurled the phrase "Free the West Memphis Three."

Arkansas officials dug in. As criticism mounted, police and state officials insisted that the film had been misleading. They pointed out that twenty-four jurors had sat through the trials, had heard and seen all the evidence, and had found the teenagers guilty. They said that anyone who bothered to examine what "really" had happened in the case, rather than form opinions based on movies and a Web site, would conclude, as had the jurors, that justice had been served.

As an Arkansas reporter focusing on crime and the courts, I began to see this as a historic case. The dispute needed to be resolved. Either the out-of-state critics were wrong, in which case the "Free the West Memphis Three" crowd could all get on with their lives, or something similar to what happened at Salem had indeed occurred again—during my lifetime and in my own state.

I decided to take my state's officials up on their challenge. I would look at what "really" had happened. I would interview participants, read thousands of pages of transcripts, touch every piece of evidence in storage, and report faithfully on what I found, regardless of whom it supported. And if what I found in West Memphis resembled what had happened in Salem, I was prepared to look further. We assume that secularism, as well as advances in science and law, distances us from colonial America. If it appeared, as critics of the West Memphis case charged, that presumably rational processes had given way to satanic allusions, it was fair to ask both *how* and *why* such a thing had happened.

PART ONE

The Investigation

CHAPTER ONE

The Murders

AT 7:41 P.M. ON MAY 5, 1993, a full moon rose behind the Memphis skyline. Its light glinted across the Mississippi River and fell onto the midsized Arkansas town aspiringly named West Memphis. Sometime between the rising of that moon and its setting the next morning, something diabolical would happen in West Memphis. Three eight-year-old boys would vanish, plucked off the streets of their neighborhood by an unseen, murderous hand. Under the glare of the next day's sun, police would discover three young bodies. They would be pulled—naked, pale, bound, and beaten—from a watery ditch in a patch of woods alongside two of America's busiest highways. But the investigation would unfold in shadow. Why had one of the boys been castrated? How to account for the absence of blood? Why did the banks of the stream look swept clean? The police would stumble for weeks without clues—until the moon itself became one.

John Mark Byers, an unemployed jeweler, was the first parent to report a child missing.[1] At 8 P.M., with the full moon on the rise, Byers telephoned the West Memphis police. Ten minutes later, a patrol officer responded.[2] She drove her cruiser down East Barton Street, in a working-class neighborhood. At the corner where Barton intersected Fourteenth Street, the officer stopped in front of the Byerses' three-bedroom house. Byers, an imposing man, six feet five inches tall, weighing more than two hundred pounds, with long hair tied back in a ponytail, met her at the door. Behind him stood his wife, Melissa, five feet six, somewhat heavyset, with long hair and hollow eyes. Mark Byers did most of the talking. The officer listened and took notes. "The last time the victim was seen, he was cleaning the yard at 5:30 P.M." That would have been an hour and twenty minutes before sunset. The Byerses described Christopher as four feet four inches tall, weighing fifty pounds, with hair and eyes that were both light brown. He was eight years old.

The officer left the Byerses' house, and within minutes was dispatched to another call, at a chicken restaurant about a mile away. She pulled up at the Bojangles drive-through at 8:42 P.M. Through the window, the manager reported that a bleeding black man had entered the restaurant about a half hour before and gone into the women's rest room.[3] The manager told the officer that the man, who had blood on his face and who had seemed "mentally disoriented," had wandered away from the premises just a few minutes before she arrived. When employees entered the rest room after he left, they found blood smeared on the walls. The officer took the report but investigated the incident no further. At 9:01, without ever having entered the restaurant, she drove away to a criminal mischief complaint about someone throwing eggs at a house.

At 9:24 P.M., the same officer responded to another call, again from Barton Street—this one from the house directly across from the Byerses'. Here a woman, Dana Moore, reported that her eight-year-old son, Michael, was also missing.[4] Taking out her pad again, the officer wrote, "Complainant stated she observed the victim (her son) riding bicycles with his friends Stevie Branch and Christopher Byers. When she lost sight of the boys, she sent her daughter to find them. The boys could not be found." Moore said the boys had been riding on North Fourteenth Street, going toward Goodwin. That had been almost three and a half hours earlier, at about 6 P.M. By now, it had been dark for more than two hours. "Michael is described as four feet tall, sixty pounds, with brown hair and blue eyes," the officer wrote. "He was last seen wearing blue pants, blue Boy Scouts of America shirt, orange and blue Boy Scout hat and tennis shoes."

By now a second officer had been dispatched to a catfish restaurant several blocks away. There another mother, Pamela Hobbs, was reporting that her eight-year-old son, Stevie Edward Branch, was missing as well. Hobbs lived at Sixteenth Street and McAuley Drive, a few blocks away from the Byerses and the Moores. She reported that her son, Stevie, had left home after school and that no one had seen him since. The officer who took Hobbs's report did not note who was supposed to have been watching Stevie while his mother was at work, or who had notified Hobbs that her son was missing. Stevie was described as four feet two inches tall, sixty pounds, with blond hair and blue eyes. The police report noted, "He was last seen wearing blue jeans and white T-shirt. He was riding a twenty-inch Renegade bicycle."

Word of the disappearances spread quickly through the subdivision. As groups of parents began searching, other residents reported that they had seen some boys—three, or maybe four—riding bikes near the dead end of McAuley Drive shortly before sunset. McAuley was a major street in the neighborhood. The house on McAuley where Stevie Branch lived was a few blocks south of the corner on Barton where the other two missing boys lived across the street from each other. From Stevie's house, McAuley wound west for a few blocks, ending at the edge of a four-acre patch of woods, a short distance northwest of the other boys' homes. The woods separated the subdivision from two interstate highways and their service roads on the north. The small sylvan space provided the neighborhood with a welcome buffer from the traffic on their northern edge. For a few diesel-fumed miles, east-west Interstate 40, spanning the United States between North Carolina and California, converges in West Memphis, Arkansas, with north-south I-55, connecting New Orleans to Chicago. For truckers and other travelers, the stretch is a major midcontinental rest stop; where the highways hum through West Memphis, the city has formed a corridor of fueling stations, motels, and restaurants. It was easy for anyone passing through not to notice the small patch of woods bordering that short section of highway. What was more noticeable was the big blue-and-yellow sign for the Blue Beacon Truck Wash that stood several yards from the edge of the woods, alongside the service road.

Just as truckers knew the Blue Beacon, kids in the neighborhood to the south were familiar with the woods. The small plot of trees represented park, playground, and wilderness for children and teenagers living in the subdivision's modest three-bedroom houses and in the still more modest apartment building nearby.[5] That the woods existed at all was an acknowledgment, not of the need for parks or of places for children to play, but of the need for flood control. Years earlier the city had dredged a channel, unromantically known as the Ten Mile Bayou Diversion Ditch, to dispose of rainwater that ordinarily would have flowed into the Mississippi River but that was prevented from draining by the great levees that held back the river. While the levees kept the Mississippi at bay, rainwater trapped on the city side of the levee had posed a different flood problem for years. The Ten Mile Bayou Diversion Ditch was dredged to direct rainwater around the city to a point far to the south, where a break in the Mississippi levee finally allowed it to drain. Part of that ditch ran through this stand of trees. In places, the ditch was forty feet wide and could fill three or four feet deep. Tributaries, such as the one that drained the land directly behind the Blue Beacon, formed deep gullies in the alluvial soil. Together, the combination of trees, ravines, water, and vines made the area a hilly wonderland for kids with few unpaved places to play.

They called the woods Robin Hood. Adults tended to make the name sound more proper, calling it Robin Hood Hills, but it was always just Robin Hood for the kids. Under its green canopy they etched out bike trails, built dirt ramps, established forts, and tied up ropes for swinging over the man-made "river." They fished, scouted, camped, hunted, had wars, and let their imaginations run. But at night, when the woods turned dark, most kids stayed away. The place didn't seem so friendly then, and the things that parents could imagine translated into stern commands.

Besides the risks from water and Robin Hood's closeness to the highways, parents worried about transients who might be lurking there. Many parents warned their children to stay out of the woods entirely. But the ban was impossible to enforce. Robin Hood was too alluring. And so it was inevitable, on that Wednesday night in May, as word flew from house to house that three eight-year-olds were missing, that parents would rush to the dead end of McAuley, where a path led into the woods. It was about a half mile from the homes of Christopher Byers and Michael Moore and only a few blocks farther from that of Stevie Branch.

The delta was already beginning to warm up for the summer. At 9 P.M., even on May 5, the temperature was seventy-three degrees. An inch of rain a few days before had already brought out the mosquitoes.[6] The insects were a nuisance everywhere, but they were especially thick in places that were moist and overgrown—shady places like the woods. The officer who'd taken the missing-person reports on Christopher Byers and Michael Moore later reported that she'd ventured into the woods near the Mayfair Apartments to help look for the boys, but the mosquitoes had driven her out. The officer who'd taken the report on Stevie Branch also said later that he'd entered the woods and searched with a flashlight for half an hour. But those two efforts were the only police action that night. No organized search by police would begin until the morning.[7]

As officers assembled at the West Memphis Police Department for their usual briefing on Thursday morning, May 6, 1993, Chief Inspector Gary W. Gitchell, head of the department's detective division, announced that three boys were missing and that he would be directing the search. A search-and-rescue team from the Crittenden County Sheriff's Office would be assisting. When a few hours had passed without sign of the boys, the police department across the river in Memphis, Tennessee, dispatched a helicopter to assist. By midmorning, dozens of men and women had also joined police in the search. Detectives and ordinary citizens checked yards, parking lots, and various neighborhood buildings, including some still damaged from a tornado that had struck the town the year before. Others fanned out across the two miles of fertile, low-lying farmland that separates the east edge of West Memphis from the levee and the Mississippi River. The most intensive search, however, remained focused on the woods. For hours, groups of as many as fifty law enforcement officers and volunteers combed the rough four acres that lined the diversion ditch. At one point the searchers gathered on the north edge of the woods, near the interstates, and marched shoulder-to-shoulder across the woods until they emerged on the other side, near the houses to the south. But even that effort turned up nothing. Members of the county search-and-rescue team slipped a johnboat into the bayou and poled it down the stream. But still, nothing. By noon, most of the searchers, their alarm increasing, had abandoned the woods to search elsewhere.

The Bodies

But one searcher stayed. Steve Jones, a Crittenden County juvenile officer, was tromping through the now empty section of the woods nearest to the Blue Beacon Truck Wash when he looked down into a steep-sided gully, a tributary to the primary ditch, and spotted something on the water. Jones radioed what he had found.[8] Entering the woods from the subdivision side, Sergeant Mike Allen of the West Memphis Police Department rushed across a wide drainpipe that spanned a part of the ditch, and clambered to where Jones was waiting. Jones led Allen to a spot about sixty yards south of the interstates. Standing on the edge of a high-sided bank, Jones pointed down at the water. Floating on the surface was a boy's laceless black tennis shoe.

The time was approximately 1:30 P.M. The area had been searched for hours. Yet here, alarmingly, was a child's shoe. Police converged on the spot. Sergeant Allen, wearing dress shoes, slacks, a white shirt and tie, was the first to enter the water.[9] It was murky, with shoe-grabbing mud on the bottom. Allen raised a foot. Bubbles gathered around it and floated to the surface. The muck beneath his shoe made a sucking, reluctant sound. Then a pale form began to rise in the water. Slowly, before the horrified officers' eyes, a child's naked body, arched grotesquely backward, rose to the surface. It was about 1:45 P.M.[10]

Word of the discovery spread like fire through West Memphis. Searchers swarmed back to the woods, but now only Gitchell's detectives were being let in. By 2:15 P.M., yellow crime tape was up. Police cars were stationed at the McAuley Drive entrance to the woods and at the entrance south of the Blue Beacon. For the detectives, in a dense and seldom visited part of the woods kids called Old Robin Hood, the job ahead was as odious as obvious. If one body had been submerged in the stream, the others might be as well. Detective Bryn Ridge volunteered for the unnerving job. Leaving the first body where it floated, the dark-haired, heavyset officer walked several feet downstream and waded into the water. Lowering himself to his knees, he spread his hands on the silty bottom. Then slowly, on all fours, he began to crawl up the narrow stream, searching the mud with his hands, expecting—and dreading—that at any moment he would touch another dead child.

He encountered instead a stick stuck unnaturally into the mud. He could feel something wrapped around it. Dislodging the stick and pulling it up, he found a child's white shirt.

Carefully, Ridge stood up and returned to the floating body. It didn't seem right to him to leave it there. He lifted the body to the bank. The officers knew from photographs they'd been shown of the missing boys that this was the body of Michael Moore. And they could see that between the time the boy was last seen and now, he had endured tremendous violence. Michael's hands and feet were behind him, bound in what some would describe as a backward, hog-tied fashion. But it wasn't that, exactly. The limbs weren't tied together. Rather, the left ankle was tied to the left wrist; the right ankle and right wrist were tied. The boy had been tied with shoelaces. The bindings left the body in a dramatically vulnerable pose. The boy's nakedness, the unnatural arch of the back, and the vulnerability of his undeveloped sexual organs, both to the front and to the back, suggested something sexual about the crime. The severity of the wounds to his head suggested a component of rage.

Once begun, the gruesome search intensified. In quick succession the ditch yielded Michael's Cub Scout cap and shirt, a pair of blue jeans, and the grim, forewarning sight of two more pairs of tennis shoes without laces. Reentering the water and resuming his search by hand, Ridge found more sticks stuck like pins into the muddy bottom. Twisted deliberately around them were other items of clothing. Before long, all the clothing listed on the three missing-person reports had been pulled out of the water, with the exception of a sock and two pairs of underpants. The detectives were especially intrigued by the trousers, two of which were inside out. Yet all three were zipped up and buttoned.

Ridge reentered the water farther downstream, and this time he felt what he had feared. Pulling against the mud's suction, he released a second naked form.[11] As it rose eerily to the surface, the detective and officers on the banks could see that this body was also naked and bent backward like the first, and like the first, its thin arms and ankles had been tied together with shoelaces. This was the body of Stevie Branch. He too showed signs of having been beaten, and the left side of his face bore other savage marks. It was hard to tell—the wounds were so deep—but on top of everything else, it looked like Stevie's face may have been bitten.

Minutes later, Ridge found the body of Christopher Byers. Like the others it was submerged facedown in the mud. He was also naked and tied in the same manner as the others, but when detectives rolled him over in the water, they were assaulted by another shock. Christopher's scrotum was gone and his penis had been skinned. Only a thin flap of flesh remained where his genitals should have been, and the area around the castration had been savagely punctuated with deep stab wounds. By now it was 3 P.M.

Detectives found the two bicycles thirty yards away, also underwater. At 3:20 P.M., nearly two hours after the first body was recovered, someone at the scene thought to call the county coroner. When the coroner arrived, he found all three of the bodies out of the water and lying on the bank.[12] He pronounced the boys dead at the scene, at approximately 4 P.M.

What had begun as a search now became a murder investigation, with Gitchell still in charge. His officers photographed and videotaped the scene alongside the stream, where the three white bodies lay. By now, however, the bodies had been out of the water for so long that they were attracting flies and other insects. Gitchell ordered the stream sandbagged above where the bodies were found, and the section below it drained, in the hopes of recovering Christopher's missing genitals, the missing underpants, and maybe a murder weapon or other evidence. Then he walked to the edge of the woods, where a large crowd had assembled. Terry Hobbs, Stevie Branch's stepfather, was ducking under the yellow police tape as Gitchell approached. Gitchell stopped Hobbs and gently reported the news. Yes, the boys' bodies had been found. And yes, it was clear that they had been murdered. Hobbs crumpled to the ground and cried. His wife, Pam Hobbs, Stevie's mother, fainted.

Gitchell spoke briefly to reporters. Then he walked over to John Mark Byers, whose stepson Chris had been mutilated. Byers was leaning against a police car. As a photographer for the *West Memphis Evening Times* aimed her camera and clicked the shutter, Gitchell held out a hand to Byers, as if to support or even embrace him. Byers, who stood almost a head taller than Gitchell, draped his arm over the detective's shoulder. When a reporter approached, Byers shook his head in a gesture of bewilderment. He had searched that very site just the night before, he said. "I was out looking until four-thirty. I walked within ten or fifteen feet of where they were found," he said, "and I didn't see them." The remark struck no one as odd. Many people had searched the area and seen no trace of the missing children. Byers then provided the reporter more information than Gitchell had divulged, information he said the detectives had given him. One of the boys had been hit above the eye, Byers said; another boy's jaw was injured, and the assault on the third child had been even "worse than that."

Eventually, onlookers saw a black hearse drive east on the service road and turn into the Blue Beacon Truck Wash, where it backed up to the edge of the lot. Police covered in dirt and sweat carried three body bags through the opening on the north edge of the woods, across a grassy field, and loaded them through the open rear door.

By then, reporters from Memphis, Little Rock, and Jonesboro, Arkansas, a city about twice the size of West Memphis sixty miles to the north, had converged on the scene. Though the reporters begged Gitchell for information, he told them he had nothing more to say. That night, however, reporters at the *Memphis Commercial Appeal* tuned in to their newsroom's police scanner and picked up a broadcast from the Arkansas State Police. It contained details Gitchell had not revealed, news that made the front page of the next morning's *Commercial Appeal*. The scoop established a dominance for that paper that would continue as the story unfolded.

The details the paper picked up from the state police report included references to how the boys were tied. It also said—incorrectly—that all three had been sexually mutilated.[13] When reporters questioned Gitchell about the sexual mutilation, the detective would not comment. He did, however, confirm that all of the victims had been bound hand to foot. He also remarked on the intensity of the search in the woods, noting, as if mystified, "That area where the boys were found was saturated hard and heavy that morning and even the evening before."

The place where the boys were last seen was just a few hundred yards from where their bodies had floated up. The site was a half mile due north of the corner where Christopher Byers and Michael Moore lived. When reporters knocked on the door of the Byerses' house, Christopher's mother, Melissa, answered. She was crying and had little to say. "I won't let them tell me what happened to them," she sobbed. "I don't want to know." Before closing the door, she added, "All I know is that my child is dead and so are the other two. I'm so sorry. I just don't want to talk about gory details. I don't know."

West Memphis went into shock. On Friday, May 7, the day after the bodies were found, teachers at the elementary school the boys attended met to discuss their students' fears.[14] "I think we can tell the children that the person who did this is very, very sick," one of the counselors advised. Adults wanted to know more than that, but Gitchell was saying little. Faced with silence from the police, the media focused on the victims' families. Of all the parents, John Mark Byers was the most willing to talk. As the weekend approached, he told reporters that besides the weight of his family's grief, the murder posed a financial burden. He explained, "I've got to find a way to bury my son."

Neighbors and sympathetic church groups began to organize collections. By Mother's Day, which fell that weekend, donors had contributed nearly $25,000 to pay for the children's funerals. And a reward fund had been started for information leading to the arrest of the murderer—or murderers. But by the weekend it was also becoming clear that this crime would not be quickly solved. On Monday, May 10, the fifth day of the ordeal, the optimistic headline in the *West Memphis Evening News* announced: "Police Still Confident They'll Solve Murders." Gitchell tried to reassure the paper's readers. His officers were tired, he said, but he added, "We're going to make it."

Enter Satan

Gitchell said little more for the next several days, though he did make one statement that caught the region's attention. He noted that his detectives were considering a wide range of possibilities, including that the murders might have resulted from "gang or cult activity"—though he quickly added that he had seen no evidence of either. To outsiders it seemed a strange pronouncement, an acknowledgment that detectives were considering an unusual explanation for the murders, despite the fact that no evidence suggested it. But readers in West Memphis understood. Within hours after the discovery of the bodies, rumors attributing the killings to satanism had begun to circulate. Two women had already reported sounds of devil worshiping in the woods. Whatever had prompted Gitchell's remark, it suggested that he and his detectives were taking the rumors seriously. Word that the case might have satanic overtones was prevalent enough that when the West Memphis Police Department assigned the case number 93-05-0666 to the murder file, reporters asked whether the last three digits had been deliberately chosen. Did the number 666 suggest a police theory of the crime? Did it refer to the Antichrist? Gitchell insisted that it did not. The assignment of that particular number, he said, had been entirely coincidental. He explained that cases were numbered according to the date the crime had occurred and the number of cases that had already been entered for the year. It was entirely by chance, he said, that this particular case, which occurred in the fifth month of 1993, just happened to be the 666th worked by the department so far. Years later, discovery of a report written by Detective Ridge and dated two days after the bodies were found would cast doubt on Gitchell's contention. That report—which was among the earliest in the case—identified it as #93-05-0555.

CHAPTER TWO

The West Memphis Police

WITHIN HOURS AFTER THE BODIES WERE FOUND, Arkansas governor Jim Guy Tucker, a former prosecuting attorney, contacted Gitchell to offer the assistance of the Arkansas State Police. The larger state police agency could have sent detectives from its Criminal Investigation Division into West Memphis to aid in what promised to be a difficult investigation. But Gitchell declined the offer, and though one state police officer did help conduct some interviews, the role of the state police in West Memphis was minimal.[15]

Gitchell's reluctance to involve the state police might have been sparked in part by the misinformation the agency had broadcast in the first hours of the case—information that had been picked up by the paper. Gitchell's strategy, from the moment the three bodies had floated up from the muck, had been to keep a tight control on information. The less the public knew, he reasoned, the better he and his detectives could work. If no one but the killer or killers knew the exact nature of the wounds, for example, the questioning of suspects would be easier. But Gitchell's attempt to control the information had been immediately undermined—by the very investigative agency that was now offering its assistance. Anyone who'd heard the police band broadcast would know how the boys' hands had been tied and the significant, if overstated, fact that "their genitals had been removed." The morning after the discovery of the bodies, when the *Memphis Commercial Appeal* published that information, Gitchell had been livid.

State and Local Police Tensions

There may also have been another, darker reason for Gitchell's coolness toward the state police. At the time the murders occurred, several officers in the West Memphis Police Department, along with officers in the Crittenden County Sheriff's Office, were themselves under investigation by none other than the Arkansas State Police. Gitchell himself had not been questioned, but much of the county's law enforcement community had, and the relationship between the local police and the state police was, at the moment, severely strained. The incident that had brought state investigators into Crittenden County arose less than four months before the murders, and the investigation into it was not over yet. It centered on drugs. It suggested corruption. And it began with another murder. The victim this time was a deputy sheriff—an undercover narcotics investigator who, the state police discovered, had been pawning evidence seized in drug arrests to buy drugs for himself.[16]

It was a tawdry story, but one that was only partly reported. The deputy was buried with honors. "He did his job," the sheriff said at his funeral. "He did a good job for us." Police in West Memphis never revealed the information, uncovered by the state police, about the slain deputy's personal involvement with drugs or that he'd pawned an undercover police car and his service revolver to get them.

Yet that murder had opened a can of worms for police in Crittenden County—especially for officers on the county's drug task force. While state police investigators were sorting through the deputy's affairs, they discovered that he was not the only narcotics detective who'd been misusing official property. Guns seized in drug arrests were found to be missing from the evidence locker. Questions were also raised about drugs and money that had been seized and not accounted for. In the months that immediately preceded the eight-year-olds' murders, the state police probe into the deputy's murder had expanded into an investigation of other officers—from both the sheriff's office and the West Memphis Police Department—who served on the county's drug task force. On March 3, 1993, two months before the children's murders, the *West Memphis Evening Times* reported mildly that the local drug task force had become "the object of an investigation by the Arkansas State Police over firearms and drugs that may be missing."

In a systematic probe, state police investigators began to polygraph members of the county's drug task force, asking each member about the missing guns and drugs.[17] During the ten weeks immediately preceding the triple murder in May, fourteen employees of the county drug task force, including four detectives from the West Memphis Police Department, were questioned by the state police.[18] Several officers, including three from the West Memphis Police Department, admitted to having taken guns from the evidence locker. One deputy told investigators that it had become common practice for members of the drug task force to help themselves to guns that were reported to the courts as having been destroyed.

The most serious statements were those made by and about Lieutenant James Sudbury, a West Memphis narcotics detective. Though Sudbury was the second-ranking officer on the county's drug task force, he would play a pivotal role in the investigation of the children's murders. Shortly before those murders occurred, however, Sudbury admitted to state police investigators that he had taken personal possession of at least four weapons that had been seized by the drug task force as evidence. Other members of the task force reported that Sudbury had taken several other items as well. All of this was reported to Brent Davis, the district's prosecuting attorney. But Davis, who would also play a key role in the forthcoming triple murder case, opted not to prosecute Sudbury or the other officers involved.[19]

In early May, after the discovery of the three boys' bodies, few people in West Memphis were aware of the tensions that had been building between police in Crittenden County and the state police. Oddly, one of the few people who may have understood the situation was the stepfather of one of the children found dead in Robin Hood.

John Mark Byers

Byers occupied an unusual position in the West Memphis community. He was a pawnbroker, a jeweler by trade, a drug dealer, a friend of police, and a confidential informant for the Crittenden County Drug Task Force. The day after the three eight-year-olds' bodies were found, Byers simultaneously praised the West Memphis police for their efforts in the search for the boys and complained about what he regarded as the sheriff's delayed response. The sheriff responded that the search had not been in his jurisdiction and that the county's search-and-rescue unit had been dispatched as soon as the West Memphis police requested it. Besides, the sheriff added, there was no reason, other than protocol, why he would have declined Byers's request, since he knew Byers and considered him a friend.

Other lawmen involved in the search—deputies and police alike—could have said the same. Several had attended parties at the Byerses' house, drinking beer, grilling burgers, and playing in the backyard pool. They knew Melissa Byers. They'd met her children, Ryan and Christopher. That may have been why, after the bodies were found, Gitchell's clasp of Byers at the edge of the woods had looked surprisingly personal. When the photo of that encounter appeared on the front page of the local paper, a spotlight fell on Byers that would shine for many months. But there were aspects of his past that it did not illuminate, although some of them were known to local officials.

Byers was born in 1957 in Marked Tree, Arkansas, about thirty miles north of West Memphis. He studied briefly in Texas to be a jeweler and, for a time after that, worked at a store in Memphis. But by 1984, he was back, living in Marion, Arkansas, a quiet farming community six miles north of West Memphis. Byers worked at flea markets in the Memphis–West Memphis area, performing on-the-spot jewelry repair until he and Melissa opened their own store, Byers Jewelry, in West Memphis in 1989. The store lasted less than a year, and when it closed, Byers filed for bankruptcy. A few months later he signed on as a partner in a pawn business that operated on the service road alongside the interstates, near the Blue Beacon Truck Wash. That venture ended quickly too, and toward the end of 1990, the disgruntled partner bought Byers out.

Byers's personal life was running no more smoothly than his career. In 1987, when he married Melissa DeFir, a Memphis woman with a history of heroin addiction, he already had two children, a son and a daughter, from a previous marriage. His first wife had custody of the children.[20] When Melissa married Mark, she brought two children to the marriage: Ryan, a shy seven-year-old, and Christopher, who was then about three. But even after his marriage to Melissa, Byers retained a stormy relationship with his first wife, who lived in Marion.

In September 1987, Byers's volatility toward his first wife had led to his arrest.[21] Shortly before 7 A.M., police in Marion received a call about "a woman screaming." The caller also reported that "there were two small kids outside by themselves unattended." That call was followed by a second, from another alarmed resident, who'd also heard the screams. The address the callers gave was that of Byers's ex-wife and her children. An officer later reported that when he arrived, the older of the two children outside told him that "his mother and daddy were inside the trailer fighting." Looking inside the door, the officer wrote, he could see "a white male and a white female on the floor. The white male appeared to have a black object pointing at the female who was crying and visibly upset." When the officer entered the house, the man, who identified himself as Byers, "got off the floor immediately and became arrogant," while the woman "was crying and begging this officer not to leave."

The woman told the officer that Byers had come to the house at 6:45 A.M., demanding to take the children. He then "began to threaten her, telling her that he wanted full custody of the kids, that he was going to kill her, and that he had an electric shocker and kept acting like he was going to use it on her." The officer's notes of the incident continued: "Mr. Byers acted strange. A few minutes he would calm down and talk normal, but then all of a sudden he would get arrogant again, advising me that he was the father and he was going to take the kids. He also became upset when I advised him that I was going to keep the Power Zapper, which he wanted back. I could not smell any type of intoxicant on his breath, but he appeared to have been either on some type of medication or intoxicant by the manner in which he was acting." The officer confiscated the electric shocker and escorted the woman and her children to a friend's home, where she could "feel safe."

That morning, Byers's ex-wife drove to downtown Marion, where she reported the incident to John Fogleman, the city attorney. Years later, Fogleman too would play a key role in events following the murder of Christopher Byers and his two young friends. But that tragedy was still almost six years in the future. In 1987, in the hours after her assault, the former Mrs. Byers told Fogleman that her ex-husband had threatened to kill her or to have someone else kill her several times in the past; that she had sought a restraining order against him; and that because of his propensity toward violence, when he had shown up at her house that morning she had turned on a tape recorder. She handed Fogleman the tape.[22] It and the investigating officer's report were convincing evidence. By the end of the day, Marion police had issued a warrant for Byers's arrest, charging that he had terrorized his ex-wife by threatening to cause her death. Byers was convicted of the offense and sentenced to three years' probation. All that was required of him was that he keep up his child support payments and remain gainfully employed.

Byers fulfilled neither requirement. Over the next few years, his first wife took him to court repeatedly seeking back child support, and twice, when Byers professed poverty, a local chancery judge reduced his court-ordered payments. Meanwhile, in 1989, Byers, now married to Melissa, bought the two-story house on Barton Street in West Memphis and moved into it with Ryan and Christopher. The house had three bedrooms, three baths, and an in-ground swimming pool. When the couple's jewelry store failed the following year, neighbors wondered how the couple afforded the house. Melissa worked as a cleaning lady, and Byers worked out of their home, mostly selling jewelry at local flea markets.[23]

Something else that puzzled neighbors was Byers's apparent chumminess with some members of the local police. One explanation for that emerged months after Christopher's murder, when it was learned that Byers had worked as an undercover drug informant.[24] But there were other, deeper mysteries that were never fully explained. One was why, exactly one year before Christopher's murder, the record of Byers's felony conviction for terroristic threatening was formally expunged. Byers had not fulfilled the terms of his probation. He had neither kept up his child support payments nor remained gainfully employed. Yet on May 5, 1992, circuit judge David Burnett signed an order absolving Byers of all legal consequences arising from the assault and death threat on his ex-wife. A year later, Burnett would become another principal player in the murder case involving Byers's stepson. But even in 1992, Burnett's role in Byers's life was important. The judge's ruling allowed Byers to state "in any application form for employment, license, civil right, or privilege or in any appearance as a witness that he has not been convicted of the offense."[25]

All of this, of course, went unreported in the local paper. Where Byers was known at all in West Memphis, it was as a failed jewelry store owner who worked at local flea markets. His ex-wife had moved away, taking her children with her, and now, even the record of Byers's conviction for assaulting her had been ordered removed from the courthouse. But some records did still exist. One, on file in Memphis, reported that on a night in July 1992—nine months before the murders—Byers had been arrested in that city.[26] Sheriff's deputies there charged him with conspiring to sell cocaine and with carrying a dangerous weapon. They booked him into the county jail. But sometime during the night, Byers was released, without explanation, into the custody of U.S. marshals. Byers was subsequently released, though—once again—records in the case were scarce. Representatives of the U.S. Marshals Service later acknowledged that records did not indicate who had ordered Byers's release or why.

Byers's financial situation looked grim in the year before Christopher's murder, but his legal situation looked remarkably good. Charges—and even convictions—didn't stick. By Christmas of 1992—five months before the murders—he was again under criminal suspicion, this time for felony theft. Again, a situation that could have landed Byers in prison was resolved to his advantage. And again, the people most closely involved with the investigation—the two West Memphis detectives and prosecuting attorney Brent Davis—would also figure heavily in the murder case ahead.

On December 8, 1992, a loss prevention agent for United Parcel Service notified Detective Bryn Ridge and Detective Sergeant Mike Allen at the West Memphis Police Department that a package containing two gold Rolex watches, valued at $11,000, had been delivered to Byers's home, but that he now denied having received it. UPS suspected fraud. But when five months passed without progress by the West Memphis police, UPS took its concerns to the Arkansas State Police. That agency was still investigating the missing Rolex watches at the time of the three children's murders.

CHAPTER THREE

The Police Investigation: Part 1

WITHIN HOURS OF THE BODIES BEING DISCOVERED, the investigation divided roughly along three lines. These were, essentially, that the children were killed by someone close to them; that they were killed by one or more strangers; or that they were killed, as Gitchell had already hinted, by members of a gang or cult. This unusual third prong of the investigation arose early and was the most sharply focused from the start, while detectives' efforts in the other two directions often appeared chaotic.

Bumbling exacerbated the problem. Though the bodies were found at about 1:30 P.M., the coroner was not called until nearly two hours later. By the time he arrived, fly larvae were starting to appear in the victims' eyes and nostrils. By 3:58 P.M., when the coroner pronounced the first of the three boys dead, the bodies had been lying in the open air for more than two and a half hours, covered for part of that time with plastic, in temperatures that approached the high eighties. The coroner reported that the water in the ditch was sixty degrees, but after the bodies were removed from it, the rate of their deterioration had been rapid. The coroner noted that it was difficult to assess the extent of rigor mortis due to the way the bodies were tied; that all three showed "signs of post-mortem staining on face and chest"; and that the bodies of Michael and Christopher showed signs that they "may have been sexually assaulted."

For the next several weeks, the location and condition of the bodies as they were found on the afternoon of May 6 would constitute almost the entirety of what police knew about the murders. The sandbagging of the ditch had turned up nothing. Though detectives had scoured the muddy bottom, they'd found no missing body parts, no underwear, no apparent murder weapon. Their search of the area alongside the stream had provided little more. They'd found one fingerprint in the mud and one partially obliterated footprint, but they'd also found what struck them as a stunning lack of blood. Detectives made casts of the prints, but though dozens of fingerprints would be sent to the crime lab, no match was ever made. Aside from the bodies, the clothing, and the bikes, police took a minuscule amount of evidence from the scene. The absence of physical evidence was surprising, especially for a triple murder that had not involved a gun and in which one of the victims had clearly lost a lot of blood.

Confusion and disorganization compounded the detectives' problems. Record keeping was unsystematic. Later, questions would be raised about the probe's scientific integrity as well.[27] The problems that would plague the investigation began to appear soon after the bodies were found. Sometime, apparently within the first day or two, an undated, unsigned "Summary Regarding the Investigation" was printed on police department stationery.[28] The summary reported the names and ages of the victims, the approximate time the boys were last seen alive, and the fact that bicycles belonging to two of the victims had been found submerged "about fifty yards away." But even that document was not reliable. It reported, for example, that "Moore"—rather than Byers—"had been obviously castrated." The mistake was repeated again where the summary noted that "analysis has determined that a knife with a serrated edge was used to castrate Moore."

Another key part of the report was oddly ambiguous. It read: "A crime scene search failed to locate any traces of blood or other evidence which would lead investigators to believe the victims had been murdered in the area where their bodies were located." That seemed to suggest that detectives' earliest suspicion was that the boys were murdered somewhere else. The document also noted that "a hammer or a round object was used to create trauma to the head of all three victims"; that "there is a possibility that Byers may have been injected by a hypodermic needle"; and that "the medical examiner also advised that evidence would tend to indicate that the victims had been struck with a belt containing studs or a raised surface." This was interesting information, but in light of the statement's obvious errors, its overall credibility had to be questioned.

The medical examiner's reference to the possibility that the children had been struck by a belt might have focused attention on John Mark Byers, since Byers had acknowledged when he'd reported Christopher missing that he'd given the boy "a few licks" with a belt just before he disappeared. But for two weeks detectives appeared to be disinclined to seriously question Byers. If they checked with the local child abuse agency to see if it had a record on Byers, no report of such an inquiry was ever placed into the file.

While that most logical prong of the investigation, the one looking at family members, was receiving scant attention, and the most unusual one—the possibility that a "gang or cult" had committed the murders— had already been announced to the media, detectives devoted hundreds of hours to examining a third possibility. This was that someone completely unknown to the children—someone not in a gang or a cult, but not in their families either—had mutilated and murdered the children.

Various Tips and Leads

As police questioned residents who lived near the woods, news of what kind of questions they were asking spread quickly by word of mouth. Although Gitchell vowed to maintain tight control over information pertaining to the case, information leaked all over. It was no secret, for instance, that detectives had requisitioned a list of customers who'd washed trucks at the Blue Beacon. And after residents reported seeing an unfamiliar white van in the area, it was widely known that police were investigating all vans in the area, white and otherwise. Descriptions of the driver had varied—some witnesses described a middle-aged white male with gray hair; others, a young white male with blond hair— and ultimately the lead had led nowhere.

Alarmed citizens called the police reporting hundreds of tips and leads. Detectives worked frantically, if utterly unsystematically, to follow up most of them. No voice was considered too small to be heard, no suggestion too absurd. On Friday, May 7, the day after the bodies were found, Aaron Hutcheson, an eight-year-old classmate of the victims, told police that he'd seen Michael Moore talking after school to a black man in a maroon car.[29] According to Aaron, the man was tall, had yellow teeth, and wore a T-shirt with "writing on it." Aaron reported that the man told Michael that his mother had asked him to bring Michael home, and that Michael had climbed into the car and ridden off with the man. Though no tall black man with yellow teeth and a maroon car was ever located, the report was a perplexing one. Aaron was a close friend of Michael's and could reasonably have been with him immediately after school. The boy's details were specific. And there seemed no reason for him to have concocted such a story. On the other hand, police knew that Michael's mother, Dana Moore, had sent no one to pick up her son. And why would she have? The Moores' house was on the lot next to the school. She told police that Michael had come immediately home. Aaron's report sounded like the product of a child's frightened imagination, and the police soon dismissed it. But as the detectives' frustrations mounted, they would visit young Aaron again— and in later interviews they would take his accounts more seriously.

For now, Gitchell's detectives cast a wide and imaginative net in their search for the killer or killers. When someone suggested that the way the boys were tied—wrists-to-ankles, behind their backs—was like the way some American soldiers had been tied when captured in Vietnam, the police checked hospitals for reports of veterans in the area who might have been treated for injuries to their penises. They checked area carpet cleaners, looking for any who had cleaned up bloodstains. They investigated a man who had once been arrested for performing surgical sex change operations without a medical license. They compiled descriptions of vagrants, strangers, mental patients, loiterers, and hoboes. They investigated one man who was said to have made "vulgar remarks" to two young girls, another who had reportedly drilled holes through his apartment wall to spy on his neighbors, and another who had aroused suspicion by failing to attend church for the past few weeks. They filed reports on men who were said to have tortured and killed animals, or who had confided having murderous fantasies, or who were said to be into child pornography, or whom a tipster had described as "brutal." They also saw to it that the outline of the crime—which was pretty much all they knew—was reported on the television show *Amer-*

ica's Most Wanted. As news of the murders spread, police across the nation tried to help by relaying information about hundreds of cases that they thought might be related.

On Wednesday, May 12, six days after the bodies were found, Gitchell's detectives belatedly tested the site by the ditch for blood. They sprayed Luminol, a product that glows luminescent in the dark in places where it has interacted with blood. Results of the test were sketchy—and minimal.[30] By the end of the first week, police found themselves struggling to separate information from the tide of rumor and speculation being phoned in by the public. A woman reported that on the evening the boys disappeared, while driving along the service road in the vicinity of the Blue Beacon between 6 and 6:30 P.M., she'd seen all three of the victims riding on two bicycles. If that report was true, it would place the boys at the opposite entrance to the woods from the one where other reports had placed them last. But some reports were more credible than others. A narcotics detective in Memphis reported that both John Mark and Melissa Byers had worked as confidential informants for both the Memphis police and the sheriff's department in Shelby County, where Memphis was located. The information was potentially important—if, indeed, the West Memphis police did not know it already. It suggested that the mother and stepfather of the most seriously brutalized child were involved, some way or another, with criminal activity. But if the West Memphis police followed up on this lead, they entered no record of it in the file.

Another interesting tip also pointed to Memphis—and to a connection with drugs. A week and a half after the murders, police in West Memphis were told that four days after the bodies were found, two young Memphis men, Chris Morgan and Brian Holland, had left town abruptly and had moved to Oceanside, California. When West Memphis police checked on the two they learned that Morgan's parents and his former girlfriend lived in West Memphis, near where the victims lived, and that he had once had an ice cream route in the victims' neighborhood. Detectives asked police in Oceanside to pick up the two for questioning. The officers in California complied, and on May 17, Morgan and Holland were given polygraph examinations. The tests indicated that both men were deceptive in their answers to questions about the murders. Oceanside police reported that at one point, after several hours of questioning, Morgan had become upset, blurted out that he had been hospitalized for alcohol and drug abuse, and stated that he might have committed the murders. He'd then immediately recanted the statement. The Oceanside police sent blood and urine samples from both men to the West Memphis police. But there the matter seemed to have ended. There was little further investigation of Morgan and Holland. The file would contain no explanation as to why such an apparently serious lead had been dropped.

Gitchell, meanwhile, was demanding more information from the state's crime laboratory and the medical examiner's office. But he was frustrated there, as well. An associate medical examiner performed autopsies on the boys the day after their bodies were found, but weeks passed and Gitchell did not receive the reports. Analysts at the crime lab provided a little more help. After examining the shoestrings binding the bodies, analyst Lisa Sakevicius sent Gitchell a report indicating that the knots used to tie Christopher and Michael were all "the same," while those used on Stevie were "all dissimilar to each other and to the other two." Sakevicius added that she had found skin, and possibly cuticles, in one of the ligatures and that there was a strong chance that this skin was "not that of the boys." But no further information was forthcoming about whose skin it might be. There was, however, this: Sakevicius reported that a fragment of "Negroid hair" had been found in the sheet that was wrapped around Christopher's body.

Byers and Other Relatives

Though detectives had not approached the boys' families as the starting point of their investigation, they had at least two important reasons to talk with the relatives. First, the families were valuable sources of information. And second, they were—or should have been—prime suspects.[31] Of the victims' three sets of natural parents, only Todd and Dana Moore were still married to each other. The Moores had one other child, a ten-year-old daughter, Dawn. On May 8, three days after the murders, Detective Ridge questioned the Moores. They had little to add to the mystery of the murders. But a friend of Dawn's told Ridge that she had seen Stevie and Michael going into Robin Hood on the evening they disappeared.[32] She said she saw their bicycles parked by the road at the entrance to the woods. Ridge wrote in his notes that the girl had stated "that she never saw Christopher that day."

Stevie's parents, Pam and Steve Branch, had divorced when Stevie was one year old. The divorce decree awarded custody of Stevie to Pam and allowed Steve Branch to visit the boy only when she was present. Steve Branch had been ordered to pay $250 per month in child support, but by the time little Stevie was seven, his father was $13,000 in arrears. Branch's wages were being garnisheed, and at the time of Stevie's murder, the state of Arkansas was also after him to collect some back taxes. Branch had once been charged with theft, though the charge was later dropped at the victim's request. But none of this background on Stevie's family was included in the murder investigation file, and notes of police interviews with Branch, or Pam, or Pam's new husband, Terry Hobbs, were minimal.

So too were notes from early interviews of Christopher's mother and stepfather. Despite the enormity of the crime, none of the early interviews with any of the parents were recorded. According to Gitchell's single page of handwritten notes, John Mark Byers had reported that his ex-wife and his two children from that marriage were now living in Missouri, but no record of the assault on her was included in the file. The report said that Christopher was John Mark Byers's "stepson," although it added that Byers had adopted Christopher when the boy was about four.[33]

Nevertheless, Byers was questioned more closely than the other two sets of parents. According to Gitchell's notes, Byers reported that he had arrived home from a medical appointment at 3:10 P.M. on May 5, 1993. At 3:50, he took his thirteen-year-old stepson, Ryan, to the police department for an appearance in municipal court, where Ryan was to testify as a witness in a traffic dispute. After leaving Ryan at the courthouse, Byers said, he drove to Memphis to pick up his wife, Melissa, at work.[34] He stated that he returned to the house with her, and at 5:30 left home again to pick up Ryan at court. Byers told Gitchell that at 6:15, when he returned with Ryan, Christopher was not at home, and that by 6:20 the family had begun its search. That was the extent of Gitchell's notes from the first reported interview with Byers.

However, two other related reports were also recorded that day. Lieutenant Sudbury, the codirector of the drug task force, interviewed a woman who had a child at the elementary school. The woman had called the police department soon after the bodies were found, saying that she had information about the Byerses. When Detective Sudbury followed up on the call, the woman told him that near the end of 1992, she had attended a parent-teacher event in the school auditorium. While there, she said, she had overheard the school's principal talking to John Mark and Melissa Byers, who were seated behind her. According to the woman, the principal was advising them "that Chris had to be put out of class that day for causing a disturbance," and that the Byerses' reply to the principal was "that they had done all they could do and thought they would send Chris away." When the principal left, the woman said she'd heard the couple continue to discuss how they needed "to get rid of Chris." Sudbury wrote that he contacted the principal, who told him that she did not remember the conversation. And that was the end of that. No records indicated that either of the Byerses were ever asked about the alleged conversation.

Another person called the police on May 8 to report "something about drugs" relating to John Mark Byers. Whoever took the call noted it not on a standard police form, but on a pharmaceutical company notepad. When a detective contacted the source, the investigator was told that "Byers is in drug re-hab in Memphis and on methadone" and may have "a brain tumor." Beneath that notation someone in the department had written "OLD NEWS" and underlined the comment twice. The entry suggested that police were more familiar with John Mark Byers than their official reports reflected.

While police were not tape-recording, much less videotaping, interviews at this stage of the investigation, they did make use of a few modern tools. One was the polygraph, or lie-detector test, administered by Detective Bill Durham. During the course of the investigation, Durham would polygraph forty-one subjects. But Durham never polygraphed any of the victims' relatives. The police also fingerprinted more than four dozen subjects, hoping that one of the prints might match the one found in the woods. But no match was ever found. And of course, they waited for information from the state's crime laboratory.

In the weeks immediately following the murders, the department submitted hundreds of items to the lab for evaluation, among them eighteen knives, three wooden sticks, one tire billy, one ice axe, three hammers, a hook, a rope, hair samples from forty-one people, blood and urine samples from eleven, footprint impressions, shoes, boxes of clothing, and a Mason jar filled with water, accompanied by a request that the water in the jar be tested to see if it matched the water found inside the children's bodies. Hair from relatives of all of the victims was submitted for analysis, as were blood and urine samples from Todd Moore and John Mark Byers.

Police briefly checked another person who was close to the Byers family. On May 11, two detectives questioned Andrew Gipson Taylor, a thirty-four-year-old mechanic who often stayed at the Byerses' house.[35] Taylor told the officers that Byers did, indeed, have a brain tumor, that he was currently on welfare, and that the Byers family had been having "a hard time financially." He also reported that there were "hard feelings" between John Mark Byers and Todd Moore. "John Mark had some pool parties," one of the detectives wrote, "and when his friends would park on his [Moore's] grass, he [Moore] would call the police." When asked what he knew about Byers's whereabouts before the bodies were found, Taylor replied that his friend had searched on "both sides of the ditch—went behind Blue Beacon in the woods."

The two officers then questioned Ryan Clark, Melissa's thirteen-year-old son. Ryan said he had arrived home from school at "exactly 3:38 P.M." on the afternoon Christopher disappeared.[36] Chris was not at home. John Mark Byers took Ryan to his 4 P.M. appearance in court, left, and returned to the courthouse at around 6 P.M. to pick him up. On the way home, Byers told Ryan that Chris had broken a seal on the window to get into the house and that he was going to be grounded for a week. When they got home, his mother told him that they were going to go to a restaurant to eat, and to go upstairs to get Christopher. Ryan went upstairs but could not find him. The family then looked for Christopher outside.

Ryan said a neighbor told them that she'd seen Christopher on a skateboard with Stevie and Michael, who were on bikes. The neighbor said Christopher had hopped onto the back of Stevie's bike, leaving his skateboard in the street. Ryan said he'd found a skateboard on the side of the street, about six houses from his own. But there was no sign of Christopher, and when the family could not find him, they'd gotten into the car to search.

That evening, Ryan said, he and three friends had joined the search in Robin Hood. Walking near the ditch, they'd heard "the grass and brush crackling" and "five real loud splashes." Ryan told the detectives that after hearing the first two splashes he'd yelled, "Hello! Is anyone over there?" There was no answer, and after the third splash, he and his friends had taken off running. When they got to the pipe, he said, they'd heard a gunshot.

Ryan estimated that he and his friends were in the woods for about thirty minutes. They then searched the neighborhood. The detectives' report on their interview concluded with Ryan's statement that he "came home at midnight and his dad made him go to bed." The next day, the two detectives interviewed Ryan's friends. All three confirmed Ryan's account.

Two weeks after the murders, Gitchell and his detectives called John Mark Byers to the station for a tape-recorded interview—his first formal interview by police. Detective Ridge, who had been asked to investigate Byers with regard to the missing shipment of Rolex watches, and Lieutenant James Sudbury, the narcotics detective who was himself under investigation by the Arkansas State Police, conducted the interview. It lasted seventy-eight minutes.

Byers described himself as a self-employed, disabled jeweler. He said he was thirty-six years old, stood six feet five inches tall, weighed 238 pounds, and was right-handed. He said he owned a blue-and-white Ford F-150 XLT truck and a silver Mark I Isuzu. Most of the interview focused on his whereabouts between the times when the boys were last seen alive and when their bodies were found in the ditch.

Byers's report generally agreed with Ryan's. He said that on the day the boys disappeared, he was at a clinic in Memphis being tested. He'd arrived home at 3:10 P.M. By then, Christopher should have been home from school, but he wasn't. Byers told the police that he and Melissa considered Christopher too young to carry a house key, so he had been instructed to wait in the carport if he got home and no one was there.

Byers said he'd left the house at 3:50 P.M. to take Ryan to court. He'd then driven to Memphis, picked up Melissa from work, dropped her off at the house, then headed back to downtown West Memphis, to pick up Ryan at court. On the way, he said, he'd spotted Christopher, belly-down on his skateboard, on the street. He drove the boy back home, made him hold on to the bar in the kitchen, and "gave him two or three licks." Byers said, "And I have, you know, if I could have took whipping him back, I'd a done it a million times. But I was just trying to keep him safe. I was just trying, you know, to keep from something like this happening."

Ridge responded, "I understand."

Byers said he instructed Christopher to clean up the carport, then left the house again to get Ryan. But when he and Ryan returned home, Christopher was gone again. His description of the search that ensued matched Ryan's. Byers said he reported Christopher missing, shortly before 8 P.M., because Christopher had "never gone off anywhere, you know, for any amount of time." He said he began searching in the woods by about 8:30 P.M. "It had got dark," he said. "Well, I had on a pair of shorts and a pair of flip-flops, so I run back to the house and changed clothes and put me on some coveralls and boots that I had on probably for the next two or three days. And I went back out there and I made a pass . . . Well, I didn't have a flashlight, or anything with me, and I thought, 'Well, I'm going to go borrow a flashlight . . .' So as I came out, I see a police car pull up." He said he and the officer searched briefly together, using the officer's light.[37]

Ridge and Sudbury did not question Byers's report that he'd driven across the river to midtown Memphis and back, at the height of rush hour, in just an hour and ten minutes. They did not press for details about the times Byers had been alone in the vicinity of where the bodies were discovered. They did not ask why he'd entered the woods in the dark to search without a flashlight. And they did not question Byers about a critical difference between his account and Ryan's of what had happened around midnight that night.

Byers stated that when he returned home from searching the woods, "it was right at eleven." He said he'd then placed two telephone calls: first, to the West Memphis police to ask "what the situation was," and next, to the sheriff's office to ask "why the search-and-rescue squad won't come out here and help me look for my boy." According to Byers, it was approaching midnight when he completed the calls. This was about the time that Ryan had told detectives that his stepfather had sent him to bed. But the account Byers gave was vastly different.

"We just went back looking," he said. "As a matter of fact, my son Ryan and I got in the car and we drove around there to Blue Beacon, and went into Blue Beacon Truck Wash." When they reached the truck wash, Byers said, he told the workers there, "Look, we got three boys missing . . . I want to go back here behind y'all's property and holler and yell in these woods, but I wanted you to know why my car's back there." He continued, "So we pulled our little silver car back there and Ryan, he's honking the horn and I'm out hollering and yelling around the edge of the woods, and he kind of drove the car around." He said the two of them "hollered and yelled there for a while" and that he had then walked toward the woods, still calling for the boys. But since he didn't have a light, he said, he had not gone all the way in. "So we hollered and yelled around there for quite a while," Byers told the detectives. "Then we went back."

Neither Ridge nor Sudbury mentioned Ryan's statement to detectives that he'd been sent to bed at midnight. Neither asked Byers why Ryan might have omitted such a major episode in his account of the night. Ryan was never questioned about the discrepancy. There is no record that police ever questioned anyone who was working the late shift at the Blue Beacon that night, nor that the issue was ever addressed at all.[38]

That was not the only opportunity for closer questioning of Byers that Ridge and Sudbury missed. During the May 19 interview, Byers told them that on the morning of the search, he'd asked officers when they were going to put a boat into the ditch, explaining, "You know, if they've drowned, you know, let's get a boat in the bayou." Neither detective asked why he suspected the three might have drowned.

Another area that Ridge and Sudbury might have explored more fully concerned Christopher's friends. Byers said that Christopher had liked to play with a "little boy named Aaron" but that Stevie Branch was his closest friend. He admitted, however, that he had not known where

Stevie lived until the night that Christopher disappeared. Neither detective asked why Byers had not known where Christopher's best friend lived. Nor did they ask him about what others had reported, namely, that Michael, across the street, had been Christopher's closest friend. Byers did not even mention Michael. And it seemed he did not want to discuss the Moores. When asked about them, he said that he and Melissa "didn't have a lot to do" with them. He explained that during the past summer, the Moores had complained to police four times about parties he and Melissa had thrown at their house, including one honoring a former sheriff.[39]

Even when Byers seemed to catch himself in a lie, the detectives did not press. That happened when Ridge asked Byers about Christopher's biological father. Byers blurted out, "I don't even know his name." He then quickly amended the statement. "He came to the funeral," he said. "His name is Ricky Lee Murray."

No one raised the subject of Byers's assault on his ex-wife. Ridge simply asked, "Anybody in your family that has a history of abuse?"

"No sir," Byers replied. With that, the topic was dropped.[40]

In other parts of the interview, Byers alluded to interactions with local officials. When Ridge asked if he thought that the killer or killers might be rehabilitated, for instance, and ever "go back on the street again," the answer Byers gave suggested that he already knew who the suspects were. "No," he told Ridge, "because from what [deputy prosecutor] John Fogleman told me, these individuals—he couldn't see how they could plead insanity 'cause they tried to cover up their crime. And he promised me in Gary Gitchell's office, with the other fathers in there, that it didn't matter what age they were, that he was going to prosecute 'em as an adult, and he would try for the death penalty."

Similarly, when Sudbury asked Byers if there was anyone police should "talk to," anyone "from Memphis, perhaps," that Byers had "talked to OCU [the Organized Crime Unit] about," Byers had responded with caution. "Who's all going to hear that tape?" he asked.

"Only us investigators," Ridge assured him. Byers then mentioned two men that he said he'd "worked with the city here on" in connection with illegal drugs.

As the interview neared its end, Ridge asked one more question.

"Okay," he began, "Well, what I want to say right now, and what I'm going to say is that, I may have information . . . This information suggests strongly that you have something to do with the disappearance of the boys. And ultimately of the murder. Okay. What is your response to that?"

Byers replied, "My first response is I can't fathom where you would get that . . ."

Ridge: "Okay."

Byers: "And it makes me so mad inside that I just kind of got to hold myself here in this chair . . ."

Ridge: "Okay. Who, of all the people you know, might make that kind of suggestion?"

Byers: "I wouldn't have the slightest idea."

Ridge: "Okay."

Byers: "If I did, it would make me want to hit 'em. You know, it would make me mad to think that someone maybe has said something like that about me. It makes me mad."

Ridge explained that these were questions he had to ask. "It was to get a response," he said. "We want to know what your response is. And I'm not saying anybody made that accusation. Okay. But I had to evoke that response from you. I had to know what your response was. You understand that? Do you understand?"

Byers said, "I probably will. I don't right now. It hurts."

"It hurts me to have to ask it," Ridge replied. "As much as I know it hurts you when I saw your response . . ."

"Just tell me one thing," Byers said. "Man to man, you tell me, man to man—I don't care, on the record or off the record—you know I didn't have anything to do with the murder of my son and those other two boys."

"Man to man," Ridge assured him, "I know that."

Two weeks had passed, and much of the investigation was an incoherent mess. The investigation of the families, such as it was, had not produced results, nor had the detectives' pursuit of the numerous miscellaneous leads. Gitchell was floundering. The city was in a state of alarm—residents were even afraid to go shopping—and local officials were expecting arrests. Yet Gitchell still had not even received written reports on the autopsies. His hopes that the lab might help him narrow the scope of the sprawling investigation were rapidly diminishing. As the investigation approached the three-week mark, Gitchell was desperate. He phoned police in Indiana and asked them to question Ricky Lee Murray, Christopher's biological father. But Murray had a sound alibi for his activities at the time of the murders.

On May 22, detectives questioned Melissa Byers. Some of what she said also contradicted what her husband had told the police. While he'd reported that Christopher had never disappeared from home before, Melissa said that Christopher had disappeared a few times recently, and that on a couple of those occasions he'd been gone for as much as two hours. One of the detectives also noted that "Melissa became concerned that maybe he had been molested." When the detectives asked Melissa who she thought might have killed the boys, she said she didn't know. But she added, "Whoever did this, the boys knew—at least one or all of the boys."

As detectives would soon learn when they saw Christopher's medical records, there was more to the child's story than either of his parents was reporting.[41] In 1990, when Christopher was only five, the Byerses had brought him to a pediatric neurologist in Memphis for evaluation of behavioral problems.[42] The doctor noted in his report, "The mother is 'at her wit's end.'" The doctor prescribed medication and saw Christopher several times in the next three years. The last time was in January 1993, less than four months before the murders. Christopher had not improved, and the neurologist wrote that he was "in a quandary" as to why.[43]

Detectives filed the information away, with little apparent interest. Nor, apparently, was their interest in Byers heightened when the Arkansas State Police reported conclusive evidence that Byers had lied about the Rolex watches. UPS officials had reported their suspicions to West Memphis police six months earlier. But they'd also put their own company investigator on the case and notified the Arkansas State Police. Now the fraud case had been solved. About three weeks after the murders, the state police informed police in West Memphis that contrary to what Byers had claimed, he had indeed received the watches—and sold them to a chiropractor in Jonesboro, Arkansas, about sixty miles north of West Memphis. The chiropractor had produced two canceled checks for the watches. The checks, totaling $9,050, were made out to—and had been endorsed by—Byers. The chiropractor and the jeweler who'd shipped the watches were willing to testify against Byers.[44] When it became clear that Byers could be prosecuted for another felony, he placed a call to Gitchell, saying he'd "made a mistake." Gitchell noted briefly that Byers had said "he wanted to be truthful and up-front about it. Hoping it would not interfere with the investigation."

Gitchell Desperate

By May 26, twenty days after the bodies were found, Gitchell still had not received the written autopsy reports. He was growing frantic. He typed a letter to crime lab officials, expressing his exasperation. He raised several questions in the letter, the answers to which, he said, were "vital" to his investigation.[45] What were the times of death? What were the causes of death? He pointed out that he still did not know. Could he get a diagram of the boys' wounds? Had "any tears or blood or punctures" been found in their clothes? Had a stick that was sent to the lab been used upon the children? Had the lab found "anything" that would indicate the involvement of a black male? Was there evidence that the boys had been forced to perform oral sex? Had they been sodomized?

The letter mentioned what was supposed to have been one of the department's most closely guarded secrets. Gitchell wrote that Dr. Frank Peretti, the associate medical examiner who had performed the autopsies on the boys, had "mentioned finding urine" in the stomachs of two of the boys. Peretti had asked that the police send "water samples" to the lab. Gitchell had done as Peretti requested, but so far the department had not been informed of any results. "What has been determined in regards to the urine?" Gitchell demanded. "Can the urine, if that is what it is, be used to eliminate any suspects—or develop any?" Additionally, he wanted to know, "Can you tell us which kid was killed first?" And, "Were the kids dragged?" Gitchell concluded: "Anything you can think to give us would be greatly appreciated. We need information from the crime lab desperately . . . without [it] our hands are tied . . . We feel as though we are walking blind-folded through this case."

Two days later, Gitchell wrote another frustrated letter, this one to John Fogleman, now the district's deputy prosecuting attorney.[46] Gitchell complained that he and his staff were "severely handicapped" by the lack of communication from the medical examiner's office. He specifically cited his need of the autopsy reports, which he had still not received. Gitchell reported that under the circumstances, he had been surprised to learn that Fogleman and another deputy prosecutor had recently driven to Little Rock to meet with crime lab officials.[47] The visit was extraordinary in at least two respects: first, as Fogleman later acknowledged, prosecutors do not normally involve themselves to such an extent in ongoing police investigations;[48] and second, the visit had been conducted without Gitchell's knowledge. "Maybe," Gitchell fumed, "you can learn something" from the medical examiner's office "to assist us"—something, he said, that the police, "for some unknown reason," had been unable to learn directly.

The prosecutors' unusual visit and the detective's testiness were signs of how the nerves of officials were fraying as the city prepared to observe the passage of a month since the murders. The triple murder case seemed to be going nowhere. And the moon was nearing full again.

CHAPTER FOUR

The Police Investigation: Part 2

Holy men tell us life is a mystery.
They embrace that concept happily.
But some mysteries bite and bark,
And come to get you in the dark.

A rain of shadows, a storm, a squall,
Daylight retreats, night swallows all.
If Good is bright, if Evil's gloom,
High evil walls the World entombs.
Now comes the end, the drear darkfall.[49]

WHILE GITCHELL WAS FEELING BLINDFOLDED and standard approaches to the case, including investigation of the families and pursuit of tips and leads, had not produced a suspect, interest in Gitchell's suggestion regarding a "gang or cult" was expanding to fill the void. Adherents to that theory focused their attention on a teenager from Marion who'd copied the lines above. While some who read those lines might see in them Gothic influences, such as those that inspired Edgar Allan Poe or Stephen King, and others might detect psychological depression or despair, law enforcement officials in Marion and West Memphis concluded that the poem suggested involvement in the occult. Though "the occult" would remain a vague term, a belief that occult, or satanic, activities were dangerously afoot in the county was already well established among some law enforcement officials by the time the murders occurred. That belief could be attributed to the efforts of Jerry Driver, a county juvenile officer, who was seen by police as the local expert on how the occult and crime converged.

Driver was not a police officer. After a career as a commercial airline pilot, he and his wife had opened a housecleaning service. When that venture failed, Driver, then in his early fifties, had taken a job with Crittenden County as a juvenile probation officer. He was supposed to keep track of kids who had gotten into trouble with the law. By the time of the murders, Driver was the county's chief juvenile officer. Steve Jones, the juvenile probation officer who'd spotted the telltale floating shoe, worked as Driver's assistant.

The murders shocked but did not surprise Driver. He'd been telling people for months that he expected something dire to happen. When it did, his first thought was of Damien Echols, a troubled kid whom Driver had been watching for about a year. From that moment on, this third aspect of the murder investigation had a clearly identified focus—something the other two approaches did not. In the weeks that followed, that focus would only grow sharper.

The boy had come to Driver's attention more than a year before the murders, when a woman called the Marion police to report that he was threatening her daughter. Damien, a high school dropout who lived in Marion's Lakeshore Estates trailer park, was seventeen at the time; Deanna Jane Holcomb was fifteen. Deanna's mother told police that her daughter had been dating Damien but that the two had ended their relationship earlier in the week. When police arrived at the Holcombs' house, Deanna reported that since she and Damien had broken up, he had been harassing her and one of her male friends. According to the police report, Deanna claimed that Echols—"five-eleven, one hundred sixty pounds, brown eyes, dark hair"—said he was going to kill the other boy "and dump him in the front yard of her house, and then come back and take care of her, and then burn the house down."[50] The girl's mother told the officer "that she was in fear for her daughter's life." Later, Driver would recall that the girl's family told him that Damien was "trying to get their daughter into black magic and this type of thing."[51]

Lakeshore was one of the poorest neighborhoods in a county that ranked among the nation's poorest 10 percent. While many homes there were neatly kept, with gardens and cheerful wind chimes, others slumped in neglect and dreary dilapidation. Most residents of

Lakeshore Estates subsisted on some form of state and federal assistance, and the Echols family was no exception. Damien lived with his sister, mother, grandmother, and stepfather in a small two-bedroom trailer. Tensions in the household were simmering. The investigating officer drove to the trailer, and when the dark-haired teenager answered the door, the officer warned him to stay away from Deanna and her family.

But problems of the Echols family had also come to the attention of social workers. Exactly a year before the murders—on the same day, as it happened, that Judge David Burnett ordered the terroristic threatening conviction of John Mark Byers expunged—a mental health worker visited the Echolses and concluded that both Damien and his sister, Michelle, needed help. A report on the visit described the family's problems as being "severe."

Damien and Michelle's mother, Pam, was thirty-four years old, twenty years younger than her second husband, Andy "Jack" Echols, who'd adopted her two children. In 1992, a caseworker assigned to the family saw it as verging on the breaking point. Damien's breakup with Deanna, which he said had come at the insistence of her parents, exacerbated the tension. Within a month after the first incident, Deanna's mother again called the police, this time to report that her daughter had begun to see Damien again.[52] An officer responded to the Holcombs' house, and while he was taking the woman's report, Deanna arrived home, accompanied by Damien. Her mother yelled at Damien to get off her property and to stay away from Deanna. The girl yelled back that she wanted to be with Damien. The officer reported, "Damien advised that he had just walked her home" after Deanna had become sick at school. But Deanna's mother was furious. The officer warned Damien once again to stay away from Deanna. He wrote in his report that the girl's mother said she was going to take her daughter to a psychiatrist.

The story of forbidden love might have ended there. But during a thunderstorm six nights later, Deanna's mother called the police again, this time to report that Deanna had run away from home—presumably with Damien. Officers headed for Lakeshore Estates, where they found the teenagers, both "partially nude from the waist down," in an uninhabited mobile home.[53] Damien's friend Jason Baldwin was with them. Damien and Deanna acknowledged that they had planned to run away. But since neither Damien nor Deanna owned a car—or even drove one, for that matter—they had sought refuge in the trailer to wait out the storm. Nothing was reported stolen, but police charged the pair nonetheless with burglary and sexual misconduct. Damien and Deanna were taken to the county jail, and Driver was notified. Someone from the juvenile office went to the Echolses' trailer and asked to search Damien's room. Pam Echols granted her permission, and the juvenile officer walked out with notebooks containing Damien's writings and drawings. Pam said she was told that they would be returned, but that they never were. The notebooks, which included the poem above, were placed into Damien's juvenile record. Driver considered them evidence that the boy was veering dangerously toward an interest in the occult.

Deputy prosecutor Fogleman filed charges against Damien for the incident at the trailer.[54] While Deanna was released to her parents, Damien was ordered to be held in a juvenile detention center about an hour north of West Memphis. Though Damien obeyed the center's rules and, according to records, treated its staff with "the utmost respect," word circulated that he and Deanna had intended to conceive a child and that after its birth, the child was to be sacrificed in a satanic ritual. When Driver heard the rumors, he contacted a psychiatric hospital in Little Rock and drove Damien there himself.

For Driver, it was a relief to have Damien in a hospital more than a hundred miles away. Driver didn't know if the rumors about Damien were true, but Damien's own statements had been enough to convince him that the boy was headed down a dangerous path. For starters, Damien had told Driver that he was a witch. "I think his claim was that he was a Wiccan," Driver later said, "and he worshiped goddesses." The boy also dressed mostly in black. To Driver, "he looked like one of the slasher-movie-type guys—boots, coat, long, stringy black hair, though he cut it short sometimes." As Driver saw it, Damien was part of an alarming trend in the county, one that was drawing not just Damien Echols but many teenagers toward Satan.

Even with Damien hospitalized, Driver noted with growing concern that "his modus operandi continued" in Crittenden County. Driver concluded that Damien was a leader or central figure in a group devoted to what Driver termed "occult-related activity." Driver and Jones found pentagrams and other "cult-related" graffiti under railroad bridges, on fortifications alongside the interstates, and in an abandoned cotton gin east of Marion that kids had nicknamed Stonehenge.[55]

Driver knew that some of the goings-on could be chalked up to adolescent mischief. He recognized that "a lot of this devil worship stuff was an excuse to drink and have sex" and that some of the kids who were involved were "dabbling, doing it as a lark." But others, like Damien, appeared to Driver to have gone beyond mere dabbling. Driver's concerns were not uncommon at that time.[56]

By the late 1980s, interest in the suspected prevalence of satanic ritual abuse, or SRA, as it became known, had grown so intense in the United States that the subject was discussed in settings as diverse as psychological conferences, religious tent revivals, police training seminars, *Ms.* magazine, and television talk shows, where the words "satanic," "occult," "ritualistic," and "paganism" were often ill defined or used interchangeably. Fantasy role-playing games, such as Dungeons and Dragons, as well as certain kinds of rock and roll music—especially heavy metal—were described as gateways to a dark world that could lead to ritual abuse. At worst, specialists in the new field of SRA warned, teenagers who started out innocently playing with Ouija boards or reading books on paganism and magic could be drawn into rites involving the use of dangerous symbols, and from there into vandalism, animal mutilations, ritualistic abuse of children, and suicide, or even murder.

By 1991, law enforcement interest in "bizarre cults and human sacrifice" had grown so intense that the FBI undertook a search of national records to determine just how widespread it was.[57] That year, an FBI specialist concluded that "after all the hype and hysteria is put aside, the realization sets in that most Satanic or occult activity involves the commission of *no* crimes, and that which does, usually involves the commission of relatively minor crimes such as trespassing, vandalism, cruelty to animals, or petty thievery." But that unsensational point of view had a hard time competing against accounts of mind control, sadism, and slaughter committed in the service of Satan. Driver was one of thousands of public officials who considered it their legal and moral duty to be on the alert for suspicious activity that might signify greater, albeit hidden, evil. So while Damien Echols was in the Little Rock psychiatric hospital, Driver contacted a consultant who lectured on crime and the occult.[58] The consultant came to West Memphis armed with photographs of graffiti and cult-related paraphernalia, which Driver recognized as similar to what he had been seeing in Crittenden County. Driver also attended seminars in Texas and Tennessee on the subject of crime and the occult, and he led seminars of his own.[59] Yet despite Driver's vigilance and Damien's absence, it seemed to Driver that the cult-related activity in his area was escalating. He kept hearing rumors that some "bad things were going to happen," and felt that the situation was headed, as he later put it, "toward some sort of crescendo."

Psychiatrists assessing Damien were not, however, so alarmed. They reported the teenager's beliefs, but only as part of a broader psychological profile.[60] And at least some of the staff was willing to acknowledge certain distinctions. A psychiatrist carefully noted that Damien "indicates he is not involved with Satanism, but witchcraft." The doctor also observed that Damien smoked a pack of cigarettes a day, had a history of asthma, and wore a "crude, rudimentary, self-inflicted tattoo" in the "shape of a scientific symbol representing the female sex" on his left upper arm. Damien's diagnosis was major depression. A psychological examiner raised the possibility of a bipolar, or manic-depressive, disorder. Whatever the cause, Damien's immediate problems were listed as "extreme physical aggression toward others, suicidal ideation and intent, depressed mood, and bizarre and unusual thinking."

He remained hospitalized for three weeks. Upon his release, the hospital notified Driver that doctors had prescribed Imipramine to treat Damien's depression. The report to Driver also noted that although Damien had drawn "numerous pictures of witchcraft type symbols" and written "some very unusual poems," he was no longer considered to be a danger, either to himself or to others. It also notified Driver that Pam Echols, Damien's mother, intended to move with him and Michelle away from Arkansas. The psychiatrist informed Driver that he had spoken with Fogleman, the prosecuting attorney, "who was in agreement with Damien's leaving the state."

In July 1992—the month that John Mark Byers was arrested on drugs and weapons charges in Memphis and released to federal marshals in the middle of the night—Damien and Michelle Echols moved with their mother to Aloha, Oregon. There, Pam reunited with Joe Hutchison, her children's biological father. Joe managed a BP gas station in Aloha, where he was able to put Damien to work. It was an ironic occupation for a teenager who had never driven a car.[61]

Aloha, Oregon, was two thousand miles from West Memphis, but Driver's interest in Damien followed the teenager there. Pam Echols and her children had barely settled into Joe Hutchison's little apartment when Driver contacted juvenile authorities in Oregon, asking that they provide "courtesy supervision" of Damien for as long as he remained on probation. An Oregon juvenile counselor wrote that in his referral on Damien, Driver had "made the following comments: a) Damien and several others of his associates are involved in a Satanic cult; b) Damien and his girlfriend were both placed in a psychiatric hospital; c) Damien threatened to kill his girlfriend's parents; d) Damien claims he is a witch; e) Damien and his girlfriend were planning to have a child, so that they could offer it as a sacrifice to Satan; and f) the authorities in Arkansas suspect that Damien's parents are involved in this Satanic belief system."[62]

With what might have been some trepidation, the Oregon counselor paid a call on the Echols family. He later wrote that Damien's parents, Pam and Joe, said they were having no problems with the boy. Damien was not enrolled in school, the counselor noted, but was working full-time at his father's gas station, earning $5 an hour. "Damien can express no hobbies or interests," the counselor wrote, "and, when asked about what he does for fun, he says he never has fun." For the record, he noted that amid other instabilities, even Damien's name seemed to be in flux. The boy was named Michael Wayne Hutchison at birth, but had changed his name entirely when Jack Echols adopted him. The counselor reported, "Damien indicated that he changed his name from Michael to Damien because, at the time, he was involved in a conversion to Catholicism, and that Damien was the name of a saint he respected. At this time, Damien indicates he is in the process of having his name legally changed from Damien back to Michael Damien Wayne

Hutchison. Damien is currently going by the name of Michael at his work place."

The juvenile counselor also checked on Driver's concerns. "Damien denies any involvement in a Satanic cult or beliefs in Satanism," he wrote.

> He expressed considerable displeasure with Mr. Driver in making such assertions. Damien did acknowledge a suicide pact that he and his girlfriend had made if the authorities or her parents attempted to keep them apart; however, he indicates that, following hospitalization, he no longer is interested in hurting himself or anyone else. Damien denies ever making threats of killing his girlfriend's parents. Damien acknowledges he is a witch, and indicates this is his religious preference. He also distinguishes his religious beliefs from Satanism, indicating he believes in a series of gods and goddesses, and he sees this as his religious preference, which should not be of concern to state authorities. Damien felt that my inquiries in this area were an intrusion into his privacy, and declined to discuss the matters further.

The meeting was uneventful, and after it the officer recommended that Damien be supervised at "a minimum level" for the next four months—until December 11, 1992—when he would turn eighteen.

But Driver was far from satisfied. Two days later, Oregon officials received another letter from him, this one reporting that Damien had been "trying to get in touch with the young lady that was arrested with him." Driver added that Damien's attempt to contact his former girlfriend was "in violation of the terms of his probation," although no records supported that contention. The Oregon authorities did not respond.

Damien could not escape Driver. He could not escape the turmoil in his family. And he could not escape the destructive forces at work in himself. Within two months of his parents' reunion in Oregon, they were calling the local police, reporting that they were afraid Damien might be about to hurt someone—either himself or them. Officers took

Damien into custody, and after discussing "his options" with him, they took him to a local hospital.[63] An examining doctor reported that Damien was responsive, coherent, and calm; denied having experienced hallucinations or delusions; denied his parents' statements that he was "into Satanism or devil worship"; and denied having threatened "to cut the throat of his mother." The physician also noted, however, that even since arriving at the hospital, Damien had "also apparently made some verbal threats to his father." The doctor had Damien admitted to a psychiatric ward under a suicide watch.

When the members of the medical staff questioned him the next morning about events the night before, Damien insisted that he had not intended to kill himself, though he admitted that he had been depressed for a long time, mostly due to problems relating to his family. He said he missed his girlfriend, Deanna, and that he also missed Jason Baldwin, his best friend. After a family counseling session, therapists recorded the same assessment that mental health workers in Arkansas had reached a half year earlier: that the Echols/Hutchisons were a severely troubled family. Joe Hutchison had volunteered that he barely knew his son. Pam had said that as a result of Damien's threats, she and Joe did not want him around. But Damien's assessment was not entirely bleak. One examiner reported that although his math skills were weak, he read at a high level, and his language skills were outstanding, even though he'd hardly attended school for the past three years. After reviewing a poem he'd written, she noted, that his "use of language is very high level and beautiful in quality, although it has a morbid appeal to it."

In the end, the question became what to do with this troubled, perhaps gifted, adolescent, whose family had no money. After two days at the hospital, the staff no longer considered Damien a threat, either to himself or others. But his family did not want him, and Damien himself wanted to return to Arkansas. In light of the fact that he would turn eighteen in just three months, Damien's physician wrote: "Plans for emancipation and return to Arkansas seem reasonable to me." The hospital notified Oregon juvenile officials. They, in turn, notified Driver that Damien would be returning by bus to Arkansas, where he planned to live again with Jack Echols, and that he would contact Driver upon his arrival.

Though the plan was approved by Oregon officials, it was not okay with Driver. Four days after Damien walked out of the Oregon hospital, Driver swore out an affidavit stating that he had violated the terms of his probation "by threatening the life of his mother and father and by refusing to obey their lawful orders."[64] At Driver's request, prosecutor Fogleman filed a petition in chancery court claiming that, in addition to the threats, "Damien Echols has since continued to violate the terms of his probation by moving from the home of his parents and returning to Marion, Arkansas."[65] Nowhere did the petition to have Damien's probation revoked mention that Oregon juvenile authorities had been notified and approved of his move, or that Driver had been formally notified as well. Upon his return to Arkansas, Damien was adjudicated a delinquent, taken into custody, and sent, once again, to the region's juvenile detention center. [66]

He was furious. A few hours after arriving at the detention center, as he was sitting in the recreation area with several other teenagers, he confirmed Driver's darkest suspicions. As the center's director reported: "One of the boys had scraped his arm a little, and it was bleeding some. Without warning, Damien grabbed the arm that was bleeding and began to suck the blood from it. The boys all stated he had been saying he had not taken his medication the night before, and he was about to 'go off' on them. Damien was asked why he did this, and he stated, 'I don't know.' He also told staff he had threatened to kill his father and eat him." The director concluded, "It is our opinion that Damien needs mental health treatment."[67]

The court ordered Damien to be returned to the psychiatric hospital in Little Rock where he had been treated before. This time, Damien's hospitalization lasted for two weeks. When he was released, at the end of September 1992, the hospital notified Driver that, as during Damien's other hospitalizations, his behavior while at the hospital appeared normal, though he "was cautioned about his behavior and how it might appear to others." He was instructed to continue taking Imipramine for depression and to avail himself of follow-up care at the local mental health center.[68]

Damien returned to Marion. He still had two and a half months before he would turn eighteen, and until then he would remain under

Driver's supervision. Driver imposed three requirements: first, that Damien was to come to Driver's office at least once a week; second, that he was to observe a curfew; and third, that he was to enroll in the local vo-tech school and obtain his GED. Damien signed a contract agreeing to all three stipulations, and by the end of December, ten days after his eighteenth birthday, he'd earned his high school equivalency diploma and satisfied the other conditions as well.

But Driver was still not satisfied, and he was far from convinced that Damien was as harmless as his doctors believed. He thought Damien was looking for power. He felt that the teenager's unusual appearance, his unconventional religious beliefs, and the satanic rituals that Damien denied—but that Driver was convinced he had conducted—were all the attempts of a social outcast to acquire some form of control. "He'd come from a horrendous family background," Driver would later explain. "He'd grown up in very poor circumstances, and he'd been picked on by other kids. I think he took on this strange persona to keep people away, to keep them from picking on him. And he progressed from that to using his oddness to serve his desire for power." In Damien, Driver saw a teenager with "a cold look to him." He believed the boy had become one of those people "who could do things without remorse." As he later told the West Memphis detectives, "The further I went with him, the more apprehensive I was getting."

Damien, meanwhile, had begun dating sixteen-year-old Domini Teer, who lived near him in the trailer park. He got a part-time job with a roofing company. And he kept his appointments at the mental health center. On his first visit there, the social worker noted that he came dressed in black, wore a silver cross, and made "intense eye contact." Damien grew to trust the therapist, and over time, in what he believed was the confidentiality of their sessions, he made several statements, which she recorded in her notes. "Damien reports being told at the hospital that he could be another 'Charles Manson or Ted Bundy,'" she wrote. Another time: "Describes self as 'pretty much hate the human race.'" And on another occasion: "Reports being harassed by local authorities, as 'they think I'm a Satanic leader.' He admits being caught with Satanic items and with handwritten books about witchcraft. Denies cult involvement. Has been interested in witchcraft for past eight years."[69]

When Echols visited the therapist on January 25, 1993, the session focused on death. Afterward, the therapist wrote that Damien had raised the subject with a poem he'd written the week before. "The theme of this poem centered around death and power," she wrote. "Damien explained that he obtains his power by drinking blood of others. He typically drinks the blood of a sexual partner or of a ruling partner. This is achieved by biting or cutting. He states, 'It makes me feel like a God . . .'" At the end of the session, the therapist encouraged Damien to continue writing as a way of communicating his feelings. She wrote, "Damien is agreeable to doing this, though he continues to question the therapist on confidentiality issues and wants to be assured that he will not be misunderstood."

Damien had reason to worry. As other parts of Gitchell's investigation, for one reason or another, dried up, the belief that the boys may have been killed by satanists began to take firmer hold. Gitchell's early remark about a cult was coming to the fore as the main theory of the case. And Damien's report to his therapist that "they think I'm a Satanic leader" was about to be proven correct.

CHAPTER FIVE

The Prime Suspects

WHILE A THERAPIST MIGHT HAVE viewed some of Damien's views as unhealthy, most people in the region, had they known of them, would also have considered them unholy. Here, as throughout the Mississippi delta, the spiritual landscape was rigorously Christian and rigorously literal. Here, to a greater extent than almost anywhere else in the country, angels were regarded as God's emissaries, hovering invisibly close at hand, and children were warned to be on guard against Satan, whose evils were just as near. A belief in possession by demons was common. It was, as one scholar noted, "an extension of the general Southern view that the devil is very real, the devil has great power and is vibrantly at work in the world."[70]

While not everyone in the Mississippi delta viewed the cosmos in such stark terms, most residents of east Arkansas did. Most attended a Christian church, and the churches most of them attended belonged to the conservative Southern Baptist Convention.[71] On Sunday mornings and Wednesday nights, in cities and along country roads, believers filed into white-steepled buildings, some grand and many humble, where preachers warned of a fiery hell and taught that redemption could be found only in the blood of the Savior, Jesus Christ. In such an environment, the ideas that Damien Echols was confiding to his therapist were beyond strange—they were blasphemous.[72] The fact that Driver had seen Damien's writings and read some of his psychiatric reports brought what otherwise might have remained privileged therapeutic conversations to the attention of police.

Driver and Jones

Even though Damien had complied with Driver's requirements that he check in once a week, obtain his GED, and receive counseling at the mental health clinic, and despite the fact that he was now eighteen and no longer the juvenile officer's responsibility, Driver's interest in Damien intensified with the start of 1993. The juvenile officer continued to find instances of what he took to be satanic rituals.[73]

When the bodies of the three eight-year-olds were discovered, one of them mutilated, Driver immediately started "to zero in on Damien and his group." He viewed Damien as a prime suspect, and he shared his opinion with his assistant Steve Jones and with Detective Donald Bray of the Marion Police Department. Bray's office stood across the street from the courthouse where Driver's office was located. "Don Bray was the first person who really listened to what was going on," Driver later noted. "He was interested in what we saw as the occult portion of the crime. I think the West Memphis police took a little longer to come around."[74]

Since Driver viewed Damien as a leader of cult activities in the region, he was also interested in Damien's friends. Besides Damien's girlfriend, Domini, the suspected cult leader was known to have only one truly close friend, sixteen-year-old Jason Baldwin, a former neighbor who shared Damien's interest in skateboarding and heavy metal music. The two had known each other since Jason was in the seventh grade and Damien was in the eighth. They had met in study hall. At the time, both lived in Lakeshore, "a dirty, grungy type place," as Baldwin would recall, where police were always patrolling.[75] "I wanted out of there," Jason later said. "A lot of people there didn't know where they was going in life. I guess they was just on autopilot. They didn't think ahead." Though Jason would later say he and Damien were both like that, at the time they met, "we thought we was the coolest people in school." Part of what drew them together was, as Jason later put it,

> Others didn't like us. They'd been accusing me of being a
> satanist since the sixth grade. It was because I had long hair

and wore concert T-shirts, with bands like Metallica and Guns n' Roses, and Ozzy Osbourne and U2. Damien and I kind of dressed different. I basically wore blue jeans or Bugle Boy jeans, with concert shirts. He liked straight clean black clothes, with nothing printed on them. But the way we dressed was one thing people criticized. Most of the other kids, they either wore sports clothes, like Tommy Hilfiger stuff, or if they were country people, they wore flannel shirts and cowboy boots and belts with giant buckles. So we stood out because, even though Damien and I dressed different from each other, we was also different from everybody else. And the music we liked was different from whatever they was listening to, too. I introduced Damien to Metallica and he introduced me to Pink Floyd. He too wasn't living his desired life, and just like my mom, he suffered from depression. I think that our friendship helped him.[76]

Jason would later recall,

Damien and I also did a lot of walking. We used to walk to the local Wal-Mart and bowling alley all the time, even when we didn't have any money. Neither of us ever had any money. We definitely *never* had twenty bucks! We could maybe get five or ten to go to the bowling alley or the skating rink, where we would just enjoy being around people, especially the girls. That is basically why we went to these places, was to meet new girls, shoot pool, and play video games. We would hear of concerts and things in Memphis, but we never had the money to go to them. Plus, my mom said that I wasn't old enough to go to one yet. My mom was very protective. At the time, whenever I went anywhere, I had to make sure to check in every hour. If I didn't I would get grounded.[77]

Jason's parents had been divorced for years by the time he met Damien. His father had disappeared from the family when Jason was four, and though the father lived in Arkansas, except for a Christmas visit eleven years after he'd left, he'd had virtually no contact with the family. "I don't care for him," Jason said. "He don't care for us." Jason was close to his mother, and as the oldest child, he felt protective of her. He appreciated how hard she worked to support him and his brothers, despite battling such severe depression that she had once attempted suicide. "It was pretty devastating," Jason wrote later in a school essay. "I was the one who found her and called 911 and kept her alive. But I am lucky. My mother is well and happy now and so am I."

While Damien had dropped out of school, Jason still attended and was a good, if unexceptional, student. His best classes were art and English, and with the encouragement of one of his teachers, he was beginning to think of studying to be a graphic artist after high school. By the tenth grade he recognized that he was something of a nonconformist, at least by the lights of Marion High. There was the way he dressed, which was linked to his tastes in music, both of which were outside the prevailing sports and country styles. He wore his hair long, pulled back in a ponytail—another departure from the norm. And if asked, he acknowledged harboring an atypical indifference to religion.

Jason believed in God, he believed firmly in right and wrong, but by high school he considered religion a comfort "for people on their deathbed." Damien, by contrast, was extremely interested in religious ideas, especially those that traced their roots to the distant past. That's why he was drawn to Catholicism and, later, to Wicca. But though Jason did not share Damien's interests, neither did he mind them.[78]

By the time Jason and Damien were in high school, they had come to the attention of Driver and Jones. Jason had gotten into trouble in 1990, when he was twelve years old and newly arrived at Lakeshore. As he related the incident, there was a tin building adjoining the trailer park, with one wall missing, a rusted roof, and rusted car frames inside. "Giant grass and weeds grew in there. You could just walk in. It was sort of a clubhouse for us kids." One day, when Jason was there with his brother Matt, who was ten at the time, and two other boys, "the police charged us with breaking in."

The official account of that episode paints a more serious picture. Police reported that the boys had broken the glass on a front-end loader, a 1969 Cadillac, and a 1959 Ford, all of which were described as "vintage cars and equipment." Baldwin was charged with breaking and entering and with criminal mischief. Fogleman, now a juvenile judge, placed Jason on probation and ordered him to pay nearly $450 in restitution, a huge sum for him and his mother. "He was going to send us to a training school for two years," Jason recalled. "But my mom said she wasn't going to let us go to a training school." Steve Jones, the probation officer, became Jason's nemesis. "He told me, 'I know you're trying to get a cult started,' " Jason later recalled. "After that, other kids would say, 'We hear you and Damien have got a cult.' We'd say, 'No, we haven't. Who told you that?' They'd say, 'The police.' "[79]

Despite the pressure, Jason could recall only one fight in which Damien was involved. That was the attack on the boy who had begun dating Deanna Holcomb, Damien's former girlfriend.[80] "From then on," Jason said, "Steve Jones would lead the 'anti-Damien' campaign across Marion and West Memphis—he and his sidekick, Jerry Driver. And after the murders, they would all go around asking people questions about the murders, but in the same interviews they would ask people if they knew Damien was in a 'satanic cult.' "

Don Bray

Before the bodies were found, as West Memphis police and county deputies were searching for the missing boys, talk of the disappearances naturally buzzed through the courthouse at Marion. In the police station across the street, Bray was confined to his office, attending to a routine complaint. The owners of a local truck stop had reported a $200 overrun on a customer's credit card and suspected a new employee, Victoria Malodean Hutcheson, who'd been on duty when the card was used. Bray was supposed to interview Vicki Hutcheson that morning. The thin, red-haired woman arrived at the appointed hour, accompanied by her eight-year-old son, Aaron.

This was the same Aaron Hutcheson who, a few hours later, would tell police in West Memphis about the black man in the maroon car who had supposedly picked up Michael Moore after school. But at this point, with the bodies still undiscovered, Bray was perturbed to see the child in his office. He would have expected a thirty-year-old woman to have had better sense than to bring her child to a police interview.[81] But Hutcheson explained that Aaron was a close friend of the missing boys. In fact, she added, Michael Moore and Christopher Byers were Aaron's two best friends. Bray sympathized and his interest in the woman and her son was piqued. It looked like there might be more to the interview than just a suspicious credit card transaction. It placed Bray near the center of what was, at the moment, the most sensational crime in the nation. Bray thought that young Aaron Hutcheson might know something about the boys that would help police search for them. He picked up the phone and called the West Memphis police to suggest the possibility. But by then it was too late. The dispatcher told Bray that the three bodies had just been found.

Bray hung up and related the news to Hutcheson. Suddenly the child with her looked both vulnerable and important. Aaron was the same age as the victims. He had been their friend. Who knew what he had seen or what he'd heard? It occurred to Bray that the boy might possess information that would help solve the murders—and no one had questioned him yet. Bray abandoned his interest in the credit card problem and turned instead to investigating the murders. Later, he told the West Memphis police that during the interview, Vicki Hutcheson reported that Chris Byers and Michael Moore had asked her to let Aaron go with them to the woods the previous afternoon but that she had refused. Bray said Aaron reported that in the past, he had been in Robin Hood with the boys on several occasions, and that Michael had gone swimming in the ditch. As for the truck stop's owners, Bray eventually told them that he believed they'd made an error in their paperwork and that no money was actually missing. Rejecting Bray's conclusion, they fired Hutcheson.

Police in West Memphis, meanwhile, were receiving some unusual calls. An anonymous informant reported that the pastor of a local Baptist church was concerned about some teenagers at Lakeshore trailer park, who allegedly worshiped the devil.[82] When police contacted the pastor, he said that a kid named Damien was suspected of being involved in cults. The minister said he'd heard that the cult held its meetings somewhere near the Mississippi River; that he had seen Damien wearing boots with the number 666 on them; and that Damien had a girlfriend by the name of Domini Alia Teer.

By now, Driver had also related to Bray the suspicions he and Steve

Jones harbored about Damien Echols and Jason Baldwin. Bray regarded Driver as "the most knowledgeable man in the county when it came to Satanic worship." During their discussions of the murders, Driver had written the names of eight teenagers on a piece of paper. He handed the paper to Bray and told him confidently that when the investigation was over, one or more of the kids whose names appeared on that paper would probably be charged with the murders. Damien's and Jason's names were there; so was Domini's. Bray folded the piece of paper and put it in his shirt pocket, where he would carry it for the next several months.[83] The reports of devil worship in Robin Hood, the pastor's concerns about cults, and Driver's interest in Damien and Jason were enough to prompt Lieutenant Sudbury and juvenile officer Jones to pay a call on the teenagers.

Sudbury, Jones, and Griffin

Although Jones was not a police officer and Sudbury normally worked exclusively on drug cases, the two teamed up. Together they conducted the first interviews in the case that focused on the murders as the work of a satanic cult. For many who learned of it, the leap from the murders to satanism was not much of a leap at all. Everything about the crime— the ghastliness of the murders themselves, the age of the victims, the castration, and the tied-up, naked bodies—struck the psyche as horrific. The murders seemed the very essence of evil. And hadn't Driver been warning about people courting the devil—about worship directed not to God but to the very prince of evil? While Gitchell and other detectives employed more standard investigative techniques, Sudbury and Jones reviewed Driver's literature on crimes related to the occult. At around noon on Friday, May 7, less than twenty-four hours after the first of the bodies had been lifted out of the creek, Sudbury and Jones went to the trailer park in West Memphis where Damien was living. His mother, Pam, was there now too, having moved back from Oregon with Damien's father, Joe Hutchison. Sudbury and Jones questioned Damien on the steps of the trailer but made no notes of the interview.[84]

By the very next day, May 8, the sense that the murders might be linked to satanism was gaining strength within the department. When a detective reported that an interview subject claimed to have seen two black men and a white man coming out of the woods, Gitchell read the report, then scribbled across the bottom: "Has been mentioned that during cult activities, some members blacken their faces."

On day three of the investigation, Driver gave Sudbury the list of names that he had already given to Bray. Sudbury passed the information to a fellow narcotics detective, Investigator Shane Griffin. Griffin then teamed up with Detective Bill Durham, the department's polygraph expert, and the two drove to Marion to question Jason.

The rented trailer where Jason lived with his mother, stepfather, and two younger brothers sat on a lot that backed up to a two-acre lake. Griffin and Durham knocked at the door at about 5 P.M. Jason opened the door wearing a Metallica concert T-shirt. He stepped into the yard, followed by Damien and Domini. What followed would mark the second time that Damien had been interviewed. The detectives asked the kids where they had been the night of the murders. "They said that on Wednesday, May 5, 1993, they had gone to Jason's uncle's house and Jason had cut the lawn," Griffin later wrote. "Damien phoned his father to pick them up at the laundrymat [*sic*] at Missouri and N. Worthington. They said they were picked up at 6:00 P.M. and Damien's father took Jason and Domini home and Damien went home."[85]

Next, Griffin and Durham took out a list of questions that Sudbury had prepared for them. Griffin questioned Damien first. The teenagers were questioned in the yard. They were not told they were suspects. They were not read their Miranda rights or told they could have a lawyer present. None of their parents were there.

Damien told Griffin that he had been in a psychiatric hospital, where he was diagnosed manic-depressive and schizophrenic; he gave them the names of his therapist and psychiatrist, and he told them that he was taking antidepressive medication. Griffin later wrote that Damien "used to be involved in Wiccan religion—Covenant of Divine Light, which practices white witchcraft," and that his girlfriend, Domini, "is four months pregnant with his child." Griffin asked Sudbury's questions and noted Damien's answers on a sheet of notebook paper.

Asked if he knew the boys, Damien said he'd "never heard of them."

He said anyone who would commit such a crime was "sick." When Griffin asked how Damien thought the boys had died, the detective wrote that Damien said, "Mutilation—cut up all three / heard they were in water drowning—cut up one more than others."

Then Griffin asked the question that had led police to Damien in the first place: "Do you believe in God, or the devil?" Damien answered, according to Griffin's notes, "I believe in a god, but a female god. Evil force not a devil."

"How does being questioned make you feel?" Griffin asked.

"Scared," Damien replied.

"Would you take a polygraph?"

"No reason I would fail."

"Why would your prints be in the area of or at the crime scene?"

"They won't be," Damien said.

Griffin then ran down the same list with Jason. But the younger boy was more cautious—or more intimidated—than Damien had been. At least, he offered shorter answers. Like Damien, Jason said he did not know the victims. He agreed that the killer or killers should receive the death penalty. He said he did not know why someone would commit such a crime. To the questions "How do you think they died?" and "How do you think the killer felt?" Jason answered curtly, "I don't know."

Jason said he did believe in God. He said that killing or watching someone die would make him feel "disgusted." And he told Griffin that being questioned made him feel "like a suspect." The detective was nearing the end of his list when Baldwin's mother, Gail Grinnell, drove up and flew out of the car in a fury. As Durham wrote in his notes, she "was very upset and accused us of picking on her son and said she did not want us talking to him." He added, "I attempted to reason with her, but to no avail. We then left."

Damien's responses to Sudbury's questions inflamed the lieutenant's interest. The following day, Monday, May 10, Sudbury asked Damien to come to the police station for more questioning. Damien went and again, unaccompanied by his parents or an attorney, answered the questions that were put to him. This time, Lieutenant Sudbury and Detective Bryn Ridge conducted the interview.

"Damien was very cold and unemotional," Sudbury later wrote in his report.

> Damien stated that the person who did the crime was sick or the act was part of a thrill kill. Damien stated that the penis is a strong symbol of power. Damien stated that the killer was not worried about the boys screaming due to there [*sic*] being in the woods. Also, he stated that the killer wanted to hear the screaming. Damien thinks that the killer thinks it's funny that he hasn't been caught and really doesn't care if he is caught. Damien stated that there would probably be stones, candles, a knife, and/or crystals in the area where the bodies were found. Damien states that the killer is probably someone local and that he won't run. Damien likes to read books by the author Anton LaVey/Satanist. Also by Steven [*sic*] King. Damien feels that sex is boring. Damien has EVIL across his left knuckles, just like his best friend Jason Baldwin. Damien considers himself to be very intelligent. Damien wants to be a writer of scary books or poems at some time.

Sudbury was proceeding on nothing more than suspicions, but Damien was doing nothing to allay them.

Ridge and Durham

Detective Ridge also wrote notes on the interview. Like Sudbury's, his began with a subjective assessment: "Damien was very calm and even cold as he answered the questions." Ridge's report was the first to record Damien's full statement of his whereabouts on the day of the boys' disappearance. "Damien stated that on Wednesday he was with Jason Baldwin and Domini Teer and that they had gone to Jason's uncle's house on Center Street in West Memphis. He couldn't give a specific address, but said that it was near Alexander's Laundromat, where he stated that he called his mother to pick him up. He stated that his mother picked him up along with Domini Teer and took Domini home." Echols said that he then went with his mother, father, and sister to a friend's house, where they stayed until about 5 P.M., at which point the family returned home. That evening, he said, he called a friend in Tennessee and talked to her until about eleven-thirty that night. He told the police that he remained at home the rest of that Wednesday night.

On Thursday, Ridge wrote, Damien said that he went to Lakeshore,

> where he stayed the night with Domini. He stated that he heard the boys were missing from Jason Baldwin while he was at Lakeshore that day. He then stated that he heard the news that the boys were missing from Jason's mother.
>
> Damien stated that Steve Jones from the Juvenile Authority had been by to see him a day or two before,[86] and that Steve had told him about how the boys' testicles had been cut off and that someone had urinated in their mouths. He stated that Steve stated that could have been the reason that the bodies were placed in the water, so that the urine could have been washed out.

This was an interesting note. Here Damien was telling the West Memphis detectives that Jones, who was neither a police officer nor part of their department, had already revealed to Damien some highly unusual—and very specific—information pertaining to the case; specifically, "that someone had urinated in their mouths." The unusual report about the urine had been relayed to Gitchell verbally by Dr. Frank Peretti, the state pathologist who'd performed the autopsies, and it was one of the few details that supposedly was known only to investigators. Yet here, just three days after the autopsies, a teenager, who might also be a suspect, was telling West Memphis detectives that when he was questioned by Jones two days earlier, Jones had divulged this peculiar information to him. If the detectives suspected that Damien might have known about the urine firsthand and was lying when he said he heard it from Jones, there was no indication of that in the record, and Damien was never questioned further on the point. Likewise, if the officers were at all distressed about this significant breach of the secrecy Gitchell had tried so hard to impose—and what it might suggest about what other details may have been released—no report of follow-up discussions with Jones were included in the record either.[87]

Ridge continued:

At this time, Damien was asked if he would submit to having hair samples taken and blood samples. He stated that he did not object to the samples being taken. It was further asked if he would be willing to take a polygraph examination if one could be scheduled, and again he stated that he would take the test. Lt. Sudbury then left the room and attempted to set up a polygraph examination to determine if he was being truthful in his statements . . . At this time Damien was turned over to Detective Durham for a polygraph examination.

Detective Durham did not record the polygraph interview. He inserted no record of his machine's electronic responses into the police record. All that remains of that episode is a one-page investigative report written by Durham that day. The full text of that report reads:

On May 10, 1993, I interviewed Damien Wayne Echols, W/M 18, of 2706 South Grove, West Memphis, Arkansas. He denied any involvement in the crime. After approximately forty-five minutes, I asked this subject what he was afraid of. He replied, "The electric chair." He then said that he liked the hospital in Little Rock. He said he had been treated there for manic depression. After a short period of time, he ceased to deny his involvement. (Admission through absence of denial.) He then said: "I will tell you all about it, if you will let me talk to my mother." Detective Ridge brought his mother in to my office to talk to him. After talking to his mother, he again denied being involved in the murders. After approximately twenty minutes, I asked: "You're never going to tell anyone about this but your doctor, are you?" He replied, "No."

Ridge wrote in his notes that after the polygraph examination, "Detective Durham came and met with me and other officers and reported that Damien had been untruthful, and according to the polygraph, was involved in the murders."

Tips and "Monstrous Evil"

Officially, few people outside of the county's law enforcement establishment knew that within four days of finding the bodies, Damien and his friend Jason were already considered suspects. But unofficially, within a day or two after the murders, talk of specific suspects, specific details of the crime, and the department's specific interest in cults already was rampant. As rumors linking the murders to satanists spread, the police began to receive reports that, whether true or not, reinforced their theory. Two aspects of the investigation—the focus on cults and the occult and on suspects outside the families—subtly began to merge.

News reports added to the speculation. As early as one week after the murders, an article in *USA Today* focused on what it called the "monstrous evil" behind the crimes. The words, quoted from a sermon the Sunday after the murders, seemed to capture the region's horror. The same words appeared the following week in *People* magazine, in an article reporting that some townspeople already suspected that a "Satanic cult" was responsible for the crimes. Ministers preaching about the crime's incomprehensible "evil" fueled the atmosphere. One clergyman expressed the views of many in the town when he described the attack on the children as the "incarnation and manifestation of evil." He told his congregation, "We're not dealing with the garden variety of sin here. Anyone who would do something like this is not like you or me. They've reached the point that they refuse to recognize that anything wrong was done."[88]

Citizens in West Memphis were scared. Donations to a reward fund created by the police swelled it to $35,000. The volume of tips increased. One tip led them to L. G. Hollingsworth Jr., a seventeen-year-old cousin of Domini Teer. A caller had reported that L.G. knew something about the murders, that he may have been involved in them, and that his aunt Narlene Virginia Hollingsworth intended to cover up for him. Durham polygraphed L.G. the next day. He reported that the teenager appeared to be lying when he said he didn't know who'd killed the boys. When police confronted L.G. with Durham's results, L.G. said he suspected that Damien was the killer.

Police also questioned Narlene Hollingsworth. She told them that on the evening of Wednesday, May 5, when she was driving just west of the Blue Beacon between 9:30 and 10 P.M., she'd seen Damien with her niece Domini, walking west against the traffic. She said she noticed that the pants on both were muddy. Now, even officers who'd tended to doubt the cult theory began to give it more credence.

Detectives turned to Driver for help. Working on his information, they contacted Damien's former girlfriend, Deanna Holcomb, who was now sixteen years old. Durham polygraphed Deanna too, and reported that—like L.G.—she'd lied when she said she didn't know who'd killed the boys. When police questioned Deanna after the exam, she—like L.G.—had changed her answer. Like L.G., she'd told police that she believed Damien had been involved.[89]

On Wednesday, May 12, a week after the boys disappeared, police questioned Pam Echols. When they asked her about Damien's whereabouts on the afternoon of May 5, she told the officers that at about 3 P.M., she, Joe, Damien, and Michelle drove to visit some friends.[90] The friends were not home, Pam said, so she spoke briefly with their daughter and left a note for the parents. Pam said that on their way home the family stopped by a pharmacy, where a prescription for Damien was filled. After that, she said, the family stayed home, and Damien talked on the telephone with two girls who lived in Memphis.

Her account was almost identical to the one Damien had provided two days before. The friends verified that they'd found the note. Pharmacy records established that a prescription had been filled for Damien that afternoon, although records did not show when it had been picked up. And the two girls in Memphis confirmed that they had telephoned Damien that night. But Driver's reports about Damien, together with Sudbury's interviews, had offered some hope that Gitchell and his weary detectives would solve the case. Their pursuit of the satanic theory intensified, even though they had not a shred of evidence on which to base an arrest.[91]

CHAPTER SIX

The Volunteer Detective

ON MAY 13, one week after the murders, Detective Bray in Marion interviewed Vicki Hutcheson again. As before, Hutcheson brought her son Aaron with her. Since Bray had already concluded that the murders in West Memphis were probably "cult-related," he asked her if she knew anything about "an occult or devil worshipers."[92] Hutcheson said she did not, but a few days later she called Bray to report that kids in her neighborhood knew something about a local cult. She said she was going to "play detective" and try to find out more.[93] Bray did not object.

Hutcheson's personal investigation began with Jessie Misskelley Jr., a scrappy seventeen-year-old neighbor who frequently baby-sat for her children. Jessie lived near Hutcheson in a Marion trailer park. Hutcheson never explained how her interest came to focus on Jessie, but it may have been no coincidence that his name was on the list of suspects that Driver had given to Bray. Misskelley's father, an automobile mechanic, shared the same name as his son. He was known around Marion as Big Jessie, primarily for his strength, because he was barely of average height. Jessie Jr., or Little Jessie as he was called, stood maybe an inch over five feet tall. Perhaps to compensate for his size, he wore his hair spiked at the top of his head, adding another two inches. Jason Baldwin had known Jessie since the two were in elementary school. "He was all right," Jason would later recall. "He just didn't learn quick, and he didn't have much common sense, either. He could be funny, but maybe we were all laughing more at him than with him."

Within a week after the murders, Hutcheson knew, as many in Marion and West Memphis did, that the police were extremely interested in Damien and his reputed involvement with cults. She saw Jessie as a way to meet Damien, in furtherance of her self-assigned role as a detective in the murder case. As she later told the West Memphis police, "Little Jessie, Jessie Misskelley, lives down the street from me, and you know, I was really close to him because he was always around. He doesn't go to school or anything. He, like, helps you mow the lawn and stuff. I'd gotten really close with him." Hutcheson said that after the bodies of Aaron's friends were found, Misskelley had mentioned to her that on the morning the boys disappeared, he had seen some boys who'd fit their description walking near the Blue Beacon Truck Wash. It was an irrelevant and erroneous statement because, as Hutcheson and everyone else knew by then, all three of the murdered boys had attended school on the day they were killed. Hutcheson glossed over the remark.

Nevertheless, she told police, she had tried to ascertain whether Misskelley knew anything about the crime. "So, you know, I just kept talking with Jessie," she said, " 'cause, ah, Jessie's—I mean, he's not a bad kid, but you know, you don't know who people know. So I just kept talking with Jessie about stuff, and Jessie told me about a friend of his named Damien and that this friend drank blood and stuff."

Jessie Misskelley Jr.

For a little guy, Jessie had already developed a big reputation as a fighter. He'd been in trouble since kindergarten, and teachers had consistently recommended that he be seen by a psychologist. He was seen by several, most of whom attributed the boy's pugnacity, at least in part, to the fact that his mother had abandoned him and the family shortly after his birth. Jessie's father had created a sizable family through a series of marriages, presenting Jessie with nine siblings, all but three of whom were older than he. Psychologists reported that the family was loving but very rough. Jessie's main memory of childhood was one of "fighting all the time."[94]

"I had to take up for myself, to let people know they couldn't run over me just because I was small," he said. "I was walking around always looking for fights, because I knew they would come. I took up for a lot of people because I had a quick temper and I knew what it was like to be picked on. I'd been picked on since I was about four or five. My brothers always picked on me, and my stepsisters always picked on me. They tried to tell me what to do." Another memory was of his father drinking beer, "like a fish, every day since I was born." The habit, Jessie said, resulted in "some bad times—but that's how it is when people drink." Despite the "bad times," Jessie was devoted to his father. He considered him "a sweet guy," a man "who would do anything for anybody," and his "role model" in life.

Almost as soon as Jessie entered school, his teachers identified him as "slow." At seven, he still could not say his ABCs past the letter *R*. He could not count past fifteen. When Jessie scored 67 on an intelligence test, an examiner reported that he was mildly mentally retarded.[95] He was placed in special education classes, but his behavior was also a concern. Teachers described Jessie as sulky, disrespectful, impulsive, indifferent, stubborn, uncooperative, and prone to rage. They complained that he would "periodically lash out physically at fellow classmates" and at them. A psychologist who saw him at the age of seven recommended that Jessie's behavioral problems were so severe that he should be treated in a hospital. But as the family didn't have money, such treatment was never given serious consideration. The psychologist advised Big Jessie and Little Jessie's stepmother to take him for regular counseling sessions at the county mental health center—the same one where Damien would go. The Misskelleys went for a few sessions.[96]

But Jessie's fighting did not abate, and the next year, after having been suspended from school, the eight-year-old was taken to a psychologist in Memphis.[97] That examiner wrote that Jessie appeared to be a boy "who is non-psychotic, not retarded, [but] who feels bad about himself and his world. He sees himself as vulnerable, unable to handle the pressures which surround him and in danger of being overwhelmed." The psychologist added, "He pulls his own hair and bites himself when agitated. He is reported to have abused animals when he rages, and has shredded his clothes while out of control. His stepmother indicates that he will 'tear up anything at hand' when he is angry, though both parents agree that there is little way to predict when Jessie will rage."

The psychologist's notes offered other glimpses into the child's home.

Jessie's father presents himself as a man who has a very "bad temper," informing the interviewer of an occasion in which he fought five men and didn't "remember anything after the first lick," though he "won the fight." . . . Jessie's father also indicates very rough "play" with Jessie, including "play punches" which send him across the room and into the wall. His willingness to continue in this type of "play" indicates to the family that he is tough and can "take it." . . . Both adults agree that Jessie will fight everybody except his father. He directs his anger toward his father at safer objects.

Like the psychologist the year before, this one also recommended "a residential facility or hospital" for Jessie and family therapy for his parents. Again, the suggestion of hospitalization was rejected, and counseling sessions, while started, were not continued.[98]

Jessie was kept in kindergarten for two years and in second grade for two more, but the maturity his teachers had hoped to see did not develop. Instead, the boy's reputation as a troublemaker grew. He daydreamed in class, often seemed confused, and bullied other kids. Despite the special education classes, he fell further behind, academically and emotionally. When the psychologist examined Jessie at age ten, he reported an IQ of 75. The score placed Jessie at the low end of normal, though the boy's verbal abilities fell into the mildly retarded range.[99]

By the age of eleven, Jessie had made it only to the third grade. His teacher reported that he did not have an adequate vocabulary and that when reading, he could not understand a passage or draw conclusions from what he'd read. By then he was also regarded as dangerous. He'd hit a girl in the head, stabbed a boy with a pencil, and severely cut his own hand by punching windows out of cars. When the school suspended Jessie for splattering ketchup around the lunchroom, a juvenile judge sent him for yet another psychological examination. Both his parents were supposed to accompany him, but this time only his stepmother could attend. Big Jessie had been arrested for selling marijuana and was serving time in prison. Little Jessie told the court that he wanted to drop out of school, but the judge ordered him to continue.

Five troubled years later, by the age of sixteen, Jessie'd been promoted to the ninth grade, but his skills were barely at a fourth-grade level. On IQ tests he ranked among the lowest 4 percent of students his age. His last psychological evaluation was administered when he was sixteen, just before he dropped out of school. A report at that time said Jessie showed deficits in his "general information, abstract and concrete reasoning, numerical reasoning, language development, word knowledge, verbal comprehension, and spatial visualization."[100]

Jessie's own explanation for dropping out was that he "just didn't care about it no more." He would later recall that by that point, he "didn't care about nothing." He figured he'd probably become a mechanic like his father, who was now out of prison on parole and working in a garage in West Memphis. Other times, Jessie would dream of becoming a professional wrestler. But mostly, he later recalled, he was living "just one day at a time." That was the state he was in when Vicki Hutcheson and her two sons moved into a rented trailer not far from the Misskelleys'.

The "Esbat"

When Hutcheson asked Jessie if he knew of a kid named Damien Echols, Jessie said yes, but that he didn't know him well. "She asked me, was he into witchcraft," Jessie would later recall. "I told her, I didn't really know. I just knowed he was a weird person." Next, Hutcheson asked Jessie about Jason Baldwin—another of the boys whose name was on Driver's list. "Yeah," Jessie told her, "I've known Jason since the sixth grade. He's a nice person. Me and him, we've always gotten along."[101]

The fact that Jessie said he wasn't close to Damien or Jason didn't thwart Hutcheson's investigation. She told Bray, and later the West Memphis police, that she had a hunch about the killings and wanted to check it out by talking with Damien alone.[102] Hutcheson, a thirty-two-year-old waitress and mother of two, told Jessie that she wanted to go out with Damien. When Jessie promised to introduce her to Damien, Hutcheson reported the news to Bray, who relayed it to Jerry Driver. The two men thought it would be a good idea if Hutcheson could carry her undercover act further by making it appear that she was interested in the occult. Driver suggested that Hutcheson get some library books relating to the occult and place them around her house. Bray even provided a list of books from the Marion library that would fit the bill. When Hutcheson told Bray that she didn't have a library card, he allowed her to use his.

Jessie did as he was asked. The next time Jason and Damien were in the neighborhood, Jessie brought them to Hutcheson's house, made the introductions, and left. He walked to his own trailer, he said, and within fifteen minutes saw Damien's mother arrive in her car to pick up the two boys. Jessie assumed that Damien had called for his mother to come, since it was well known that Damien did not drive. As far as Jessie knew, that was the only contact Vicki Hutcheson ever had with Damien and Jason.

But Hutcheson would tell Bray—and later the West Memphis police—that a relationship had developed between her and Damien after that meeting and that it was the start of an eight-day romance—one that she said was entirely calculated on her part, passionate on Damien's, but sexless from beginning to end. She said the relationship had been strictly part of her "private detective" work.[103] "We talked about lots of different stuff," Hutcheson reported.

> He's not real, real talkative. You kinda have to pull things out of him. But he kept telling me about the boys' murders and how he had been—he never said "questioned," he always said that "I was accused for eight hours, I was accused of killing those three little boys." And I said, you know, I just acted like it was no big deal, and I said, "Well, you know, why would they pick you in West Memphis? You know, there are beaucoups of people. Why would they just pick you out?" And he just looked at me, I mean, really weird, and said, "Because I'm evil."

Far from being frightened by her association with someone who allegedly had proclaimed himself evil—and who was suspected by police of having committed a triple homicide—Hutcheson said she'd told Damien that she wanted to see him again to learn more about satanism. She reported to Bray that she expected to get that opportunity soon, as

Damien had invited her to attend something that he called an "esbat." Hutcheson said that she'd looked the word up in a dictionary, learning that it referred to a gathering of witches.[104] Later, Bray said that when he heard of this plan, he warned Hutcheson that it would be too dangerous for her to attend such an event. But, he said, she told him that she didn't care about the danger, if it would help catch the killers. If Bray instituted any protections for the young mother as she prepared to enter a realm that police suspected might harbor vicious murderers, neither he nor she ever mentioned them.

Hutcheson later reported to Bray that on the night of Wednesday, May 19—two weeks after the night the children disappeared—Damien picked her up at her house in a red Ford Escort. Beyond the description of the car, her details of the experience were thin. Jessie was in the car, she said. Damien drove them to a field north of Marion. They'd approached it by a dirt road, and she'd heard water running in the distance. When she climbed out of the car, she saw about ten young people, with faces and arms painted black, taking off their clothes and "touching each other." Offended, she asked Damien to take her home, and he agreed. Damien drove the car, leaving Jessie behind at the orgy. Hutcheson said she could not identify anyone she'd seen at the esbat because of the paint on their faces. She could not provide any names, because attendees had only used nicknames, such as Lucifer, Spider, and Snake.

Though Hutcheson did not mention it, there was no moon that night. Police apparently did not ask how the scene was lighted, or how she'd been able to see what little she'd described. Nor did police question her claim that Damien had driven the car, despite their awareness that he did not have a license and had never been known to drive, and that no one in his family owned a red Ford Escort.[105]

By the third week after the murders, the sheer number of allegations that Damien had taken part in the killings was beginning to have an effect. On May 26, the day that Gitchell complained to the crime lab that he felt "blind-folded," Detective Ridge interviewed yet another young man who reported that Damien had told him that he'd raped the boys and then cut them with a knife that was eight to ten inches long. By now, even if Gitchell had harbored reservations about information provided by a juvenile probation officer, a detective from another department, and a waitress turned self-appointed investigator, he was willing to set them aside. With little to show after nearly a month of investigation, the police in West Memphis were ready to talk to Vicki Hutcheson and to her little son Aaron.

"Nasty Stuff"

On May 27, Gitchell, Ridge, and Allen drove to Marion, where they questioned Vicki Hutcheson in Bray's office. She was a striking figure: five feet ten, 130 pounds, with red hair and green eyes. Aaron was there again with her. Under questioning by the West Memphis police, Hutcheson repeated much of what she had reported to Bray, and Bray added some details from the several interviews that he had by then conducted with Aaron.[106] Bray informed the visiting detectives that Aaron had told him that he and the murdered boys had often visited the woods together. The boy said they had a clubhouse there, and that on some occasions they'd spied on five men who gathered in the woods. Bray said Aaron told him that the men would sit in a circle, chant, sing songs about the devil, and do "what men and ladies do."[107]

The questions arising from Vicki and Aaron Hutcheson's statements were many and serious. But their allegations supported the theory that a cult was behind the crime, and at this rather desperate point in their nearly month-old investigation, the police were ready to overlook a few difficulties presented by their stories. They arranged to interview the mother and child again.

The next day, Vicki Hutcheson handed the police an object that seemed to reinforce the connection between her account and Aaron's—and also to link Damien to the reported rituals in Robin Hood. The object was a cheap pewter earring cast in the shape of a human skull. It featured a snake slithering out of one of the eye sockets and coiling around the skull. Vicki said that the earring had belonged to Damien, and that she had it because he'd dropped it while visiting her at her house. She said that when Aaron saw it, he'd told her that it was exactly like one worn by one of the men he'd seen chanting in the woods.

On the second day of interviews, Sudbury and Ridge asked Hutcheson if she would let them hide a tape recorder in the bedroom of her trailer. The idea was that she would invite Damien to her house during the coming weekend, get him into the bedroom, and lure him into discussing some of the activities she had reported. Hutcheson agreed and the trap was set. Hutcheson later said that Damien did come to her house, and detectives reported that a recording was made. But, they said, the recording was of poor quality and Damien's voice was not discernible on it. The tape subsequently disappeared.

After nearly a month on the case, the police still did not have a single piece of evidence that would tie anyone to the crime. On Wednesday, June 2, they decided to polygraph Hutcheson. Durham reported that she was telling the truth.

To Gitchell, the news was a breakthrough. From that moment on, there was only one thrust to the investigation, and it was directed toward Damien Echols.

CHAPTER SEVEN

The Confession

JESSIE HAD NO IDEA, as May 1993 slipped into June, that his neighbor Vicki Hutcheson was discussing him with the West Memphis police in relation to the murders. He would later say he was surprised when told the extent of what she'd said, particularly the part about Damien driving Hutcheson and him to the orgy.[108] He said no such trip had taken place and that, besides, "everyone knew Damien didn't drive." But Jessie's version of events during that last week of May agreed with Hutcheson's on a few points. Here's what he said happened:

"When I first heard about the kids come up missing, it was early in the morning, about nine o'clock. I was going to work with a friend of mine." Jessie said he heard the news on the radio as he and a friend drove east on I-40 toward Memphis, where they'd gotten a roofing job. When he returned from Memphis that afternoon, another friend told him that the bodies had been found.[109]

A few weeks later, Jessie said, Hutcheson asked him to introduce her to Damien Echols and Jason Baldwin. He found the request odd in light of her age, but he liked to help her out. The next time he saw Damien and Jason he told them that she wanted to meet them and brought them to her trailer. Jessie did not know that Hutcheson was in contact with Detective Bray or that Hutcheson believed she was doing undercover work for Bray.[110] He was not aware, by the end of May, that the West Memphis police considered Damien a suspect. Nor did he realize that information provided to the West Memphis police by Driver, Bray, and Hutcheson connected him to their prime suspect. He was so unaware of the circumstances that were closing around him that, on the night of June 2—four weeks exactly after the night the boys disappeared—Jessie agreed to stay at Hutcheson's house because her boyfriend was at work and she'd heard reports of a prowler in the neighborhood. According to both Jessie and Hutcheson, he slept on the couch with a gun nearby.

The next morning, Jessie was awakened around 9 A.M. by the sound of banging on the trailer's door. It was his father. "He said [Detective Sergeant] Mike Allen wanted to talk to me," Jessie said. "Did I have a problem with that?" Seeing that Allen was with his dad, the teenager answered no, he had no problem talking with the detective. He dressed and drove off with Allen at about 9:45 A.M.[111]

As Misskelley later recalled, "He said we was going to the police department. I didn't know what was going on. But I wasn't scared. At that time I didn't know what he wanted to talk to me about." Once inside the station, Allen filled out a standard form. Along with the usual height and weight, he noted that Jessie had several tattoos, including one on his right arm that said "FTW" (it was noted that that stood for "Fuck the World"), one of a skull and dagger on his left arm, and the word "bitch" on his chest. Allen explained that he wanted to ask Jessie some questions about the murders.

> But then he told me he couldn't ask me no questions without my dad signing papers. I told him my dad wouldn't have a problem with that. So we left the police station to go where my dad was at. While we was on the way, he told me if I knew anything, that there was a $35,000 reward, and if I could help them out, we'd get the money. We met my dad down on the service road. I talked to my dad about it. He said if I knew anything, to tell the police, and then my dad could buy him a new truck. We went back to the police station. I just told them what I knew—about the kids I seen on the side of the service road and what my friend told me. That's all I knew. That's when they gave me a polygraph.[112]

Allen was dispatched to get permission from Big Jessie, because Jessie Jr. was still a minor. The elder Misskelley was found at a McDonald's restaurant, where, without consulting an attorney, and apparently without reservation, he signed the form the police needed to polygraph his son.

Durham's Polygraph Exam

But the elder Misskelley did not sign a form agreeing to let Little Jessie waive his constitutional rights. According to police records, Jessie was read his rights twice within the next hour: once at 11 A.M., by detectives Ridge and Allen, and again at eleven-thirty, by Bill Durham, the department's polygraph expert.[113] Each time, Jessie was advised that he had the right to remain silent, the right to have a lawyer appointed, and the right, if he decided to answer questions, to stop at any time. Ridge reported that Jessie said he understood and signed the Miranda forms. But that is an overstatement. Never having mastered cursive, Jessie could only print his name.

Detective Durham administered the polygraph exam. "It was just me and him," Jessie later recalled.

> Mike Allen, Gary Gitchell, and Bryn Ridge—they were in another room. Bill Durham asked me some questions and I answered 'em. He asked me did I know who killed 'em. I told him no. He asked me would I tell him the truth. I told him yes. He asked me did I ever do drugs. I told him no. He asked me three times, over and over, and then when I was through, he told me I was lying. I told him, "Okay, I have done drugs before." He said, "I know you have because I've seen you sell them." And that's when I really got mad, because I told him, "I have never sold drugs. I've used them, but I ain't never sold them." That's when he told me I was lying. He told me that my brain was telling him so.

Here is Durham's account: Jessie was questioned briefly before the polygraph interview began. Durham wrote that in that pretest interview, Jessie "said that he has never participated in a Satanic ritual and has never observed one. He denied being involved in the murders and does not know who killed the three boys. He also said he does not suspect anyone." During the polygraph test, Durham asked Jessie ten more questions. After the test, Durham wrote that Jessie had recorded "significant responses indicative of deception" on these five critical questions: "Have you ever been in Robin Hood woods?" "Have you ever took part in devil worship?" "Have you ever attended a devil worship ceremony?" "Are you involved in the murder of those three boys?" And "Do you know who killed those three boys?" According to Ridge's notes, Durham came out of the interview room and announced, "He's lying his ass off."

Jessie later said that Durham had insisted his polygraph machine could read people's minds, and that it could tell if what was in their minds was different from what they said. "I didn't know what was going on," Jessie said. "Because how could my brain be telling him that I was sitting there lying? It got me confused. Then he stood up and he was talking. He kinda spit on me. I don't know if it was on purpose or not, 'cause he was yelling when he did it. I drew back. I was going to hit him. Then Mike Allen came in and grabbed me."

Jessie said the detectives moved him to another room while they talked to Durham. By now it was almost 12:30 P.M.

> Then Gitchell came and got me and took me to another room, and that's when he started talking to me. The whole time, the same questions that they'd already asked me, they kept asking over and over again. When Gitchell asked me what the boys looked like, I told him all the stuff I'd heard. I kept telling Gary Gitchell I wanted to go home. He said I could go home in a minute, then he kept asking me the same questions, over and over again.
>
> From that point, it just got rougher on down. They asked me, how did I know so much about the murder if I didn't do it? I kept telling him I didn't know who did it—I just knew *of* it—what my friend told me. But they kept hollering at me. Gary Gitchell and Bryn Ridge both. They kept saying they knew I had something to do with it, because other people done told 'em. After I told 'em what the boys were wearing, Gary Gitchell told me, was any of them tied up? That's when I went along with him. I repeated what he told me. I said, yes, they was tied up. He asked, "What was they tied up with?" I told 'em a rope. He got mad. He told me, "God damn it, Jessie, don't mess with me." He said, "No. They was tied up with shoestrings." I had to go all through the

story again until I got it right. They hollered at me until I got it right. So whatever he was telling me, I started telling him back. But I figured something was wrong, 'cause if I'd a killed 'em, I'd a known how I done it.

The Circle

The interrogations so far were not tape-recorded, and neither was the one that followed. The only accounts of what transpired are Jessie's, and two written reports by Ridge—a handwritten version and a later, type-written one. According to Jessie, the interview hinged on a moment when Gitchell literally drew him a picture. It was of a circle surrounded by Xs. Inside the circle, Gitchell drew three dots. As Jessie recalled the exchange, "Gitchell pointed to the dots and said, 'This is you, Damien, and Jason. The Xs are police all around you. You can be in the circle or you can be out.' I said I wanted to be out."

Ridge made no reference to any such circle in his typed report, but he did in his handwritten notes. According to his notes, the polygraph examination had produced a change in Jessie. As police continued to question him after his experience with Durham, Jessie made several accusatory statements about Damien and Jason. Now, according to Ridge, Jessie said that he had "received a call from Jason Baldwin the night before the murders. They were going to go out and get some boys and hurt them. . . . He knew what they were going to do." After that, Ridge wrote, "Jessie began to say something, and then says he doesn't want anything to do with it." But Jessie's hesitancy did not last. Following that expression of reluctance, Jessie reportedly told the detectives

—that he had seen a picture of the murdered boys at a meet-ing of a "Satanic cult"
—that "all meetings are held on Wednesdays"
—that the group "has had meetings in Robin Hood"
—that at the meetings, members built fires "of paper and wood and stuff," and "someone brings a dog, and they usually kill the dog . . . and eat part of it"
—that the animal killings were "part of a ritual"

—that on the Wednesday the boys were killed "there was no meeting"

—that "a friend of Jason's" would "bring a briefcase" containing "a couple of guns and drugs—marijuana and cocaine"

—that the picture he'd seen of the three victims standing "in front of a home" had come from the briefcase

—that he didn't know who had the briefcase now

—that "Jason and Damien are having sex with each other"

—that "Jason has a folding knife"

—that "Damien has watched boys in the woods where they were killed"

—that Damien and Jason had called him three times about the murders: once, the day before; again, on the morning of the murders; and a third time, soon after the murders, "after dark," when he'd heard Damien in the background saying, "We did it."

The statements sent a thrill through the station. But claims of a photograph, satanic rituals, a teenager with a folding knife, and even Damien's alleged shouts of "We did it" were not enough to claim a solution to the murders. On the other hand, Jessie's account had changed considerably since his arrival at the police station more than four hours earlier. He'd said initially he knew nothing of the murders. Now his statements were getting more elaborate, more accusatory, and more focused on Damien. The detectives upped the ante. According to Ridge's handwritten notes, they showed Jessie "a picture of one victim in the coroner's office." The notes continue: "Jessie knew it was one of those killed by Damien. Jessie looked hard at the picture and said it was of the 'Moore boy,' and that it was one of the boys in the Polaroid." This was apparently a reference to the photograph that was reported to have been in the briefcase seen at the esbat. Alongside this section of notes, there appears a circle, with the words "the circle" written inside. The next line of the text continues: "Jessie stated that he didn't want to be a part of this, that Damien and Jason killed, he did not."

With Jessie clearly shaken, Ridge wrote, "I left the room, at which time Jessie informed Gary Gitchell of his being present during time of the murders, [of his having] witnessed the murders by Damien and Jason." Having tape-recorded nothing so far, the detectives decided it was now time to record what Jessie was saying. Ridge's handwritten notes conclude: "Taped statement began after time given to get self composed."

Jessie later said that after the session with Durham, he had decided to start "telling 'em back whatever they told me." He said there were three reasons for that decision. The circle was one of them. The photograph of the murdered child laid out on the slab at the crime lab was another. "It was just a kid that was beat up in the face," he recalled, "but when I looked at it, it shocked me." His third incentive was a tape recording. After drawing the circle for Jessie and showing him the photo of the murdered boy, Gitchell had also played him a tape recording featuring the eerie, disembodied voice of a child. The voice said spookily, "Nobody knows what happened but me." Jessie was not told—and would not know until much later—that the voice was that of Aaron Hutcheson. The six-word segment of tape that Gitchell played for Jessie had been extracted from an interview with Aaron that police had recorded a few days earlier.

Ridge made no mention of the photo, the circle, or the child's voice in his typewritten report.[114] He did note, however, that, "at about 2:20 P.M., Jessie told Inspector Gitchell that he was present at the time of the murders. . . . We then prepared for the interrogation to be taped."[115]

Self-Incrimination

Until this day, Jessie's most serious experience with the police had been an incident involving the theft of several flags belonging to the Marion High School marching band. After years in special education classes, Jessie had dropped out of school, but he had dreams of building a speedway, and he needed some flags for it. Not too cleverly, he had gone back to school to steal flags from the band. Driver had recognized that Jessie was "kind of slow mentally," but Jessie's age and intellectual limitations were of little concern to the police. Except for the permissions they'd sought from his father to question and polygraph him, Jessie's claim that he understood his constitutional rights was treated the same as if he were a lawyer. Now, with the tape-recording about to begin, he was read his rights again, and again, without benefit of parents or counsel, he waived them.

The taped part of Jessie's interrogation began at 2:44. For thirty-four minutes, while tape fed through the recorder, Jessie answered questions for Gitchell, Ridge, and Allen. Most of his answers were vague. Many were contradictory. Almost all began with a prompt by one of the detectives.

"Okay, Jessie," Ridge said. "Let's go straight to that date, May 5, 1993. Wednesday. Early in the morning. You received a phone call. Is that correct?"

Jessie: "Yes, I did."

Ridge: "And who made that phone call?"

Jessie: "Jason Baldwin."

Ridge: "All right, what occurred, what did he talk about?"

Jessie: "He called me and asked me if I could go to West Memphis with him, and I told him, no, I had to go to work and stuff. He told me that he had to go to West Memphis so him and Damien went and then I went with them."

Ridge: "All right, when did you go with them?"

Jessie: "That morning."

Jessie said that he, Damien, and Jason had walked the three or four miles from Marion to West Memphis, and into the Robin Hood woods. Ridge asked what happened there.

Jessie answered: "When I was there, I saw Damien hit this one boy real bad, and then he started screwing them and stuff . . ."

Ridge showed him a newspaper clipping of the three victims and asked him which boy Damien had attacked. Jessie pointed to one of the pictures and said, "Michael Moore." But the boy Jessie pointed to was not Michael Moore. Gitchell, pointing to one of the photos, interjected, "This boy right here?" When Jessie answered, "Yeah," Gitchell said, "All right, that's the Byers boy. That's who you're pointing at?" Jessie said that it was.

Ridge continued: "Okay, so you saw Damien strike Chris Byers in the head?"

Jessie had not said he'd seen Damien strike Chris in the head. Nonetheless, he answered, "Right."

Ridge: "What did he hit him with?"

Jessie: "He hit him with his fist and bruised him all up real bad, and then Jason turned around and hit Steve Branch . . . and started doing the same thing. Then the other one took off. Michael Moore took off running. So I chased him and grabbed hold of him, until they got there, and then I left."

The statement marked a turning point, both in the questioning of Jessie and in the case. Jessie was saying that he had witnessed at least part of the crime. Not only that; Jessie was admitting his own participation. But like so much about this case, the statement was riddled with problems. The most serious centered on the crucial factor of time. Jessie said the incident he described had occurred in the morning. Yet the police knew that Chris, Michael, and Stevie had been in school then—and that they had remained there until school let out at 2:45 P.M. Another problem was that even in this self-incriminating version, Jessie was saying that he'd left the scene without having witnessed the murders. Ridge tried again, taking Jessie back to the moment when he'd said Michael had "took off running."

"Which way does he go?" Ridge asked. "I mean, does he go back toward where the houses are? Is he going to the Blue Beacon? Is he going out toward the fields? Where's he running to?"

Jessie: "Toward the houses."

Ridge: "Toward the houses?"

Gitchell: "Where the pipe is that goes across the yards?"

Jessie: "Yes, he run out there and I caught him and brought him back, and I took off."

It happened repeatedly: Jessie saying he'd left the scene without witnessing the murders.

Ridge tried again. "Okay," he prompted. "And when you came back a little later, now all three boys are tied?"

Jessie had said nothing about returning to the scene. But he answered, "Yes."

Ridge: "Is that right?"

Jessie: "Yes, and I took off and run home."

Ridge: "All right, have they got their clothes on when you saw them tied?"

Jessie: "No, they had them off."

Ridge: "They had already gotten them off? When he first hit the boy—when Damien first hit the first boy—did they have their clothes on then?"

Jessie: "Yes."

Ridge: "All right, when did they take their clothes off?"

Jessie: "Right after they beat up all three of them, beat them up real bad."

Ridge: "Beat them up real bad, and then they took their clothes off?"

Jessie: "Yes."

Ridge: "And then they tied them?"

Jessie: "Then they tied them up, tied their hands up, they started screwing them and stuff, cutting them and stuff, and I saw it and turned around and looked, and then I took off running. I went home. Then they called me and asked me, 'How come I didn't stay?' I told them, 'I just couldn't.' "

Ridge: "Just couldn't stay?"

Jessie: "I couldn't stand it to see what they were doing to them."

Still, Jessie was not saying that he'd witnessed a murder.

Ridge asked, "Okay. Now when this is going on, when this is taking place, you saw somebody with a knife. Who had a knife?"

"Jason," Jessie said.

In answers to a half dozen more questions, Jessie said he saw Jason cut one of the boys in the face and another boy "at the bottom," in what Gitchell established was "his groin area." Then Ridge asked, in a rare acknowledgment of Jessie's limitations: "Do you know what a penis is?"

"Yeah," Jessie answered. "That's where he was cut."

The officers established that the boy in question was "the Byers boy again." When Jessie confirmed, "That's the one I seen them cutting on," Ridge asked again: "All right. You know what a penis is?"

Again, Jessie said yes, and that that was where he'd seen Jason cutting, "right there real close to his penis and stuff, and I saw some blood, and that's when I took off."

The officers asked a few questions about where Jessie was standing as this bloody scene unfolded. He told them that he was on one of the banks overlooking the drainage ditch. "I was looking down, and after I seen all of that, I took off."

Ridge acknowledged Jessie's claim to have left the scene. "All right," he said, "you went home, and about what time was it that all of this took place? I'm not saying when they called you. I'm saying what time was it that you were actually there in the park?"

"About twelve," Jessie said.

Ridge: "About noon?"

Jessie: "Yes."

But the police knew that noon was no good. So Ridge's next question was: "Okay, was it after school had let out?"

Jessie: "I didn't go to school."

Ridge: "These little boys . . ."

Jessie: "They skipped school."

Every detective in the room knew, even if Jessie did not, that the statement was absurd. But the detectives persisted. And Jessie said it again: the boys had skipped school. In this version, he had met Jason and Damien in the woods "early in the morning," at about 9 A.M., and the victims, who had skipped school, had been murdered by noon.

Exasperated, Ridge asked Jessie if he wore a watch. When Jessie said that it was at home, Ridge suggested: "So your time period may not be exactly right is what you're saying."

"Right," Jessie answered.

As the interview progressed, Jessie's version of events grew more convoluted. At one point he told the detectives that "after all of this stuff happened, that night that they done it, I went home about noon, then they called me at nine o'clock that night." He said Jason placed the call, but that Damien was at Jason's house with him at the time. "They asked me how come I left so early and stuff, and I told them that I couldn't stay there and watch that stuff no more . . . And Damien was hollering in the background saying, 'We done it. We done it. What are we going to do if somebody saw us? What are we going to do?' "

But now Gitchell was growing impatient. He told Jessie, "I've got a feeling here you're not quite telling me everything. Now you know that we're recording everything, so this is very, very important to tell us the entire truth. If you were there the whole time, then tell us that you were there the whole time. Don't leave anything out. This is very, very important. Now just tell us the truth."

Jessie responded, "I was there until they tied them up and then that's when I left. After they tied them up, I left."

Gitchell: "But you saw them cutting on the boys."

Jessie: "I saw them cutting on them . . ."

Gitchell: "So what else is there, after that?"

Jessie: "They laid the knife down beside them, and I saw them tying them up, and that's when I left."

Ridge: "Were the boys conscious or were they . . . ?"

Jessie: "They were unconscious then."

Ridge: "Unconscious."

Jessie: "And after I left they done more."

Ridge: "They done more?"

Jessie: "They started screwing them again."

Jessie went on to describe a scene that, again, did not conform to the facts. The detectives knew that all of the bodies had been found in a highly unusual posture, backs arched and hands tied to ankles. Yet just as Jessie had failed to mention the removal of their clothes, he now ignored the peculiarity of how the boys were bound. He repeatedly mentioned only that their hands were tied. He even said that "one little boy" was "kicking" his legs "up in the air." When Ridge asked, if "just their hands are tied, what's to keep them from running off?" Jessie still did not say anything about the feet having been tied. The only reason he could offer for why the boys had not run off was that the assailants had "beat them up so bad so they can't hardly move."

Ridge tried again: "You said that they had their hands tied up, tied down. Were their hands tied in a fashion that they couldn't have run? You tell me."

But Jessie didn't get it. "They could run," he said.

Gitchell took another tack, asking: "Did you ever use—did anyone use—a stick and hit the boys?" Jessie volunteered that Damien had hit one boy with a "kind of a big old stick." He also said he'd seen Jason cut one of the boys on the face, using a "fold-up knife." And he said he'd been involved in the "cult" for about three months. Asked by Gitchell what the cult's members did "typically in the woods," Jessie replied, "We go out, kill dogs and stuff, and then carry girls out there. . . . We screw them and stuff. . . . We have an orgy and stuff like that."

Jessie had provided the detectives with a few details they could use. But they still lacked the crucial one. Ridge made a delicate move. "Okay," he said. "Let me ask you something. Now this is real serious, and I want you to be real truthful, and I want you to think about it before you answer it. Don't just say yes or no real quick. I want you to think about it. Did you actually hit any of these boys?"

Jessie: "No."

Gitchell: "Now, tell us the truth."

Jessie: "No."

Ridge: "Did you actually rape any of these boys?"

Jessie: "No."

Ridge: "Did you actually kill any of these boys?"

Jessie: "No."

Ridge: "Did you see any of the boys actually killed?"

Jessie: "Yes."

Ridge: "Okay. Which one did you see killed?"

Jessie: "That one right there."

Gitchell: "Now, you're pointing to the Byers boy again?"

Jessie: "Yes."

Ridge: "How was he actually killed?"

Jessie: "He choked him real bad and all."

The police had not seen—and the medical examiner had not mentioned—any indication that the boys had been choked, much less that that's how they died. But Ridge carried on. "Choking him? Okay, what was he choking him with?"

Jessie: "His hands, like a stick. He had a big old stick, kinda holding it over his neck."

Ridge: "Okay, so he was choking him to the point where he actually went unconscious, so at that point, you felt like he was dead?"

Jessie: "Yeah."

Jessie had claimed to have witnessed at least one of the murders. But again there was a problem, and not a minor one. Christopher Byers clearly had sustained a profound injury—one severe enough to have killed him—yet Jessie was not mentioning that. Instead, he was attributing the boy's death to strangulation with a stick. The trouble was that Christopher's neck was one of the few parts of his body that had shown no signs of trauma. Aside from a few scattered scratches, his neck appeared to have been untouched.[116]

Ridge and Gitchell did not press the point. They had an eyewitness to the murders. They opted not to be picky. But there was still the nagging problem of Jessie's times to be addressed. Ridge approached it once again. "Okay. They killed the boys," he said.

Jessie had not said he'd seen the other two boys killed, but Ridge glossed over that point. He continued. "They killed the boys. You decided to go. You went home. How long after you got home before you received the phone call? Thirty minutes or an hour?"

In an interview full of misrepresentations of what Jessie had said, this was one of the greatest. Jessie had repeatedly stated that he'd arrived at the woods at about 9 A.M. and that he had left there at "about noon." He said the phone call from Jason had come at about nine o'clock that night. Yet now Ridge was giving him a choice. How long after he'd left the woods had the phone call from Jason come? Thirty minutes, or an hour?

Jessie was silent for a moment. Then he said, "An hour."

The police decided to end the interview there. Ridge noted the time, 3:18 P.M., and the tape recorder was turned off. By now, Jessie had been at the police station for almost six hours. He had been questioned, polygraphed, questioned, and then questioned once again. Of all that questioning, only the past thirty-four minutes had been recorded.

"Discrepancies"

But Jessie's interrogation was not over yet.[117] Police took a twenty-minute break, during which Jessie smoked two cigarettes. Then Gitchell began another interview—and this one he also recorded. The time of this second interview is disputed, but a police report listing the chronology of the day's events noted it was conducted "to clear up some discrepancies concerning time and events in the first interview."[118]

This time, only Gitchell was in the room with Jessie, and for reasons that are not explained, the interview began with Jessie offering a dramatically different account of the time at which he, Damien, and Jason allegedly arrived in the Robin Hood woods. Throughout the first interview, he had maintained that they were there in the morning and that he had left by noon. Now, after a twenty-seven-minute break, during which the tape recorder was off, all of that had changed.

Gitchell: "Jessie . . . when you three were in the woods and the little boys come up, about what time was it?"

Jessie: "I would say it was about five or so. Five or six."

Gitchell: "Did you have your watch on at the time?"

Jessie: (Shakes his head no.)

Gitchell: "All right, you told me earlier around seven or eight. Which time was it?"

Jessie: "It was seven or eight."

Gitchell: "Are you . . ."

Jessie: "It was starting to get dark."

Gitchell: "Oh. Well, that clears it up . . ."

With that troublesome matter now quickly and neatly "cleared up," Gitchell turned to another of the problems with the earlier confession, the part in which Jessie'd said that the boys had been tied with ropes. The correct answer would have been shoestrings, some white, others black, that had been removed from the children's own shoes.

Gitchell: "All right. Who tied the boys up?"

Jessie: "Damien."

Gitchell: "Did Damien just tie them all up, or did anyone help Damien?"

Jessie: "Jason helped him."

Gitchell: "Okay. And what did they use to tie them up?"

Jessie: "A rope."

Gitchell: "Okay, what color was the rope?"

Jessie: "Brown."

Quickly abandoning that line of questioning, Gitchell moved on to the question of rape. Because the boys were naked and tied the way they were, police had suspected that sexual violation might have been part of their murders. Jessie said he saw Damien and Jason rape two of the boys, whom he identified oddly—and incorrectly—as "the Myers" and "the Branch."[119] Gitchell asked about several forms of sex. Jessie said that, in addition to raping them, Damien and Jason had had oral sex with two of the boys or, as he put it, "They stuck their thang in their mouth."

At one point, Gitchell rose from his seat, apologizing to Jessie.

"Okay. All right," he said. "Hold on just a minute." There was a pause, during which Gitchell left the room. When the chief detective returned he explained, "I'm sorry I keep coming back and forth, but I got people that want me to ask you some other questions . . ." When the questioning resumed, he asked, "Did anyone go down on the boys and maybe sucked theirs or something?"

Jessie said, "Not that. I didn't see neither one of them do that."

Probable Cause

Whether anything had been "clarified" or not, that concluded the second session. Though the time was not mentioned on the tape, a police time chart noted that at 5:05 P.M., Jessie was offered food, and that an hour later he was brought a "burger and Coke." But while Jessie was getting to relax, detectives Ridge and Gitchell—along with deputy prosecuting attorney John Fogleman and municipal court judge William "Pal" Rainey—were busy preparing an affidavit.[120] At 9:06 P.M. they appeared in municipal court, this time in front of Judge Rainey, for a hearing to explain why they had probable cause to arrest Jessie, Damien, and Jason and to search their houses. By then, Jessie had been at the police station for more than eleven hours.

Years later, Jessie would recall that his questioning by police had seemed to him like a game. He said that when the detectives refused to accept his answers to their questions, he didn't know what to do. Then he figured out that they were giving him clues, and that when he provided answers that conformed to the clues, things went better for him. Though the questioning had seemed serious, it had also struck him as silly. "I figured they knew I was lying from the git-go," he said, "because the police, they knew me. They knew me for a long time. They knew I wasn't that type of person, to go killing little kids. I figured they knew I was lying 'cause they was lying, too."

There was an easy way to test the accuracy of Jessie's statements. Gitchell himself had told the *West Memphis Evening Times* just a few weeks earlier that "in the initial stages [of the investigation], people were calling and confessing. But by what they said, they were eliminated quickly." Gitchell told the paper that his officers had "escorted some potential witnesses or suspects into the area" to test their statements against elements of the crime the police knew to be true. It would have been easy to have subjected Jessie to a similar test, to have brought him to Robin Hood and had him point out to officers where the events he described had transpired. During the first recorded interview, Detective Ridge had, in fact, suggested doing just that.

"Are you willing to go down there with us," Ridge had asked Jessie, "and us having a camcorder, and show us where these things took place? Would you do that?"

Jessie's response was inaudible, but the boy apparently nodded his head.

Ridge wanted to get his answer on tape. He asked, "Wouldn't have any problem with that?"

Jessie: "Not that I know of, I wouldn't."

Ridge: "But you would be able to point out where these things took place?"

Jessie: "Yes."

But Jessie was never taken to the woods. Despite the numerous inconsistencies and flat-out errors in his statement, Gitchell and his detectives decided not to put it to the simple test of questioning Jessie at the site while someone videotaped the excursion. The detectives were satisfied with Jessie's account. That, or they were unwilling to expose it to the risks that a trip to the woods would entail. Ridge adopted a stance of certainty, writing in his final report, "Jessie Junior, during the course of the interview, gave specific information that only a person with first-hand knowledge could have had. Jessie Misskelley Junior stated that he did take part in the apprehension of the victims and that he was an eyewitness to the murders by Jason Baldwin and Damien Echols."

When the detectives were through with their questions, they took Jessie to a holding cell. Later, he recalled, "After they turned the tape recorder off, I was too tired to talk. I just wanted to lie down. I figured I was just supposed to wait there until my dad come to get me." No one had explained to Jessie that he had implicated himself in the triple murder by saying that he'd caught and held one of the boys, or that he was about to be arrested. "I figured they knew I needed a ride home," he said. "But my dad never did show up."

CHAPTER EIGHT

The Arrests

IT IS RARE THAT JUDGES ISSUE WARRANTS for nighttime searches. Arkansas law requires police to show that extraordinary circumstances necessitate invading a home after dark. These circumstances are well defined and narrow: the home to be searched must be difficult for police to approach by day, or there must be a threat that officers will be harmed or evidence destroyed if a daytime search is attempted. None of the trailer homes where the three suspects lived were difficult to approach, day or night. And police had questioned all three of the teenagers without a hint of threat. As for the likelihood that evidence would be destroyed, thirty days had already passed since the murders. If evidence remained at the suspects' homes, the chance that it would be destroyed within the next twelve hours might have struck oddsmakers as slim. But June 5, when the town would mark the passage of a month since the murders, was only a day and a few hours away, and now that police had Jessie's confession, they did not want to wait.

While Jessie waited for his father, deputy prosecutor Fogleman was appearing before municipal judge Rainey to explain why it was essential that the homes of Damien, Jason, Jessie, and Domini be searched that very night. Fogleman's reason, as he'd written in the sworn affidavit he handed to Rainey, was that the suspects were "close friends" and "members of a close-knit cult group." Rainey signed the search warrants, as well as the warrants authorizing the arrests of Damien and Jason. At 10:28 P.M., with a full moon high above them, dozens of police cars from several agencies pulled into three trailer parks. Officers burst out and their urgent searches began.

It was a Thursday night. Usually, on weeknights, Jason had to stay at home with his younger brothers, while their mother worked the evening shift at a trucking firm in Memphis.[121] But today had been the last day of classes at Marion High. Jason had finished his exams and completed the tenth grade. To congratulate him, and to thank him for the work he'd done, both at school and taking care of his brothers, his mom had made arrangements for him to be off that night. He was at Damien's house, celebrating with his friends.

Damien's parents, meanwhile, had planned a night out for themselves at the new Splash Casino, which had recently opened in Mississippi, about fifty miles south of Memphis. Pam Echols and Joe Hutchison were headed there for some fun. They'd rented a television and a VCR for Damien and Michelle while they were away. Jason had come to the house, and so had Domini. The four teenagers were watching a video called *Leprechaun*, a recent horror movie, when Michelle heard sounds outside. Pulling aside the curtain, she yelled at her brother and his friends, "Go hide!"

"We thought it was a game," Jason would later recall. "But it was the police."

Jason ran to Damien's room, while Michelle went to the door. When Jason returned to the living room, the officers had Damien in handcuffs. "I was, like, 'What's going on?' " he recalled. "I told them, 'I know Damien. He doesn't do drugs. He wasn't doing anything wrong.' But they just told me and Michelle and Domini to sit on the couch. When we asked why, they told us to shut up. Then a cop came in and asked me if I was Jason Baldwin. I said I was. He said, 'Well, you're under arrest too.' I asked, 'For what?' He said, 'For murder.' I said, 'No. You've got the wrong people!' "[122]

Damien later said that he was not surprised. In the weeks between the murders and this night, he said, "The cops camped in our driveway. They had spotlights on the house. I could not sleep at night." Now, surrounded by police, he was led away without resistance.

Police charged Damien and Jason with three counts each of capital murder. Damien was listed on the arrest record as an eighteen-year-old roofer without a driver's license. On a line for "peculiarities," someone had written: "earrings, two left, one right." Jason was listed as a sixteen-year-old student, five feet eight inches tall, weighing 112 pounds. No "peculiarities" were noted for him. According to the arrest reports, police read both boys their rights but the suspects "made no statements about the charge."

Jason later said that though he remembers having been read his Miranda rights, they'd "meant nothing at the time."[123] He soon sat handcuffed to a chair at the police station battling shock, anger, and fear. "I didn't know what to do, what to say, where to go," he recalled. "I was in there trying to tell them where I was at that day, and they said, 'No. We know you're lying.' I said I was at school that day. They said, 'You mean, if we get your school records, they'll show you were there?' I said, 'Yes. Get them.' "[124]

The police booked Charles Jason Baldwin on suspicion of murder and took him to a cell. They told him to get out of his clothes and handed him a set of police-issue clothes that were so large they almost fell off him. He was driven to a local hospital, where technicians took dental X rays and samples of his hair, blood, and saliva.[125] From there, West Memphis police drove him to the county jail and put him into a cell. By now it was well past midnight. Sixteen-year-old Jason had not been allowed to place a telephone call. His mother had not been informed of his arrest. He had no attorney. And his questioning by police had not been recorded.

On a Scale of One to Ten

As soon as Jessie, Damien, and Jason all were behind bars, the department notified the media that the killers had been caught. The next morning—June 4, 1993—people on both sides of the Mississippi River awakened to the news. At 9 A.M., Inspector Gitchell held a press conference to announce his department's success. Television stations throughout the delta broke into their regular schedules to carry Gitchell's statement live. Cameras showed the balding inspector sitting alone behind an array of microphones, his detectives in a line behind him. Gitchell announced the names of the three teenagers who'd been arrested during the night. He said they'd been regarded as suspects since early in the investigation. "It was like a big puzzle," he said. "The pieces started falling in place to make a clear picture." He reassured viewers that the suspects were securely in custody. And he praised his officers for the work they'd done on what he said had been the most difficult case of his career.

Reporters fired questions. What could he tell them about the accused? Had they known the victims? How had police cracked the case? Gitchell would not comment. Did he know the motive for the killings? Gitchell said that he did, but would not elaborate. One reporter zeroed in on the rumor that had dogged the case since the first body floated to the surface. Were the defendants members of a cult? Gitchell shook his head. "I can't comment on that."

The sensational press conference was drawing to an unsatisfying close. Finally a reporter asked the chief detective, "On a scale of one to ten, how solid do you feel your case is?" This one Gitchell could answer. He smiled and said confidently, "Eleven."

But Gitchell's confidence was overstated. At the time of the arrests, he and his detectives had Jessie's convoluted confession to hold against the three—and little else. Later, Fogleman would acknowledge that "the only thing" police had against Jason "was Jessie's statement," and in a trial, "an accomplice's statement alone is insufficient; there has to be something else connecting a person to a crime." Although the prosecutor recognized that he could use Jessie's statement as probable cause for an arrest, he would later admit that "if we had tried the case the day that Jason was arrested, he would have been acquitted. There would have been a directed verdict of acquittal." As a result of the dearth of evidence against Jason, Fogleman later explained, Jessie's "statement had to be investigated further, to see whether or not more evidence could have been developed."[126]

From a legal point of view, the case against Damien was not much better. As with Jason, Jessie's statement alone was insufficient. And despite the abundant rumors about Damien, by the time of the arrests, police had found no physical evidence linking him to the crime. They'd taken hair samples, blood samples, and urine samples from him and sent them to the crime lab, but none connected him to the murders. They had a polygraph examination that Bill Durham said Damien had flunked, but polygraphs are considered too unreliable to be admissible in court.

The police had no evidence at the time of the arrests other than an array of statements: Jessie's statement, Vicki Hutcheson's statements, and a half dozen statements from young people between the ages of twelve and seventeen saying that Damien had done it.[127] Except for Hutcheson's, all of the statements had been given to the police by minors. And many of those, including Jessie's, had become incriminating only after police had administered a polygraph test, which Durham said the teenager had failed. Though reporters had no way of knowing it at the time, this was the entire basis of Gitchell's claim that his department's case was an "eleven."

"So Close to Perfect"

Jason's mother was no lawyer, but she assessed the arrest of her son much the way Fogleman later acknowledged he had. She did not believe there was any evidence that could be used to prosecute Jason. After Gitchell's press conference, she stormed into Ridge's office, demanding to know why Jason was being held. Ridge explained that Jessie had accused him of the murders. By then, the family members of the victims, as well as those of the accused, had been shown a copy of Jessie's statement.

"I've got proof that Jessie Misskelley is lying," Gail Grinnell exclaimed. Focusing on Jessie's repeated claims that the murders had happened early in the day, she told Ridge that Jason had attended school that day. "If he was in school," Grinnell said, Jessie's claim "cannot possibly be true."

In contrast to Jason's later recollection that he had talked to the police, Ridge complained to Grinnell that he had not. She replied that if Jason wasn't talking, it was because she had advised him not to, after the detectives had come to their house. She told Ridge that she'd been "scared, 'cause you all put words in his mouth and make things . . . make a mountain out of a molehill."

Ridge countered, "Well, that's the reason we got tape recorders. And I'm not putting words into your mouth." Grinnell persisted, until Ridge finally told her, "It's like this. If you would listen to me for just a second, I'll try and clear something up for you. We've got one person that told us the story that is very believable. If Jason doesn't tell us the story, a story, if Jason doesn't tell us what his side of things are, we will never know what he has to say."

Grinnell replied, "Well, I'll get him a lawyer so that he can tell the lawyer. I want him to have a lawyer with him because I've never been involved in anything like this before and I don't want to see my son go away for my mistake. I know he's innocent. He is innocent. But I don't want him being made out not to be innocent because he don't have a lawyer."

Ridge was condescending. "Do you understand," he asked, "that we tape our conversations, we don't put words into people's mouths? It's exactly on tape what is said, and we would welcome the opportunity to talk to Jason and he will not talk because his mother has told him not to talk."

"One of the reasons I told Jason not to talk to the police," Grinnell replied, "is because I was told that the police was going around and telling lies about Jason before they came and arrested him. After police questioned Damien, there was rumors started. People were saying that the police told them this and told them that. And I thought in my mind then, the police are trying to make him out to be the guilty one. And I told him not to talk to them, to anybody. And I said, if you hear of anybody else saying something that a policeman said, get his name, 'cause I am going to go to the police station with it, because there has been policemen going out there in the trailer park telling kids lies."[128]

Gail Grinnell said again that Jason was innocent, that he had been in school, and that she had obtained a statement to that effect from the principal. Finally, she sighed, "I'm so tired. My whole family has been up all night."

At that, Ridge defended the midnight arrests. "It's a situation that couldn't be avoided," he said. "We had to look for evidence, and if it's there, then it's going to look bad for Jason, and if it's not, then Jason is cleared because of it. So it's the only way to get the answers, is to do what we did. We didn't want to make things hard on you. We don't want to make things hard on Jason. But these are the only tools we have to get to the truth sometimes."

Grinnell asked when she could see her son. "I'm worried about him because I know that he is scared," she told the detective. "I know that he's real scared. He's alone."

Ridge said he did not know when she would be permitted to see Jason. Grinnell asked how he could base Jason's arrest on nothing more than the statement Jessie had made, with all its discrepancies. "There are so many different stories in that story he gave," she exclaimed. "I don't see how anyone could believe it."

"It's like this," Ridge replied. "We've got a story that is very, very believable. It is so close to perfect that we have to believe it. So we're going to believe it until we can break that story, and we cannot even start to break that story apart until Jason tells us something."

When Grinnell tried to protest again, Ridge silenced her. "You don't have the point of view that we got," he said. With that the meeting ended.

"Sensitive and Inflammatory"

Over at municipal court, meanwhile, the case was taking another turn. Municipal judge Rainey, who had signed the warrants for the searches and arrests just the night before, now issued an order denying public review of those documents.[129] But by the time Rainey issued his order, sensitive information about the investigation had already been leaked—and now Jessie's confession was too. While refusing to comment about the case, other than to say that it was an "eleven," police had allowed people outside the department to see transcripts of Jessie's confession. Gail Grinnell had seen it, and so had many others. A television news director reported that a woman called his station the day after the arrests, offering to sell a copy for several hundred dollars.[130] The day after Rainey sealed the records, a copy reached the *Commercial Appeal.* Rainey issued his order on Friday. On Monday, the paper ran a copyrighted front-page article outlining what Jessie had said. The headlines read: TEEN DESCRIBES "CULT" TORTURE OF BOYS and DEFENDANT MISSKELLEY TELLS POLICE OF SEX MUTILATION.[131]

The leak of Jessie's confession created a sensation, but Rainey's order sealing the affidavits prevented reporters from discovering how little the police had to back it up. The effect was that news outlets focused on the three defendants and on what Jessie had said about them. For days, a blizzard of news broadcasts and articles blanketed the area. Even someone who did not buy a paper could read headlines such as these, just in passing a newsstand:

ONE SUSPECT WAS "SCARY,"
TALKED OF WORSHIPING THE DEVIL

OUTBURST IN COURT BY VICTIM'S DAD REFLECTS
COMMUNITY'S SHOCK, RAGE

WORSHIP OF EVIL DEBATED AS MOTIVE IN KILLINGS

ARK. YOUTHS COULD FACE THE DEATH PENALTY

The articles that accompanied the headlines told a public hungry for information that Damien "carried a cat's skull around with him at school and routinely dressed in black"; that Jason was said to be "shy and artistic" but "into that devil stuff"; and that Jessie was "tough" and "a bit troubled" but had been considered "kind to kids." Gitchell maintained his position that he could not comment on the case.[132]

But Rainey's order sealing the records did not sit well with newspaper editors on either side of the Mississippi River. The battle for information suddenly became part of the story. In response to the official clamp on information, the *Commercial Appeal* of Memphis filed a formal request for the records, citing Arkansas's freedom of information law. The paper's managing editor said that the records were needed "to help sort out facts alleged in the case from a growing supply of rumors." The smaller *West Memphis Evening Times* echoed the complaint.[133]

But editors' cautions changed nothing, and shortly after Rainey sealed the records, a state judge affirmed the unusual order.[134] Like Rainey, the state judge said that the information contained in the records was "sensitive and inflammatory" and that "it would be prejudicial to the defendants to have those documents released to the public prior to the trial." In fact, the records contained nothing more inflammatory than the statements of Jessie Misskelley, which had already been reported. But the public did not know that.[135]

Spiritual Warfare

But by and large, for most of the media, reporting on satanism beat skepticism, hands down. The West Memphis paper reported that Damien wore the number 666 and "a sign of the devil" inside his boots. It quoted two boys who claimed to have heard of ghosts in Jason's house. It quoted an unnamed girl who claimed that she had seen Damien drink Jason and "Dominique's" blood, and another who said Damien had once "threatened to cut a boy's head off and put it on a doorstep." It quoted a woman who lived in the Lakeshore area who'd noticed that "last year, there were some dogs that turned up missing out here," adding that "the Echols boy always wore black." In editions on three consecutive days, the *Jonesboro Sun*, in northeast Arkansas's largest city, quoted a local Baptist minister who said that Damien had made a pact with the devil and would be going to hell.[136] "I've never witnessed to anyone any harder," the minister was quoted as saying. "He didn't reject me. He rejected Christ." An article in *USA Today* began: "Michael Echols, who calls himself 'Damien,' once told a pastor he couldn't go to heaven because he's already committed—to going to hell." The *USA Today* piece did, however, also quote a few of the suspects' defenders. Joe Hutchison, Damien's father, said, "I thought the law of this land was that the accused were considered innocent until someone proved them guilty." A friend of the Misskelley family said that Jessie "wasn't into Satanic worship, he was into country music."

With the devil so prominent in news reports, ministers were quoted as experts. Six hundred people turned out two weeks after the arrests when the Missouri Street Church of Christ offered a free lecture on what advertisements said were "the six indicators of Satanic involvement." They were an obsession with death, possession of "Satanic paraphernalia," kidnapping, sexual abuse, cannibalism, and cremation. Reporters for the West Memphis paper covered the event. They also contacted "experts" in the occult, such as Driver and a Memphis psychiatrist and writer.[137] Based on those interviews, the paper reported that "Echols' reading habits could help determine the nature of his thinking and possible cult activities. People who knew Echols said he dressed in black, called himself 'Damien,' and carried a cat's skull." The

Memphis psychiatrist reportedly confirmed that those were common signs that teenagers were "delving into Satanism."[138]

While preachers railed against Satan and reporters examined library books, police were coming to terms with the reality underlying the arrests. That was, as Fogleman would later delicately acknowledge, that Jessie Misskelley's statement "had to be investigated further, to see whether or not more evidence could be developed." The police had suspects, but did Fogleman have a case? With the three teenagers in custody, the West Memphis police entered the second phase of their investigation: a scramble to find evidence against them.

Aaron Revisited

Detective Bray of Marion had introduced Vicki and Aaron Hutcheson to the West Memphis police. The Hutchesons had led them to Jessie Misskelley. And Jessie had handed them their big break in the case. Now, as detectives turned to the task of supporting what Jessie had said, Bray tried again to help. Again he turned to eight-year-old Aaron Hutcheson.

By the time of the arrests, Aaron had made several statements, many of them highly conflicting. But Bray was convinced that Aaron knew more than he'd yet acknowledged. A few hours after Gitchell announced the arrests, Bray interviewed the boy again. And now, Aaron's account of what he'd seen took another dramatic turn. For the first time, the boy told Bray that he had been in the woods with the victims on the afternoon they disappeared. In fact, he said, he'd witnessed their murders. Suddenly, Aaron was now also clear as to the identities of his friends' killers. The men he'd seen in the woods, Aaron said—the men he'd seen murdering his friends—were Damien, Jason, and Jessie.

In a long, disjointed statement, Aaron told Bray that on the afternoon the boys disappeared, he'd ridden his bike to Robin Hood. He said he'd seen five men in the woods: the three defendants and two others, whom he could not identify. They all wore black T-shirts with dragons on them and had knives "like Indians in the jungle have." Jessie was holding Stevie down in the water, telling him, "I don't want to kill you yet until what my boss says." Damien was the boss. Michael and

Chris found two guns lying on the pipe. They hid behind a tree. They planned, on the count of three, to jump out and shoot all five of the men. They counted to three, but when they began shooting, they discovered that the guns were not loaded. By then, Michael's neck had been cut and blood was pouring out all over his T-shirt. After Michael was dead, Damien removed the boy's clothes and raped him. Jessie cut the private parts off all three boys. Aaron began to run. Jessie saw him and started to chase him, but Aaron tripped him and got away.

Bray had long believed that Aaron had witnessed the murders, and now he was sure he'd been right.[139] Four days later, on June 8, he questioned Aaron again. This time, Aaron's details were even more preposterous. This time Aaron said that Jessie had called him the night before the murders. Jessie told Aaron to bring his friends to the woods, and that they would all "do something." When Aaron arrived, Michael and Chris were behind a tree. (Later he said they were in a tree.) Jessie got hold of Stevie. Damien was standing in front of Stevie, holding a knife. Jessie ran Stevie into Damien's knife, cutting him in the stomach. Then Jessie caught Aaron and tied him up for about forty seconds, but Aaron was able to kick his way free. After Aaron escaped, the assailants allegedly raped the other boys.

It was a messy, sad account, offered by a child who had been interviewed repeatedly by police and whose mother, with police approval, had appointed herself an unofficial investigator.[140] But Bray recognized the potential importance of what young Aaron was saying. So far, police had only Jessie's account of the murders. A second eyewitness account, even if it contradicted the first and was growing more fantastic by the day, might be invaluable, especially since it named the three teenagers who were in custody.

Gitchell apparently agreed, because on June 9, two days after the details of Jessie's confession were reported by the media, the West Memphis chief inspector questioned Aaron again. Aaron repeated that he'd witnessed Damien, Jason, and Jessie murder his three friends. And now, Aaron added one more important detail: he told Inspector Gitchell that he'd seen all three of the victims tied up with rope.

PART TWO

The Trials

CHAPTER NINE

The Defendants

ALMOST AS SOON AS HE HEARD about the arrests, Ron Lax, a Memphis private investigator, decided to get involved in the case. A meticulous dresser, a self-described "anal-retentive" organizer, a collector of French antiques and books on art, Lax was not a stereotypical private eye. He headed his own investigations company, Inquisitor, Inc., with offices in Memphis and Nashville. Most of Inquisitor's work focused on insurance and financial fraud. But in the past five years, Lax had widened the scope of his work. Defense lawyers had sought his help on cases where clients faced charges of capital murder. Lax had agreed, though he considered the death penalty an appropriate punishment for persons found guilty of some kinds of murder.[141] Lax's investigative work helped get some defendants acquitted. His experiences also convinced him that bad police work often resulted in charges against innocent people. By the time of the sensational West Memphis murders, Lax had moved from a position supporting the death penalty to one of opposition. He believed that people who committed terrible crimes should be locked up for life. But he no longer considered the legal process reliable enough to warrant the imposition of such an irrevocable sentence. By 1993, Inquisitor had grown big enough that Lax was able to assign himself a few singularly but personally important investigations of capital murder cases every year. Now, with news of the West Memphis arrests, he asked his assistant, Glori Shettles, to drive across the river and inform the court-appointed defense lawyers that if they wanted him, he was willing to help.

There had never been any question about the boys hiring their own defense. Jessie was the only one who even had a job, and that was intermittent work as a roofer. All lived with their families in rented mobile homes. Though Jason's mother had told Ridge in desperation that she would "have to hire a lawyer," there was no way she could have afforded to pay for even a few hours of legal advice, let alone the kind of help needed to mount a legal defense against death.

At a hearing on June 7, 1993, a state judge appointed a pair of lawyers to represent each of the three defendants. The judge appointed Val Price of Jonesboro, chief public defender for Craighead County, and Scott Davidson, also of Jonesboro, to represent Damien. He appointed Paul Ford and George Robin Wadley, both of Jonesboro, to represent Jason. And he appointed Dan Stidham and Greg Crow, law partners from Paragould, to represent Jessie. Most were in their mid-thirties. Stidham was twenty-seven. None had much experience representing clients charged with capital murder.

Jason

Jason, stunned by his arrest, hardly knew where he was, much less where his case was headed. He'd later recall that on the night of his arrest, he was driven first to the jail in Marion, then to the hospital in West Memphis, and finally to the juvenile detention center sixty miles north in Jonesboro.[142] At their first meeting, Jason later said, his court-appointed lawyers told him that the state appeared to have little evidence that implicated him. According to Jessie's confession, Jason had been the most vicious of the killers—the one who'd castrated Christopher Byers. But other than that, there was nothing. And unlike Damien, Jason did not even appear to be weird or mentally unstable. Jason had no history of violence. His entire criminal record consisted of having broken glass on cars stored in the derelict shed and having shoplifted a bag of M&M's. He was an average-to-good student at Marion High, where he'd received certificates for punctuality and attendance. The police had obtained essays he'd written for an English class shortly before the murders, but they had a humorous, optimistic tone and held no hint that Jason had been harboring murderous impulses.[143]

When Ford and Wadley read the essays, the men were struck by their mildness. In one assignment, when students had been asked to write about a classmate who had recently killed herself, Jason had written: "I didn't know the girl very well. I seen her around every now and then. But I know how people that knew her feel, because once my mother tried to commit suicide, and I know how I felt when that happened. It was pretty devastating, since I was the one who found her and called 911 and kept her alive. But I am lucky. My mother is well and happy now, and so am I."

Ford and Wadley noted that Jason had written those lines on April 5, 1993, a month to the day before the murders. Nothing about the kid seemed to fit the profile of someone who was about to commit a multiple murder. The lawyers knew what Jason had been accused of doing in Jessie's confession, but so far, if the police had any corroborating evidence, no one had mentioned it.

Jessie

If Jason felt bewildered, Jessie was in a panic. While Jason was taken north to Jonesboro, Jessie was removed to a jail west of West Memphis, in the small town of Wynne. Within hours after being locked in the jail there, he'd sent a desperate letter to his parents.[144] In the letter, Jessie repudiated the statement he'd made to the police. "I hope that y'all don't hate me because I did not do it," he wrote. He added, "I can not stand [it] in here much longer. I will go crazy." He begged, "Please try to get me out. I will die in here."

Jessie's father showed the letter to reporters, and the *Commercial Appeal* printed portions of it. When reporters asked Gitchell about Jessie's attempt to recant, the detective would not comment. Now, when reporters once again asked Gitchell to assess the strength of his case, he dismissed the question. "We just have to keep on working," he said.[145]

Jessie's lawyer did not believe what the boy had written to his father. Dan Stidham believed Jessie was guilty and doubted his attempt to recant. "Of course, initially, my take on the situation was that anybody who would confess to such a crime obviously did it," Stidham later recalled. "It was unfathomable to me that anybody would confess to a crime who had not committed it. I figured my client was obviously guilty, and so my initial thought was that my only goal was to prepare him to testify against his codefendants and, hopefully, to work the best possible plea bargain I could for him. That was the only thing I figured we had going for us. We were hoping simply to avoid the death penalty."

But Stidham's hopes of negotiating a plea bargain would be jeopardized if Jessie persisted in claiming that his confession had not been the truth. "It kind of made me angry," the lawyer later said. "I demanded that Jessie take a look at this. I reminded him that he was facing the death penalty, and that he needed to tell me what happened." But Jessie vacillated. "When his father was there," Stidham said, "Jessie'd insist that he didn't do it. And when his father was gone—when it was just Jessie and me—he'd try to recite what he'd told the police. But every time he'd tell the story, there'd be major inconsistencies." Stidham could not figure out what he was dealing with.

Finally, on one visit near the end of the summer, Stidham recalled,

I went back to the jail and said, "You've got to level with me. Were you there or were you not?" And he said he was not. And I said, "Why would you have told me all this time that you were there?" He said, "Well, because I didn't want to die in that electric chair." I explained to him that Greg [Crow] and I were on his side. And that's when I began to realize that he didn't understand what a lawyer was. He had no idea what a defense attorney was. He didn't understand the concept. To him, a lawyer was just a person who was part of the justice system. He thought we were detectives. He didn't understand that we were on his team. That's when I began to see Jessie Misskelley in a different light. At that time, he had a weird haircut and tattoos. He looked like an ordinary, everyday street thug. But the kid was handicapped. Bill Clinton had just been elected president of the United States, and everybody in the state of Arkansas knew who Bill Clinton was, but Jessie Misskelley didn't.

Stidham would eventually conclude that Jessie had had nothing to do with the crime, and that his confession had been coerced. But by the time Stidham reached this "epiphany," Jessie had been in jail for two months. Stidham abruptly altered his strategy. He began to study the phenomenon known as false confessions. After what he called his epiphany, Stidham told a reporter, "We don't believe the state has any evidence except this wild story Jessie made up." And he added, "The world has a right to know what kind of investigation these cops pulled."

If Stidham had any lingering doubts about his revised view of his client, they were allayed during a visit when Jessie asked him who "Satin" was. Stidham didn't understand. "He handed me a pamphlet a preacher had given him that was all about Satan," Stidham would recall, "but Jessie could barely read it. And what he could read he thought was about somebody named 'Satin.' " Now, with a jolt, Stidham got it. Jessie was referring to Satan, but never having read the unfamiliar name before, he was mispronouncing it as "Satin," like the fabric. Stidham was dumbfounded. As he discussed the pamphlet with Jessie, Stidham realized that the boy had heard of the devil, but never that he was called Satan. "It was one of the most ironic moments of the entire ordeal," the lawyer later said. "There I was, sitting in a jail cell with this confessed satanic killer, and he's asking me who 'Satin' is."

Damien

After discussions among the attorneys, it was decided that private investigator Ron Lax would work with Val Price and Scott Davidson, who were representing Damien. In the beginning, Lax, like Stidham, assumed that all three defendants were guilty. He also assumed that any investigation he and his assistant, Glori Shettles, did on behalf of Damien would likely benefit all three. His approach, as always, would be organized and methodical. It would begin with an interview of Damien in the jail where he was being held in the town of Clarendon, Arkansas. But that interview almost never occurred. On Tuesday, June 8, four days after his arrest, Damien took an overdose of Elavil, his antidepressant medication.[146] His mother had brought the medicine and left it with the jailers. On Saturday, Sunday, and Monday, the jailers had dispensed Damien's pills to him, and by Tuesday, without their knowledge, he had saved up twelve of them. He swallowed them en masse and was rushed to a nearby hospital, where his stomach was pumped.

Lax met with Damien several times as Damien's lawyers prepared for trial. But most of the work with Damien would fall to Glori Shettles, a former parole officer and prosecutor's assistant who held a master's degree in counseling. For the next nine months, Shettles visited Damien almost once a week. In the beginning, she and Lax were uncertain about Damien's name. The media seemed to love "Damien," but the investigators opted for "Michael," which they'd been told was his legal name.[147]

Damien told Shettles that his family had moved frequently when he was young.[148] Though he was unaware of it at first, Damien said, his family had been desperately poor, living at times in shacks with dirt floors and no indoor plumbing. He said he'd grown used to being picked on at school, and that once he'd made it to high school, he'd begun carrying a dog's skull he'd found because kids tended not to bother him when he did. He discovered that being ridiculed for being strange—something he could choose for himself—was better than being ridiculed for things he could not control.

It seemed to her that Damien had had a hard time making sense of his life, and that he'd turned to religion for help. When the Protestant influences of his childhood failed to satisfy or comfort him, he'd turned to Catholicism, and then to more earth-based, pagan beliefs.[149] As Damien grew more comfortable with Shettles, the investigator tried to explore the behaviors that had attracted Driver's attention. Shettles noted:

> Michael reports his wardrobe of black clothing originated as a result of Deanna telling him that she thought he "looked good" in black clothing. He stated he began purchasing black pieces of clothing to please her and before long, all of his articles of clothing were black. He states he regrets the day he began wearing his trench coat, which he wore every day; however, he thought at the time that it looked "cool" . . .
> Michael briefly described a period of time, apparently while he was still in school, that he described as his "vampire

look." He stated during this period of time he put white powder on his skin and wore very dark, small glasses and gave the appearance he was a vampire. He stated schoolmates would ask him if he drank blood and he stated he did drink blood, but only of those persons he knew . . . Michael also stated that, as time grew, he was earning more and more of the reputation by schoolmates, teachers, and persons in the community as being a devil worshiper. He stated that right before he was sent to Charter Hospital by the juvenile authorities he was brought in and asked by Jerry Driver and Steve Jones if he could read a Latin inscription that was on a gold ring that Michael described as a wedding band that was in a glass pyramid. He stated he could not read Latin and had no idea what the inscription was. He was asked by these men if he could remove the ring by "willing" it or through some ritual, and he told them he could not.

Damien told Shettles that he, Jason, and Domini had been "harassed" by police for almost a year and a half before the murders.[150] After one of Lax's visits with Damien, the private investigator wrote:

Before his arrest, Steve Jones, his probation officer, came by and asked why Echols had not been around. Echols responded he had not been around because his probation was over. He stated Jones acted very suspicious during this visit. Jones gave Echols some information regarding the murders. He told Echols someone urinated in the mouth of one of the boys. Then, when the West Memphis Police Department asked him what he knew about the murder and he stated someone had urinated into one of the victim's mouth, they denied Steve Jones knew this and stated that only someone at the murder scene would be aware of this information.

Ron Lax found the story peculiar. The prosecutor's office had just begun to provide documents from the police investigation to the defense attorneys, through the legal process known as discovery. To Lax's and the lawyers' frustration, the flow of records throughout the summer amounted to only a trickle. But at least the trickle had included copies of the autopsy reports, which the West Memphis police had finally received after the arrests. Lax scoured the reports, but they contained no mention of urine having been found in the stomachs of any of the bodies.[151] Since Lax and the lawyers had so far been provided with but a fraction of the police department's file, the private investigator had no way of knowing that the file contained two documents, both from early in the investigation, in which Gitchell and an unidentified West Memphis Police Department official had, in fact, referred to Peretti's reported statement about finding urine in the victims' stomachs.

Meanwhile, it became clear to Shettles that until the night of their arrests, Damien and Jason had never fully appreciated the seriousness of their situation.[152] To the irritation of the police, Damien had maintained an attitude of arrogance. He told Shettles that he'd felt safe; that he'd believed the police would never find evidence against him, since he had not committed the crime; and that eventually they would be forced to realize how stupid they'd been to hound him. With evident satisfaction, Damien told Shettles how, during one interrogation, he'd finally said that if officers would let him speak with his mother, he'd tell them everything he knew about the murders. Detectives had gotten excited and brought Pam to the station, and while Damien was speaking with her, they'd hastily set up a video camera to tape his expected confession. Damien had then smugly announced that everything he knew about the murders was "nothing." Damien thought it was funny. The officers had been furious.

But Shettles suspected that Damien's haughtiness had always been a facade. She noticed that his hands shook when he talked. Sometimes he cried. He told her he had little hope of being believed by a jury. She wrote, "He stated many times he prays that if there is a God, he will not allow him to live another day. He further stated he feels that he is going insane, but is not certain of what will happen to him mentally should this process occur."

For the investigators, Damien's psychiatric background was legally important, as well. At the time, Arkansas was one of five states that held bifurcated trials; that is, one part dealt with the question of guilt or innocence, and if a defendant were found guilty, the second part of the trial was held to determine his sentence. If Damien's trial went that far, his mental health history might be used as a mitigating factor; evidence of mental defect might be presented to persuade a jury to spare his life or to reduce his time in prison. Part of Shettles's assignment was to closely explore Damien's mental health history.

He told her that he had suffered severe headaches as a child, some so intense that he would pull clumps of hair out of his head in an effort to ease the pain. Pam Echols reported that Damien had suffered several blackouts but that they'd never been diagnosed. There'd been his stays, as a teenager, in psychiatric facilities, and the outpatient counseling in West Memphis. Pam reported that after Damien's last hospitalization, he'd been declared totally disabled by the Social Security Administration. Three months before the murders, he had begun receiving Social Security disability checks of $289 per month. These were stopped after his arrest.

Descent into Madness

As the summer intensified, so did Shettles's concern for Damien's mental state. By mid-July he told her that he was sleeping as little as two hours a night. Noting that he was "noticeably shaky," she wrote, "He can quote many songs and relates lyrics of songs to his feelings. He quoted lyrics from a Pink Floyd song called 'Comfortably Numb' and an Ozzy Osbourne song called 'Road to Nowhere.'"

The titles were sounding increasingly apt. By August Damien was hallucinating. Soon he was showing signs of full-blown paranoia. He wrote in a letter to Shettles, "I think the police are up to something. They are doing something to the food and putting some kind of gas in the vents. I think they are doing something to my medicine." When Shettles visited the jail in mid-August, the sheriff informed her that Damien had begun a hunger strike. When she went to Damien's cell, he told her that "the reason he had gone on the hunger strike was he had no desire to go to trial and he did not feel he would receive a fair trial." She wrote, "As I left, one of the older jailers asked when Michael might be moved to the state mental hospital for an evaluation. He stated he did not understand why the attorneys had not already moved him, as it was inevitable that he would need to be transferred for an evaluation. There are several jailers there that apparently take Michael's condition very seriously and they appear to be sympathetic and concerned for his welfare."

The jailers had reason for concern. Damien told Shettles he felt like "a walking razor blade." He knew that, mentally and legally, his situation was dire. He knew he was perceived as "a devil worshiper or a nut case or something." In his fitful journal he wrote, "I might lose my mind and I might lose my head." Despair was taking its toll. He alternated between utter delusion and acute awareness. In a desperate letter to his family he wrote: "I need a doctor. I think I'm having a nervous breakdown, and I'm afraid to tell the people here. They wouldn't care anyway. Don't worry about me. I'm okay. Just tell Val Price [Damien's lawyer] or Glori [Shettles] I need a doctor. *Don't forget!*" At the bottom of the page, he pleaded again, "Don't forget the *doctor!*"

But no doctor ever came. Damien later wrote, "I am walking the borderline of insanity. . . . I don't like it. I am helpless to stop it." Later: "Help me. They have invaded and destroyed my world. It seemed harmless enough. Now it's a contest: who can destroy me first? Them or myself." Later still: "Mother Night, wrap your dark arms around me. Protect me. Lord of Chaos, guide me. Father Death, embrace me. I am the half man who dwells in both worlds. I walk in shadow and light and am cursed by both."

CHAPTER TEN

Release of the Police Files

As FURTHER PROOF of Damien's unstable mental state, while he was contemplating his death, he was also planning his marriage. Domini was pregnant and was expecting to deliver the baby in the fall of 1993. If Damien was coming apart, as he feared, the parts were greatly at odds. His writings, which the private investigators did not see, verged on madness and despair. When Shettles and Lax visited, they saw a severely troubled teenager who they feared might be suicidal. But Damien's letters to Domini and his family were, by contrast, almost sunny. He wrote to Domini, "I told my mom to buy you an engagement ring with my next check. Remind her. Tell your mom I said hi, and I may be out by Christmas." Reflecting on Domini's pregnancy, he wrote, "I hope I get out in time to see our baby be born!"

Whether he realized it or not, the wish was preposterous. The defendants' trial dates had yet to be set, and the prosecutor had barely begun to release information about the case to the defense lawyers.[153] As none of the defendants had even finished high school (though Damien had obtained his GED), their understanding of the legal process gearing up around them was severely limited. Their lawyers had to explain that a defendant has a right, through the process of discovery, to know what evidence the prosecution intends to present against him. He also has a right to any evidence the prosecution might have that would point toward his innocence. Sitting in their cells, Damien, Jason, and Jessie could not imagine the scale of the job their lawyers faced.

Organizing the File

As a private investigator working for Damien, most of Lax's time, from June to the end of 1993, was spent compiling information for the attorneys and trying to understand the police files that Fogleman was gradually releasing. Lax scrutinized Jessie's confession and identified several parts he considered "questionable." Jessie's belief that the victims had skipped school, his report of rope ligatures, his confusion about the times, and his claim that the boys had been choked to death all suggested to Lax that Jessie had been clumsily making up answers based on misinformation and faulty assumptions. The investigator concluded that the entire statement appeared to be "a 'leading type' interview." In letters to the attorneys, he pointed out a half dozen points at which, he said, the officers seemed to provide Jessie with answers. Moreover, Lax observed, "The statement does not appear to follow any logical progression." Lax noted that though Jessie said Damien had "bruised" one of the boys "real bad," he found it "difficult to conceive of this incident lasting long enough for bruises to become visible to Misskelley." Lax wondered "if the police allowed him to look at the crime scene photographs, or the autopsy photographs." Elsewhere he noted that Jessie "first stated Michael Moore began running toward the service road, which would be north of the ditch; however later, on the same page, he stated Moore ran toward the houses (this would be south)." Lax pointed out that "Misskelley sounds real confused regarding when he was present and when he was not." Finally, noting that "Misskelley said he returned to the crime scene two or three days after the bodies were found," Lax wrote, "I find this very difficult to believe since the area should have been sealed off and was probably being guarded, or at least closely watched, during this time."

Three or four times a month, throughout the summer and into the fall, the lawyers received batches of records from Fogleman. But there was no continuity to the material, no organization that would have given them a sense of how the investigation had proceeded. Lax spent much of his time sorting through hundreds of names on hundreds of reports, trying to determine the significance—if any—of each. He summarized every document that was received, though he admitted to uncertainty about what many of them meant.[154]

As records naming Vicki Hutcheson began to filter in, Lax asked Damien about "the girl Misskelley tried to fix him up with." Lax wrote that Damien "stated he stayed at the trailer for an hour to an hour and a half and the girl named Vicki made a couple of passes at him but nothing occurred." Lax set out to locate Hutcheson. Neighbors told him that she'd moved, and directed him to an area south of Marion, where he found her living "on a street that has no sign, in a house that has no number." There was a Pontiac "jacked up in the drive," a pickup parked in the drive, and another in the yard. After noting the license numbers of each, Lax knocked on the door. When Hutcheson appeared, she "became very nervous and upset," he later wrote in his notes. She then "informed me she did not want to talk to me and did not want to become involved. I explained she was already involved." Eventually Hutcheson gave Lax her version of events, which Lax described as "fuzzy." He wrote, "I then quizzed Vicki as to why she would have been with Misskelley and Damien after her son identified them as being involved in the murders and her answer was never clear. She attempted to avoid that question but finally ended up saying, 'I would try to get anything from them I could to help the police.' "

Lax would later recall, "We were interviewing everybody we could find, and nobody had detrimental information, with the exception of Vicki and Aaron. We kept wondering what the police had that we still hadn't seen."[155]

"Evil People"

For much of the public, the matter was not so complex: three teenagers who worshiped Satan had sacrificed three younger boys.[156] Religion permeated the case. Damien told Shettles that due to publicity about the case, Baptist ministers came to the jail to preach to him at least twice a week.[157] Now, Lax and Shettles learned, that publicity was about to widen. Damien and Domini's baby was due at the end of September. In mid-August Pam Echols called Lax to report that a production company from New York, Creative Thinking International, had called seeking permission to film a baby shower that was being planned for Domini. The company's owners, filmmakers Bruce Sinofsky and Joe

Berlinger, had promised to contribute a high chair, and Domini's mother, who was hosting the party, had agreed to let them come. Pam reported that Sinofsky and Berlinger said they'd contacted Damien's lawyers, who'd given their permission.[158]

Piecing Together the Police Investigation

As deputy prosecutor Fogleman released more records, Lax found himself working harder to organize and to understand what the police department had produced. To him, much of it looked chaotic. Records from the investigation were being provided in no discernible order. They were not organized by time, names, or place. Different reports on the same individuals came filtering in over several months, and because many were out of sequence, Lax found it difficult, as he processed the material, to get a clear picture of how police had worked the case. He filed the records in the order they were received, providing a caption and summary of each.

Normally, the summaries were brief: "INFORMATION REGARDING MOORE'S PARENTS—05/10/93. The police spoke with the Moores regarding their activities on the evening of May 5, 1993 and May 6, 1993." Or "INFORMATION REGARDING BYERS' PARENTS—05/12/93. Det. Lt. Martello, Memphis P.D. Narcotics, informed the West Memphis Police Department that the Byerses have both been confidential informants for Memphis and Shelby County Sheriff's Department." But occasionally Lax commented on items in the file. After reading a magazine article entitled "Satanic Cult Awareness," Lax wrote that it made him feel like he "was back in the dark ages." He commented, "With the exception of the castration of the Byers victim and the fact that the bodies were nude and in a wooded area, I have seen no evidence of anything connected with the case which even remotely resembles the discussions in this article."

Lax was particularly interested in a list of forty people who had been fingerprinted by police. But he was frustrated to find that "There are no accompanying sheets discussing these individuals [and] we do not know why these individuals were fingerprinted." As his review progressed, Lax was even more disconcerted to realize that, aside from Jessie's confession, he still had not received anything that constituted evidence against the defendants. From June until well into September, the only records the defense attorneys received were those that had been generated *before* the arrests, and the release of even these was slow. They did not learn of Narlene Hollingsworth's claim that she had seen Damien and Domini on the service road until August 25, and they received no records of interviews with Vicki and Aaron Hutcheson until the first week of September. Lax found Hollingsworth's statement confusing, since Domini was never mentioned as a participant in the crime; what was perplexing about the Hutchesons' statements was that the police had not quickly dismissed them.

Gradually, the defense teams began to receive records showing what the West Memphis police had done *since* the June 3 arrests. To his amazement, Lax read that on July 1, nearly a month after Damien, Jason, and Jessie were in custody, Detective Ridge had returned to the site where the bodies were found. Ridge's purpose, as stated in his report, was "to look for evidence which may have been missed." To Lax's greater amazement, Ridge reported that he'd found some evidence. Recalling Jessie's claim that the victims had been beaten with a stick, Ridge reported that on his visit to the scene in July, he'd found two sticks that had previously gone unnoticed. There was nothing about the sticks that connected them to the crime, other than their location in the woods where the bodies were found. Nonetheless, Ridge took them back to the station and marked them as evidence.

Other records showed that while the police had reportedly polygraphed thirty people before the arrests, since the arrests, they had polygraphed eleven more. Records also revealed that police had sent dozens of items from the defendants' homes to laboratories, to be tested for genetic material. Realizing how many reports he'd seen about items that had been sent off for testing, Lax prepared a review of the physical evidence the police had collected. The twenty-eight-page memo covered nearly six hundred items. In addition to numerous fingerprints, blood, and urine samples, Lax counted more than one hundred items of clothing, eighty-seven samples of hair, seventeen knives, three sticks, three hammers, three ropes, two razors, an ice axe, a candle, a hook, a mask, and a Mason jar full of water. Out of all that, the crime lab had reported finding only a few fibers that analysts said were "microscopically similar" to fibers found in the homes of two of the defendants. In light of the bloodiness of the crime, its hands-on physicality, and the number of victims and defendants, the discovery of a few mass-produced fibers from items available in Wal-Marts and other clothiers all over the country struck Lax as an infinitesimal amount of evidence, which was also highly circumstantial. But he knew that Fogleman would use it, just as he knew the prosecutor would use the part of Hollingsworth's testimony that placed Damien near the scene of the crime.

As the outline of the case slowly became more clear, Lax tried to focus on elements that would be essential to Damien's defense. He interviewed two girls in Memphis with whom Damien said he'd spoken by phone on the night the children disappeared.[159] Lax wrote that "both girls stated they did remember this and were positive of the day." He interviewed Narlene Hollingsworth and noted that despite the apparent problems her account posed for both the prosecution and the defense—placing Damien at the scene, but with Domini rather than Jason—she seemed to be "unshakeable" in her recollections. On October 7, Lax met with Detective Bray in Marion. During their conversation, Lax noted, "Don Bray reached into his shirt pocket and produced a sheet of note paper. He held this up and told me that when he first learned of these murders and what had happened to the victims, he wrote down the names of people he knew to be responsible. I asked him how he came by this knowledge, and he stated he had been in this business a long time and in the area for quite some time and, because of the particulars of what happened to the victims, he knew the ones who were on the sheet and who were responsible." Bray showed Lax the paper. There were eight names on it, including those of Damien, Jason, Jessie, and Domini. "Further conversation revealed Don Bray compiled this list after he spoke with Jerry Driver," Lax wrote. "I continued to question Detective Bray as to the reason these individuals would have come to his mind in regard to this murder. He could not be specific, but he referred to rumors which had been circulating throughout the community."

Lax next met with Gitchell and Ridge.[160]

I asked them how Damien Echols' name had first been presented in connection with this investigation, and they discussed all the rumors and talk in the West Memphis area regarding Damien and his interest in Satanic worship. Further conversation revealed they spoke with Jerry Driver, who provided them with a great deal of information regarding Echols and Satanic cults. . . . At this point I asked Gitchell and Ridge what they found at the crime scene which was indicative of a cult killing. Their response was the fact that the scene was so clean, with no available evidence. . . . During the conversation, Ridge and Gitchell stated it was their impression that Jason Baldwin was a pretty good kid and had never been in trouble before, but Jessie Misskelley was "mean as a snake." They also felt Damien was the ring-leader of the bunch. When I reminded them that Damien had no prior arrest record, with the exception of the problems he had with his girlfriend, they agreed to this fact, but cited Damien's psychological problems. At this point, they expressed their expectations for Damien's defense to be insanity. They are firmly convinced Damien is insane.

CHAPTER ELEVEN

The Pretrial Motions

THE WORDS "OBEDIENCE TO THE LAW IS LIBERTY" are etched in stone above the entrance to the Crittenden County Courthouse at Marion. On August 4, 1993, two police officers led Damien, Jason, and Jessie, all wearing handcuffs and shackles, into the heavily guarded building for their first pretrial hearing. The courtroom was called to order, and Judge David Burnett, with black robes flowing and cornsilk-colored hair curling slightly at his collar, climbed to his seat at the bench.[161] Burnett told a reporter he'd read a book about satanism "for information purposes," in preparation for the case. Now, in his official capacity, he told the defendants that they were each charged with three counts of capital felony murder. He asked them, how did they plead? Each replied, "Not guilty."

Burnett cut a familiar and genial figure at the two-story courthouse. Earlier in the summer, he and the three other judges in Arkansas's Second Judicial District had met to discuss who would officiate in the already sensational case. The fifty-two-year-old Burnett had been selected. He was a native of the region, the son of a tire dealer in Blytheville. After high school, where he was an Eagle Scout, Burnett attended the University of Arkansas and then its school of law. As soon as he'd graduated from law school, in 1966, he'd entered the army, not as a military lawyer but as a police officer. His first tour of duty was at Fort Ord in California, where, he once said, "I was essentially the police chief for the base." He was awarded a Bronze Star for later service in Vietnam.

After leaving the army, Burnett returned to northeast Arkansas, where he started a private practice. He soon ran for and was elected prosecuting attorney for the Second Judicial District, and eight years later, in 1983, he was elected to the bench.[162]

One Arkansas reporter described Burnett as "a low-intensity judge whose idea of a good time is raising prize-winning tea roses."[163] Within his profession, opinions were mixed. While he was regarded in some circles as affable, smart, and one of the best of the region's good ol' boys, critics complained that he was still a policeman and prosecutor at heart, and one local politician called him "a political alligator." Burnett made no secret of his skepticism toward testimony in the field of psychology. As the West Memphis case headed toward trial, Burnett was working on his thesis for a judicial master's degree. He unabashedly told a reporter for the *Commercial Appeal* that his thesis centered on his belief that the expert opinions of psychiatrists and psychologists "shouldn't be given the great weight that it's normally given by courts, juries, and what have you."[164]

The first ruling Burnett made was that Jessie would be tried separately from the two teenagers whom he had accused.[165] Another concern Burnett promptly addressed dealt with mental competency. Perhaps anticipating that one or more of the defendants would plead not guilty by reason of insanity, the judge noted that so far, none of the lawyers had sought mental evaluations for their clients, and he gave them fair warning. "Gentlemen," Burnett announced, "I'm concerned with the possibility of a motion to seek mental examinations and the inevitable delay that that causes. . . . If you don't request it within thirty days, you're waiving it. You're on notice that the court is drawing a deadline as far as that defense goes." The deadline came and went. By then it had been decided that none of the teenagers wanted to plead not guilty by reason of insanity.[166] The lawyers planned to base their defenses on claims of actual innocence.

In the months ahead, Burnett would wade through a stack of motions more than a foot thick, and he'd issue more than fifty pretrial rulings. Most concerned the trials ahead. But one addressed an issue that was of personal concern to the lawyers. It asked Burnett to explain how—and how much—the court-appointed defense attorneys were to be paid. At the time, the matter was extremely murky.[167] The six court-appointed lawyers told Burnett that they expected to spend hundreds of hours on the case, and that they wanted the question cleared up. Jessie's attorney argued that he was already working full-time on his client's defense, and that not being paid would impose a serious hardship on his family and on his legal partner. Jason's lawyer pleaded, "I don't feel we should have to self-finance this case until it's over and then be reimbursed." Burnett told the lawyers not to worry.[168] "Obviously," he said, "the attorneys are going to be paid reasonable fees." But he offered them no specifics about when those fees might be paid.

"The Discovery Mess"

Four times between August and November, Damien, Jason, and Jessie were hauled back and forth from the boredom of their respective jail cells to various scenes of fury as they were led into court. Jessie, the smallest of the three, hunched, as though trying to make himself even smaller, as deputies marched him past the crowds. Jason walked head down and silent. But Damien seemed unable to ignore the angry taunts. Onlookers lining the sidewalks at the courthouse remarked that he looked sullen. Lax and Damien's attorneys warned him that his demeanor could harm his defense. When Shettles visited Damien after one of the hearings, she showed him a copy of that morning's *Commercial Appeal*.[169] Afterward, she wrote:

> The picture of Michael which appeared in this paper was very detrimental and depicted Michael looking behind him and giving the appearance he was sneering. I reminded Michael once again the community's and law enforcement's perception of him is a major aspect of this trial and pre-trial proceedings and should be taken very seriously. Michael stated a female photographer called his name several times before court began and indicated to him to smile. I advised Michael that in all future proceedings he should make no response. He admitted he had "blown a kiss" to the victims' family members following court. The family members and their friends were calling him a Satan worshiper and yelling he would burn in hell. He told me they were throwing rocks

at him as well. We discussed at length the fact that, although he maintained his innocence, the families had endured tremendous grief and pain and their feelings must be taken into consideration. By reacting in the manner he did, he reinforced the belief he was involved in Satanic activities.

Damien told Shettles that the sheriff's deputy who'd transported him from the jail to the courthouse and back had been "very kind" to him. Damien chuckled that the media had wanted to take his picture, but that the photographers had seemed to be afraid of him. Recalling how, upon his arrival to court, a "circle of guards" had surrounded him, one with a sawed-off shotgun, Damien marveled to Shettles that he was considered so dangerous. As tactfully as she could, Shettles let Damien know that rather than protecting people from him, the guards had been protecting him.

Later she wrote, "Michael stated that once inside, there was no holding area, and he, Jessie, and Jason were placed in an office with guards. He said Jason smiled and shook his head, but Jessie never looked up at either of them. Once again, Michael did not display open hostility toward Jessie and stated he felt the police had put words into Jessie's mouth to implicate him and Jason."

While Damien's lawyers worried, Jason's lawyer Paul Ford became furious. During one of Ford's visits with Jason, the boy had told Ford that Detective Ridge had recently come to the jail, to collect court-ordered samples of hair and blood from him.[170] The incident that Jason then described struck Ford as "extremely troubling." Ford fired off a letter to Gitchell, in which he explained:

My client informed me that Officer Ridge began to tell him that I was a nice guy and would try to make him like me; however, that I really didn't care about him and that I could not be trusted. He further told my client that he knew me when I was an attorney in Wynne and he was a police officer in Wynne. He told my client that I could not be trusted and that I really did not have his best interests at heart. He also told my client that I would not do a good job for him, and

that I would ultimately sell him out. He then tried to get my
client to come clean, confess, and that he could be trusted to
take care of him.

Ford continued:

> Immediately upon learning this event, I called John
> Fogleman to express my anger. He agreed with me that I had
> a right to be angry, but was not convinced that the event had
> occurred. I recognize that clients make up such stories from
> time to time, and many times these are totally fictitious.
> However, what troubles me the most is that I never told my
> client that I knew Officer Ridge as a police officer in Wynne
> while I practiced law there. I know of no way that he would
> have been able to obtain this information other than the fact
> that it was told to him by Officer Ridge.

But neither Damien's behavior nor the behavior of the police concerned the defense lawyers as much as the condition of the discovery
files that Fogleman was slowly releasing. One of the defense attorneys'
earliest motions—and one that would be often repeated—urged Judge
Burnett to order Fogleman or the police to help them clarify what they
called "the discovery mess."[171]

"The state has presented us literally mounds of evidence," Ford told
Burnett. "There's no heads or tails of it. There's no consistent order to
it." Ford asked Burnett to order Fogleman to reveal to the defense what
portions of the police investigation were relevant to the prosecution.[172]

The other lawyers joined with Ford in arguing that the state should
reveal its theory of the case so that they could prepare their defense,
but Fogleman objected. He maintained that the law did not require
him to reveal either what material was relevant or his theory of how
the crime had been committed. Burnett listened. Then he addressed
the prosecutor: "I understand you're giving them everything that is in
the file."

"That's correct, Your Honor," Fogleman replied. He then promised
that by the end of August, the defense would have everything the police

and prosecutors had developed to that point. Judge Burnett considered that was good enough and denied the defense lawyers' motion.

The Search Warrants

From then on, the defense launched motions like arrows at a fortress, and most were easily deflected. At one of the hearings, attorneys attempted to suppress evidence taken in the nighttime search—a search that they argued had been both unnecessary and illegal. Jason's other attorney, Robin Wadley, noted that the warrant itself had been vague. He pointed out that the "blue, green, red, black (or) purple fibers" listed on the warrant were items that could generally be found "in any home in Crittenden County." Moreover, he said, police had misled Judge Rainey by claiming that the accused were "friends and members of a close-knit cult group." Arguing that nothing in Jessie's statement had indicated that Jason was Jessie's friend or had "ever participated in occultic activities," Wadley called Detective Ridge to the stand. To Wadley's surprise, as the officer was being questioned, he testified that municipal judge Rainey had not only approved the search warrant but had come to the police station to advise police on how to prepare it. This was highly unusual, as it later placed the judge in the position of ruling on the legality of a document that he had helped prepare. "Judge Rainey was assisting in preparing the search warrant affidavit," Wadley said incredulously to Ridge. "Is that what you're telling me?"

"Yes sir," Ridge responded.

As the questioning continued, Ridge also disclosed that Rainey had reviewed Jessie's statement and found some problems with it. Wadley asked Ridge: "You would agree with me Judge Rainey had some serious, serious concerns about discrepancies in Mr. Misskelley's statement at the time he was to issue this search warrant?" Again Ridge replied, "Yes sir."

Wadley next attacked the document's ambiguity with regard to the search for "cult materials." Wadley asked Ridge what that phrase "cult materials" meant to him. "As a definition," the officer stammered, "a cult material, as a cult would be a group, and the cult materials would be any kind of groups with symbolism, writing, paraphernalia, that would agree with that cult."

"Be specific," Wadley demanded. "What are you talking about? You have 'cult materials' and then in parentheses you have 'Satanic materials.' Are you talking about specific items?"

"Books," Ridge answered. "Reading materials. Drawings. Knives. Anything of that nature." He then added that during the search at one home, police had found a poem that was "of a questionable nature."

Still trying to suppress items found in the search, the defense lawyers called to the stand Lisa Sakevicius, an analyst from the state crime lab. She revealed that, in yet another unusual turn of events, she had driven from her office in Little Rock to assist the police in their search. Under questioning by Paul Ford, Sakevicius acknowledged that she would have been "surprised" if any of the fibers found with the dead boys' bodies had been found at Jason's house.[173]

When Ford asked, "Was there any scientific reason that this search needed to be conducted at night?" Sakevicius answered, "Not to my knowledge."

To refute the assault on the warrants, Fogleman called Judge Rainey to the stand. The municipal judge contradicted the testimony by Ridge. Though Rainey admitted that he had been called to the police station after police finished questioning Jessie, he insisted, "I had no participation in the preparation of the affidavit. I had no participation whatsoever." Rainey told Judge Burnett that he had approved the search warrant because of the "close relationship between the alleged perpetrators" and "the fact that the evidence possibly could be removed or destroyed if it was not attempted to be gathered immediately."

Ford argued further that, as a judge, Rainey had not been independent and detached enough to properly rule on the warrant. He insisted that the U.S. Supreme Court "has been quite strict" in setting limits on nighttime searches. But Judge Burnett rejected both arguments. "It is the court's opinion and ruling," he declared, "that Judge Rainey was on very sound ground."

"A Level Playing Field"

Nevertheless, Ford pressed on. Arguing that all he and the other defense lawyers wanted was a "level playing field," he pointed out that

Fogleman had recently taken the unusual step of issuing prosecutor's subpoenas, a seldom-used tool that allowed him to question witnesses under oath before the trials. "It's rare that you do what I did in that case," Fogleman later acknowledged.[174] But he added, "The prosecutor has a right to conduct their own investigation . . . and through the subpoena power, a prosecutor can compel people to give testimony, just like in a grand jury. . . . And there were things that I needed to know." Most of Fogleman's mandated interviews were conducted in September, four months after the murders. First, he questioned members of the family that the Echols family had reported visiting on the evening of May 5. The Echolses' friends confirmed their account. Fogleman next questioned members of Damien's and Jason's immediate families. They too supported the boys' accounts of their whereabouts on May 5. Fogleman then questioned L. G. Hollingsworth, the teenager who, after being polygraphed by Detective Durham, told police that he believed Damien was the killer. But L.G. told Fogleman that he knew nothing about the crime. When Fogleman questioned Damien's girlfriend, Domini Teer, she testified that contrary to what her aunt Narlene Hollingsworth had claimed, she had not been with Damien on the service road near the Blue Beacon on the night the boys disappeared.

Lax attended the interview when Fogleman questioned Damien's family, along with a lawyer from West Memphis who had been appointed by Burnett to represent them for that procedure.[175] Lax later wrote in his notes that when he introduced himself to the court-appointed lawyer, the attorney informed him that he knew that Damien was guilty. "When I asked him what knowledge he had to lead him to believe this," Lax wrote, "he stated, 'They found that boy's penis and testicles in a glass jar in Damien's bedroom.' I attempted to explain to him that that was not true, and he repeatedly told me I needed to check my sources, because it was true." In fact, Chris Byers's severed body parts never were recovered. Lax wondered how the attorney had come to be so certain. What "sources" had given the lawyer his misinformation? The exchange suggested to Lax how deeply rumors had taken root in the town. And it made him wonder if some of them had originated with the police.

Since Fogleman was questioning potential defense witnesses under oath before the trials, the defense lawyers wanted a similar opportunity to question Gitchell, Allen, and Ridge. "I am asking it in the interest of a fundamentally fair trial," Ford said, "the right to due process, that if Jason Baldwin's mother can be questioned under oath by Mr. Fogleman, the least I can do is to be able to question under oath Inspector Gitchell." But Fogleman argued that the defense had already been given the officers' reports, and he again assured Judge Burnett that the defense would receive everything the state had produced. Noting that the state faced the greater burden of proving the defendants guilty, Burnett again denied the defense lawyers' motion. He ruled that the police would be made available to answer questions for the defense, but that he would not order the detectives to submit to questioning under oath.

Some of the defense motions were long shots, such as those asking Burnett to rule Arkansas's death penalty statute unconstitutional,[176] to prohibit so-called death-qualified juries,[177] and to instruct the juries that they could return a finding of first-degree, rather than capital, murder.[178] Others, such as attorney Stidham's attempt to suppress Jessie's confession due to tactics the police had employed, were thought to at least have a chance. But they failed nonetheless. Stidham took the defeat hard. He felt that the West Memphis police had "scared Jessie Misskelley to death" by showing him the photograph of a corpse and then playing him the eerie recording of Aaron Hutcheson's disembodied voice. Stidham considered it a tragedy that the court was willing to admit a confession made by a minor under such circumstances.

Jason's lawyers were just as dismayed by Burnett's unwillingness to separate Jason's trial from Damien's. They did not want Jason's case to be affected in any way by evidence or perceptions that might apply to Damien alone. "There has been considerable media coverage of Mr. Echols and particularly his having taken the nickname of Damien," Ford told the court, "and that nickname has been associated overwhelmingly with a movie by the name of *The Omen*, where the main character in that movie, Damien, is the Antichrist." Pointing out that "there has been an awful lot of publicity and speculation as to occult activities and whether or not this was a killing that was associated with an occult type ritual," Jason's lawyer argued that "the publicity as to that occultic type activity has been predominantly centered around Mr.

Echols, as opposed to Mr. Baldwin." He added, "If the two cases are tried together, Baldwin could be associated with activity that there is no evidence he ever participated in." He did not want Jason to be painted with the same broad brush as Damien.

Though Burnett refused to sever, or separate, the trials, Ford continued to raise additional issues to support that contention. At another pretrial hearing, he raised the subject of Narlene Hollingsworth's expected testimony that she had seen Damien, not with Jason but with Domini, on the service road on the night of the murders. Noting that Arkansas law required that cases be severed when their defenses were antagonistic, Ford explained that Hollingsworth's testimony "places Mr. Echols at or near the crime scene" and that because of that, Jason's trial strategy was at odds with Damien's. The lawyers representing Damien asked that the trials be severed, as well. But Burnett was not persuaded. Citing the need for "judicial economy" and stating that he could find "no reason that either defendant would be unduly jeopardized by a joint trial," he denied all motions for severance. He addressed the lawyers' concerns by advising them that "the jury, of course, will be instructed that they are to treat each defendant separately in viewing and evaluating the evidence."

Juveniles as Adults

Another major battle, waged by the attorneys for both Jason and Jessie—and another that was lost—concerned their status as minors. Since Jessie was seventeen and Jason just sixteen, their lawyers wanted them to be tried as juveniles, rather than as adults. Though Arkansas law allowed the state to prosecute juveniles as adults when they were accused of serious crimes, Ford argued that the court should consider Jason's record and try him in juvenile court. "In this case, there is a bare minimum, if not an absence, of criminal activity on the part of Jason Baldwin," Ford said. "And also, Your Honor, Mr. Baldwin is a good student. He has not been a discipline problem at home. He has not been a discipline problem in the school system. He has made good grades . . . all of which would indicate an ability to live up to certain codes of conduct." But Burnett was unimpressed. "I find that the seriousness of the offense was most serious, grievous, heinous," he said. "The fact that there were three eight-year-old boys murdered in the fashion depicted to the court, the violence exhibited—that certainly alone is enough to warrant that this charge be heard before a jury in circuit court."

Stidham fought the same battle for his client, only he argued that Jessie was not mentally mature enough to stand trial as an adult. "I am convinced," Stidham told Burnett, "that Mr. Misskelley is of limited intellect." To make the point, he called Dr. William E. Wilkins, a psychologist, to testify at one of the pretrial hearings.[179] Wilkins, who had examined Jessie, told the court that the boy's IQ scores hovered at around 70 and that, scholastically, he had achieved a "maximum level" no higher than the third grade. "He's never passed the Arkansas minimum standards test," Wilkins told the court.

Burnett asked Wilkins if he believed Jessie had developed what Burnett called "street smarts." "Even though his intelligence capacity is borderline," the judge asked, "did he not function in society well?" Wilkins answered that he did not. "He functioned marginally," the psychologist said.

Fogleman sought to counter Wilkins's testimony by calling Jerry Driver, who recited Jessie's record, which included the theft of band flags from the school. Fogleman then called Detective Ridge, who described the injuries he'd observed on the victims. As with Jason, Burnett ruled that due to the seriousness of the crime, Jessie would have to "answer to the circuit court as an adult."

Location of the Trials

None of the defendants waived their rights to a speedy trial, so Burnett announced that they would be tried early the next year.[180] By November 1993, the defense lawyers mounted a series of last-gasp pretrial efforts. They achieved partial success on only one of them: the motion to get the trials moved—at least out of Crittenden County. Jessie's lawyers, Stidham and Crow, argued that large parts of Jessie's confession had been printed in the *Memphis Commercial Appeal* and quoted repeatedly in other media throughout the district. They told the court that when they'd asked residents of the region to sign affidavits in support of moving the trials, they'd met with intense hostility.[181]

Arkansas law allowed for the trials to be moved to another county within the judicial district but Stidham asked for more. "It is quite possible," he wrote in one of his motions, "that this case has attracted more media attention than any other criminal case in the history of the Second Judicial District, and perhaps even in the entire state." Noting that members of Jessie's family had received death threats, he reported, "People say we don't need a trial, we need a lynching." Claiming that Jessie could not get a fair trial anywhere in northeastern Arkansas, due to the extent of the pretrial publicity, Stidham argued that the law requiring that he be tried there was unconstitutional. Later he told reporters that he would like to see Jessie's trial moved "as far away from West Memphis as possible."

Jason's lawyers took another approach to the publicity problem. Worrying that the pretrial motions they were filing might "reveal the essence of the defendant's defense," Ford and Wadley asked Burnett to seal all subsequent filings in the case. The *Commercial Appeal* was already concerned about the level of secrecy shrouding the case. When reporters learned of efforts to further restrict access to information, the paper filed a lawsuit. It objected to any future seals and asked Burnett to remove those that had been imposed at the time of the arrests. Burnett split the difference; he left the earlier, state records sealed but refused to seal pretrial motions.

Damien's lawyers filed affidavits showing results of a mini poll they'd conducted, in which all twenty-six of the respondents said they doubted the defendants could get a fair trial anywhere in the judicial district. Asked what "the motive for the murder is believed or known to be," those questioned in the survey had answered: "cults," "devil worshiping," "Satan worship," "hate," and "cruelty."

Jessie's lawyer asked, "Would the Court consider moving the case outside the district?"

"I don't really see the need to do that," Burnett responded. "Granted, I keep seeing these revealing reports on all the TV channels, and the *Commercial Appeal* is having a field day. It would seem to me that the news media could exercise a little restraint and maybe we could go on with the business at hand."

"Your Honor, that is the exact point," Stidham implored. "That is why I want to leave the district."

But Burnett would not be moved. He announced that Jessie would be tried in January, in the tiny town of Corning, a few miles south of the Missouri border. Damien and Jason would be tried the following month, in Jonesboro, the district's largest city.

"Every Note—Everything"

As 1993 drew to a close, the defense attorneys were still begging Judge Burnett to let them question detectives Gitchell, Ridge, and Allen under oath. The lawyers wanted to understand precisely what had led the police to these three particular defendants. Stidham argued that Fogleman, through the use of his subpoenas, had "the right to go out and force people to come into their offices and put them under oath, ask them questions and have a court reporter there. We don't have that power, and it inhibits our ability to represent our client." But again, Fogleman insisted that the state was reporting everything it learned to the defense attorneys.

"Your Honor," the prosecutor complained, "they keep talking about a level playing field. We've provided them everything that we have. We have no right to find out what their investigation discloses, and so the playing field is not level, and it is balanced in their favor, as far as discovery is concerned."

"Judge," Stidham countered, "Mr. Misskelley was interrogated by the West Memphis police for somewhere around twelve hours, yet the transcript is nowhere near twelve hours long. We should be entitled under due process, equal protection, and other constitutional requirements and safeguards to talk to these officers and find out what happened in this other time."

"You have got my permission to talk to them," Burnett responded.

"Do we have permission to ask them questions under oath and have a court reporter present?"

"No. No, you don't. . . . I would like to know if there is any Arkansas case where you are permitted to do that."

"Your Honor," Stidham began again, "even a civil defendant has the right to conduct depositions. It seems like someone who is facing the death penalty should be afforded the same opportunity to depose the witnesses against them."

Jason's lawyer joined in the request to depose Gitchell, Ridge, and Allen. Ford told Burnett, "I want to have the opportunity, just like Mr. Fogleman has the opportunity, to question them under oath, and then, if necessary, send out that dragnet to poke holes in their story the way they are trying to do to the parents of my client."

"Your Honor," Fogleman interrupted, "they have got that. They have got everything that we've got. Every note—everything."

"But it is not under oath, Your Honor," Ford insisted. "It is not under oath. If it is not under oath, we are limited in how we can use those notes to impeach them on the witness stand."

But Burnett stood firm. The police would not be questioned under oath before the start of the trials.

Glori Shettles sat through the hearing with Damien and his lawyer Val Price. She was troubled by the behavior of John Mark Byers, who, she said, sat nearby, "glaring" at Damien, except when he occasionally "nodded off." She wrote in her notes that she suspected that he was "under the influence of drugs and/or alcohol."

At one point, while Price was at the bench consulting with Fogleman, the other lawyers, and Burnett, Damien leaned over to her and whispered that members of the victims' families had yelled and cursed him again as he'd entered the courthouse. They'd called him a "faggot murderer," he said. He told Shettles that despite her cautions, he had not been able to control himself. He'd turned to them and said, "Fuck you." But at least, he noted, he had not yelled the words. Shettles wrote afterward that Damien had "appeared frustrated and angry at himself." When Damien reported the jeering to his lawyers, one of them, Scott Davidson, decided to accompany Damien as he walked out of the courthouse after the hearing. Shettles wrote in her report, "Scott returned shocked at the verbal assaults he'd witnessed."

After the hearing, the courtroom was empty except for Inspector Gary Gitchell, the judge, the lawyers, and her. Shettles later reported to Lax that in that more informal atmosphere, Burnett asked Damien's lawyers if their client had decided to testify against his codefendants. She said Judge Burnett had observed that such a turn of events would make the case "more interesting." Damien's lawyers replied he had no such intentions. Shettles told Lax that Fogleman then commented that something would have to be done about Damien's eyes for him to be credible. "As comments such as these are made," Shettles wrote in her report, "I continue to have great concerns regarding any possibility of Michael Echols receiving any semblance of a fair trial."

Fogleman's Idea

The defense attorneys had many concerns, but Fogleman harbored some too. Six months had passed since the murders, and though much of the public believed that the teenagers were guilty as charged, other than Jessie's confession, all of his evidence was circumstantial, and there was not much even of that. Jessie had retracted his confession and vowed not to repeat any part of it. The crime lab had reported a similarity between some fibers found with the bodies and fibers taken from the defendants' homes, but similar fibers could have been found in almost any house in Arkansas. The police had found two young girls and a couple of teenage boys who said they'd heard Damien brag that he'd committed the murders, but that wasn't much of a foundation from which to argue for the death penalty. The prosecutor faced going into court with only Jessie's retracted confession to present against him, with only Damien's weirdness to present against him, and with virtually nothing to present against Jason. Then Fogleman had an idea.[182]

He decided to search the lake behind the trailer where Jason lived. He said that as he drove around the trailer park, "I said to the officers I was with, 'What better place to dispose of evidence than in a lake?' "

Fogleman contacted the Arkansas State Police, which dispatched a team of professional divers. On November 17, one of the divers entered the littered water of what was known as Lakeshore Lake at a point between the trailers where Damien and Jason had lived.[183] A short time later, he emerged holding a nine-inch survival knife, with a distinctly jagged blade. It was exactly the type of knife that Deanna Holcomb, Damien's former girlfriend, had told police he sometimes carried. The diver said he'd found the knife, buried up to its hilt in mud, at a point forty-seven feet behind Jason's house.

Fogleman later described the find as "quite a coincidence."[184] He said he considered the possibility that "somebody could have planted it" but had dismissed the idea because, as far as he knew, "the only people who knew we were going to do that search were the police." Fogleman said there were two reasons he was sure the knife had been thrown into the lake by the murderers. First, he said, no one other than the investigators knew that Deanna had told police that Damien had owned such a knife. And second, anyone planting the knife would have had to know, as Fogleman put it, "not just that we were going to look, but when we were going to do it."

He regarded the knife as a coup. The crime lab had reported that the wounds on Christopher Byers had been inflicted by a knife with at least one serrated edge, and this knife had a serrated edge. The knife resembled the one Deanna had described. And there was the "coincidence" of where it was found—almost directly behind Jason's trailer. With one inspired move, Fogleman had directed police to evidence that would become the centerpiece of his case—evidence that had eluded police, evidence he could link to Jason.

But there was more than "coincidence" in Fogleman's account of the knife's discovery. For one thing, it was contradicted in part by Gitchell. Despite the court order prohibiting release of information about the case, the day after the dive, the *West Memphis Evening Times* ran a front-page story about the sensational find. Gitchell even talked about it with reporters. But he did not say that the search of the lake had been Fogleman's idea. To the contrary, he said, his department had wanted to search the lake for several months but had not previously had an opportunity.

The matter of who would get credit for the discovery—the police or the prosecutor—amounted to a minor difference. What was not minor, in light of Fogleman's claim that no one but the police knew "that we were going to look" and "when we were going to do it," was the photo that ran with the page-one article. It showed a diver, still neck-deep in the water and wearing his diving mask, holding up a large serrated knife. The article offered no explanation as to how the reporter who'd taken the photograph had known about the search.[185] The photo's caption simply read: "Knife found near suspect home."

CHAPTER TWELVE

The Private Investigation

WHILE THE LAWYERS WRANGLED, private investigator Ron Lax delved deeper into "the discovery mess." At the end of November 1993, despite Fogleman's repeated assurances to Judge Burnett that the defense would have the entire police file by the end of August, the prosecutor suddenly released another large batch of material. One item in the batch, in particular, had sparked the defense lawyers' interest: a transcript of the interview that detectives Ridge and Sudbury had conducted with John Mark Byers on May 19, more than six months earlier. This was the first the defense had seen of it. This lengthy interview, which was conducted *before* the arrests, had inexplicably been withheld, not just past August but for more than three months after that. Until now—three weeks before the Christmas holidays and with Jessie's trial just six weeks away—the three defense teams had known nothing about the John Mark Byers element of the investigation.

As with all the documents received, Lax summarized the transcript for the attorneys. He outlined Byers's account of his whereabouts on May 5, beginning early in the evening, when he began searching for Chris and reporting the boy's disappearance. Lax noted, "It was not clarified why Byers became worried so quickly." But coming late as it did, with the trials looming, the transcript did not receive the scrutiny it otherwise might have. Neither Lax nor the defense lawyers caught the points on which Byers's account had differed from the statements given by Melissa and Ryan to police, partly because those reports had been released months earlier. Byers may have looked like a shady character, but so far as the defense teams knew, he had not been a suspect in the murders. So Lax focused on what the transcript implied about the conduct of the investigation—and the significance of that for the defense.

"On page thirty-one of the interview," he wrote with emphasis, "Byers tells Ridge that John Fogleman had promised him and the other fathers that he would seek the death penalty for the individuals responsible, *regardless of their age*. Fogleman also allegedly told the fathers he did not see how the responsible parties could claim insanity since they had tried to cover up the crime." Noting that this interview was conducted on May 19, two weeks after the murders and two weeks before Jessie's confession, Lax asked pointedly, "Why would Fogleman refer to the age of the responsible party(ies) this early in the investigation?"

Damien

Lax felt unusually unprepared as the trial dates drew nearer. He still did not see how Fogleman was going make his case. At the same time, however, he and Shettles shared deep concerns about certain aspects of the defense. Damien's mental state was one. Although his mother and sister, and both Joe Hutchison and Jack Echols, had stood by Damien since his arrest, Lax and Shettles worried that his obvious psychological problems would cloud his prospects at trial. As the date of his trial approached, those concerns grew more acute.

Becoming a father had not helped. Damien and Domini's son, Seth Damien Azariah Teer, was born, as expected, in September.[186] Domini brought him to the jail soon afterward, but the sheriff would not allow Damien to touch the baby. The following month, Damien's maternal grandmother died.[187] When Lax and Shettles visited Damien during the first week of November, Shettles noted that "he appeared frightened," he was "biting his nails," and "his hands were shaking rather violently." Lax brought a pack of cigarettes, which, Shettles observed, Damien "practically snatched from his hand." She noted, "He began chain smoking and consumed at least eight cigarettes in our hour to hour-and-a-half visit." Lax asked what was wrong, but Damien did not answer. When Lax asked Damien if things were "getting to him," Damien answered, 'Sometimes.' "

Lax wrote in his notes following the visit that he believed Damien was "suffering from great depression." Nonetheless, Lax felt he needed to confront Damien about a key issue in the case. Had Damien ever told people that he'd committed the murders? Shettles had posed the question to Damien on a visit a few weeks before. She'd explained to him that some girls at a softball game had reported that they'd heard Damien claim responsibility. Shettles advised Damien that the girls might be witnesses against him. Shettles wrote that Damien "admitted that prior to his arrest, he made remarks to various persons, when asked about the murders, that might be misconstrued." However, she added, "He stated he did not make any remarks in a serious nature, although some of his comments could have been misinterpreted." Now that Lax was visiting, he pressed Damien to be more specific. But Damien seemed unwilling or unable to acknowledge to the investigator that he may have hurt his own case. Lax wrote, "When I asked him about the numerous references in the police files regarding individuals who say Damien either told them he was responsible, or they overheard Damien say this, he does not answer, but merely sits there and stares."

When Shettles visited the following week, Damien said he was feeling better, although she noted that his hands were still shaking.[188] In December, Shettles brought cupcakes to the jail, along with a couple of books, for Damien's nineteenth birthday. But the event was overshadowed by discussions of the upcoming trial. Shettles recalled Damien saying that if the jury found him not guilty, he wanted to "move out of state, and would like to own a bookstore. However, he informed me, if he is found guilty, he will throw himself 'out of a third story window.' Michael is anxious to have his trial over, 'one way or another.' "

Loose Ends

In late December, Fogleman released the transcript of an interview that Detective Bill Durham had conducted with Jerry Driver earlier in the month. According to the transcript, Driver reported that for as much as a year before the murders, he'd been closely watching seven kids who'd exhibited what he called "all the earmarks" of satanic involvement. He described the suspicious earmarks as "the tattoos and the devil rings and this and that and the other." Driver considered Jessie's "spike hair and stuff" as a sign of his involvement.[189]

Lax next tracked down Marty King, the manager of the Bojangles restaurant. King reported that on the evening after the boys' bodies were found, an off-duty West Memphis police officer had come into the restaurant to eat. King said he told the officer about the bloody man who'd come in the night before. The officer checked the rest room, found some remaining flecks of blood, and called the police department. A short time later, King said, Detective Allen and Sergeant Ridge arrived. The visit marked the first time since King's call to the police about the bloody man that detectives had entered the restaurant.

King said that he gave Allen and Ridge a pair of sunglasses he'd pulled out of the commode, and that the detectives then took blood scrapings from the rest room wall. After that, King said, he never heard from them again.

"Has any police officer contacted you since that incident to show you photographs or to discuss this incident any further with you?" Lax asked.

"No sir." King replied.

Another of Lax's interviews was with a teenager who'd known Jessie Misskelley. Fogleman had listed the boy as a potential witness. Police reports indicated that they had questioned the eighteen-year-old for close to five hours, during which Durham had administered a polygraph exam. They had then videotaped a statement in which the boy said that Jessie had admitted to him that "he was with Jason and Damien when they sacrificed them little kids."

On December 30, Lax drove to the teenager's house. He introduced himself as a private investigator and spoke briefly with the boy and his uncle. After that, with the uncle present, Lax tape-recorded an interview with the boy. In his summary of the taped interview, Lax wrote that the boy had "stated he attempted to tell the police the truth about what he knew regarding the murders of the three boys, which amounted to nothing. He stated the police continued to yell and scream at him until he told them what he thought they wanted to hear. He informed me Jessie Misskelley had never said anything to him about the young boys, nor had anyone else, and he had no knowledge whatsoever of the murders."[190]

This was not the only interview Lax conducted with a teenager who described a disturbing experience with police. Christopher Littrell, a neighbor of Damien's, told Lax that he had been questioned twice.[191] The first interview, on May 10, five days after the murders, had lasted for three hours. The boy's mother had been present and, Lax wrote, the boy stated that "everyone treated him cordially." However, on May 27, police picked up Littrell from school and questioned him for another two hours, this time without his mother present. The boy told Lax that Durham had been "nice" to him throughout the interview but that Inspector Gitchell had become "extremely upset on occasions and would yell and scream at him." At one point, Lax reported, the boy said Gitchell had "grabbed his chin" and put his face close to the boy's, threatening that "he would have no reservation about keeping him in the holding tank if he wouldn't tell the truth."

Lax also revisited Vicki Hutcheson. On this visit, he was particularly interested in an altercation that had taken place between 5:30 and 6 P.M. on the evening of the murders, in the trailer park where Hutcheson and Jessie lived. Because of the apparent importance police had placed on Aaron Hutcheson, his whereabouts at that time were crucial. Marion police had responded after a woman living in Hutcheson's trailer park had reported that a neighbor had slapped her son. An officer had come to the trailer park, but left a few minutes later. Then the neighbors had argued again, and this time, three squad cars had responded.

Lax interviewed five residents of Hutcheson's trailer park.[192] All reported that Vicki Hutcheson had participated in the events that night when the police were called, and that Aaron had been with her. Lax didn't know what Fogleman intended to do with Aaron's many statements, but he felt better after talking to the neighbors.[193] Since he was there, he also asked the women about their experiences with Vicki Hutcheson in the days after the murders, and if Hutcheson had ever mentioned the $35,000 reward. One of the neighbors told Lax that the subject had come up twice. "At one time she told me that they were going to split the reward money between Aaron and another little boy," the woman said. "Another time she told me they were going to give Aaron all the reward money."

Another woman said she also recalled hearing Hutcheson discuss the reward. "She had told me that Aaron was receiving it," the woman said, "and she told me how she was going to spend the money, what she was going to buy with it."

"Did you ask her why Aaron was going to receive the money?" Lax asked.

"Yes sir."

"And what did she say?"

"She said because he had seen the murders."

"Did you believe it?"

"No sir."

"Why not?"

"Because he was out here in the trailer park."

Byers on Film

Family members of the victims were also listed among the witnesses Fogleman said he might call. Since they seemed to have no information that implicated any of the defendants, Lax did not interview them. The filmmakers Berlinger and Sinofsky, however, were very interested in the families. Their request to film the shower for Domini's baby had been only the start.

Since then they had contacted all of the principals in the case: the families of the victims, the defendants and their families, the police, the lawyers, and the judge. They'd offered money to the defendants and to family members of the victims who agreed to be interviewed. Damien was offered $7,500 if he would agree to two interviews. His defense attorneys, and the others, were reticent.[194] But the filmmakers noted that the finished documentary would not be released until several months after the trials, and ultimately, the lawyers gave their clients the go-ahead for a couple of interviews each.[195] Though Judge Burnett withheld his decision on the filmmakers' request to videotape both of the trials, he too relented shortly before the trials began.

From the summer of 1993 through the end of the year, filmmakers Sinofsky and Berlinger were able to record moments with members of both the victims' and the defendants' families as they grappled with what had happened—and contemplated what lay ahead. Michael's parents,

Todd and Dana Moore, seated together at a table in their house, were the quietest in front of the camera. After describing some of the questions that haunted them as parents—"Was he calling for me?"—Todd Moore said simply that Michael had been killed "by real monsters."

Pam Hobbs, Stevie Branch's mother, was filmed in front of the elementary school as she was being interviewed by a local TV reporter. Chewing gum, giggling, and fiddling with a yellow Cub Scout scarf that had belonged to Stevie, she looked, at turns, delighted to be on camera and sobered by the subject of her son's murder. Microphone in hand, the reporter asked, "Do you feel the people who did this were worshiping—"

Hobbs finished the question for him. "Satan? Yes, I do. Just look at the freaks. I mean, just look at them. They look like punks." She fairly spat the last word.

But no one's rage or venom compared to that expressed by the Byerses. Melissa was filmed seated at a kitchen table. She had dark circles under her eyes. "Christopher never hurt anybody," she said. "He had a gentle, loving, and giving heart, and they crucified him in those woods. And they humiliated his little body. They took his little manhood before he even knew what it was. And I hate 'em for it. I never hated anybody in my life, and I hate those three"—then, hammering the table with her finger, she added emphatically, "And the mothers that bore them."

Her husband, Mark, wearing overalls, accompanied the filmmakers to the gully where the boys' bodies were found. There he delivered a monologue in language that was as brutal as it was sentimental. Full of religious allusions, it was shockingly profane. Even with editing, Byers's speech, as it appeared in the film, was long and rambling. Later the filmmakers reported that when they'd shown the unedited segment to their wives, the women had found it so disturbing they'd left the room.

"Yea, though I walk in the valley of the shadow of death," he began, "I shall fear no evil. And I'm not scared of the devil. I know who my comforter is. Thy rod and thy staff comfort me. And I thank you, Lord, for letting me be able to believe in that with all my heart."

Apparently turning his attention from God to the defendants, Byers continued, as though addressing them directly, "I hope you all really believe in your master, the Satan, sleuth-foot devil himself, 'cause he's not going to help you. He's going to laugh at you, mock at you, and torture you. He doesn't need your help. The devil's got all the devils he needs."[196]

At another point he railed: "Jessie Misskelley Jr., Jason Baldwin, Damien Echols, I hope your master the devil does take you soon. I want you to meet him real soon. And the day you die I'm going to praise God. And I make you a promise. The day you die, every year on May 5, I'm going to come to your graveside. I'm going to spit on you. I'm going to curse the day you were born. And I'm sure, while I'm standing there, I'm going to have to have other bodily functions let go on your grave. I promise you, as God is my witness, I'll visit all three of your graves."

Compared to the speech by Byers, what the families of the defendants said to the filmmakers sounded subdued. Jessie Misskelley Sr., weathered and wearing a work shirt, told them simply, "Little Jessie told me he didn't do it, he didn't have anything to do with it, he wasn't there. And I believe him. I think the cops just can't find who done it, and they've got to put it on somebody."

Jason's mother, Gail Grinnell, looked gaunt and nearly distracted as the camera rolled. "I want to tell the whole world my son is innocent," she said, "because I know he is innocent. I know where he was, and I know he's innocent, and I want to tell the world, and I want the world to know."

Damien's biological father, Joe Hutchison, said, "This boy is not capable of the crime he's been arrested for. I've seen him take a little kitten and love it just like you'd love a little baby. It's like a nightmare you can't wake up from. Our son is innocent. We intend to prove it."

But while most who had parts in the tragedy appeared anguished and subdued, John Mark Byers seemed to relish being in front of the cameras. Berlinger and Sinofsky filmed him seated in front of the pool in his backyard, expounding on angels and demons; at the pulpit of a local Baptist church, singing a hymn; and with his neighbor Todd Moore in a field shooting pumpkins with handguns. In that scene, Byers, wearing a cowboy hat, did most of the talking, as he loaded his gun. "There's a few people I wouldn't mind going on and shooting with it," he said, "but hopefully, the courts and the justice system will take care of 'em."[197]

CHAPTER THIRTEEN

The Bloodstained Knife

BY THE SECOND WEEK OF JANUARY 1994, reporters were gathering in Corning, Arkansas, where Jessie's trial was about to begin. One of them asked prosecutor Fogleman about some of the questions that had been raised at the pretrial hearings. Citing professional ethics, he said he could not discuss the police investigation, the rumored lack of physical evidence, or attorney Stidham's contention that Jessie's statement had been coerced. "I can't comment on specifics," Fogleman said, "because I sincerely want these defendants to receive a fair trial." He added, however, that he had "never seen a police department work any harder on a case" than the West Memphis police had worked on this one.[198]

On January 17, the day before jury selection was scheduled to begin, Fogleman released more documents to the defense attorneys. Most of them showed how the police had been working to bolster their case as the two trials drew near. Among other activities, the records indicated that as recently as New Year's Eve, Fogleman, Ridge, and Bray had met for yet another interview of Aaron Hutcheson. No transcript of that meeting was produced or supplied to the defense, but according to notes taken by Ridge, Aaron reiterated his statement that he had watched his friends being killed, though some of the details he now offered differed again from prior accounts. When Ron Lax reviewed the material, he was surprised to see that the police and Fogleman were still trying to wrest a coherent statement from the child. But Lax was dumbfounded by two other reports contained in the latest batch of discovery materials. These were release forms signed by Dana Moore and John Mark Byers—forms dated December 20, 1993, granting the West Memphis police, along with staff from the Arkansas crime lab, permission to search their houses. No explanation accompanied the forms, but they raised a disturbing question for Lax. Why, on the very eve of Jessie's trial, had the police suddenly decided to search two of the victims' homes? What could they have been looking for, more than eight months after the murders—and nearly seven months after the arrests?

"Additional Discovery"

A possible explanation—or a hint of one—came in a phone call two days later. By then, Jessie's jury had been seated. Damien's lawyer Val Price telephoned Lax at home to report that Fogleman had just released more records from the West Memphis police. These last-minute records concerned a knife that the police said they'd received eleven days earlier, on January 8, 1994. Lax immediately made a note of what Price related in the call. "The knife had been Federal Expressed," Lax wrote, "but the package had been discarded. The knife was eight and three-fourth inches in length and was sent to the Arkansas crime lab for analysis. The results reflect there was blood on the knife which was consistent with the blood of Chris Byers. The results also stated this blood was consistent with eight percent of the population. The knife was given exhibit number E178."

With Jessie on trial for his life, his attorneys, Stidham and Crow, were focused on events in the courtroom. But now the remarkable news of the FedExed knife became a serious distraction. As the lawyers waded into the trial, Lax worked outside of court, trying to learn what he could about the mysterious knife. Bit by bit, he managed to find out that it had been sent to Gitchell by the New York filmmakers Sinofsky and Berlinger. The two later explained how the knife had come into their possession—and why they'd sent it to the West Memphis police. It was a remarkable tale.

"A few days before Christmas," they wrote,

> Mark Byers gave a member of our crew a used hunting knife as a gift. We later discovered that the knife appeared to have traces of blood on it. Naturally, we were shocked and found ourselves in an extremely difficult situation. We felt it

was strange that Mr. Byers had given us a used knife that seemed to have blood on it. However, it could have easily been an innocent gesture of friendship, so we did not want to carelessly hand it over to police, creating controversy for Mr. Byers, particularly in the local press.

On the other hand, since the investigation had yet to recover a definitive murder weapon, and since it was Byers' stepson who had been castrated with a knife, we had no way of knowing if the knife was involved in the murders. We had to weigh our responsibility as journalists against our moral and civic responsibilities. We didn't want it to create the false impression that we were manipulating the outcome of our film, nor did we want an innocent man to be falsely accused. And, on a practical level, we feared that the tremendous access and trust that people had placed in us would be destroyed if we turned over the knife—the press might play it up, and if the knife did not play a role in the case, our subjects might not trust us any longer. But the most important consideration kept floating to the top: if there was even the remotest possibility that the knife was involved in the case, we had a moral obligation to turn it over. After several meetings with HBO on the subject, we decided to turn it over to the local police.[199]

The sudden appearance of a knife—one owned by John Mark Byers and bearing traces of blood that was consistent with Christopher's—was the most significant development in the case since Jessie Misskelley's contorted confession. Its connection to people related to the crime was clear. Unlike the knife police said they'd taken from the lake, which they claimed linked two of the defendants to the murders, this knife had indisputably belonged to the father of one of the victims. And blood on it was consistent with the blood of his murdered stepson.

For the defense attorneys and Lax, the timing of the knife's appearance could hardly have been worse. The knife cast serious suspicion on Byers. But until now, no one on the defense had ever focused on him as a suspect. That was partly because of the size and condition of what they called "the discovery mess." It was partly because, despite Fogle-man's assurances to Judge Burnett that "everything" would be turned over to the defense by the end of August, notes of the interview detectives had conducted on May 19 with Byers had not been released until the middle of November. And it was partly because other records, such as those concerning Byers's activities as a drug informant and his conviction for threatening to kill his ex-wife, had never been released at all. Now, faced with the startling appearance of the bloodstained knife, Lax and the defense lawyers felt handicapped by all they did not know about the stepfather of the castrated victim.

For Stidham and Crow, who were already deep into Jessie's trial, the situation was especially acute. They had to decide whether to introduce the knife, in an attempt to suggest that there was reasonable doubt that Jessie was the killer. At the time, the defense attorneys did not even have a clear idea about how the police had reacted to the knife's appearance. Only gradually, and amid the pressures of the trial, were they able to fill in some critical details.

According to the filmmakers, Byers had presented the knife to a member of their crew six days before Christmas, on December 19, 1993.[200] The next day, December 20, police had conducted the search of Byers's house and of the Moores' house, across the street. It looked to Lax as if the two events were probably related. His suspicion was strengthened when he spoke with Sinofsky and Berlinger, who told him, as he wrote, that they had "spoken with Fogleman and Gitchell in December 1993 . . . and apparently provided them with details of the knife."[201] No record of that discussion was supplied by the West Memphis police. The knife's existence was not reported to the defense attorneys until almost a full month later—after Jessie's trial had already started. And the FedEx packaging in which the knife had been sent, which would have confirmed the date, had reportedly been discarded.

Gitchell said the knife was received on January 8 and that he sent it out the same day to a North Carolina laboratory for testing.[202] Gitchell sent a memo with the knife noting that it had what might be blood and another unknown substance in the fold. (It would later be learned that the other substance was a red fiber.) Gitchell asked that the lab test the knife and compare any results with DNA from the victims. The lab had returned its results just as Jessie's trial was beginning. That's when Fogleman had informed the defense attorneys about the knife's existence—and that the blood on it was consistent with that of Christopher Byers.

Questioning Byers

Jessie's lawyers wanted Byers questioned immediately—and by someone other than Inspector Gary Gitchell. But the West Memphis police were reticent. "State police CID [Criminal Investigation Division] officers were present," Stidham later recalled. "I begged Judge Burnett to have one of them interrogate Byers, but Judge Burnett refused."[203] Finally, the judge instructed that Byers would be questioned—but only by the West Memphis police. Since Gitchell, Ridge, and Byers were already at Corning to attend Jessie's trial, an interview was hastily arranged. It took place on Wednesday January 26—with Jessie's trial now already in its second week—in a room at the county sheriff's office. The interview, which was recorded, lasted forty-five minutes.

It began with Gitchell reading Byers his rights and advising him that anything he said could be used against him in court. Byers said that he understood and waived his right to a lawyer. He then told Gitchell that, yes, he had owned a Kershaw knife—"You know, it's got like a serrated edge, like a Ginsu knife"—which he had given to a member of the film crew "as a Christmas gift." Byers said he believed that had been in November.[204] He told Gitchell that he had never used that knife for hunting; that, in fact, "that knife had not been used at all"—and that no one in his family had ever been cut with it. He said, "No one's been cut with the Kershaw."

Detective Ridge asked Byers, "Did you use the knife?"

"I never used it," Byers replied. "I would have used it. Hopefully, I was going to use it for deer hunting—that's all I do is deer hunt—but I never had an opportunity to use it on a deer." He told the detectives that the knife had "stayed put up" in the top drawer of his chifforobe.

Gitchell: "Did, um, any of your kids, Ryan or Chris, know where that knife may have been at? I mean, could they have gotten it out?"

Byers: "No sir. I don't think they could have. . . ."[205]

Gitchell then showed Byers the knife that had been sent from New York. He described it as a Kershaw knife with a nine-inch blade, a Pachmayr grip, and an inscription that read "Cannon City." Byers identified it as the knife he had given to the cinematographer, a knife that, he said, his wife, Melissa, had given to him a few years before as a Christmas present.

"Okay," Gitchell said. "Let me explain a problem we had, and you need to answer this for me: we have found blood on this knife."

Byers: "I can tell you where I might assume it might have come from."

Gitchell: "All right."

Byers: "Uh, I got a deer this year, and I was cutting it up to make some beef jerky and I had a filleting knife, a Ginsu filleting knife, and I thought of that knife, and I tried to cut some of the deer as thin as possible, and when I found out that it wouldn't cut as thin as the skinning knife was, I put it up. But that would be the only time it's been around anything bloody. . . . I was cutting some deer meat at home."

Neither Gitchell nor Ridge asked Byers to explain why, only a few minutes before, he had stated that he had "never used" the knife and, even more specifically, that he'd "never had an opportunity to use it on a deer." Instead, Gitchell proceeded, almost deferentially, to point out another "problem."

"Okay," he told Byers, "let me, let me go a little bit further and say there's a problem with that. I mean, I'm not saying that's not true. The problem is we have sent this knife off and had it examined, and it has the blood type of Chris on it."

Suddenly Byers began addressing the detective by his first name. "Well, Gary," he responded, "I don't have any idea how it could be on there."

"That's our problem," said Gitchell.

Byers: "I have no idea how it's on there."

Gitchell: "Why? Why would this knife have blood on it?"

Byers: "I have no idea, Gary."

Gitchell: "That's what scares me."

When Lax and the defense attorneys saw a transcript of the interview, they were appalled by the tenor of the exchange. Byers was in an ex-

tremely compromising situation. Blood consistent with that of his mutilated son had been found on his own knife, a knife he'd said had never
been used and that he'd given away to someone who was leaving the
state. Yet when this was pointed out to Byers and he had no good explanation, the chief detective on the case had remarked that *he* was scared.

Byers, meanwhile, was reduced to stammering. "I have no idea, I
have no idea, how it could have any human's blood type on it at all," he
said. "I don't even remember nicking myself with it, cutting the deer
meat or anything."

Finally, hesitantly, almost apologetically, Gitchell asked Byers the
central question. And now he too was stammering. "I got to, I got to ask
you point-blank, I've got to ask you point-blank, Mark," he said, "I've
got to ask you point-blank: were you around or participated in these
deaths of these boys?"

"No," Byers responded. "Not in any shape, form, or fashion . . . Absolutely not. Positively not. Unequivocally not. No. Not at all."

"Well," Gitchell said, "there are other tests being run on this knife,
and we should, may have the results right now. We've been waiting on
them the last several days." Gitchell added that blood had recently been
taken from Melissa and Ryan, and that since a sample of Mark's blood
had been taken in May, tests were being run to see if any matched the
blood on the knife. "That's what we've been trying to do," Gitchell explained, "is see if it could have been . . . if you have similar blood. We
don't know. We don't know if there's a similarity. We don't know."

It seemed to Lax that Gitchell sounded worried in the interview and
almost apologetic. Gitchell had certainly not been as confrontational as
in the interview with Jessie Misskelley, when Gitchell had demanded of
Jessie, "Now tell us the truth." But if Gitchell had, indeed, been worried that his case might suddenly implode, he was reassured later that
day when further results came in from the lab. Fogleman's report on the
findings left the defense teams stunned. The amount of blood on the
knife was small, Fogleman said, and because of that, only a limited
analysis could be performed on it. The science of DNA testing was relatively new in 1994, but working within the constraints of the small
sample and the emerging science, the lab had conducted what tests it
could. Its results indicated that while the blood was consistent with

Christopher's, it was consistent with that of Christopher's stepfather, John Mark Byers, as well.

Lax and the attorneys wondered, could the DNA of two people who were not biologically related be utterly indistinguishable? Or—the thought arose—was John Mark Byers actually Christopher's biological father? Was that why he'd always claimed to have "adopted" the boy, but not Christopher's half brother, Ryan? Those questions would hang over the case, unresolved, for years to come.

But with Jessie's trial under way and another trial soon to start, there was no time for speculation. And soon after Gitchell received the ambiguous lab results, Fogleman notified the defense teams that upon reflection, and despite his earlier statements to the contrary, Byers now recalled that he had, after all, cut himself with the knife.

Ignoring the Knife—and the Stun Gun

This knife, with its uncanny traces of blood and Byers's self-contradictory statements, related more closely to the crime than any piece of evidence the police had recovered so far. Yet without further question, Gitchell and Fogleman accepted Byers's final statement. Lax viewed the decision as another example of the investigators picking and choosing which statements to believe. They'd done it with Aaron—ignoring his contradictions while accepting his claims of having witnessed wild satanic activities in the woods. They'd done it with Jessie—ignoring his contradictions while accepting any statements he made that implicated Damien, Jason, and himself. And now, with the blood evidence rendered inconclusive, they were doing it with Byers—ignoring his contradictions while accepting only his statements that made the knife appear less suspicious. Rather than reopening their investigation, they seemed relieved to believe that Byers had, as he now remembered, cut himself with the Kershaw knife.

Lax hurried to consult with experts in DNA evidence. He contacted a forensic science lab and tried to explain what had happened.[206] As he later noted, "I also explained we had been informed a DQ Alpha test had been conducted on the victim's (Chris Byers's) blood and the blood of the owner of the knife (John Mark Byers) and they were consistent with each other. I asked if there was any other test which could be conducted to further that identification." The scientist

> explained that a DQ Alpha test is not a very powerful test; however it is a test which can be done very quickly and with very little quantity of blood. She stated the next step to more specifically determine if the blood belongs to a particular individual is called a DNA-RFLP test, but that test requires six to eight weeks and a significant quantity of blood. I asked her if a significant quantity would be an amount which could be found on the inside of a knife after it was folded. She stated what she would consider a significant amount of blood for that test would be if the knife had been covered with blood and not been wiped off.

To the defense teams, the situation was maddening. The quickness with which the police and Fogleman had been willing to dismiss not only the knife but Byers's peculiar interview about it renewed long-simmering frustrations. If Byers had, in fact, owned the knife for a couple of years, and kept it in his bedroom, that meant that, in May 1993, when the West Memphis police had searched his home, they had failed to find a weapon marked with blood matching that of one of the victims. On the other hand, if the knife had not been in the bedroom, as Byers claimed, the questions raised were even more serious.

As Lax and the defense attorneys discussed Byers, Damien's lawyer Val Price mentioned having heard that Byers had once been convicted of terroristic threatening after taking a stun gun to his ex-wife and threatening her life. This was the first Lax knew of the incident, and the news left him deeply disturbed. Only later would he learn that Fogleman had prosecuted the case against Byers and that Burnett had been the judge who'd ordered Byers's conviction expunged.

The Prosecutor's Suggestion

If Lax had known more at the time about officials' handling of the Rolex case involving John Mark Byers, his concerns would have multiplied. That investigation had been handled quietly. No word of it had reached the media. The only mention of it that was included in the murder case file was Gitchell's note that Byers had called to say he regretted the incident. The state police reports about their investigation of Byers were never made part of the file.[207]

If reports on the Rolex case had been included, Lax and the defense teams would have learned that Byers had confessed to the crime—and that Fogleman's boss, prosecuting attorney Brent Davis, had suggested that he not be prosecuted.[208] Among the records relating to Byers that the defense teams never saw was a memo dated June 24, 1993—seven weeks after the murders—in which a state police investigator outlined a plan proposed by prosecutor Davis that would allow Byers to pay $7,400 in restitution in lieu of facing prosecution.[209] How Byers was expected to repay the money was a question. Davis had proposed the plan just a couple of weeks after Byers, who was bankrupt and years behind on his child support payments, had publicly appealed for money to help pay for Christopher's funeral.

CHAPTER FOURTEEN

The First Trial

WHILE THE FUROR OVER THE BLOODSTAINED KNIFE played out behind the scenes in the Clay County Courthouse, the life-and-death drama of Jessie's trial was unfolding in the courtroom. Heat in the building was cranked up high as the region coped with a rare winter storm. Outside the one-story cinder-block courthouse, the streets of Corning sparkled under a coating of ice. Usually, this corner of northeast Arkansas, nestled into the Missouri boot heel, didn't experience severe winter weather. But this January of 1994 was an exception. Just before the trial began, bitter cold had swept through the Mississippi River valley, cracking trees and making travel hazardous. Even now, on January 18, as heavily armed sheriff's deputies led Jessie, hunched and handcuffed, from a squad car into the building, broken tree limbs still littered the lawn.

Stidham expected a fight as intense as the weather. He'd battled unsuccessfully to keep Jessie's confession out of the trial. Now, with the confession in, he looked ahead to a difficult defense. While he doubted that Fogleman had much evidence other than the confession, that alone was formidable. For Jessie to be acquitted, the confession had to be discredited. Everything Stidham did—both as he cross-examined Fogleman's witnesses in the first part of the trial, and then as he presented Jessie's defense—would have to chip away at the jury's confidence in the truth of what his client had said.

Despite the hazardous roads, more than ninety of the one hundred prospective jurors who'd been called had made their way to the courthouse. They were men and women accustomed to stern conditions, including the demands of distance. Of Clay County's seventeen thousand residents, seven thousand clustered in its two biggest towns, one of which was Corning, with a population of about three thousand. One in four of the county's children lived below the federal poverty level; fewer than seven hundred Clay County residents had graduated from college. The religious attitudes that kept the sale of liquor banned in the county were a point of pride for many residents, as was the county's claim to a population that was almost totally white. When Judge Burnett welcomed the potential jurors to his court, he began by asking if any of them would hesitate, due to moral or religious scruples, to impose the death penalty. No one raised a hand.

Only thirty-six people had to be questioned to impanel a jury of seven women and five men, plus two male alternates. One man was dismissed when he said he had discussed the case with a close friend who lived in the West Memphis area. When Burnett asked if he could set aside what he had heard, the man answered straightforwardly, "It would be hard for me to." Corning's postmaster was one of the jurors chosen. Others included a housewife, a clerk at the local Wal-Mart store, a loan officer from the bank, a factory worker, and a plant manager. The youngest juror was twenty-three years old. That made him five years older than Jessie, who'd spent his eighteenth birthday in jail a month after his arrest.

The thirty-year-old courthouse had never hosted such a high-tech drama. There were television trucks with satellite hookups, a mobile telephone bank, a room full of closed-circuit television monitors for the dozens of reporters. Inside the courtroom, two television cameras, one for the New York film crew, the other for the local news pool, stood near the jury box, though Judge Burnett had issued a warning that no one was to photograph the jurors. Amid all the hubbub, members of the victims' families sat quietly in the first few rows of spectators' seats, just behind the table where Stidham sat with Jessie. During a break, Stevie Branch's mother told a reporter that she was "still enraged" and would like to "jump at" all the defendants. "Sometimes," Pam Hobbs said, "I just have to hold myself back." Another spectator commented that Jessie's trial struck her as a waste of time. "We all know he's guilty," the woman said. "They ought to just fry him and get it over with."

Inside the courtroom, Jessie seldom raised his eyes. He seldom cast so much as a glance in the direction of the jury. Most of the time he sat bent over, chewing gum, head near the edge of the table, eyes directed at the floor. A reporter from Little Rock described Jessie as "a strange-looking little character, small and frail, giving the impression of being deformed in some elusive Dickensian way, his manner that of some furtive rodential creature—a tranquilized squirrel perhaps." The writer went on to note that there was "a passivity about him so profound it strains credulity; he sits all day facing away from the judge and jury, staring at his feet; slumping farther and farther forward in his chair, as if he might ooze down and become a puddle between his shoes."[210]

Stidham had advised the posture; he didn't want anyone to think Jessie looked cocky, but some observers thought it reflected the defendant's shame and guilt. Jessie also wore a more conventional haircut than when he was arrested. A front-page article in the *Jonesboro Sun* called attention to the change. The paper ran photos of all three defendants, taken at their arrests, along with more recent photos, from when they'd appeared in court for pretrial hearings. An article describing the "metamorphosis" noted that when Jessie was arrested, he'd had "the look of a late 1950s Bohemian, more often known as a beatnik," though now that he was on trial, he presented "more of a schoolboy look."

Opposite where Jessie sat with his lawyers, Dan Stidham and Greg Crow, Fogleman sat with the district's main prosecutor, thirty-six-year-old Brent Davis. Though Davis would play a significant role at both Jessie's trial and the one to follow, Fogleman was the lead prosecutor. Fogleman was well known in Crittenden County, the scion of a family that was one of the oldest in the region. Near the courthouse in Marion, a monument commemorated the role the deputy prosecutor's great-great-grandfather had played in what remains to this day the greatest maritime disaster in American history. At the end of the Civil War, in 1865, pioneer John Fogleman was operating a ferry on the Mississippi River between the Arkansas side and Memphis. In April of that year, the steamship *Sultana* was traveling upstream, loaded with newly released Union prisoners of war. The ship exploded in the middle of the night, near Fogleman's Landing. Though the ferryman rescued those he could, more than eighteen hundred men burned to death in the explosion or drowned in the freezing water. More lives were lost than in the sinking of the *Titanic*, but the catastrophe was overshadowed by the assassination of President Abraham Lincoln, only a few days before. The monument near the Crittenden County Courthouse reflected the Foglemans' place in local history from that early day to the present. The deputy prosecutor's relatives had been prominent in the region's commercial, civic, and legal affairs. They had worked as grocers, farmers, lawyers, bankers, deputy sheriffs, and circuit clerks. Fogleman's father had served on the Marion school board for forty-five years; one of his uncles had served on the Arkansas Supreme Court, and his father had once been president of the Arkansas Bar Association. The John Fogleman who now faced the jury had been a deputy prosecutor for the past ten years. A respected and strait-laced teetotaler, he was seen as a rather formal fellow.

Opening Arguments

Fogleman rose to present his opening argument to the jury. In a slow, emotionless drawl, he recounted the nightmare of the previous May—how the little boys had disappeared, and the horror the next day. He reported the medical examiner's findings that Michael and Stevie had died from drowning, while Christopher had died from "multiple wounds," which included his brutal castration. Fogleman told the jury that a young woman who had a son the same age as the victims had been so disturbed by the murders that she'd decided to "play detective" to help police solve the crime. "Ultimately," he reported, "Victoria Hutcheson would lead police to Misskelley, and Misskelley would confess."

What the deputy prosecutor did not tell the jury was that Jessie Misskelley's confession was virtually the only piece of direct evidence that he had. It was a compelling piece, to be sure, but it was also seriously flawed. Fogleman's next task, if the jury was to believe the confession, had to be a preemptive one: to address the numerous weaknesses—and the outright errors—in Jessie's statement to the police. Fogleman acknowledged to the jury that not everything Jessie had said in his confession was true. There were discrepancies, he admitted, between some of Jessie's statements and the facts of the crime. But Fogleman said these were easily explained. They were the results of Jessie's bungled attempts to minimize his involvement. Fogleman urged the jury to focus instead on things Misskelley had said that "only the true killer" would have known: that one of the boys had been cut in the face, that another had been sexually mutilated, and that all three of the boys had been beaten. These incriminating details, combined with Misskelley's own admission of personal involvement, would prove more than enough, Fogleman predicted, for the jury to find him guilty of three counts of capital murder.

Dan Stidham lacked Fogleman's polish. More heavyset and more loosely tailored, he looked like a man whose favorite pastimes were hunting ducks or fishing, which is what he was. Stidham liked practicing trial law, and despite the glares he'd received from neighbors who couldn't understand why he'd represent a murdering satanist, he felt passionately about the case—and Jessie's innocence.

"Ladies and gentlemen," Stidham said when it was his turn to address the jury, "this whole case is a sad, sad story. But what's even sadder is the way the West Memphis Police Department decided to investigate this crime." Recalling the anxious month that had passed between the murders and the arrests, Stidham noted the strain the police had been under. "Ladies and gentlemen," he said, "there was a public outcry. The public was demanding that someone be arrested for this crime, and the police department was trying to respond to this tremendous amount of pressure." Besides offering a reward, he said, they had developed what he called "Damien Echols tunnel vision." That meant that "from day one," the West Memphis police had Echols "picked out as the person responsible." Jessie, he said, had merely been caught in a net spread to ensnare Echols.

But as he spoke, Stidham knew that the most crucial battles in Jessie's trial had already been lost. During the months of pretrial motions, he'd argued repeatedly that Jessie's confession had been coerced and should for that reason be kept out of the trial. But Judge Burnett had rejected that claim, as well as Stidham's parallel arguments that the confession should not be admitted because Jessie was mentally retarded, and that since Jessie was a minor, his case should be tried in juvenile court. Stidham's only hope now was to make the jury believe that Jessie would not have said what he did but for the psychological pressure being applied by the police. It would be a hard sell, he knew. Most adults cannot imagine confessing to a crime they did not commit—especially one as horrendous as this. At the start of this case, even Stidham had found it hard to believe that anyone would confess to a murder that he did not commit. But Stidham felt that he had learned a lot since then. His education had taken a while. He wouldn't have that much time to change the minds of the jurors.

What Jessie told the police was "a false story," Stidham told them. He argued that Inspector Gitchell and Detective Ridge realized that what Jessie was telling them was "factually incorrect in many, many important areas . . . but they kept right on interrogating. . . . They didn't care that what he was telling them was wrong." Stidham insisted that details of the crime, including those the police said "only the killer would have known," were in fact widely known. Instead of acknowledging that crucial information had been repeatedly leaked, Stidham told the jurors, detectives had been willing to terrify Jessie until he'd told them what they'd wanted to hear.

"They broke his will," he said. "They scared him beyond all measure."

Foundation for the Confession

The trial that followed would last for two weeks. Fogleman called Dana Moore and Melissa Byers to the stand, to give their grief-stricken accounts of the night their sons disappeared.[211] Stidham barely questioned Melissa. There were a lot of questions he would have liked to ask her, and still more that he would have liked to put to her husband. What about that beating Christopher had received just before he disappeared? What about the notation in the police report on the night that Christopher disappeared that he had not taken his Ritalin that day? Why not? (The drug, which calms hyperactive children, is known to act as a stimulant when taken by adults.) Had one of Christopher's parents helped themselves to the drug instead? Had Christopher left home in the past for several hours at a time, as Melissa had told the police? Or had that never happened, as her husband claimed? And what about John Mark's account of his activities on the night of the murders? Why had he entered the woods after dark on the evening the boys disappeared without a flashlight? And why had he then left to go home and change his clothes?[212] Most of all, Stidham would have liked to grill the couple about the mysterious bloodstained knife. But the lawyer held his tongue. Despite Stidham's mounting concerns that Byers might have been the killer, he considered it far too risky to suggest that possibility in court. Long after the trial was over, he would admit that his decision might have been different had he known more about Byers's background. Under the circumstances, he concluded that "pointing the finger at a stepparent without blatant proof" would probably "inflame the jury" and "insure the death penalty for Jessie."[213]

When Fogleman questioned Ridge about his hands-and-knees search of the ditch, the detective cried on the stand. To emphasize the sadness of that day, and the loss, the prosecutor had the boys' bicycles wheeled into the courtroom and introduced as evidence. The bikes remained in the front of the courtroom, leaning against a wall, throughout the rest of the trial. Next, Fogleman handed the jury more than three dozen photographs showing the victims' bodies as they lay, white, bound, and uncovered, on the muddy, shaded bank. Fogleman then called Dr. Frank Peretti of the Arkansas Crime Laboratory to report on his autopsy findings.

As jurors were handed another batch of photos, these showing the boys' bodies on the autopsy table, Peretti explained that there'd been limits to what his examination could reveal. Citing the length of time that the bodies had lain exposed to the warm air, for example, he said he had not been able to estimate the time of the boys' deaths. The matter of time was important, in light of Jessie's widely varying statements regarding time.

But when Stidham cross-examined Peretti, time was only one of the discrepancies the lawyer wanted to explore. Had Peretti found evidence that the boys had been choked, as Jessie had told the police? No, the doctor said. Was there evidence that they'd been sodomized, as Jessie had described? Again Peretti said no.[214]

Fogleman then called Gitchell to explain the circumstances that had led to Misskelley's confession. Gitchell testified that during the interview, Jessie was "very relaxed" and was under no pressure from officers.[215] The chief inspector described how he had played a tape recording for Jessie to see how the boy would react. Fogleman asked Gitchell to play the tape, exactly as he'd played it that day. Gitchell clicked on a tiny tape recorder and held it to the microphone. The voice of a child filled the courtroom, saying, "Nobody knows what happened but me." That was all. Gitchell clicked the tape recorder off. Nobody asked him to explain whose voice was on the tape or how it had come to be made, or to put the words in any context. All the jury learned was that the tape had shocked Jessie and that shortly after hearing it, he had confessed. With that, Fogleman asked Gitchell to play the tape recording of what Jessie had said. For the next thirty-four minutes, as another tape recorder played in the hushed courtroom, the jury listened to Jessie confess.

When Stidham cross-examined Inspector Gitchell, the detective admitted that, yes, Jessie's statement did contain several errors. The victims had not skipped school, as Jessie had reported, and they could not have been killed at noon.

"And you knew that that was incorrect when Jessie told you that?" Stidham demanded.

"Yes sir," Gitchell responded.

Stidham recalled that Jessie had said he'd seen the boys tied up with brown rope. That was inaccurate too, Gitchell acknowledged.

"These seem to be pretty important issues," Stidham said. He asked if it ever occurred to Gitchell, while he and Ridge were questioning Jessie, "that his entire story was false?"

Gitchell repeated Fogleman's explanation that Jessie had merely smudged the facts to minimize his involvement. But these were major errors, Stidham pressed. Calmly, the detective deflected any suggestion that the errors presented a problem. "Jessie simply got confused," Gitchell said. "That's all."[216]

Now Fogleman tackled the delicate question of how the boys were tied. Jessie's insistence that the ligatures were ropes posed a major problem for the prosecution. "Was there," Fogleman asked Gitchell, "any evidence that would indicate that there had been some sort of binding other than the shoestrings?" Gitchell, to Stidham's amazement, answered yes. The police department's chief detective then testified that he had personally seen a wound on one of the boys that had "indicated" to him that, at some point, the boys could have been tied with a rope.

It was a stunning statement—one that was utterly unsupported by the police notes of the case or by any of the medical examiner's findings. Stidham jumped to object. "I think that calls for pure, unadulterated speculation on the part of a witness, who is not qualified to render such an opinion," he told the judge. But Burnett overruled Stidham and allowed the testimony. And despite Stidham's further objections, Burnett also allowed Gitchell to draw a picture for the jury of the injury he re-membered thinking might have been made by a rope.

Vicki Hutcheson to the Stand

Perhaps the biggest problem with Jessie's confession was that it con-tained no explanation of why he had helped Damien and Jason kill the three little boys. In case any juror was wondering what might have mo-tivated Jessie, Fogleman was ready with an answer. He called Vicki Hutcheson to the stand.

Again, Stidham objected. Judge Burnett told the lawyers to approach his bench for a discussion that the jury could not hear. The short *in cam-era* hearing would be one of dozens that would punctuate the trial.[217] Re-porters listened in, as was allowed, although the jury did not, as Fogleman explained to the judge his intentions in calling Hutcheson. He said he planned to have her describe the trip she'd reportedly taken with Damien and Jessie to the orgiastic "esbat." Stidham countered that if the trip had occurred at all, it had, according to Hutcheson's testimony, taken place *after* the boys were killed. More important, he argued, testi-mony about an alleged cult meeting was not relevant in any event, since nothing at the site where the bodies were found had indicated that the murders were the result of satanic or cult activity. Fogleman shot back that in Jessie's confession he had referred to meetings "when we had that cult," at which a photograph of the victims had been shown. No such photograph had ever been found, but based on that statement, Judge Burnett allowed Fogleman to put Hutcheson on the stand.

Looking demure, her red hair in a bun, she related how Damien had invited her to go with him to an esbat. She said that she looked the term up in "one of the witch books," whereupon she'd learned that it meant "an occult satanic meeting." Fighting back tears, Hutcheson explained that she began to "play detective" because the victims were friends of her son. "I loved those boys, and I wanted to see their killers caught," she said. But like so much of the case, Hutcheson's testimony was prob-lematic. Not wanting Stidham to bring up the most damaging question, the prosecutor raised it himself. He let Hutcheson tell the jury that de-spite her suspicions about Damien and her claim that Jessie had accompanied Damien and her to the esbat, she had never suspected that Jessie might have been involved in the murders. In fact, she said, she'd felt "very close" to him. She'd felt so comfortable with Jessie, she admitted, that the night before his arrest she had asked him to spend the night in her trailer, to protect her and her children from prowlers.

Under Stidham's cross-examination, Hutcheson admitted that she'd been convicted of writing hot checks, and that her involvement in this case had begun because Detective Bray had called her in for questioning about another alleged fraud, the one that had resulted in her being fired from her truck stop job. But Hutcheson dismissed the incident as just "a credit-card mess-up." And anyway, she added, "all the charges" had been dropped. Was it true, Stidham asked, that part of her motivation for getting involved in the case was the $35,000 reward? No, Hutcheson said. "The reward money never entered my mind."[218]

The Absence of Aaron

Aaron Hutcheson, the alleged eyewitness on whom the police had relied so heavily, was never called to testify. Later, Fogleman explained his reason. "I had some police officers that were absolutely convinced of his story," he said, "and I talked to him a couple of times. The first time, I was a little bit believing him. The last time, I guess when he started talking about draining the blood into a bucket, or whatever it was he said, it was so inconsistent and stuff that I got real concerned."[219]

Stidham had his own reasons for not calling Aaron. The boy was wildly unpredictable. He'd already given Fogleman and the police a number of escalating accounts of what he claimed to have seen in the woods. Recently, since the start of the trial, he'd elaborated even further. Now the boy was telling Detective Bray that he had personally dismembered Christopher, having been forced to do it by a black man who'd stood over him, holding a gun to his head. Stidham did not want the jury to hear even one of Aaron's stories, however fantastic it might be. He did not want a nine-year-old boy to point to Jessie, saying he was one of the killers. And just as important, Stidham did not want to place himself in the position of appearing to pressure, embarrass, or bully a child who'd been a playmate of the victims.

So the jury never heard from Aaron, the boy who some of the detectives were "absolutely convinced" had witnessed the murders. Given the child's role in the development of the case, his absence from the trial was remarkable. Aaron's friendship with the victims was what had first caught Bray's attention. Bray, Gitchell, and Fogleman had questioned Aaron about events in the woods almost a dozen times. Aaron's accounts of things he'd allegedly seen there, coupled with his mother's reports, had prompted police to question Jessie. His enigmatic taped statement, played during Jessie's questioning, had led Jessie to confess.

In one way or another, Aaron had been present at every critical juncture in the police investigation—from the moment his friends' bodies were discovered until the day of the three arrests. He'd been a catalyst for key events, yet now that those events had culminated in a trial, Aaron's potential testimony was being dismissed as too unreliable. In some respects, Aaron was, along with his friends, one of the crime's young victims. He could not have witnessed or participated in all the bloody things he'd described, but somehow, the more investigators had listened, the more he'd imagined that he had. And too many adults, with agendas of their own, had been willing—even anxious—to believe him.

Fibers

Jessie's confession was powerful evidence. But Fogleman knew that if Stidham could make the jury even consider that it had been coerced, the rest of the state's case was precariously circumstantial. He bolstered it where he could. For that, Lisa Sakevicius, of the state crime lab, was Fogleman's most important witness. She testified that a green polyester fiber analysts had lifted from a Cub Scout cap found at the scene was "microscopically similar" to fibers from a polyester and cotton shirt that she and the police had found during their search of Damien's house. She further testified that fibers from the shirt were microscopically similar to fibers found on a pair of blue pants that had been submerged near the bodies. In addition, Sakevicius told the court, a single red rayon fiber found on a white shirt that had been recovered near the victims' bodies was "microscopically similar" to fibers from a woman's red bathrobe found during the search of Jason's house.

Neither the shirt found at Damien's house nor the bathrobe from Jason's were items the teenagers would have worn—a point that Fogleman acknowledged. "Just so the jury understands," he said, "you're not suggesting that Damien wore this little shirt or that Jason wore the bathrobe?" Sakevicius said she was not. She explained that fibers can be moved from one place to another by either "primary" or "secondary" transfer. Primary is direct. Secondary transfer, she explained, occurs when a person picks up a fiber from one place and deposits it in another. In other words, Fogleman suggested, Damien and Jason had picked up fibers from items in their homes and inadvertently left them with the bodies.

For three hands-on murders, one of which involved a castration, the fibers amounted to very bare threads of evidence. The claim of secondary transfer made them highly circumstantial, and Sakevicius's repeated and careful statement that they were "microscopically similar" made them more circumstantial still. The fact that the fibers were similar did not signify with any degree of certainty that they had come from the garments in question, a point which Sakevicius noted. "I should say that they were similar fibers," she emphasized while on the stand, "not that they came from them." Later, under questioning by Stidham, Sakevicius acknowledged that many fibers are "microscopically similar," and that the "discovery proved nothing."

Sakevicius also described for Fogleman how the boys were tied—Michael with a combination of square knots and half hitches; Stevie with a combination of half hitches, a figure eight, and loops; and Christopher, most consistently, with four double half hitches. Fogleman would later suggest that the different types of knots pointed to multiple killers.

Stidham asked her about other fiber evidence as well; specifically, the mysterious fragment of "Negroid hair" that had been found on the sheet in which Christopher's body had been wrapped when it arrived at the lab. Sakevicius said that the origin of the hair remained unknown. Whatever else Stidham had accomplished in his cross-examinations, he had demonstrated that none of the state's evidence—not Jessie's confession, not Vicki Hutcheson's testimony, not even the crime lab's conclusions—was what anyone would call a clincher.

But Fogleman was saving one of his strongest witnesses for last.

When the witness's appearance failed to work out as he'd hoped, the deputy prosecuting attorney was, by one account, "furious."

William Jones

Toward the end of Fogleman's case, he planned to call a teenager named William Jones, who would support Vicki Hutcheson's testimony. More than that, Fogleman expected William to link Damien to the satanic cult Hutcheson had described, and to the murders as well. Fogleman had a videotape in which William was shown telling West Memphis detectives that once, when Damien was drunk, he had confessed to him that he was a member of a satanic cult and that he had raped the three eight-year-old boys, then killed them with a knife.

While the trial was under way, Lax had located William and asked him about that interview. William said he wanted to consult first with his mother and stepfather. The three had gone into another room of their trailer, while Lax waited for almost a half hour. When they rejoined him, William's mother asked Lax what would happen to William if he had lied to the police.[220] Lax said he was not an attorney and could not be sure, but it was probably a good thing that the boy had not been placed under oath by the police. William then told Lax that he did not like Damien and that he'd falsely boasted to his mother that Damien had confessed to the murders. To his surprise, he said, his mother had believed him and called the police. William, being unwilling to admit to his mother that he'd lied, had expounded on his claim to Detective Ridge, and he'd continued to lie when he gave his videotaped statement.

Lax asked if William wanted to correct the situation. When William said he did, Lax asked if he could record a new videotape. The boy and his parents agreed, and both parents sat with William as he answered Lax's questions. Lax began by asking William what he had planned to do when called to testify. "I was going to get up there and tell the truth," he said.

Lax: "And what is the truth?"

William: "That I don't know nothing about it. . . ."

Lax: "Has Damien ever said anything to you at all about this murder?"

William: "No . . ."

Lax: "Has Jason Baldwin?"

William: "No sir. None of them have. . . ."

Lax: "In this statement, you had some fairly, uh, specific information regarding what happened to the boys when they were killed. Where did you get that information?"

William: "Rumors, and the papers, and what I was told."

William Jones was one of several teenagers questioned by Lax who'd admitted making a false statement to the police. The first had been Buddy Sidney Lucas, who'd said he'd been frightened by Durham and had told the detective what he thought he wanted to hear so that he wouldn't "get in trouble."[221] But the testimony of William Jones had been the most damaging, and his decision to recant his statement was the most important to the defense. Lax informed Stidham, who reported the news to Fogleman.

One of Lax's investigators, Cheryl Aycock, drove the nervous teenager to the courthouse. Detective Ridge met them in a hallway and escorted them to a room where the deputy prosecutor was waiting. Fogleman told Aycock that he wanted to talk to William alone, but William insisted that he wanted her to stay. Fogleman asked Aycock what her relationship was to William. Aycock later stated in a sworn affidavit that when she told him that she worked for Lax, "Fogleman became visibly agitated and hostile."

"Fogleman turned to [William] Jones and asked what was 'going on,' " Aycock said in the affidavit.

> Jones said he had told his mother something that he didn't know anything about. Fogleman asked Jones what Mr. Lax (pointing at me) had done to make him change his story. Jones replied, "Nothing." Fogleman asked if Mr. Lax threatened him, to which Jones replied, "No." Jones explained he "just wanted to tell the truth. . . ." Fogleman insisted Mr. Lax had "done something" to Jones. He told Jones not to be afraid, that ". . . no one can touch you. Mr. Lax can't touch you, Jessie can't touch you, Damien can't touch you, the cult can't touch you." Jones stated he understood this and repeated his desire to simply tell the truth. Fogleman then asked Jones, "Did Lax threaten to send the cult out after you? Did he say they'd cut

your (pause) off?" to which Jones replied he had not. I believe it was [prosecuting attorney] Davis who said, "Come on, son. Something's wrong with you. We can tell." Jones again denied anything was "wrong. . . ."

Fogleman asked Jones something to the effect of what would he [Jones] have done if Lax had not come to talk to him. Jones replied he was just going to wait until he got on the stand and tell the truth when [Fogleman] asked him. Fogleman again became visibly agitated, widening his eyes, slamming his palm on the table, and raising his voice, asking, "You were going to wait until you got on the stand today to tell me this?" to which Jones answered, "Yeah, I didn't know what to do." A man I assumed to be Inspector Gitchell (white male, slender, balding) approached and asked Jones, "How much is he paying you?" Jones emptied his pockets and produced some coins and said, "Nothing, see? This is all the money I have."

Fogleman's demeanor continued to be hostile, and I, personally, found him to be physically threatening. During this conversation, Davis and Gitchell drew nearer and nearer to Jones, ending up approximately three feet from Jones, shoulder-to-shoulder with Fogleman, which made me very uncomfortable. Fogleman made a comment to the effect Lax had to be "doing something" to intimidate witnesses because every time he spoke with them, they changed "their story." Fogleman asked Jones whether he realized it was a criminal offense to lie to police. Jones replied, "I don't know. All I know about the laws is this," and he held his wrists together behind his back. Fogleman informed Jones he could be prosecuted for filing a false statement to police and indicated he intended to prosecute Jones.

Lax said that after the encounter,

All the attorneys went into chambers to talk to Burnett. From what I heard of that meeting, Fogleman, Davis, and Burnett were all pissed. Fogleman reportedly made statements about my having intimidated witnesses—something to the effect of, "We don't need an investigator from Tennessee who drives a Mercedes coming in here and intimidating our witnesses." If I'd been there, I would like to have pointed out that I did all the interviews in front of the boys' mothers, which is more than the police had done. But the result was they had *me* investigated. I was going through a divorce at the time, and my wife called me and said an investigator for the Arkansas State Police had contacted her about me. She told him to get lost. We brought that up to Burnett. He asked Fogleman and Davis. They said that another prosecutor in their office had initiated the investigation. In chambers, the state police investigator reportedly told Burnett that I was the only person he'd found involved in the case who had not done something wrong. The matter was dropped there.

Faced with little choice, Fogleman moved on with what he had. He introduced pairs of black boots that belonged to Damien and Jason, because Jessie had mentioned in his confession that his accomplices had been wearing black boots. He introduced the book *Never on a Broomstick*, which Damien had bought at a library used-book sale a year before the murders. Driver had found the book in Damien's house a year before the murders. It was, Fogleman suggested, evidence of "cult-related" motivation. And to establish that Damien and Jason were close enough friends of Jessie Misskelley that they would have included him in their murderous orgy, he called Jerry Driver, who testified that he had definitely seen the three teenagers together, walking down a street in Marion. With that, Fogleman rested.

The trial was not half over, but Jessie felt almost victorious. He recognized that Fogleman's case against him rested on his confession. But since, as Stidham explained, Fogleman's evidence to support the confession had been slim and circumstantial, Jessie believed he was practically free. "At the time," Jessie later recalled, "I thought a statement weren't nothin'. If that was the only evidence against me, I figured it wouldn't be no good. Because, the stuff I'd seen on TV, if you convict somebody, you've got to have some kind of physical evidence. Anybody can say anything."

CHAPTER FIFTEEN

The *in Camera* Hearings

STIDHAM WAS FAR LESS CONFIDENT than his client. He recognized, as he began his defense, that he faced several hurdles. Some, like the trouble he expected with Jessie's alibi, he'd seen coming for several months. Others that lay ahead would take him by surprise.

The problem with Jessie's alibi had arisen the previous summer, when Stidham was first appointed to the case and believed that Jessie was guilty. At the time, Stidham was communicating with Fogleman, hoping to work out a plea bargain in which Jessie would get a reduced sentence in exchange for his testimony that would convict Damien and Jason. "It was about that time," Stidham later recalled,

> when Mr. Misskelley Sr. began to raise issues about Jessie being in a different county on the night of the murders.[222] Jessie Sr. began to hold almost nightly news conferences on the front porch of his mobile home, and basically, laying out his [son's] alibi. That was making the prosecuting attorney very angry. We were wanting to work with him, but when Misskelley was holding these press conferences, that was making the prosecution's case weak, and Mr. Fogleman was telling us, "You've got to shut this guy up."
>
> So I talked to Mr. Misskelley, and he asked me when we were going to come and check out the alibi. And I kept putting him off, because in my mind the kid was guilty. Then we went to the first hearing, and Fogleman told me we had a DNA match—that there was a T-shirt found in Misskelley's trailer that had a speck of blood on it, and the

prosecutor claimed that that speck of blood matched Michael Moore's. To me, that cinched it. He was guilty. There was no doubt about it.

But then two things happened simultaneously. When I confronted Jessie about the blood on the T-shirt, he said, "That's my blood." He said he busted a Coke bottle with his hand—that was one of his favorite pastimes to show how tough he was: he'd throw a Coke bottle up in the air and bust it with his fist. A day or two later, Fogleman called me and said, "We were wrong. That blood wasn't Michael Moore's." And Mr. Misskelley Sr. was getting hot because we weren't questioning these alibi witnesses. So when Fogleman told us the blood *didn't* match, I decided I'd go to West Memphis and question these people. And it became obvious that Jessie had an alibi for up to midnight the night the boys disappeared.

Most of the time, alibis are successful. But in this case, all of the witnesses had been interviewed by police, because Jessie Misskelley Sr. had been holding these press conferences. The police wouldn't have gone to interview them, but when they did, the witnesses were afraid of getting involved, and basically, they couldn't remember the exact night. When we sat down and started going through the tedious process, they said, "Yeah, that was that night. . . ." But when we got to trial, and called these witnesses to testify, the state was able to stand up and say, "Well, you told Officer So-and-So that you couldn't remember, so how are you so sure now?" And they'd say, "Well, because Mr. Stidham talked to us." And of course, it looked to the jury like we were cooking this up. I know Mr. Misskelley Sr. was frustrated that nobody—not even I—believed him. But those press conferences came back to haunt us. In fact, they may have made the difference in the case.

Fogleman saw the development in exactly the same light. "Alibis are real tough," he said. "It would be tough for anyone to say, 'Well, I was with so-and-so a month ago.' They're real tough. But if you try to put on an alibi defense that's not good, then the jury's going to sit up there and say, 'Well, they're lying.' And it hurts the credibility of the entire defense case."

Stidham had tried to present Jessie's alibi, but the net result was probably a loss. Under other circumstances, he might have put his client on the stand so the jury could see him speak up for himself. But as Stidham saw it, with Jessie, that approach was out of the question. On one hand, Jessie would not be able to articulate much on his own behalf, and on the other . . . Well, Stidham cringed at the thought of Jessie being cross-examined by Fogleman or Davis. To call Jessie as a witness, Stidham thought, would be to hand him to his prosecutors on a silver platter.

No, what Stidham had to do, he figured, was to raise doubts for the jurors, as to both Jessie's abilities and the conduct of the police. First he tried to show that by the time Jessie was questioned, the police were desperate, and that that was partly due to the shoddy work on the case. As illustrations, he introduced testimony from the crime lab analyst of the "Negroid" hair that was found in the sheet wrapped around Christopher Byers—the hair whose presence there was never explained. Then he called Marty King, the manager of the Bojangles restaurant, to testify about the bloody man whom he'd reported to the police, and about the officers' lack of follow-up. When Stidham questioned Detective Ridge, the detective admitted that the blood scrapings that had been taken from the restaurant the following day had been lost and that, as a result, DNA that would have been recovered from them could not be tested against DNA from the hair. Stidham felt that all of this made an important point, but he also realized that it was an abstract one. Abstractions, he knew, could be hard to convey to a jury who sat looking, day after day, at two bicycles bearing evidence tags and a defendant accused of killing their owners.

Along with suggesting deficiencies in the police investigation, Stidham wanted the jury to know about Jessie's deficiencies, too. But now it was the prosecution's turn to score a behind-the-scenes coup.

Dr. William Wilkins

In an attempt to establish Jessie Misskelley's intellectual vulnerability, Stidham wanted to have him evaluated by a psychologist. "But," as he later recalled, "we didn't have money to go out and hire a psychologist. We had no budget at all for experts. We filed a motion to ask for experts, but for the state to approve anything, we would have had to spell out everything we wanted to do. We would have had to lay our cards on the table. Later the state created a public defender's office with a budget just for that. But in 1993, essentially all we had was my gold card and the ability to beg people to come in." The expert Stidham begged was William E. Wilkins, Ph.D., a local psychologist whom Stidham had met in a child custody case. Wilkins was interested in examining Jessie and agreed to work without pay.

The report Wilkins prepared depicted Jessie as a teenager who bordered on being mentally retarded, whose maximum scores for academic achievement were in the third and fourth grade levels, and who had never passed any of the Arkansas minimum performance tests.[223]

Stidham expected that Wilkins's testimony would be crucial to his case. "But on the eve of his testimony," the lawyer would later recall, "[Prosecutor] Davis dropped the bombshell that Wilkins was about to lose his license. There were allegations that he had made some little boy drop his pants to look for a birthmark, when there were no witnesses in the room." To Stidham's great dismay, he learned that Davis's information was correct. (Wilkins did, in fact, have his license revoked a few weeks after Jessie's trial, when the Arkansas Board of Examiners in Psychology found that he had engaged in "serious professional misconduct.") But even knowing that Davis would roundly discredit his witness, Stidham put Wilkins on the stand. He felt that he had no choice; he needed someone to let the jury know about Jessie's intellectual limitations, and there was no time to find a new examiner. "It's hard to find a psychologist who will work for free," Stidham explained, "and it's even harder the night before he's supposed to testify. It became a very embarrassing and horrible thing for us. He hurt us, no doubt about it."

Wilkins had been one of three main witnesses on whom Stidham planned to base his defense. The other two were Warren Holmes, a nationally recognized expert on polygraph techniques, and Dr. Richard Ofshe, a nationally recognized expert on coerced confessions. But as it turned out, the jury would never hear much of what Holmes and Ofshe had come to say. Fogleman and Davis vigorously objected when each of the men started to talk, prompting Judge Burnett to hold lengthy sessions between the witnesses and the lawyers without the jury present. These *in camera* hearings, where lawyers debated before Judge Burnett what testimony should and should not be allowed to be presented in front of the jury, constituted a significant part of Jessie's trial. For Stidham, they were also among the most disappointing.

Warren Holmes

As part of his attack on the police, Stidham wanted to persuade the jury that, whether deliberately or not, Detective Bill Durham had played a dirty trick on Jessie. Stidham believed that a turning point in Jessie's interrogation had come when Durham told Jessie that he had failed the polygraph test. Stidham believed Jessie had been telling the truth, but that when confronted with Durham's technological "proof" that he was lying, he'd felt trapped and overwhelmed. Once again needing an expert, Stidham got on the phone, and as before, he went begging. The expert he wanted was Holmes, a veteran homicide detective and polygraph examiner. Holmes had served as a consultant to the FBI, the Texas Rangers, and the Royal Canadian Mounted Police, and he'd conducted polygraph examinations in some of the nation's best-known cases, the Watergate break-ins and the Kennedy and King assassinations among them.

"When I called Mr. Holmes, I explained to him that I had been appointed to represent an indigent kid in Arkansas charged with killing three boys," Stidham later wrote.[224] "I explained to him that I had no money to pay him, but that I really needed his help because I felt my client was innocent." Holmes agreed to look over the polygraph charts from Jessie's examination by Durham. "About a week later, Mr. Holmes phoned me and told me that Jessie had only showed signs of deception on one question—the drug question. Jessie had passed all the questions about the homicides, showing no signs of deception on the charts. It was clear that Officer Durham had lied to Jessie."

Holmes paid his own expenses, which were later reimbursed by the court, to travel to Arkansas to testify. He contributed his time free of charge. But even before the trial began, Fogleman and Davis lodged strenuous objections to the prospect of letting the jury hear Holmes.

When the time came, Burnett held an *in camera* hearing on whether Holmes's testimony should be suppressed—that is, withheld from the jury. With the jury gone from the room, Burnett began the discussion by noting that results of polygraph tests, though frequently used by police, have long been considered too unreliable to be introduced as evidence in trials. Burnett announced that the results of Jessie's polygraph exam were, therefore, "not admissible under any circumstances" in court. Because of that prohibition, Burnett said he would sharply define what testimony from Holmes would and would not be allowed. He would not allow "speculation" as to "the machine's results," he said, "or whether or not the results apply to guilt or innocence, or whether or not the person [who interpreted the results] was truthful or deceitful." He would, however, "allow testimony about whether or not the polygraph could have induced a person to make a statement that they would not have otherwise made."

The pronouncement put Stidham in a bind. It meant that he had an expert witness who was not going to be allowed to offer his expert opinion. Holmes could not tell the jury that, as he read Durham's test results, Jessie was telling the truth. Stidham argued that the testimony should be allowed. "We are talking about the voluntariness of the confession," he began. He told Burnett that Holmes should be allowed to testify "so the court can determine the totality of the circumstances regarding this confession." And he cited case law to show that other courts had held "that any evidence tending to show the innocence of the accused is admissible."

"In other words," Burnett asked, "you want him [Holmes] to testify in his opinion that the accused was *not* showing deception? That's totally and completely irrelevant and inadmissible. . . . My ruling is that the results of the polygraph test are not admissible evidence and, therefore, no expert—state or defense—is going to be able to testify to the veracity of the polygraph machine, because it's not accepted in this state as credible evidence. I won't accept it one way or the other. I don't care whether he says he was telling the truth or whether he says he was lying."

Stidham asked the judge to let Holmes "proffer" his testimony in the hearing, that is, to state for the record what he would have told the jury, had that been allowed. If Jessie was convicted, Stidham would use the record of Holmes's proffer as part of his appeal. Burnett agreed, and with the jury still gone, Holmes was sworn in. Stidham asked Holmes about factors that might indicate to him that a suspect was giving a false confession. Holmes cited three.

"Number one," he said, "they don't tell you anything you don't already know. Number two, what they do say doesn't jibe with the crime scene analysis or the physical evidence or any investigation that has been done up to that point. And number three, if they don't relate it in narrative form, you have to be suspicious." Valid confessions, on the other hand, are marked by what Holmes called "an emotional release."

> You don't have to question him because he wants to get it off his chest. . . . They relive some of the sensations at the time of the crime. . . . And if the confession is really valid, they will offer some incidental detail which lends credibility to their story. Maybe they'll say, "At the time we were doing this, some man was walking his dog off in the distance." Or, "Just at the precise moment I was doing this there was an automobile accident," and later you will find out that actually occurred. You look for those incidental details they can offer. If it is a valid confession, and you make a supposition and you're wrong, they will tell you you're wrong. They'll answer every question directly. You don't have to correct them. . . . You don't have to lead them in any way. . . .

When asked specifically about Jessie's confession, Holmes replied, "What I don't like about his confession is he doesn't attribute any conversation during the crime to the boys. I don't like it that he doesn't express any feelings about the crime, how he felt at the time, how he feels now. I don't like the fact that he's giving wrong information about the ligature which should absolutely stand out in his mind, and I don't like the time factor. It would seem to me that despite his IQ level, he should know the difference between 9 A.M. and 5 P.M. And he somehow should know the difference between a rope and shoelaces. Those things bother me a lot."

"Can a polygraph examination contribute to a false confession?" Stidham asked.

"Unfortunately it can."

"How is that?"

"Because with some people, it is a last hope," Holmes explained. "They think, 'Okay, if I take this test and I pass it, you're going to get off my back,' and then when they are told that the test indicates they are lying, that's the straw that breaks the camel's back, and then their will is beaten to a pulp, and then they just give up."

"Mr. Holmes, you have had an opportunity to examine the polygraph test that was performed on Jessie Lloyd Misskelley on June 3?"

"Yes."

"Can you tell us what your findings were?"

"Well, they were different from the other examiner," Holmes replied. "He indicated he thought there was deception at the points in the graphs where the pertinent test questions were asked. I evaluated the charts, and I have come up with just the contrary opinion. I didn't feel that at the point where the pertinent test questions were asked that the defendant was deceptive in nature."

"In your report you list some factors that trouble you," Stidham said. "Could you explain those to the court?"

Well, this was an ideal case for what we call a peak attention test, where you set up a series of questions, where one is the key detail, and in this case there should have been a peak attention test regarding whether or not the boys were tied up with plastic tape or wire or shoelaces. And the theory being, of the items listed, if the examinee reacts to the key one, he definitely has pertinent information with regard to the crime in question. So you keep taking that key detail and you shift it around in a series of different tests, and statistically, if he reacts each and every time to the key detail, there's a large probability that he has intimate knowledge of the crime. Also, a peak attention test could have been conducted regarding the location of the clothes.[225]

"Is it true," Stidham continued, "that if an examiner didn't interpret the test results properly, that that might cause the interrogator to become more assertive and produce a false confession?"

"It's a catalyst. If the examiner goes out and says this guy is deceptive, he's involved, that's all those interrogators have to hear. That gives them the enthusiasm to be more assertive in their accusatory format. Sure. It is a catalyst."

"Is it important," Stidham asked, "when you're trying to corroborate a confession, that you find things independent of the confession linking the suspect to the crime?"

"Absolutely," Holmes replied. "That's one of the things that disturbs me about the defendant's confession in this case. There's nothing you can hang your hat on."

"Does it bother you that they didn't take him to the crime scene?"

"That's the first thing you do. When you get a guy to, so to speak, verbally crap out what he did, you take him right to that crime scene. In this case, there was some dispute as to what side of the creek he was on, where he was standing, where the bikes were. That could have been re-solved if he had been taken to the crime scene."

Judge Burnett listened to the testimony but was not persuaded by Stidham's arguments that the jury should hear it. After hours of negoti-ation, Burnett allowed Holmes to take the stand in the presence of the jury. But Stidham was warned to ask him only a few, very general ques-tions. The closest Holmes was able to come to addressing the issue at hand was to observe that Jessie Misskelley "certainly knows the differ-ence between shoelaces and a rope." That was essentially all the jury heard from Warren Holmes.

"The thing that concerned me most," Stidham said later, "was that the judge would not permit us to tell the jury about the polygraph, and the fact that Jessie had passed instead of flunked. But the jury never knew that Jessie had passed. So the issue becomes, if the police can use this as a tool to beat up on retarded kids and scare them into confessing, why can't the jury know about this tool?"[226]

Dr. Richard Ofshe

Stidham's last hope was to present a witness with expertise on the subject of coerced confessions—and that too was all but shot down. Richard Ofshe was a social psychologist with a doctorate from Stanford University.

He specialized in interpersonal dynamics, particularly in police interrogations.[227] Stidham believed Ofshe's testimony was so critical to his defense that he talked Jessie's family into releasing the $5,000 they were to receive from their contract with HBO to pay Ofshe to come to Arkansas.[228]

As the trial neared its conclusion, the professor took the stand. He had barely recited his credentials in order to be qualified by Judge Burnett as an expert witness when the prosecutors again objected. After sending the jury out of the room one more time, Judge Burnett held another *in camera* hearing. "Well," Burnett began, "I'm going to be honest, gentlemen. I'm real interested in knowing what a sociologist is going to testify to that would aid and benefit the jury and what is the scientific basis of that testimony. It seems to me that you've called this witness to give an opinion that the confession was coerced and that it was involuntary."

"That's exactly right, Your Honor," Stidham said.

"And I think that's a question for the jury to decide," Burnett reiterated, "and I'm not sure I'm going to allow him to testify in that narrow framework. I can see him having value testifying that these are common techniques employed by the police to override one's free will, and that I found such-and-such conditions prevailing here, and things of that nature—or maybe group dynamics of a cult. But I'm not sure I'm prepared to allow him to testify that in his opinion it's coerced and therefore invalid. I mean, what the hell do we need a jury for?"

"He's not going to testify whether or not the confession is false or true or whether the defendant is guilty or innocent," Stidham said. "He's going to testify to the voluntary nature of the confession—the statement to the police—whether or not it was coerced. That's an issue that the jury has to decide, and that's what an expert witness is for, to help the jury decide these issues."

"No. No, Judge," Davis interrupted. "That's the real crux of the matter. Whether the confession was coerced or not doesn't make—whether it was the truth. It's whether it was the truth—and they're trying to get through the back door what they can't get through the front door."

Stidham begged. "Your Honor, that's not the correct statement of the law."

"No. I mean, of course, I've ruled that it was voluntary," Burnett declared. "The jury, I guess, could go back and decide that it wasn't, if that's what you're talking about. But the question of whether or not psychological ploys or tools were used to get a guilty person to give a true statement, now that's another issue."

Stidham said, "Your Honor, that's not what he's going to testify to."

Burnett was growing impatient. "I don't know what you've got him here for. What is he going to testify to? I want to know."

"Your Honor," Stidham said, "he has an opinion as to whether or not the statements made by Mr. Misskelley to the West Memphis Police Department were voluntary."

"Well, we might as well get on with it," said the judge. "I'm going to let him testify, but I'm not about to let him testify that in his opinion, Misskelley is innocent. . . . Don't even try to ask him whether or not he has an opinion whether the confession was true or false, because I'm ruling that he cannot do that. . . . And I'm not going to allow him to testify that, in his opinion, these officers illegally exacted or coerced a confession from him either. I'm not going to allow him to testify to that. So what's he going to testify to?"

When Stidham described a line of questioning that he thought conformed to Burnett's demands, the judge agreed to call the jury back and let Ofshe testify. But first, Burnett advised the jury on a rule of law. "An expert witness," he told the jurors,

> is a person who has special knowledge, skill, experience, training, or education on the subject to which his testimony relates. An expert witness may give his opinion on questions and controversies. You may consider his opinion in the light of his qualifications and credibility, the reasons given for his opinion, and the facts and other matters upon which his opinion is based. You are not bound to accept an expert opinion as conclusive, but you should give it whatever weight you think it should have. You may disregard any opinion testimony if you find it to be unreasonable.

With that, Ofshe was allowed to speak. He explained that he believed Jessie Misskelley had provided what he called a "coerced compliant" statement—"a false statement, one that comes about because an individual can no longer stand the strain of the interrogation and knowingly gives a statement that they know to be untrue."

"Doctor," Stidham asked, "is it possible for police interrogation tactics to produce a false confession?"

Ofshe answered that it was, and began to describe a recent study, reported in the *Stanford Law Review*, which he said had identified 350 cases in which the jury had found someone guilty who was, in fact, innocent. "In that study," Ofshe reported, "19 percent of the miscarriages were caused by false confessions. . . ."

But Davis jumped up to object, and once again, the lawyers held a discussion with the judge that the jury could not hear. In this *in camera* hearing, Davis complained that the answer had broken the ground rules Burnett had established for Ofshe's testimony.

Burnett agreed. "I'm interpreting this as an attempt to use coercive techniques on the jury to suggest to them that this is a false confession, and that there is danger in their considering the confession, and that it suggests to them that they have to be very careful not to make a 350 error—whatever the percentages were."

"What they did," Fogleman said, referring to the defense, "is exactly what the court told them not to do."

"No, Your Honor," Stidham said. "I asked the witness if there were empirical scientific studies, and he was simply relating those to the jury."

"Well, I don't care," Burnett said. "You're still making inferences that, by these statements, that this particular statement was false and untrue."

"Judge, and that's what's going to happen," Davis agreed, "because of this witness, as you surmised. He's very astute. He's very smart, and he's going—he's going to slip around the ground rules, and we're sitting here talking to a jury in terms of percentages of cases in which there's been a false confession."

Burnett ruled. "I'm going to sustain the objection."

Returning to the courtroom, Stidham tried again to establish that Jessie's confession had been false. "Dr. Ofshe, are certain individuals more susceptible to coercive police tactics than others?" he asked.

"Generally, it's been found that individuals who are lacking in self-confidence, who have low self-esteem, are more persuadable, and also more likely to respond to coercive tactics," Ofshe answered. "Individuals who are mentally handicapped are also at risk to responding to coercive and overly persuasive tactics."

After Ofshe had explained a bit more, Stidham asked him if he had formed an opinion about the voluntariness of Jessie's confession. But before Ofshe could respond, Judge Burnett interrupted. Again he dismissed the jury.

"Are we going to start calling sociologists and psychologists to second-guess a court?" he stormed. "I've already ruled it was voluntary. Now, am I going to let a witness get up here and contradict my ruling?"[229]

Davis agreed. He pointed out that while Burnett had ruled that Jessie's confession had been voluntary, which was why it could be admitted as evidence, the prosecution was not allowed to report the judge's finding to the jury. Since the prosecution could not present the judge's "expert opinion" with regard to the willingness of Jessie's statement, Davis argued, nobody else's expert opinion should be admitted either. Burnett said that it was up to the jury to decide whether or not the confession had been voluntary, and that he would not allow any witness to give an opinion that would "supplant the jury's function."

Stidham explained that he wanted Ofshe's point to be "crystal clear" to the jury. He asked the judge if he would be allowed to question Ofshe whether the tactics used by police in their interrogation of Jessie had been coercive or psychologically overbearing.

Burnett said he would allow that question. So with the jury back in the courtroom, Stidham said, "Dr. Ofshe, I need to rephrase the question for you. Do you have an opinion as to whether or not some of the interrogation tactics employed by the police against Mr. Misskelley were coercive in nature?"

"Yes, I do."

"Could you tell the jury what that opinion is?"

Again, prosecutor Davis was on his feet. "Your Honor, I—wait—wait—wait," he sputtered. "We—I hate to object, and I apologize for this, but the court just told Mr. Stidham . . ."

"That I could ask that question," Stidham said.

But Burnett turned to the jury. "All right, ladies and gentlemen," he said. "You're going to be instructed to disregard the last question and the last answer."

In desperation, Stidham asked Burnett if he could write down a question and get the judge's approval for it before he asked it of Ofshe. Burnett agreed and Stidham wrote down a question. When he handed it to the judge, Burnett read it and said, "I think I'll go along with that." But Fogleman objected, and Burnett called the court into recess.

Stidham faced the same situation he had encountered with Holmes. The testimony he wanted his witness to give would not be allowed to be heard by the jury. As before, Stidham asked Burnett to let him present Ofshe's testimony as a proffer of proof, to at least get it into the record for consideration by a higher court upon appeal. Burnett agreed. "Let's be sure that I know what I'm excluding and that I know what you're attempting to put in," he said, "and then maybe I'll change my opinion."

Finally, with the jury still out of the courtroom, Stidham was able to ask Ofshe his opinion, and the witness was allowed to express it. That opinion was "that the statement made by Jessie Misskelley was a product of the influence tactics brought to bear on him, and that it overbore his initial stated intention to maintain that he had nothing to do with this crime and was not there." Ofshe cited what he regarded as an escalating process that had begun with Durham's inaccurate report that Jessie had been "lying his ass off" in the polygraph exam. Ofshe said the circle diagram, in which Jessie was told he could be either "with the killers" or "with the police," intensified the pressure. Additionally, Ofshe said, the officers' "repeated refusals to believe his statements about where he was contributed again to his sense of helplessness." Showing Jessie the photo of the murdered boy increased the pressure to the point where Jessie began to cry. After that, Ofshe said, Gitchell further intensified it, playing the tape of Aaron's voice. It was after Jessie told the detectives that he wanted "out" of the circle Gitchell had drawn that detectives recorded his first statement.

"We now have the first undisputed record in the case," Ofshe testified,

and in that part of the interrogation it's possible to demonstrate how relentless the questioning was, the leading, the suggestions, and the unwillingness to accept anything other than what the police knew the facts of the crime to be. Even then, there were still gross inaccuracies in the statement. The next thing that happened is that Mr. Misskelley is left alone, and Detective Gitchell meets with Prosecutor Fogleman, and some of the specific gross inaccuracies in the recorded statement are now discussed, and according to Detective Gitchell's statement, Prosecutor Fogleman sends him back in to work on these particular statements. And then we can look at the second statement and show how precisely that happened and how, again, Jessie Misskelley is conforming to the demand placed on him and is changing his statement from direct response to suggestions and direct instructions by Detective Gitchell.

Ofshe concluded that "these statements are far more likely to be the product of influence than they are based on any memory that Mr. Misskelley has of the crime."

Stidham then turned to the subject of cults, Ofshe's other area of expertise. He asked for Ofshe's opinion: did the eight-year-olds' murder have "anything to do with satanic rituals or anything of the occult?"

Ofshe replied that, as far as he could tell, they did not. "And as far as the satanic panic tips that were given to police," he added, "my understanding is that none of them have panned out. Apparently, there is one individual who claims to have attended a cult meeting," he said, referring to Vicki Hutcheson, "but apparently her report is equally unconfirmed. As far as I can tell, there is an absence of hard information suggesting that such a satanic cult exists in this area, and in addition, I know of nothing about the crime scene that suggests that this is an occult ritual killing."

When Ofshe concluded his statement, Burnett decided that he would not allow the jury to hear it. The judge ruled that if Ofshe's testimony were admitted, it would, in effect, tell the jury "what their finding should be." So when the jury came back into the courtroom, Stidham asked Ofshe only one question: was it his opinion "that the tactics used by the police were suggestive and led the defendant to make a statement?" Ofshe answered: "Yes, and that the statement—the content of the statement—was shaped by these techniques."

When Prosecutor Davis cross-examined Ofshe, he attacked the suggestion that Jessie's questioning had been coercive. "Did you find any evidence," Davis asked, "as to physical coercion?" Or "that any of the officers yelled or used a loud voice or were degrading to the defendant?" Or that "there was any undue influence, pressure, or loud voices and demands made on the defendant?" Ofshe answered no, that "in the limited set of materials you're allowing me to testify on," there was not.

"And is what you term coercive," Davis asked, "that the officers asked at times leading questions?"

Ofshe answered, "The questions were more than leading. The questions were very directly specifying what the answers should be."[230]

When Davis sought Ofshe's acknowledgment that Jessie could be heard on the tape making self-incriminating statements in his own voice, Ofshe agreed. But, Ofshe noted, Jessie could also be heard making statements that were clearly false. "The statement about the time at which this crime occurred is a statement that comes up and is manipulated eight different times over the course of this interrogation, and over the course of those eight manipulations one sees a pattern of unrelenting pressure on Mr. Misskelley."

Before Stidham questioned Ofshe again, he asked Burnett, "Your Honor, may I use the word 'coercive,' like the prosecutor used?"

"I guess that's the goose and the gander thing, isn't it?" Burnett replied. "Go ahead."

Now that Davis had introduced the word he'd been fighting to keep out, Stidham attempted to explore its nuances. He asked the witness, "Could you give some examples of the police being coercive and leading or suggestive during the course of the interrogation?"

"Yes, I can," Ofshe said. "Perhaps the most powerful example in my opinion is the example of the eight revisitings of the question of the time at which the crimes occurred." Ofshe noted that Jessie began by saying he'd gone to the woods at nine o'clock in the morning. The next time Ridge raised the question, Jessie said he was in the woods at "about noon."

"Ridge now says something that, in my opinion, was an attempt to manipulate Mr. Misskelley's statement about the time," Ofshe testified, "because Detective Ridge now says, 'Okay, was it after school had let out?' This is immediately after Jessie saying, 'It's at noon.' He's now suggesting it must be later by saying, 'Is it after school let out?' "

Gitchell had next raised the question of time, and then Ridge had brought it up a fourth time. Ofshe noted,

> And this time Detective Ridge says, and I quote, "Okay. The night you were in the woods, had you all been in the water?" Jessie replies, "Yeah, we'd been in the water. We were in it that night playing around in it." This is the first time in the record, according to my analysis of it and according to Detective Ridge's testimony, that it is directly suggested to Jessie that the correct answer is, "This happened at night."
>
> Immediately upon that being suggested Jessie responds by accepting and now he starts to use the word "at night," where he had never used it before, where he had consistently said it was during the day. That is an influence tactic. It is a way of getting someone to accept something out of pressure and out of suggestion.

Ofshe pointed out three other points in the interview when Jessie was asked about what time he was in the woods. Finally, Ofshe noted, "Jessie replied, 'I would say it was about five or so—five or six.'

"So Jessie is now moving in the direction of later, but it's as if there is the original statement that he made about the morning, and he's being slowly moved towards the evening. But clearly, in this statement, he has not gone far enough, because five or six, I gather from what I've been informed, is too early for the boys to have shown up at the woods." So, Ofshe said, there was one more attempt to move Jessie's account of the time. This came when Gitchell told Jessie, "All right, you told me earlier around seven or eight. Which time is it?"

"There are two important things about this," Ofshe observed.

> The first one is it's obvious that Detective Gitchell is giving Jessie a choice. Pick one and I win, or pick two and I

win—either seven or eight. Gitchell can live with either answer, and he's giving Jessie only those two choices. But
what's even more important about this is that nowhere in the
record—including the record of what the detectives say, the
notes, the specific statements by Detective Ridge, the transcript of the first interrogation—is there any indication that
Jessie ever said, as Detective Gitchell says, "You told me earlier around seven or eight." There is an absolute absence of
anything indicating that. So it's my opinion that this is a tactic, and it's a very effective tactic, because Jessie now simply
repeats back to Detective Gitchell what Gitchell told him.
He says, "It was seven or eight." Jessie doesn't even make a
choice. He just tells Gitchell everything that Gitchell told
him. That's an indication of someone who is willing to com-
ply and does not want to take any chances of making a mistake and therefore being punished for it through pressure.

When Stidham sat down, Davis asked one more question. "Doctor,
when the person is being asked questions and they don't know anything
about it, and they don't know any of the details, they can always say, 'I
don't know. I don't know anything about it. I don't know the details
you're asking me about.' They can always say that, can't they?"

"They can," Ofshe replied. "And sometimes they get to the point at
which they can no longer do that and so they simply give up."

The Verdict

Fogleman presented his closing argument, stressing the confession in a
controlled, unemotional voice. Stidham cited the inconsistencies in
Jessie's statement and the lack of physical evidence in hopes that the
jury would find reasonable doubt. He concluded, "Killing one human
being by another is only exceeded by the state killing an innocent man."
Then Davis, who had the final argument, used it to lash out. Vehe-
mently and emotionally he reminded the jurors of what the police had
concluded was the motive for the crime. "I don't know what the definition of a cult is," Davis sneered. "I don't know if it has to mean that they

go once a week and worship the devil or what. But when the evidence is that all three of them are involved in this type of activity—that's a cult in my book." Then, standing behind the defendant, where he held a photo of Michael Moore over Jessie's head, he told the jury emphatically, "He chased him down like an animal and brought him back. And, as a result of his action, Michael Moore is dead, Stevie Branch is dead, and Chris Byers is dead." He asked the jurors to find Misskelley guilty of three counts of capital murder, a verdict that would allow the state of Arkansas to execute him.

By noon the next day, the jury had reached its verdict. Jessie kept his head bowed as Judge Burnett read the forms. In the death of Michael Moore, he was found guilty of first-degree murder. In the deaths of Christopher Byers and Stevie Branch he was found guilty of murder in the second degree.

Stidham felt the breath knocked out of him. The verdicts of first- and second-degree murder meant that the death penalty could not be imposed, as Fogleman and Davis had wanted. But Jessie had been found guilty. In the sentencing phase of the trial, the jury sentenced Jessie to life in prison without parole for the murder of Michael Moore. The jurors tacked on an additional twenty years each, to be served consecutively, for the murders of the other two boys.[231] When Judge Burnett asked Jessie if he had anything to say, the teenager answered, "No."

Afterward, one of the jurors said that allegations about Jessie's ties to the occult had not factored into the verdict. "To be honest with you, it wouldn't have mattered to us if there was a cult or not," juror Lloyd Champion told the *Commercial Appeal*.[232] Champion said that jurors considered Stidham's arguments that Jessie's confession was coerced, but that they'd concluded Jessie's statement about chasing Michael Moore and holding him had not been solicited. "The police didn't ask him that," Champion said. "Boom! That was out of nowhere." In the same interview, Champion added that he was not surprised that Stidham didn't have Jessie testify. With irony that was apparently not intentional, Champion explained, "I think that prosecuting attorney could have tore him apart and made him say anything."

Gitchell exulted that the conviction had vindicated his department.

Jessie's stepmother told reporters that she hoped the prosecutors would be able to sleep at night. "They're all a bunch of liars," Jessie Sr. said. The elder Misskelley added that Jessie had been terrified and near despair as sheriff's deputies had led him away for his trip to prison. Jessie was crying, Jessie Sr. said. "He told me, 'I'll never make it down there. I'll never get out and come home.' "

Years later, sitting in prison, Jessie would recall, "When that verdict came in—eeee-yewww!—I just knew my life was over right then."

CHAPTER SIXTEEN

The Allegations
of Official Misconduct

TODD AND DANA MOORE were characteristically reserved as they left the courthouse. They did not speak to reporters. Pam Hobbs, Stevie Branch's mother, expressed her hope that Jessie's life in prison would be a long and tormented one. The Byerses, as usual, were unrestrained. Expecting that Jessie would end up at the infamous Cummins Unit of the Arkansas Department of Correction, they described in rough and suggestive detail the future they wished for him there.

"I hope he never sees sunlight again," John Mark Byers said. "Life plus forty—that's fine with me. That means Cummins keeps his dead ass forty years after he dies."[233] Melissa Byers, with dark circles under her eyes, ranted in front of the cameras. "This doesn't change anything," she said. "Christopher's dead. And he was tortured to death by three murdering bastards on a ditch bank. He was eight years old, and guilty is guilty, and I hope the little sucker, when he hits Cummins, they get his ass right off the bat, because he deserves to be tortured and punished for the rest of his life for murdering three eight-year-old children!"

The couple walked a few steps away. Then, as though Jessie were there, Melissa added, "Prison's not a safe place, Jessie, sweetie." To the photographers who were following her she offered a last aside. "I'm going to mail him a skirt."[234]

Judge Burnett complimented the news media, noting that he was "well pleased" with the way they had covered the trial. Jessie's lawyers announced that they'd appeal. And prosecutors Davis and Fogleman dropped the word to reporters that Jessie's sentence of life without parole might not be exactly final. Noting that Damien and Jason's trial was just eighteen days away, they explained that Jessie's sentence would not become final for about four months. During that time, if Judge Burnett chose to do so, he could reduce Jessie's sentence. They said such a thing might happen if, for instance, Jessie agreed to testify against Damien and Jason at their upcoming trial.

The day after Jessie's conviction, Glori Shettles visited Damien in a new jail. He'd already been moved to the jail in Jonesboro, the city where he and Jason were to be tried. "He may watch television for a limited number of hours from his cell floor," Shettles wrote, "but has not been allowed to see the news. His books have been taken from him; however, he has been allowed to choose books to read from the jail library. Great efforts have been made to ensure he and Jason have had no contact; however, Michael laughed and stated he heard Jason 'howling' one night."

Pretrial Concerns

Shettles wrote that one of Damien's lawyers had visited him earlier in the day and informed him of Jessie's conviction. She noted that Damien did not seem to be "negatively affected" by the news, but rather "spoke of his hope of having a larger, more educated jury pool, who would consider the evidence with a more open mind." However, Damien also told Shettles that if his own trial ended with a conviction, "he had no interest in an appeal. He stated he would not be taken out of the courtroom guilty, as Jessie had been, but would attempt to grab one of the deputies' guns to kill himself or to force the deputies to shoot him."

Damien's lawyers let him hold on to his hope that a trial in Jonesboro, the district's most populous county, would produce jurors more receptive to his case. It was true that Jonesboro was home to Arkansas State University, and that the average income and educational level in Craighead County was higher than in mostly rural Clay County, where Jessie had just been tried. But Val Price and Scott Davidson also knew that Craighead County was one of the most religiously conservative places in the state, and that Jonesboro, the county seat, was home to several large and powerful churches, almost all of them housing fundamentalist Christian congregations. Jessie's just-concluded trial had dominated the region's news. Now, after that and months of publicity about Damien's interest in the occult, Price and Davidson worried that the odds of finding jurors who had not been influenced was not as great as they had allowed Damien to hope.

They also worried about Jessie. He'd been sentenced to life without parole. But now, fresh on the heels of his conviction, the prosecutors were offering him a chance to shorten his time in prison, just for saying a few words. If, as Jessie's lawyer had contended, the boy had buckled under pressure from the West Memphis police when they'd questioned him for a few hours, how would he react under the greater pressure of prison? Would he grab the offer Fogleman and Davis were holding out to him? Would he accuse Damien and Jason again, this time on the witness stand, under oath, in front of the jury?

Jason's lawyers had those worries, and an additional one. They still believed strongly that Jason's trial needed to be separated from Damien's. They did not want Jason's trial to be tainted by the stories of satanism, cult or occult practices, or general weirdness that were attached to Damien. They wanted to be free to take any approach they felt was needed to defend Jason's life. If that meant arguing that Damien might have killed the children but that Jason certainly did not, they wanted to be free to say that. In a last-ditch pretrial motion, they told Judge Burnett that presenting their case would be difficult, if not impossible, if the two boys were tried together. But as in the past, Judge Burnett rejected the motion.

Prosecutors Davis and Fogleman had serious worries of their own. They had had virtually no evidence against Jessie, other than his tape-recorded confession. But the jury had considered that confession to be sufficient. Now they were heading into a trial with a similar dearth of evidence, but against defendants who had not confessed. Jessie had accused Damien and Jason, and that accusation had been the basis for the arrests. But if Jessie would not repeat his accusation at the upcoming trial, under oath, as a witness for the state, Davis and Fogleman would not be allowed to mention it. Even to play the tape of Jessie's confession, in which he implicated Damien and Jason, without Jessie himself taking the stand, would violate the constitutional requirement that defendants be allowed to face their accusers at trial.

Fogleman and Davis realized that if Jessie accused Damien and Jason in court, the blow to the defense case would be devastating. On the other hand, even if Jessie did not testify, and no mention of his confession could be made, the defense teams would still have immense damage to overcome. Jessie's confession had been leaked to the press within two weeks after his arrest, and his damning accusations against Damien and Jason had been intensely publicized. Jessie's just-concluded trial, with all its attendant publicity, had again riveted public attention on the confession. It was almost inconceivable that any twelve jurors could be seated who were not already well aware both that Jessie had confessed and that he had accused Damien and Jason of the murders.

However much they might have been helped by the backdrop of publicity to the case, the prosecutors did not want to count on it. Facing a trial where there were no confessions, no direct physical evidence, and no clear motive, they wanted an eyewitness—even one whose story had changed repeatedly. But talk of reducing Jessie's sentence did not sit well with the victims' families. Davis and Fogleman met with them to explain why, now that they'd just gotten Jessie convicted, they were trying to offer him a deal. "Unfortunately," Davis explained, "we need his testimony real bad."

"All is not lost if he doesn't testify," Fogleman quickly added. "But the odds are reduced significantly. I mean, we've still got *some* evidence." Fogleman then summarized the evidence they had against Damien and Jason, if Jessie's confession was excluded. He listed

—Three fibers. Fogleman said he considered fiber evidence strong but added, "We can't say it came from that particular garment to the exclusion of all others."
—The Hollingsworths' claims that they'd seen Damien and Domini on the service road. These reports presented two problems: they placed Domini at the scene, and they failed to place Jason there.[235]
—The statements of the "kids at the girls' softball game," who said they'd overheard Damien saying that he'd killed the three boys and was going to kill two more.
—"A guy that was in jail with Jason, who says Jason made

some incriminating statements." Fogleman warned, however, that the witness—a teenager named Michael Carson—might not be believed by the jury.

—"Oh, yes," Fogleman concluded. "And the knife in the lake."

"So that's what we've got," he told the victims' families. "But that's *all* that we've got." When someone asked Davis what the odds were of convicting Damien and Jason if Jessie did not testify, the prosecutor did not sound confident. "Fifty-fifty might be good," he said.

The defense lawyers were well aware of the prosecutors' dilemma. Without Jessie's testimony, Davis and Fogleman would be trying to win a death penalty conviction with scant and circumstantial evidence. If Jessie did testify, the defense lawyers would make sure the jury realized how much he stood to gain by talking. Still, both the defense teams ardently hoped that Jessie would not appear. As Jason's attorney told him, "If that's their best evidence and they can't use it against you, then this dog-and-pony show is over."

Jessie's Next Statement

With only eighteen days to go until the start of the next trial, the possibility that Jessie might testify frayed nerves on both sides of the case. Jessie vacillated. But everyone knew that the prosecutors held a distinct advantage. Jessie was scared as sheriff's deputies led him to a car that would take him to prison, three hours away, in south Arkansas. He told his father that he'd "never make it down there." By the time the sheriff's car arrived in Pine Bluff, the intake site for the prison, the deputies who'd driven Jessie had good news for Fogleman and Davis. As one of them reported, "Jessie was asked if there was anything he wanted to say, and after being assured we could not use anything he said against him in court, he chose to talk."

According to one of the deputies, Jessie had admitted once again his involvement in the murders, and he'd renewed his accusations against Damien and Jason.[236] The details of this statement, as reported by the deputy, were different in several respects from anything Jessie had said before. Still, Fogleman and Davis were excited.

According to the deputy, Jessie did a lot of talking on his long ride to the prison. He told his drivers he'd met Damien and Jason on the "evening" of May 5. Before that, he'd been drinking whiskey that Vicki Hutcheson had bought him. Damien and Jason were drinking beer. Earlier in the afternoon, they all had smoked marijuana. The three teenagers went to the woods, where they were sitting in the water, when they saw the three young boys at a distance. Damien told Jessie and Jason to hide, then Damien grabbed Michael Moore. Michael's friends started hitting Damien, whereupon Jessie and Jason jumped out and helped Damien "beat them" with sticks. Damien and Jason took turns raping the boys. The boys were not tied at that time. Jessie helped hold the boys and beat them, but had no part in raping or killing them. "Blood flew everywhere" as Jason castrated one of the boys with a "buck-type locking knife." Jason threw the dismembered part of the unidentified boy's body into "the weeds." That boy was then thrown into the water, where he was "still squirming around" when Jessie decided to leave. The other two boys were, at that point, unconscious but not in the water.

The deputy reported that Jessie said that he'd lied when he was questioned by the police about the time the murders took place and about the children being tied with rope. He said he'd wanted "to trick the police and to see if they were lying." The deputy concluded, "Jessie claims he has felt sorry for what happened and talks as if he wants to testify against the other boys so they will not go free and to help himself."

Prosecutor Davis later said that when he heard the deputy's report, he called Jessie's lawyer to discuss a postconviction plea bargain. Four days after Jessie arrived at the prison in Pine Bluff, attorney Stidham, Inspector Gitchell, and prosecutors Davis and Fogleman drove there to talk with Jessie. Before anything else happened, Stidham wanted to meet with Jessie alone. Fogleman later recalled: "Well, Stidham stays in there forever. He finally comes out, all white-faced, wanting a Bible. Dan just could not believe what Jessie was telling him, and he wouldn't let us talk to him. He kept saying, 'If only there were some more corroboration. And he did tell us some of the details of what Jessie told him, including that he had been drinking, and the brand of whiskey, and the particular person who'd given him the whiskey."

Jessie had also reported that, on his way home, after witnessing the murders, he'd thrown the bottle of whiskey away, near a highway over-pass. "And so, we went back there," Fogleman said,

> practically in the middle of the night, searching this overpass Jessie described. We found this neck of a whiskey bottle. It was the largest piece of whiskey bottle that we could find, that you could identify, and it's the brand that Jessie has de-scribed. Of course, we're talking about what—a year later? And so we say to Stidham, "Dan, is that enough corrobora-tion? Here's the kind of whiskey." And he said, no, that wasn't enough. So we go back to the police department, and Gitchell calls the person who allegedly gave Jessie this whiskey, and she's on a speakerphone. Gitchell says, "So-and-So, I've got a real important question to ask you. Did you ever give Jessie any alcohol?" And there's this long pause and she says, "Well, yes, I did." And he says, "What kind was it?" And she says, "Well, it was whiskey." And he says, "What kind?" And she goes through three or four and then she says, "No, that wasn't it." Then she says the brand of what Jessie told Dan it was. Of course, that still wasn't enough to convince Dan.

Stidham attributed Jessie's sudden willingness to talk to the prosecu-tor to his fear of being in prison and to his corresponding desire to please authorities. While Stidham was chagrined by Jessie's decision, he was less than impressed by the fact that prosecutors had found a broken Evan Williams bottle alongside an overpass near one of the nation's busiest highways. Stidham decided to meet with Jessie again at the prison, and now it was the prosecutors' turn to be dismayed. On Febru-ary 15, eleven days after Jessie's conviction, Stidham informed the state that Jessie would not testify against Damien and Jason.

Tensions were palpable the next morning. All the lawyers met in Judge Burnett's courtroom in Jonesboro for a pretrial hearing. The prosecutors were not convinced that Jessie was going to stay silent. Ja-son's lawyer was pressing again to have Jason's trial severed from Damien's. And now Damien's attorneys wanted Judge Burnett to order the HBO filmmakers to surrender footage they'd heard had been shot of John Mark Byers. The lawyers told the judge that in the segment they wanted, Byers was reportedly shown standing at the site where the boys' bodies were found, "talking about being accosted when he was eighteen or nineteen years old, tied up, sodomized, and thrown into a ditch." Burnett rejected the request.[237]

After the hearing, Fogleman called Jessie's father, asking that he speak to his son and persuade him to testify. Big Jessie told Fogleman bluntly that Little Jessie had no interest in the deal. Davis then asked Jessie's lawyer to let the prosecutors put the question to Jessie themselves. Stidham refused. But the prosecutors were not thwarted.

Incident at Rector

They went to Burnett. Without notifying either Stidham or Jessie's father, they asked the judge to issue an order for Jessie to be taken out of prison and brought to Jonesboro. Information was leaked to the media that Jessie was moved so that he could be available to testify at the Echols-Baldwin trial, which was still a week away. Stidham learned that his client had been moved while watching the television news. He was furious. He later complained that Judge Burnett had issued the order for Jessie to be moved ex parte, after consulting only with the prosecutors, while Jessie's attorneys had been excluded. Stidham said the first he'd seen of Judge Burnett's order was the copy shown on television.

All hell broke loose, legally, during the next three days. On February 17, five days before Damien and Jason's trial was to start, Jessie was driven from the prison at Pine Bluff to Rector, a town of about three thousand, some forty miles northeast of Jonesboro. At about 5 P.M., a sheriff's deputy drove Jessie to the law office of one of Davis's assistant prosecuting attorneys.[238] Davis was already there waiting. At about six-fifteen, the local deputy prosecutor called attorney Stidham at home to report that Jessie was now in Rector—and that he was prepared to make a statement.[239] Stidham could not believe what was happening. He told the deputy prosecutor that neither he nor Davis were to take any statement from Jessie. Then Stidham picked up his partner, Greg Crow, and the two men sped through the dark to Rector, in the far northeast corner of the state. Forty-five minutes later, they pulled up in front of the office where Jessie was being held.

Stidham and Crow demanded to speak with their client in private. When the prosecutors left the room, Jessie happily told his attorneys that the deputy who'd driven him to Rector had promised to bring Jessie's girlfriend to see him in the local jail. Stidham had never encountered a situation anything like this. As he later recalled the night, he and Crow had had fifteen minutes in the conference room alone with Jessie when Davis opened the door, insisting the session must end. He said that Jessie had agreed to make a statement and it was time for him to make it. Stidham and Crow objected strenuously to having their meeting with their client interrupted. Davis left the room but returned a few minutes later. This time, in front of Jessie, he and the deputy prosecutor expressed their concern that Jessie's two defense lawyers would convince him not to talk. As the argument ensued, Jessie stood up. He announced that he *did* want to make a statement, then, turning his back on his own lawyers, he walked out of the conference room with the prosecutors.

Stidham rushed to a phone to call Judge Burnett at home. He complained that the prosecutors were violating his client's constitutional rights. He told the judge that Jessie had requested psychiatric help upon his arrival in prison, and asked that Judge Burnett delay any questioning until a psychiatric evaluation could be performed. Burnett refused. Then prosecutor Davis took the phone. Burnett told him that he could inform Jessie that anything he told the prosecutors would not be used against him in court. And that was that. At 8:02 P.M., with Jessie's lawyers in the room, Davis turned on a tape recorder and placed Jessie under oath.

This time Jessie said that he went to the woods with Damien and Jason after he got off work, which was around "dinnertime." He'd been drinking whiskey Vicki Hutcheson had bought him. It was "still daylight" when he arrived at the woods "by a bridge . . . on the service road." He, Damien, and Jason heard "some noise." All three of the teenagers hid. "Then three little boys come up and we jumped 'em." In this recounting, Jessie did not identify any of the victims by name, but he did recall some dialogue. He said that as the younger boys were being attacked they'd yelled, "Stop! Stop!" but that Damien had yelled to Jessie and Jason, "No! No! Don't stop!"[240]

Jessie also supplied another detail of the attack, but this one posed a problem for Davis, as it contradicted Fogleman's theory that the knife taken from the lake behind Jason's trailer had been the murder weapon. When Jessie told Davis that Jason had been "swinging" a knife at the boys, sending blood "flying," Davis asked what the knife looked like. "I can't remember," Jessie said. Then he added, "All I know is it's a lock blade." The knife from the lake was not a folding type, but a fixed-blade survival knife. Davis asked, "When you say a lock-blade, one that folds out and locks?" Jessie answered, "Yeah."

Davis asked Jessie about his earlier statement to police that the boys were tied with rope. "I made that up," Jessie said. This time Jessie was clear that the boys were tied with "shoestrings," but he was vague about how the laces had been removed from the shoes. This time he recalled seeing all three boys thrown into the water, after which he left, still carrying the whiskey bottle. He said he "busted" the bottle on the way home, on "like a slope going down over the overpass," then he went to a wrestling match with a friend. Davis asked if there were "events that took place that night" that were difficult to remember. Jessie answered, "I can't remember."[241]

The next day, Stidham formally notified Judge Burnett that neither Davis nor Fogleman were to have any further contact with Jessie. But Stidham's outrage affected nothing. Every day until the start of the trial, one or the other of the prosecutors continued to visit Jessie in jail. Stidham was not told of the visits. Burnett did not intervene.

"The Bottom of the Truth"

The furor surrounding Jessie was still raging behind the scenes as prospective jurors arrived at the Craighead County Courthouse for Damien and Jason's trial. It was February 19, and northeast Arkansas was crackling beneath a second blast of ice. As media and spectators gathered for the long-awaited trial, lawyers on both sides met in the chambers of Judge Burnett for another intense confrontation. Stidham spoke first. He argued that Jessie was being used and that his future appeals were being compromised by the state. He wanted the prosecutors stopped. He handed Judge Burnett a motion citing all of the contacts state officials had had with Jessie, in which the boy had been urged to talk, since the moment of his conviction.

Stidham complained that as Jessie's attorney, he had notified Davis and Fogleman repeatedly that Jessie *would not* testify at Damien and Jason's upcoming trial. The prosecutors' "improper contact" with Jessie, he said, was a "conscious and calculated attempt" to circumvent the boy's rights to remain silent and to receive the assistance of counsel. Stidham said, "They even promised to bring his girlfriend to see him at the jail, Judge. I think that is the most abhorrent, ridiculous, flagrant violation of my client's rights that I have ever seen."[242] Again, Stidham asked Burnett to order the prosecutors "not to have any contact whatsoever, directly or indirectly," with Jessie without Stidham's knowledge and consent. He also asked that the prosecutors be held in contempt of court and "punished accordingly." Finally, he asked that a special prosecutor—"preferably one from outside the Second Judicial District"—be appointed to investigate the prosecutors' behavior.

Davis countered that Stidham had become unreasonable and that Stidham's interests and Jessie's "were no longer consistent." Davis told Burnett that once Jessie started talking after being sentenced to prison, Stidham had "lost his objectivity as to what was in his client's best interest." Davis said Stidham no longer understood what to do "to get to the bottom of the truth."

Judge Burnett quickly settled the matter. He walked into the courtroom, seated himself at the bench, and dealt with the issue in public. Noting that word of the discussions about Jessie Misskelley—and criticisms of the prosecutors' behavior—had already reached the media, Burnett announced that no prosecutors had engaged in misconduct. As reporters scribbled their notes, the judge added that Jessie would be allowed to testify "if he chooses to do so."[243]

CHAPTER SEVENTEEN

The Witness List

A FEW DAYS BEFORE the start of Damien and Jason's trial, the *Memphis Commercial Appeal* reported that a "club" with what appeared to be blood and hair on it had been found in the mobile home where Damien lived at the time of the murders. The trailer's new renter had found the club and notified police. But though the report created another sensation, it was quietly proven untrue. The stick turned out to be an old axe handle that had been used to stir red paint. The hair was from a dog.

To Damien's private investigator, the story typified what the defense had been dealing with throughout the case: wild suspicions, false claims, and convenient leaks from police to the press. Ron Lax had been trying since the beginning to find a consistent theory of the crime, a clear motive—something the defense could attack. But the state's version of the crime had kept changing. Too much about this case was vague, contradictory, confusing. It was hard to find a clear path through it. To Lax, nothing about it seemed fixed. Stories and testimony had kept changing. Documents, such as the first police interview of Byers, had been inexplicably withheld, while possible weapons, such as sticks and the lake knife, had popped up long after the arrests. Amid so much uncertainty, it had been hard for the defense to prepare.

But however crazy the case appeared, Damien and Jason's lives were now on the line, and with the trial about to start, Lax dove for one last time into the discovery records. Lax had arranged them chronologically and by subject, and added his and Shettles's notes. While jurors were being selected to judge Damien and Jason, Lax methodically reviewed the now organized police file. In the process, he noted references to several documents that he had never seen, records that should have been part of the file but that had not been turned over to the defense. Among the items Lax would have expected to find but did not were notes from the patrol officer who'd searched the woods with John Mark Byers on the night the boys disappeared; a behavioral profile of the killer that Inspector Gitchell had requested and that had apparently been prepared by the FBI; Don Bray's notes from his interviews with Vickie and Aaron Hutcheson; any notes, reports, or photographs of the place where Vicki Hutcheson told police she'd attended the alleged esbat, the tape recordings made when detectives had wired Vicki Hutcheson's trailer; and follow-up notes to the report from Memphis police that both Mark and Melissa Byers had been confidential drug informants. Working with what they had, Lax and Shettles assessed, visited, and in some cases revisited the witnesses whose testimony might prove most damaging.

The Hutchesons

Vicki and Aaron Hutcheson topped the list—not because Lax found their statements compelling but because the police and prosecution had placed so much stock in them. As recently as the last week of Jessie's trial, Bray had tape-recorded yet another statement from Aaron, and it had turned out to be the most elaborate yet. This time, Aaron stated that his friends had been beaten with long sticks that had a dragon carved on them, and that Damien and Jessie had poured blood into a glass and made him drink it. The inconsistencies in Aaron's numerous statements were so many and so profound that Lax could not imagine that Prosecutor Fogleman would call the child to testify, no matter how sympathetic an eight-year-old friend of the victims might appear. But on the other hand, Lax reminded himself, the prosecutors were working feverishly to get Jessie to testify—and his statements had been profoundly inconsistent too.

Aaron's mother was a different matter. Vicki Hutcheson had already testified at Jessie's trial, and she would probably be called again. Lax urged Damien's and Jason's attorneys to press Hutcheson about her past and about her own inconsistencies, especially with regard to her reports of the esbat. At one point she'd said that she, Damien, and Jessie had arrived at approximately 6 P.M. In another, she'd said that it was "really dark" when they arrived. Lax also wanted someone to zero in on her claim that

Damien had driven the car. The investigator noted that in the police inter-views, "there was no discussion regarding the fact that Damien is not capa-ble of driving any type of vehicle." Recalling Bray's report that Hutcheson told him in advance that she was going to attend the esbat, Lax wrote, "It seems odd that if she was conducting this 'investigation' and she informed the police that she was going to attend a Satanic cult meeting with their primary suspect, they would not have placed surveillance on her."

Byers

The question of how to treat John Mark Byers was vastly more complex. Since the appearance of Byers's knife, additional bits of information about Byers's past had come to light. Among the police records that were turned over to the defense was a tip from the television program *America's Most Wanted*, which had aired a segment on the West Memphis murders. An unidentified woman had called in to report that Byers had beaten his wife and children in the past, and that on the night the boys were missing, he and Melissa had argued and he'd hit her several times.[244] By the end of Jessie's trial, Lax and the defense attorneys had also learned of Byers's conviction for terroristic threatening. Lax located Byers's ex-wife, Sandra Slone, who had remarried and now lived in Missouri.

She was cooperative but reserved when he telephoned her.[245] In his notes on the call, Lax wrote that when Byers's ex-wife heard about the West Memphis murders, she'd said, "she immediately suspected Byers was responsible. She described him as extremely violent and said her children were deathly afraid of him. She stated he used to beat her and the children, but did so in a way which left no visible marks or bruises, when dressed." Lax wrote that the woman told him she had reported her fears for herself and her children to Inspector Gary Gitchell, but that the detective had "assured her Byers was not a suspect and was not connected with the mur-ders. He told her any problems with Byers were personal problems, with which she would have to deal and he could not help her further."

Accustomed as he'd become to peculiarities in the case, Lax found the woman's statement astonishing. Byers's attack on her six years earlier had been proven in court, his stepson had been brutally murdered, his ac-count of his activities on the night of the murders conflicted with accounts of other family members, and a knife belonging to him had recently turned up with blood on it that might have been Christopher's. Yet here was Byers's ex-wife saying that when she told Gitchell that she feared for herself and her children, her concerns had been rudely ignored.

The conversation illustrated what had become a fundamental dilemma for the defense—the question of how to handle Byers. His status as a police informant, combined with Gitchell's delicate questioning of him about the bloodstained knife—and now Slone's reported suspicion that he'd long had police "connections"—heightened Lax's and the lawyers' suspicions. But they shared the same concern that had dogged Stidham in Jessie's trial—that if they even hinted that Byers was the killer, without hard evidence to prove it, they risked inflaming the jury.

One More Juvenile Witness

On the eve of the trial, Lax also tracked down another teenager who'd told police he'd heard Damien discussing the murders.[246] The sixteen-year-old was one of the witnesses Fogleman had subpoenaed to testify at the upcoming trial. After the boy admitted to Lax that what he'd told the police was "wrong," Lax videotaped an interview with him and his mother. The woman said that she'd been asked to bring her son to the police station in September 1993, four months after the murders. She said Detective Bryn Ridge questioned him briefly, then had him take a polygraph test. After that, Ridge and Durham had questioned him again.[247]

The mother told Lax that though she went to the police station with her son, she'd been asked to sit in the hall. The woman said she did not know—and police did not tell her—that she had a right to be with her son while he was being questioned. Lax noted in his taped interview that statements the boy made to the police before he was polygraphed differed from those he made after. Lax asked him why that was. The teenager answered, "Because in the first part, I was telling the truth, that I didn't know nothing. The second part, they took me to the, uh, polygraph, and went downstairs and got fingerprints, and when I came back, they told me I was lying and everything. Just kept on and kept on and kept on about Damien this, Damien that . . ."

The boy said the officers had not hit him, but that they had "kept on and kept on" yelling, "like I was fixing to get arrested or something." In his statement after the polygraph, the boy told Ridge and Durham that he'd heard Damien say he'd been present "when the little boys got killed." Lax asked if he'd been frightened, and the boy nodded yes. He said he was afraid "that they was going to try and say I was there and . . . that I knew them. Then I thought I was going to, like, get involved and have to go to court, you know, like they are."

The list of prospective witnesses that Fogleman had given the defense contained more than two hundred names. More than a tenth were police officers; a few more worked at the state crime lab. One of those would deal another blow to the case Fogleman was trying to make.

Dr. Peretti

From the first day of the investigation, police had acted on the assumption that the victims had been sodomized. One reason for that was that the crime looked sexual. The boys' nakedness suggested that, as did the way they were tied: bound behind their backs, with their genitals prominently exposed and their backsides accessible. Of course, Christopher's castration was a violent sexual assault. The other factor that led police to believe that the boys had been sodomized was that their anuses had appeared dilated, or unnaturally open, when the bodies were removed from the water.

Though the autopsies were performed the next day, the medical examiner's inexplicable delay in releasing the autopsy reports forced Gitchell and his detectives to proceed on their suppositions. Weeks passed without a definitive answer on the question of rape, which was why, in his letter to the medical examiner almost a month after the murders, Gitchell still had had to ask, "Were the kids sodomized?" He did not have an answer when Jessie was interrogated. But the strength of the detectives' assumption that the boys had been sodomized was reflected in Detective Ridge's questions. Jessie told the police he'd seen Damien and Jason "screwing" the boys, and that aspect of his statement had contributed to the loathsomeness of the crime. Yet after the arrests, when the belated autopsy reports finally arrived, all three of them stated that "no injury" had been found to the boys' anuses.

At Jessie's trial, Dr. Peretti, the associate medical examiner who'd performed the autopsies, testified that while he could not rule out that the boys had been raped in the attacks, there was no physical evidence to support the contention. When Stidham asked Peretti if he would expect to find injuries to the children's anuses if an eyewitness had reported seeing them raped, the pathologist said he would. "If it were forcible, I would expect to find injuries," Peretti said. "If the penis enters the anal canal, I would expect to find bruises and abrasions to the opening. I couldn't find any physical evidence of that."

Because of Peretti's testimony, the defense lawyers had asked Judge Burnett to bar the prosecutors from claiming that the boys had been raped—an allegation that, the defense lawyers knew, carried intense emotional weight with the jury. But Peretti's testimony posed no problem for the prosecutors because, despite the lack of evidence to support the claim, Judge Burnett allowed them to say that the boys had been sodomized.

The sodomy question remained one of the case's numerous ambiguities. Jessie's most recent statement had made it even murkier. In Jessie's confession to the West Memphis police, given at a time when the police believed the boys had been sodomized, Jessie's story had conformed to that belief. He said he'd seen Jason and Damien "screwing" the victims "in the ass" and "in the mouth." But a few nights before, in Rector—after Jessie'd heard Peretti testify at his trial that he'd found no evidence of sodomy—Jessie's story had changed. "They didn't do it," Jessie'd told Davis, when the prosecutor asked. "He was going to do it, then they didn't." If Jessie decided to testify at the trial that was about to start—a question that was still not completely resolved—Lax and the defense lawyers had a hard time trying to imagine what the state's contention on the sodomy issue might be.

Michael Carson

Another question concerned what evidence the state planned to present against Jason. Lax knew that Lisa Sakevicius, the crime lab analyst, would testify, as she had at Jessie's trial, that fibers found with the victims bodies were "microscopically similar" to fibers from a shirt found in Damien's house and from a bathrobe found at Jason's. But Lax anticipated that the fibers would be easy to discount. They were too common, for one thing. For another, Lax found it a stretch to think that the only evidence Jason had left behind at the crime scene was a fiber from a garment that did not even belong to him. Lax figured that even the prosecutors probably realized that this argument for secondary transfer of fibers was a skimpy one, at best.

As evidence, the knife from the lake didn't look much better. Lax figured that Fogleman would tell the jury that that was the knife used on Christopher Byers, and that its location, in the lake behind the trailer where Jason lived, connected him to the crime. But again, if Jessie testified, the knife would present new problems, since it bore no resemblance to the folding knife that Jessie had described to police. To try to connect Jason to the murders with nothing more than the lake knife and a fiber from his mother's bathrobe looked to Lax like a long shot. But then, less than a month before the start of Damien and Jason's trial, in a turn of events almost as remarkable as the discovery of the knife, a new witness suddenly emerged. Like the knife, the witness would link Jason to the crime.

Sixteen-year-old Michael Roy Carson was a kid in serious trouble. He was on probation for earlier crimes when police in Jonesboro picked him up in November 1993, on suspicion of burglary. At the time, Michael seemed to have no connection to the West Memphis murders, and Val Price, the city's chief public defender—and Damien's court-appointed lawyer—was appointed to represent Michael. But in January 1994, at the start of Jessie's trial, Michael abruptly informed authorities that he did know something about the murders—and that, in fact, his information might be crucial. He said that three months after the murders, in August 1993, he'd been in the same jail where police were holding Jason and that Jason had bragged to him about the murders. The boy told police that Jason had given him "gory details" of the murders. He also said that Jason had told him he'd like to "whip Misskelley's ass" for divulging the trio's involvement.

Everything about this newly arrived witness struck the defense lawyers as suspicious. They found it hard to believe that Jason, who had steadfastly maintained his innocence, would confide the "gory details" to Michael, whom he'd known for less than twenty-four hours. Michael had a long record of drug abuse, in addition to his burglary charges, and the defense teams noted that he had not reported Jason's extraordinary boast until five months after it had allegedly occurred—five months during which Michael's own troubles with the law had deepened.

Another new name on Fogleman's list was that of a Dr. D. W. Griffis. Apparently Griffis was going to appear as the prosecutors' expert on cult-related murders. It seemed that in preparing for his appearance, Griffis had asked the West Memphis police to describe the evidence of cult involvement they'd found with the bodies. Fogleman provided the defense attorneys with a copy of Detective Ridge's responses, but they showed that Ridge had had little to offer Griffis beyond the wild statements of Aaron Hutcheson.[248]

It had become clear in Jessie's trial that the police had found almost no blood at what they regarded as the murder site. Lax noted that in his letter to Griffis: "Ridge stated the victim who was cut in the area of his penis was known to have died from bleeding to death; however, they had found no blood at the crime scene. He attempted to explain this by stating the cutting could have been done in the water, or if it was done on the bank, it was cleaned off with water before the murderers left the area. He also stated he had testified in court about the absence of blood and that the friend of the victims [Aaron] reported that a bucket was used to catch the blood."

Writings

More than speculation about buckets of blood, certain writings gave Lax cause for concern. He and the defense lawyers knew that Fogleman had dozens of pages of Damien's personal writings—many that had been confiscated by Driver—and that he would use what writings he could to portray Damien as a killer. Shettles reviewed the writings for content in an effort to anticipate what Fogleman might introduce. "In my opinion," she wrote, "there is very little material in the text of these writings that is damaging. . . . The major themes noted are despair, loneliness, and thoughts of death and suicide."

But it was not only Damien's personal writings that now appeared to be aimed against him, but his reading choices as well. While Jessie's trial was under way, West Memphis police served a search warrant on the

Crittenden County Library, looking for all books that had been checked out by Damien, Jason, Jessie, or Domini. The two books that had apparently interested police had both been checked out by Damien. They were *Magic*, by Maurice Bouisson, and *Cotton Mather on Witch-craft*, by the colonial minister Cotton Mather. Lax advised the defense teams, "Along with our attack on the inept police investigation, I feel that every opportunity should be taken to show correlation between the Salem witch-hunts in the seventeenth century and the persecution of Damien Echols, Jason Baldwin, and Jessie Misskelley."[249]

CHAPTER EIGHTEEN

The Second Trial

JUST AS ICE HAD GRIPPED NORTHEAST Arkansas at the start of Jessie's trial, another unusual blast of cold heralded the start of Damien and Jason's. Television crews encircled the Craighead County Courthouse, a building that reminded a reporter from Little Rock of "a Reconstruction mausoleum, smack in Jonesboro's busy business district." Inside, in Judge Burnett's courtroom, prosecutors Davis and Fogleman and the defendants' four attorneys were still questioning prospective jurors. The courtroom crawled with armed policemen, the Little Rock reporter noted: "three state troopers, five sheriff's deputies on a normal day—surveilling us spectators as if seventy-five percent were convinced of an imminent attempt at a lynch."[250]

Outside the courthouse, Jessie's lawyer stood talking to reporters on the building's icy steps. "Mr. Misskelley made a decision last night that he is not going to testify against his codefendants," Stidham announced.[251] Reporters hollered questions. Had Jessie been offered a reduced sentence if he testified—one that would give him an opportunity for parole, as Damien's lawyers claimed? Or had no such deal been offered, as Fogleman contended? Stidham declined to answer but did say, tellingly, that the decision Jessie had reached the night before had been "the most difficult decision he will ever make." Stidham said that as he spoke, Jessie was being driven back to the prison at Pine Bluff.[252]

Years later, in an interview in the prison, Jessie described the pressures he'd been under.[253] He said that when he was brought back to northeast Arkansas after his own conviction, he was told that if he did not testify against Damien and Jason, they would not be convicted, and that while he rotted in prison, they'd go after his girlfriend. "They told

me that if I didn't testify, Damien and Jason would walk free," he recalled, "and they was going to go see Susie; they was going to get to her.
That's when they told me: talk or Damien and Jason was going to walk
free and I was going to be locked up." Jessie credited his father and
stepmother with helping him to understand his situation. They told
him that if he lied at Damien and Jason's trial, "That's something I'd
have to live with the rest of my life." That, he said, was when he decided
not to testify. "This way, if I ever do get out," he explained, "my name
will be clear, and I can live pretty much a decent life."[254]

Secret Voir Dire[255]

Inside the courthouse, the process of seating a jury was not proceeding
quickly. When Burnett asked if anyone on the jury panel had not heard
about the case, not a hand was raised. By the second day, several
prospective jurors had already been dismissed because they'd admitted
they could not hear the case impartially.[256] On the first day, only one juror, a Jonesboro housewife, had been seated.

The *Jonesboro Sun* reported that the demeanor of the defendants in
this second trial was as different as "night and day" from that of Jessie at
his. Whereas Jessie had appeared meek, the paper noted, Damien was
"furtively staring at the ceiling one moment, the next guffawing" at
comments by the judge. The article noted that the defendant "tosses his
long black locks around in search of the next prospective juror approaching the jury box," "often looks at those in the press box out of the
corner of his eye," and "holds his head high, almost proudly, as he walks
by the media." The Little Rock reporter, meanwhile, was focusing on
Judge Burnett, who, he wrote, struck "an occasional John Barrymore
profile" for the cameras recording the event.

By the third day, as Damien and Jason were led into court, wearing
the standard bulletproof vests, nine jurors had been selected. As
Damien passed, a reporter shouted, "Who did it?" Damien answered, "Byers." Though questions were shouted at Jason too, the
younger boy did not respond. Inside, Burnett told a reporter that it
was proving "almost impossible" to find citizens who could say they
were impartial.[257] Then, noting that some prospective jurors had said

that they were afraid, Burnett introduced another unusual element into the already remarkable proceedings. He told reporters that as jurors were selected, their names would be made public, but he asked that they not be published. "Because of the magnitude of this case," he said, "some are fearful that it could affect their business. One or two have asked to remain anonymous." Partly because of the prospective jurors' concerns, Burnett explained that he was taking the further unusual step of having prospective jurors questioned privately in his chambers, rather than in open court.

The move represented yet another layer of secrecy imposed upon the proceedings, and as it had in the past, the *Commercial Appeal* protested. Lawyers for the Tennessee newspaper cited Arkansas law, which, they argued, provided for all trial and hearings to be held in public.[258] But the prosecutors, as well as Jason's attorney Paul Ford, argued for keeping the process secret. "The potential jurors are not the people on trial," Ford said during a hearing on the request. "We're far more likely to get a fair jury, which is what we're after, in private." The judge agreed.[259] The *Commercial Appeal* appealed the issue to the Arkansas Supreme Court, which scheduled an emergency session for the following Monday morning. But by then, a jury of eight women and four men had been impaneled. The jury included a nurse, three housewives, a building contractor, two factory workers, an air force airman, a bookkeeper, a speech pathologist, a state highway department worker, and a self-employed businessman.

Now that Jessie had been convicted, the *Commercial Appeal* also filed a freedom of information request, seeking access to the investigative file police had compiled on him. Arkansas's freedom of information law required release of police investigative files when a case was closed, a point that is clearly marked when a defendant is sentenced. But Burnett denied that request too. He said that the files of all three defendants were combined and that "the right of a fair trial supersedes the right for the press to have access."

Days later, the Arkansas Supreme Court finally ruled that Burnett's questioning of prospective jurors in private had been in error.[260] But coming when it did, the decision had no impact on the trial that was already under way in Jonesboro. The improperly impaneled jury remained seated and the trial continued.

"Negative Evidence"

At 5 A.M. on the Sunday morning before testimony was to begin, a reporter driving by the courthouse noticed a crude sign stuck into the courthouse lawn. It featured a picture of the Grim Reaper, below which someone had written, HE WANTS YOU DAMIEN. The reporter notified police, but the sign's maker was never found.[261] Later that morning, subscribers to the *Commercial Appeal* found several articles about the case in their Sunday papers. One, datelined Marion, Arkansas, began: "The legend of Damien Echols blows through the trailer parks and flatlands around this Delta town like a brisk winter wind, chilling listeners with tales of vampires, Satanism and ritual murder."[262]

The next morning, Damien and Jason's trial opened much as Jessie's had, with Fogleman describing the crime scene to the jury. Pointing to a map of Robin Hood, he described an area along one bank that appeared to have been "slicked off." He said police found "lots of scuff marks, unnatural marks," in the spot. But, he added, "There's no blood. No blood at all.

"Now as the proof develops," Fogleman told the jurors, "I want to tell you in advance, there's going to be some—there's going to be a lot of testimony from the Arkansas Crime Laboratory. And some of this evidence is going to be what we call—I guess you call it 'negative evidence.' It doesn't really show a connection to anybody. . . . For instance, there will be proof, like on the bicycles, there aren't any fingerprints; on some things in the kids' pockets, no fingerprints. Things like that. And you may wonder why we're putting on evidence of a negative, but we'll explain that to you later."[263]

In his opening statement, Jason's lawyer Paul Ford described his client as an average student, "not a troublemaker," who "comes from a poor background." He described how, because Jason's mother worked a night shift, Jason was responsible for getting himself and his two younger brothers up, fed, and dressed in the mornings, and that they caught the bus for school. Ford said Jason was arrested for the murders only because the police had done a sloppy investigation. "As you'll see from their own testimony," he told the jurors, "they found nothing. Not even a drop of blood." He related several of the tangents that police investigated—truckers, veterans, known child abusers—but "there were no answers to their questions. There was no solid evidence pointing to anyone. And the pressure began to build. . . . The evidence will show that as late as the twentieth day of May, the police admitted they were blindfolded. They had no answers. But suddenly an arrest is made."

Ford described how police "swarmed" into Jason's life, taking clothes, shoes, schoolwork, and school records.

> They obtain samples of his hair. They obtain samples of his blood. They obtained his saliva. They take his fingerprints. They take his handwriting samples. They take footprints, and they made casts of his shoes for shoe prints—all looking for something to link him to this crime. And they begin to take all this evidence and send it out to the experts. Sent it to Little Rock to the crime lab. Sent it to the FBI in Virginia, in Quantico, for them to assess it. Sent it to experts in Alabama for their opinion. And you'll see, there was no substantiating evidence to link him to the crime. But before that ever occurs, and before that is made public, Inspector Gitchell goes in front of that same press who had once been the source of pressure and said that, on a scale of one to ten, the proof against this young boy is an eleven. And from that point forward, nobody believed him no matter what he said.

Damien's lawyer also zeroed in on "police ineptitude" in his opening remarks. Val Price echoed the claim Stidham had earlier made, that detectives had developed "Damien Echols's tunnel vision." But in addition, Price attempted some damage control regarding Damien's well-publicized image. Gesturing toward Damien, the lawyer said, "Well, I'll be honest with you. He's not the all-American boy. He's kind of weird. He's not the same as maybe you and I might be. That'll be negative. But I think you'll also see that there's simply no evidence that he murdered these three kids."

Motion for Mistrial

The state began calling its witnesses. Again, as in Jessie's trial, Dana Moore and Pam Hobbs described the last times they saw their sons, and Melissa Byers went into detail about how, shortly before Christopher disappeared, her husband had found him riding his skateboard on a busy street. "He brought Christopher home and gave him three swats with a belt," Melissa said, "because he could have been run over by a car."

But now reporters who'd covered Jessie's trial noticed something different. Ron Lax and the defense lawyers noted the change too. In one of the prosecutors' opening moves, they called a witness who testified that on the evening of May 5, he had seen not three, but "four kids" enter Robin Hood woods.[264] Lax and the defense teams understood what was going on. One of the few consistencies that had run through Jessie's many statements was that he, Damien, and Jason had seen *three* boys in the woods. And that was the account the prosecutors had presented at Jessie's trial. But here—since Jessie would not be testifying, and all the evidence was circumstantial, and there was no apparent motive or eyewitness to the crime—the prosecutors seemed to be altering their version of what had happened. It looked like they were laying groundwork for testimony from Aaron Hutcheson.[265]

As in the first trial, Detective Allen recounted how he had almost literally stumbled upon the first body, and then how he had recovered the others. Allen cited the absence of blood on the ground, but testified that the water around where Christopher's body was found "had a lot of blood in it." This struck Lax as preposterous. None of the police reports had noted "a lot of blood" in the water, and one would have thought that Detective Ridge might not have had to search the ditch on his hands and knees if the water around the bodies had been so noticeably bloody. Once again, pictures of the victims, naked, pale, and bound, were shown to the jury, as Ridge described how the boys were tied and what he'd seen of Christopher's mutilation.

On the second day of testimony, Jason's attorney asked Ridge to describe how police had handled the evidence found with the bodies. Ridge explained that since the clothing and shoes were wet, they'd "had to be dried before they could be sent to the crime lab." He said the articles were placed in used paper grocery sacks and taken to the police station. There, he said, the articles were removed from the sacks and "air-dried" overnight on the floor of Inspector Gitchell's office. Ridge said they were "resacked" and delivered to the crime lab in Little Rock the next day.

When Damien's attorney cross-examined Ridge, he asked about two sticks that were marked as evidence but that police had not taken from the crime scene until nearly two months after the murders. Handing Ridge one of the sticks, Price asked, "You did not take that stick into evidence at the time that y'all recovered the bodies?"

"No sir," Ridge replied. "I didn't take this stick into evidence until the statement of Jessie Misskelley, in which he said—"

Price swirled toward the judge, interrupting the detective to object. He demanded, "I move for a mistrial, Your Honor."

In a conference before the bench, which the jury could not hear, Price complained that the question he'd asked the officer "did not call for him blurting out the fact that Jessie Misskelley gave a confession." He said the judge should declare a mistrial because "the whole purpose for our trial being severed from Mr. Misskelley's trial in the first place was the confession that Jessie Misskelley gave. That's the entire reason for the severance."

The discussion at the bench was brief. "He shouldn't have volunteered that," Judge Burnett acknowledged. "But," he added, "I certainly don't see any basis for a mistrial." Price's motion was denied.

Then Jason's lawyer moved for a mistrial. But Burnett was adamant. He noted, "There isn't a soul up on that jury or in this courtroom that doesn't know Mr. Misskelley gave a statement." He said he would caution the jury to disregard Ridge's statement, and ruled that the trial would continue.

"Cult Activity"

Back in front of the jury, Damien's lawyer resumed his questioning of Ridge. Price asked the detective about the blood scrapings that Ridge and Sergeant Allen had taken from the wall of the Bojangles rest room after the boys' bodies were found. "What is the date that you sent the blood scrapings off to the crime lab to be analyzed?" Price asked.

Ridge answered, "They were never sent."

"They were never sent?"

"That's correct."

"Where are the blood samples at this time?"

"I don't know, sir. They are lost."

"They're lost?

"Yes sir."

Price then attempted to ask Ridge about his note, written a few days after the murders, about an area resident who'd told police that "some black men" had been seen in the woods. Beneath Ridge's note on the call, Gitchell had added his own comment that "it has been mentioned that during cult activities, some members blacken their faces." Price mentioned the report to Ridge so that jurors would realize how early in their investigation Gitchell and his detectives had begun looking upon the murders as possibly "cult related." But Fogleman interrupted and the lawyers approached the bench. Fogleman said he wanted to know where Price was heading with the question. When Price explained, Fogleman said he wouldn't object to the question, because "that would open the door" for prosecutors to ask Ridge "about whatever evidence he has that there was cult activity involved."

Now it was Jason's lawyer's turn to object. He pointed out that, months ago, he had filed a motion asking that no one on any side be allowed to mention "cult activity," and a special hearing had been held before Judge Burnett. Paul Ford wanted anyone attempting to assert that cult activity had been involved to have to demonstrate beforehand that some "factual basis" existed for the allegation.

Damien's lawyer's trial strategy was different. Price told Burnett that he wanted to be free to use the term in order to show that the police had focused on the possibility of cult activity to the exclusion of other, more reasonable ones during their investigation.[266] The disagreement between the two defense teams highlighted the differences that had dogged them from the start, and that had prompted their repeated requests that Damien's and Jason's trials be severed. Price wanted to attack the detectives' focus on cults and satanism, which he believed had drawn unwarranted attention to Damien. Ford, believing that Jason could not be connected to anything relating to cults or satanism—and that Jason would be harmed if the subjects were introduced—did not want the words even mentioned.

The question was what position the prosecutors were going to take. Burnett asked Fogleman, "Are you going to bring up cult activity as a possible motive? Do you plan to develop that in this case?"

"We have not made that decision," Fogleman replied. "It depends on how the case develops."

Noting that the law did not require the prosecutors to prove motive, Burnett reflected that whether or not the murders had been cult-related did not "really have a whole lot to do with anything here, unless that was a possible motive." He asked Fogleman, "Do you want to prove motive?"

Without directly answering the judge's question, Fogleman responded, "If Mr. Price and Mr. Davidson will stipulate that Damien Echols was involved in satanism and devil worship, then we don't have any objection to them going into that." Price and Davidson declined.

Burnett then issued a highly significant ruling. He told the lawyers for all sides that he would allow Price to question police about their interest in cult activity—but only if the prosecutors decided that they were going to introduce cult activity as a motive. Burnett told Ford that if the prosecutors did introduce cult activity as a motive, and Damien's lawyers attempted to combat it, he would issue "a very strong cautionary instruction to the jury that that evidence should be taken to Echols only, and not to Mr. Baldwin."

"Is the court aware," Damien's lawyer persisted, that "we have a thousand pages of discovery from the state alleging a cult-related killing?"

Judge Burnett only replied, " That doesn't mean they have to prove motive."

Change of Procedure

The question of whether or not Fogleman and Davis would raise the occult or satanism as a motive for the crime remained unsettled as the proceedings resumed in open court. Detective Ridge was questioned further, without the word "cult" being mentioned. Then Dr. Frank Peretti, of the medical examiner's office, took the stand. Prosecutor Davis's questioning was brief. Handing Peretti the knife that was discovered in the lake on Fogleman's hunch, Davis asked Peretti if Christopher's wounds were "consistent with the serrated portion of that knife." Peretti answered that some of them were. That was all. The prosecutor sat down.

On cross-examination, Jason's attorney got Peretti to admit that most serrated knives—not just this one in particular—could have caused the injuries. Then Damien's lawyer got up and handed Dr. Peretti what he called "the John Mark Byers knife." He asked if Christopher's injuries were consistent "with wounds being inflicted by this type of knife." Peretti again said yes, and that "some of the smaller serrated wounds" were consistent with the serrations on that knife.

Davis turned the questioning to certain injuries on Michael Moore. He asked about bruises that Peretti said he'd found on the boy's ears and about abrasions inside his mouth. Peretti said the injuries were of a type "we generally see in children who are forced to perform oral sex." Davis asked if there could have been other causes. "Well," Peretti said, "you can get them by—the lip injuries—by putting an object inside the mouth. You can get those type of injuries also from a punch or a slap. Or you can get those type of injuries from the hand over the mouth and pressing the hands very tightly up against the mouth." Peretti also said that Michael had "defense type wounds" on his hands indicating that he had fought his attacker. He testified that the boy had suffered "multiple fractures" to his skull, causing bruising of "the entire brain." In addition, he said, the boy's lungs were filled with water, indicating that, "when he was in the water, he was breathing."

When questioned about Stevie Branch, Peretti noted that "multiple, irregular, and gouging type cutting wounds" were evident on his face. When Davis asked for possible causes, Peretti said "an object such as a knife or glass or any sharp object" could have made the marks, if the object were twisted or the child had been moving. "What is important to note," Peretti elaborated, "is that on the forehead region, we have an abrasion or scrape that left a pattern. And inside the pattern, you can see, it's almost like a dome shape. And that injury, you see, it's typical of a belt injury. The belt has a little buckle. . . . That type of injury we typically see with belts." Peretti said that Stevie Branch's body showed injuries to the ears and mouth similar to Michael Moore's. He said that like Michael, Stevie had fluid in his lungs, and had also suffered a massive blow to the back of his head. "The base of the skull, the back of the skull, showed a three-and-one-half-inch fracture, which had multiple extension fractures." He added graphically: "If you have ever dropped an egg, and you see how you have fractures of the egg; that is basically what happened."

Davis asked Peretti to "generally describe" Christopher's wounds. "Well," the doctor replied, "Christopher also had head injuries, as well as neck injuries, genital-anal injuries, right leg injuries, left leg injuries, back injuries, right arm injuries, and left arm injuries."[267] The doctor said that Christopher had "a contusion or black eye" and that other facial wounds had "the appearance of, like, the stud on a buckle." Peretti described the wounds to Christopher's genital area as "antemortem," meaning that they had been inflicted while the boy was still alive.

Pointing to a photograph, he continued. "Here we can see that the skin of the penis has been literally removed or carved off," Peretti said. "And what we have here is the shaft of the penis without the skin on it. And all around it we have all these cutting, gouging wounds. The scrotal sac and testes are missing."

Christopher's skull was fractured, as were the other boys', but there was an additional fracture on his skull, not found on the other two: a round, quarter-inch hole had been literally "punched out" of his skull, just above where it joined the spine, where, Peretti said, something had been literally "punched into the brain." It was a dramatic statement, and one that bore no relation to anything Jessie had said. But no explanation was sought—or offered—for the remarkable injury.

As the questioning continued, Peretti also reported that he had not found any mosquito bites on the three children. That absence had troubled Lax and the rest of the defense teams from the beginning, because of the numerous reports about how thick the mosquitoes had been in the woods on the night the boys disappeared and the association of mosquitoes with blood. But having asked the question, Davis quickly moved on. "Now, Doctor," he said, "I have noted in your autopsy report that there's no mention as to time of death. Did you deal with that issue, or did you mention that in your autopsy report?"

"No, I didn't," Peretti answered.

Estimating the time of death is an important part of a medical examiner's work, and Peretti offered a only weak explanation for his failure to report one. "Determining the time of death is more of an art, not a science," he said. "Realistically, it is not possible, unless you were there and you witnessed the person who died." He said the best anyone could provide would be an estimate, but in this case, not even that had been possible.

"Now, Doctor," Prosecutor Davis said, "you said that part of your job is to prepare an autopsy report. In this particular case, were you particularly cautious about who you released that information to and when you released it?"

"Yes, I was."

"Normally, where do your reports go to, as far as who gets a copy of it?"

"What we do in the crime lab," Peretti explained, "is, the day we do the autopsy, we issue a sheet. It is called a 'Cause of Death' sheet. This sheet automatically goes to the prosecutor of the county of death, the coroner, and the investigative agencies handling the death investigation."

Davis asked, "Did you kind of change that procedure a little bit in this case, in order to insure that the information obtained in your autopsy report wasn't disseminated in the general public?"

"Well, what I did was—normally what we do . . . for example, if I do someone who died of a heart attack, I would write on it 'heart attack, coronary artery disease.' But because this case generated such intense media coverage, and there was rumors—a lot of rumors—people calling for all of these circumstances, I elected on the Cause of Death sheet just to put the causes of death on the sheet. I did not say anything about any of the injuries. I didn't tell the prosecutor. I didn't tell the police. And I didn't tell the coroner. I just kept it to myself."

Lax, who sat listening to the testimony, was astonished. A standard element of crime lab reporting—information that was usually "automatically" sent out—Peretti had "just kept" to himself. Lax wondered how many deviations from normal procedure could arise in a single case.

Newspapers the next day reported that Damien had spoken briefly with reporters during a break in the proceedings, before his attorneys "led him" away. The exchange was long enough, however, that Damien had managed to describe the charges against him as "bullshit" and to observe that he was finding the trial "pretty boring, most of the time."

"Very Difficult"

When court resumed, Jason's lawyers cross-examined Peretti. Jessie's confession was not to be mentioned at this trial, but since the arrests and the state's theory of the crime were based on that critical but unmentioned confession, Ford wanted to explore a few of its central features. "Was there any evidence of strangulation?" he asked Peretti. "There was no evidence of strangulation," the doctor responded.

Ford next examined the claim that the boys had been sodomized. Peretti answered that he had found no evidence that any of the boys had been raped. Had the boys been tied with rope? "No," Peretti said, he'd found no evidence of that. As for the wounds to the boys' heads, the doctor acknowledged that "hundreds of items" could have been used to inflict the injuries, not just the sticks police had retrieved from the site. As the cross-examination continued, Peretti also acknowledged that "any serrated knife" could have caused Christopher's wounds.

When Ford asked if it would have taken "some skill and precision" to perform Christopher's castration, Peretti replied, "I would think so."

Ford then asked Peretti how long it would take a doctor such as himself, with all "the skill and the precision and knowledge" that he had, to do what had been done to the boy.

"That's a difficult question," Peretti replied. "It would take me some time. It's not something I think I could do in five or ten minutes."

"It would take you longer than five or ten minutes?" Ford asked.

"I would think so."

"And that is in your lab?"

"I would think so."

"With a scalpel, is that correct?"

"That's correct."

"Now, Doctor," the defense lawyer persisted, "if we added to the equation that you were in the dark, could you do this in the dark? You, Doctor. Could you do it in the dark?"

"It would be difficult."

"Could you do this in the water? You, Doctor. Could you do this in the water?"

"It would be very difficult to do."

"And if you were in the water and it was dark, it would take even longer, is that correct?"

"That's correct."

"And if you were doing it in the dark, in the water, with mosquitos all around you, would that make it even much more difficult?"

"I would think so." In fact, Peretti added, he doubted that he could have performed such a procedure under those circumstances.

As the questioning continued, Dr. Peretti testified that Christopher had bled to death from his injuries; that the blood was gone from his body, his internal organs were pale. Asked if he thought that Damien and Jason, in the dark, could have cleaned up the amount of blood Christopher had lost, Peretti said: "I think it would be quite difficult. It's not easy to clean up blood. It would soak into the ground."

"Doctor," Ford said, "with this homicide we are talking about here today, would you agree with me that this could have happened in one of three ways? These injuries could have happened in the water. These injuries could have happened there on the bank, there by the side of the ditch. Or, they could have happened somewhere else. Would you agree with me, those are the three possibilities of how this could have happened?" Peretti agreed.

"Okay. Now, would you also agree with me that, based upon what you saw that was done to these boys, that it would be highly improbable for it to happen in the water?"

Once more Peretti agreed. It would have been "very difficult," he admitted.

Time of Death

Now Ford returned to the elusive matter of the time of death. At Jessie's trial, Dr. Peretti had stated that he could not give an opinion as to the time of death. But now, with Damien and Jason on trial and their lawyers pressing hard for an estimate, Peretti shocked everyone in court.

"Okay," he said. "Based on what I know, it would be a very broad range: between 1 A.M. and, you know, five or seven in the morning." In contrast to the vague statement he'd given earlier, Peretti was suddenly more specific. He said that in arriving at the estimate, he had taken into account factors such as the temperature of the air, the temperature of the water, the time the boys disappeared, the time their bodies were found, and the causes of their deaths. Jason's lawyer asked him if he had consulted any of the other medical examiners regarding his conclusion. Peretti said he had discussed it with two other doctors.

"Do they concur in your opinion?" Ford asked.

"They were in agreement," Peretti answered.

The surprise testimony flew in the face of the state's theory of the crime. It contradicted everything Jessie had said in his confession—the confession that had led to the arrests and then to Jessie's conviction. It meant that the little boys may have been alive during the nighttime search of the woods—alive somewhere else. It called into question everything the police had surmised: about the lack of blood at the scene, where the boys were killed, and who might have been with them between midnight and dawn.

Many of the questions Peretti's estimate raised could not now be answered. But as Lax reflected, one thing about it was obvious: Peretti's latest testimony represented one more piece of late-coming evidence; one more element an official had withheld; one more contradiction of the police scenario—one more ambiguity in a case already riddled with them.

When Jessie's lawyer heard that Peretti had now testified as to the time of death, he was stunned. Stidham's mind raced with thoughts of how he could have used that information, had he had it at Jessie's trial. The defense lawyer noted that twice during Jessie's trial, he had asked

Peretti if he could determine the approximate time of the victims' deaths, and that each time Peretti had told the court that he could not. But now, with Jessie's codefendants on trial, Peretti was offering an estimate—and the estimate did not fit with anything in Jessie's confession. Arguing that Jessie had been denied a fair trial because the jurors were not told of the discrepancy, Stidham filed a motion with Judge Burnett, asking him to overturn Jessie's conviction and grant the boy a new trial.

Damien's and Jason's lawyers regarded Peretti's admission as a minor coup. On top of the admissions of foul-ups by the police and Peretti's admission that he had treated this case differently than most, here now was the state's own medical examiner saying the murders appeared to have been committed at least four hours later than would have been possible according to the state's own scenario.

Fogleman was livid. Peretti's testimony had come as an unexpected and unpleasant surprise. "I will say this," Fogleman later fumed. "If you rely on Dr. Peretti for a time of death opinion, it's a mistake. Dr. Peretti is another book."[268] Fogleman said that he and Davis learned that Peretti planned to testify as to the time of death shortly before he returned to the stand. The two prosecutors and Peretti had been standing outside the courtroom, Fogleman said, when Peretti volunteered that he was "going to have to express an opinion." Fogleman said he and Davis were astonished. "We said, 'Why? You told us you didn't have enough information.' " Fogleman said Peretti never answered his question, but that over time the prosecutors surmised what had happened. According to Fogleman, Jason's lawyers had discussed the case with Peretti sometime before the trial, and they'd tape-recorded the session. "I'm not sure whether Dr. Peretti knew that," Fogleman later said,

but that's neither here nor there, because they had the right to tape-record him anyway, whether he knew it or not. But I suspect—now, again, this is suspicion—that, just in talking and playing to Dr. Peretti's ego, you know, they said something like, "Surely you have some idea about the time of death," and he did, and they had him on tape giving an opinion, and he was going to be faced on the witness stand with them saying, "Well, you gave us an opinion before.

Why can't you give us one now?" That's my suspicion of what happened. I do know they taped him. They told me they had him on tape. And I know Dr. Peretti made a sudden shift in giving an opinion.

As the questioning of Peretti continued, Davis attempted to minimize the damage. He dropped the matter of time of death and asked Peretti about the effect that water might have had on the evidence. Yes, Peretti answered, water could have washed away sperm from the boys' anuses, if they had been raped. And, yes, it was possible that not every rape of a child leaves lacerations on the victim. The beleaguered pathologist was then allowed to leave the stand.

"Getting to Be Absurd"

Next, the state called sixteen-year-old Michael Carson, the young burglar who'd recently come forward with a damning story about an encounter he said he'd had months earlier with Jason in jail. Michael's testimony would prove critical. It, along with the knife removed from the lake and the fiber found with the bodies that was said to be "microscopically similar" to fibers in a woman's bathrobe in Jason's house, would constitute the entirety of the state's case against him.

"He told me how he dismembered the kids," Michael told Prosecutor Davis. "He sucked the blood from the penis and scrotum and put the balls in his mouth."

Spectators in the courtroom gasped. Davis pressed on. Noting that Michael did not report what Jason had said until almost six months later, the prosecutor asked, "What caused you to come forward at that point in time?"

"Because I saw the family on TV," Michael said, "and saw how brokenhearted they were about their children being missing. And I have got a soft heart. I couldn't take it."

Next, the prosecutor questioned Detective Sergeant Allen about the knife that was removed from the lake behind Jason's house. When the prosecutor produced a map of the trailer park, Allen showed the jury where Jason lived, then pointed to a spot in the lake, a short distance away, where he said divers had found the knife. On cross-examination, defense lawyers attacked the tenuousness of the links, not only between the knife and Jason, but between the knife and the crime. Jason's lawyer asked Allen, "Are you telling this jury that this knife is the murder weapon? Is that what you're telling this jury?"

"No sir." Allen replied. "I am not telling the jury that."

When Detective Ridge returned to the stand, he acknowledged that contrary to what Gitchell had told reporters, the suggestion to search the lake had been Fogleman's. Damien's lawyer picked up the folding knife that John Mark Byers had given to the filmmakers—the one weapon that could be directly linked at least to the family of one of the victims. But when Price tried to question Ridge about his interview with Byers after blood was found in the knife's fold, the prosecutors objected. They did not want the jury to hear that within the past six weeks, the police had formally read Byers his rights and questioned him about the murders—a revelation that might make him look like a suspect. Burnett immediately dismissed the jury and held another *in camera* hearing with the lawyers.

Both sides questioned Gitchell in the hearing. He maintained under oath that he and Ridge did not consider Byers a suspect. He said that they had questioned him about the bloodstained folding knife only because Stidham had insisted. Asked why, if Byers was not a suspect, they'd read him his rights before the interrogation began, Gitchell said that he was just trying to be cautious. It was the kind of catch-22 that the defense attorneys felt they'd been dealing with since the case began. And the absurdity did not stop there. When Damien's lawyer asked Gitchell if, during their questioning of Byers, the detectives had been "trying to determine whether or not Mark Byers was involved in this homicide," Gitchell responded, "Yes sir." But when Price then asked, "So, at that time, you still had a question as to whether or not there might be other parties involved in this homicide than the three people charged?" Gitchell replied, "No sir."

Judge Burnett said he couldn't see the defense lawyer's point. Price said he wanted to introduce evidence collected by the West Memphis police showing that Byers had been a suspect and that there had been others as well, but Burnett would not allow it. Besides Byers, Price argued, there was young Christopher Morgan, the Memphis teenager who'd told police in California that he had committed the murders. Morgan had quickly retracted the statement, but then, so had Jessie Misskelley. Price wanted to question Morgan as a way of suggesting to jurors that the police case had been far from certain.

But Burnett asked why Morgan's testimony would be relevant. Price was incredulous. "A man who confessed to these murders? A man who knew all three of the victims? A man who left West Memphis within a week after the murders? I think it is definitely relevant, the fact that he went out to California and confessed." Moreover, the defense teams argued, they wanted to question other witnesses whom the police had viewed as suspects. But Burnett had heard enough.

"Gentlemen," he said, "this is getting to be absurd. I mean, I'm not going to let you drag in every possible suspect in this case, unless you've got something to tie those persons to some event in this case."

The defense lawyers argued that a suspect's confession, even if retracted, ought to suffice as a tie-in. But Burnett ruled that testimony about other suspects would not be allowed. He told the defense attorneys that he was not going to let them "confuse the issue" with "things that aren't relevant."

CHAPTER NINETEEN

The Motive

THE TRIAL WAS ENTERING ITS THIRD WEEK. Prosecutors Davis and Fogleman had welcomed the judge's decision to bar evidence about other suspects. Still, their case was thin. In Jessie's trial, they'd had a confession. Here they did not. Unable to call Jessie and unwilling to call young Aaron Hutcheson, the prosecutors had no eyewitness to the crime. And for physical evidence all they had were a few ordinary sticks from the woods, a couple of "similar" fibers, and the knife that was taken from the lake—nothing that directly linked the defendants to the murders. To some observers, their case was looking tenuous. Then, abruptly, Fogleman announced a motive. PROSECUTION SAYS KILLINGS CULT RELATED, the *Jonesboro Sun* proclaimed.

The prosecutors had not suggested a motive in their opening statement to the jury. But now, the paper reported that Fogleman was expected to call "an expert in cult-related crimes" to testify. The decision triggered another *in camera* hearing, as Jason's lawyer Paul Ford tried to block the approach. With the jury out of the room, Detective Ridge testified that he had believed from the start that the boys' murders were linked to the occult. "The fact that there was overkill, more injuries to the boys' bodies than what was needed to kill them," he said, had led him to suspect a cult-related crime. The boys' ages—eight, which Ridge said was a number used by witches in the Wicca religion—and his observation that "in cult-related killings, the victims will be males," had supported his suspicion. Aaron Hutcheson's statements had reinforced his belief. "Plus," he said, "there was damage to the left side of one of the boys' faces, which is a sign of the occult." Ridge testified that when he'd questioned Damien, the teenager's responses had further heightened his suspicions.

Burnett asked Ford and Fogleman, "Can either one of you define 'occult' for me?"

"Well," Ford said, "we can get Webster's dictionary, Your Honor."

"I don't know what an occult is," Burnett grumbled. "It sounds like something bad, but I'm not sure what it is."

Price asked, "Is the state now stating that the motive is occult killing?"

"We have not made a final, firm decision," Fogleman replied, "but at this point, I would say yes."

Burnett asked Fogleman if he expected to link Jason "to occult activities."

"Your Honor," Fogleman said, "that is something that will have to be talked about with the expert. It is my understanding that part of the involvement deals with obsession with heavy metal music, change in forms of dress, wearing all black. And I believe the proof would show that he had fifteen black T-shirts with the heavy metal thing. And he had some kind of animal, either claws or teeth—I think they said they were claws—in his possession."

Jason's other lawyer, Robin Wadley, shook his head in disbelief. "Judge, if it's the state's position that owning black T-shirts with rock bands on them meets the court's burden . . . is that fact alone enough?"

But Fogleman said there was more. "We have the testimony that Michael Carson gave related to the sucking of blood from the penis," he said, "and I think the evidence would show that drinking of blood is something that these people believe gives them power."

Jason's lawyers were disappointed but not surprised when Burnett sided with Fogleman, ruling that he would allow questions about the occult. But in light of that decision, they again beseeched Burnett to separate Jason's trial from Damien's, as they anticipated that there would be extensive testimony about Damien's acknowledged interest in the occult, but that there would be none for Jason. Again, Burnett refused to sever the trials. He said he would warn the jury "that this testimony—I hate to dignify it by calling it occult testimony—but testimony relative to Wicca religion" could be considered only against Damien.

"Save Yourself"

Ford's requests that Jason be tried separately from Damien had been widely reported. But what the public never knew—and what, in fact, almost no one in the courtroom, including the jurors, knew—was that while the prosecutors were trying to win sentences of death for the accused child killers, they themselves had secretly offered Jason a separate deal. They had offered not once, but twice. As Jason later recalled, the offers were relayed to him by his attorneys, Ford and Wadley, and were similar to the deal that the prosecutors had offered Jessie. Instead of asking the jury to sentence Jason to death, they would seek a sentence of forty years—a term that would allow for his eventual parole—if he would plead guilty and testify against Damien. If Jason accepted the deal and exhibited good behavior in prison, he could expect to be out in ten to fifteen years.[269]

In some respects Jason presented the biggest threat to the prosecutors' case. They had little evidence against him, and Fogleman and Davis worried that if the jury harbored doubts about Jason, his status as a codefendant might lead them to question Damien's involvement, as well. On the other hand, if Jason were to testify against Damien, one of their biggest liabilities would be transformed to their advantage. Jason's lawyer Paul Ford recalled that the first approach to Jason was made before the trial began. It presented a tremendous challenge to a boy whose seventeenth birthday was still a month away. But his response was swift and sure.

"They said, 'Just say something. Save yourself,' " Jason recalled. "Ford was encouraging me to do it. But I was, like, 'Nah. This isn't right.' I made the decision on my own, right then and there. It was a flat-out no. Ford said, 'Well, I still had to ask.' "

Like much about Jason's role in the trial, the drama played out quietly and was ultimately ignored. But the episode was revealing. It showed a lot about the prosecutors—and about the character of the sixteen-year-old who, in turning them down, risked being put to death.

"The Credibility of the Witnesses"

Damien did not know of the offer that had been made to Jason, or of Jason's refusal to "lie," as Jason put it, about his friend. What Damien did know was that he risked hearing his own words used against him. Damien's lawyer was trying to prevent that.

The prosecutors wanted to introduce the reports West Memphis police had written about interviews with Damien in the weeks before his arrest. Price argued that the statements had been obtained illegally. Burnett considered the disagreement in another *in camera* hearing, and here, with the jury out of the room, Damien himself was called to testify. After he was placed under oath, Price asked him if he had requested an attorney when he was questioned by police on May 10, five days after the murders. Damien said that he had asked for an attorney—not once but three times—but that Detective James Sudbury had argued against it. "He told me that I didn't need an attorney," Damien testified, "because he would end up costing me a lot of money and would quit anyway." Damien said he was questioned for eight hours that day. "At first," he said, the detectives "were pretty nice. But later they started cussing me. And they said they were going to 'fry my ass,' that I might as well go ahead and confess."

Damien's mother, Pam, testified that at about 5:45 P.M., while police were still questioning Damien, she'd called an attorney from a nearby town who happened also to be a state senator, and asked that he come to West Memphis and represent her son.[270] Later in the hearing, the senator testified that after receiving the call, he drove to the West Memphis police station, where he'd asked to see Damien, but that his request had been "refused." The state senator said that he'd repeated his request a short time later, and that this time he was told that the "building was closed" and that he "could not go upstairs" where Damien was being questioned.

Detectives Ridge and Durham swore, however, that Damien had never asked for an attorney. Davis argued that the senator's role was irrelevant anyway, because no statements from the part of the interview conducted after he'd arrived would be presented as evidence.

"It's relevant to the way they harassed this kid," Damien's lawyer responded. He argued that the jurors needed to know that Damien had been denied access to a lawyer.

But Judge Burnett was not impressed. He noted that if the police investigation itself was challenged, literally hundreds of people could be called to testify, and that that would, as he'd said before, be "absurd."

Based on the "credibility of the witnesses"—Ridge and Durham—Burnett ruled that the statements Damien made during his nearly eight-hour interrogation would be admitted at trial. The trial moved back to open court, where, in the presence of the jury, Fogleman was now allowed to ask Ridge about what Damien had told the police. Ridge related Damien's comments about the mystical significance of water, about three being "a sacred number in the Wicca religion," and about the "demonic forces" that, Ridge reported, Damien said all people have "inside them."

Then it was Price's turn to cross-examine Ridge. "When you asked him about what his favorite book of the Bible was," Price asked, "that's when he told you it was Revelations?"

Ridge agreed.

"Was that a question that you asked other suspects in this case?"

"I don't remember asking that of anybody else. No sir."

"When Mr. Echols—you asked him what type of books did he enjoy reading?"

"Yes sir."

"And he told you, I think it was Anton LaVey and Stephen King?"

"Yes sir."

"In your opinion, is there anything unusual about those being the type of books Mr. Echols likes to read?"

"Anton LaVey is a book of Satanic rules and involvement. Stephen King seems to be horror movies, horror books, and if you're asking if I felt that was strange, yes sir, I did."

To further explore how Damien was "strange," Fogleman called to the stand Deanna Holcomb, Damien's former girlfriend. "During the time y'all went together," Fogleman asked the seventeen-year-old girl, "how did Damien dress?"

"He wore all black," Deanna said.

Fogleman asked, "During the time that you went with him, did Damien carry any type of weapon?" Deanna said he carried "knives."

Fogleman showed her the knife from the lake, asking if she had ever seen one like it before. "Yes sir," Deanna replied. She said that once when she'd given Damien a hug, she'd seen a knife like it in his trench coat pocket.

The defense lawyers tried to discredit the police by showing that their investigation had been unreliable in several ways. Again, in a hearing away from the jury, they told Judge Burnett that detectives had compiled a ten-picture photo lineup, which they had shown to several people, including Aaron Hutcheson, but that the detectives had kept no records of whose photos were included. Fogleman said the issue was unimportant, since Aaron had never identified anyone from the photos. Damien's lawyer argued, "Judge, if they showed this alleged eyewitness my client's picture and he didn't pick out my client, that's exculpatory, and we are entitled to know who the ten photos are." But Burnett announced once again that "the police reports and investigation" were "not the subject of this trial." And again he sided with Fogleman.

Occult, or Cult?

Having decided to pursue the cult-activity motive, the prosecutors pulled out all the stops. Fogleman asked Burnett "to consider taking judicial notice that there was a full moon on May 5, according to an almanac." The defense objected, but Burnett said he found the request "appropriate," and took official note of the full moon on the night of the murders.

With that established, the prosecutors called Dale Griffis, a Ph.D. "cult expert" from Tiffin, Ohio. They wanted Griffis to elaborate on Ridge's contention that the killings had been cult related. But the defense teams objected to Griffis being qualified as an expert. With the jury dismissed yet again, this time for more than three hours, Burnett listened as Griffis was questioned by attorneys for both sides. How, the defense wanted to know, does one become an expert in something like the occult? Griffis answered that he had twenty-six years of law enforcement experience, a doctoral degree "from Columbia Pacific," and a consulting practice relating to satanism. Because of his expertise, Griffis said, Jerry Driver had contacted him about satanic activity in West Memphis long before the murders had even occurred. The two had spoken about a half dozen times.

Jason's lawyer asked Griffis what classes he had taken in order to obtain his Ph.D. After avoiding an answer for several rounds, Griffis finally acknowledged, "None."

Finally, Damien's lawyer had heard enough. "On behalf of my client," Price told Burnett, "it's our position that the mail-order Ph.D. in which a person doesn't have to take classes . . . from a nonaccredited school doesn't qualify as an expert in Arkansas."

"I disagree," Judge Burnett replied. "I'm going to allow him to testify in the area of the occult."

Fogleman later stated that he had not realized until the hearing that Griffis's degree was "from a correspondence school." Years after the trial, Fogleman admitted that the revelation had "probably" been his "most embarrassing moment as a lawyer."[271] But at the time, the prosecutor's embarrassment had not been so severe as to prevent him from questioning Griffis as the expert that Judge Burnett had just ruled he was.

"What is the difference in occult or cult?" Burnett asked Griffis. "What is it? Is there any?"

"Yes," Griffis answered. "An occult group is a group that is involved in some form of esoteric science, and they have been around prior to Christianity. A cult group usually is a group that I deal with—the ones who are breaking the law—are those who follow a particular belief style under a charismatic leader and in and among their belief style they do break the law."

"Does the number three—three victims—have any significance?" Burnett asked.

"One of the most powerful numbers in the practice of satanic belief is six-six-six, and some believe the base root of six is three," Griffis replied.

But when Damien's attorney asked Griffis if he would agree the number three was "also significant in Christianity, for example, and other religions," Griffis answered, "I cannot make that statement."

Price asked, "Are you familiar with the Christian belief, the Trinity, the Three in One?"

Griffis said that he was, but added that his belief that the murders were cult related had been confirmed for him by some of Damien's drawings, particularly one of "an individual that had the head of a satanic goat."

Price objected that any materials Driver had taken from Damien's home before the crime were confidential juvenile records. But Fogleman argued that the materials related to Damien's "belief system, his state of mind."

"Judge," Price argued, "we have the First Amendment in the United States. A person is entitled to believe—they can practice the freedom of religion."

"I don't have any problem with him practicing whatever belief he wants to," Burnett responded. "That doesn't mean that belief is not a part of relevant evidence in a proceeding against him."

Price countered, "If it is a writing he had a year before the murders, it is obviously not relevant."

But Prosecutor Davis returned to the theory of motive, arguing that the timing of Damien's beliefs was not relevant. He argued that a person's ideas, which might be "a motive for causing them to act," continued "over a course of time."[272]

Ultimately, Burnett ruled in favor of the prosecution: that the books, writings, and drawings taken from Damien's home a year before the murders would be admitted as evidence. "I'm also going to rule," he said, "that, inasmuch as the state has the burden of proof in this case, and inasmuch as a good portion of the case is circumstantial, that it's necessary and appropriate that the state prove motive if they can . . . [and] that the probative value of the testimony with regard to motivation outweighs any possible prejudicial effect."

Still in the hearing, Ford asked Griffis, "Do you have any evidence that establishes a link between Jason Baldwin and the occult?"

"No."

"Are all crimes of this nature occultic in nature? Are all murders where these type of injuries happen, are they all occultic?"

"No sir."

"What separates this one from those that aren't?"

"First of all, the dates, the full moon."

The defense lawyers protested that there was no scientific basis to Griffis's proposed testimony that the murders were cult related. But Judge Burnett ruled against them. The judge said he was qualifying Griffis as an expert "based upon his knowledge, experience and training in the area of occultism or satanism."

Eleven Black T-shirts

When the jury returned, Fogleman called a few witnesses in preparation for Griffis. Lisa Sakevicius, from the crime lab, testified that she'd found "a trace of blue wax" on one of the victims' shirts. Other witnesses said that they'd found a book titled *Never on a Broomstick* and the skull of a dog in Damien's home, and that eleven black T-shirts had been found in Jason's home. With that, Fogleman called Griffis, who told the court how, based on the fullness of the moon and the lack of blood at the scene, he had detected "the trappings of occultism."

"In looking at young people involved in the occult, do you see any particular type of dress or jewelry or body markings, anything like that?" the prosecutor asked.

"I have personally observed people wearing black fingernails, having their hair painted black, wearing black T-shirts, black dungarees, that type of thing," Griffis said. "Sometimes they will tattoo themselves. Then they'll use some earrings which have occult symbols on them that you can buy through mail-order houses."

Then Fogleman asked about the types of artwork he'd seen associated with "people involved in occultism." Griffis answered that what he'd seen involved "necromancy, or love of death." Artwork attributed to Damien qualified as that, he said. Similarly, he said that Damien's writings indicated involvement in the occult. And so did books in his possession. As Griffis testified, he sharpened his opinion further, stating that the crime showed trappings, not just of vague occultism, but of satanic worship in particular.[273]

The State's Final Evidence

The next day, Fogleman and Davis mounted their final attack. They called two young girls and the mother of one of the girls to testify about what they'd heard at a softball game. One of the girls, a twelve-year-old, said, "I heard Damien Echols say that he killed the three boys."[274] She said that Jason Baldwin was with Damien at the time, and that after she heard the remark, she'd reported it to her mother.

On cross-examination the girl acknowledged that she had never seen

Damien before the encounter at the ballpark. She said he was talking in a group of people, but that the confession to murder was the only part of what he'd said that she'd heard. She also acknowledged that she was at least fifteen feet away from Damien when he made the remark. Although the girl said she had told her mother about the remark, and the crime had not been solved, she acknowledged that neither she nor her mother had reported the information about Damien's alleged boast to the police until after Damien's arrest.

The other girl was a year older than the first witness and a friend of hers.[275] She testified that at the same softball game, she'd heard Damien say "that he killed the three little boys and before he turned himself in that he was going to kill two more and he already had one of them picked out." She too said that she'd never seen or heard of Damien prior to that event. She also said that she'd reported the incident to her mother, though again, neither the child nor her mother had alerted officials until after the arrests. When defense attorneys questioned the girl, she acknowledged that, although "six or seven" other people had been with Damien that evening, she would not be able to recognize any of them if they were in the courtroom.

And that marked the end of the prosecutors' evidence.

Damien's Defense

When the prosecutors sat down after calling their last witnesses, a reporter jotted impressions in his notebook of the case they'd just presented. "A pervasive vagueness . . . ," he wrote. "Just couldn't get through it or past it; simply impenetrable."[276]

Later the reporter wrote, "When the prosecution rested the state's case, about all it had proved was (1) that the murders had indeed occurred, and (2) how the victims died. It had proved the deed and the how, but not the who, the why, the where, or even the when. Its who, why, where, and when were supposition, guesswork, rumor, and bad courtroom Vaudeville. No motive, opportunity not clearly established, time of death disputed, and not a single shred of tangible evidence linking any of the defendants to the crime."

Not surprisingly, the defense lawyers also regarded the evidence as paltry, especially in a case where the prosecutors were seeking the death penalty. Arguing that "there's been a lack of evidence to place Jason Baldwin at the scene of the crime"; "there has been no eyewitness to identify him as being a perpetrator"; "there's no evidence whatsoever to tie him to the act of homicide"; and "there's been no introduction of any scientific evidence to link him to this homicide," Jason's lawyer asked Burnett to issue a directed verdict, acquitting Jason on the spot, which a judge is empowered to do when the evidence is deemed glaringly insufficient. But Burnett refused, announcing in open court, "I feel it is more than sufficient."

Damien's lawyer then made a similar motion, and Judge Burnett made a similar ruling. Jason's lawyer appealed again for a severance, noting that "there has been overwhelming evidence introduced in this case that the court has instructed the jury to apply *only* to Damien." And again, the request was denied.

While Judge Burnett ruled that he considered the state's case "more than sufficient," Damien's lawyers found little in the state's case to contest. Now that the ball was in their court, and it was time to present their defense, they felt they were battling shadows. How were they to counter allegations linking Damien to Satan and thence to murders beneath the full moon? They began with his alibi.

Damien's mother testified about her activities on the previous May 5, ending with her claim that Damien had been with the family from 4 P.M. on. But on cross-examination, Davis lacerated her testimony, forcefully suggesting that, at the very least, she was confused about her times. Michelle, however, corroborated her mother's account, as did three of the family's friends.

With that, Damien's lawyers put him on the stand.

Sound and Fury

Damien stepped into the witness box. His coal black hair was unevenly cut. When Shettles had seen him before the trial, he'd been in bad need of a haircut, and with no better barber available, she'd done the job herself. As Val Price asked Damien some preliminary questions, the nineteen-year-old answered in a voice that, oddly, sounded neither confident nor afraid. Price asked how Damien came to have his name. Damien explained that he'd changed his last name when Jack Echols adopted him and how, at the time, he'd been "very involved" in the Catholic Church. "And we was going over the names of the saints," Damien said. "Saint Michael's is where I went to church at—and we heard about this guy from the Hawaiian Islands, Father Damien, that took care of lepers until he finally caught the disease hisself and died. I was inspired by what he did."

"Did the choosing of the name Damien have anything to do with any type of horror movies, satanism, cultism, anything of that nature?" Price asked.

"Nothing whatsoever."

Price suggested, "Tell the ladies and gentlemen of the jury a little bit about the types of things you enjoy doing, your interests, hobbies, and things of that nature."

"For a few years I really enjoyed skateboarding," Damien said. "It was like all I did for a while. I like movies, about any type of books, talking on the phone, watching TV."

"Do you like to read a great deal?"

"Yes."

"What types of books do you like to read?"

"I will read about anything, but my favorites were Stephen King, Dean Koontz, and Anne Rice."

"During this time period, did you develop an interest in different types of religions, or what beliefs were you studying?"

"I have read about all different types of religions because I've always wondered, like, how do we know we've got the right one, how do we know we are not messing up."

"After the time period you were really into the Catholic religion, did you start focusing in on another particular religion?"

"Wicca."

Price asked Damien about some of his writings, which the prosecutors had already introduced. Damien identified one of the books as his personal journal. Pointing to quotes on the inside front cover, the lawyer asked Damien to read them to the jury "and then tell them where they came from."

Damien began to read. " 'Life is but a walking shadow. It is a tale told by an idiot, full of sound and fury signifying nothing.' That's from *A Midsummer Night's Dream* by William Shakespeare.[277] 'Pure black looking clear. My work is done here. Try getting back from me that which used to be.' That is off a Metallica tape called *And Justice for All*. It's about how warped the court systems are and stuff like that. The other one was from a *Twilight Zone*. 'I kicked open a lot of doors in my time, and I am willing to wait for this one to open and when it does I'll be waiting.' "

Damien identified other items the state had introduced against him as a cover from the Metallica tape *Master of Puppets* and "a bootleg Metallica tape that most people didn't even know existed, called *Garage Days Revisited*. Damien explained that he and Jason "used to get copies of them on copy machines and get them enlarged bigger and have them for decorations in our rooms." He said he'd kept the dog's skull he'd found because "I just thought it was kind of cool." Another picture the state had introduced was of a gold skull with wings. Damien identified that as a Harley-Davidson emblem he had.

Price asked why Damien had borrowed *Cotton Mather on Witchcraft* from the library.

"Just to read it," he said. "Most people by looking at the cover, they would think it was a witchcraft book. It's really an antiwitchcraft book. It was wrote by a Puritan minister. It was on different ways that during the persecution era, they used to find ways to torture people or keep them locked up until finally they would say, 'Yeah, I'm a witch,' and then they would kill them."

When Price asked if Damien had a driver's license or had ever driven a car, the teenager answered no to both questions. When Price asked if he'd discussed the murders at a girls' softball game, Damien replied that he had been at the ballpark, but that he had not talked about the murders there. When Price asked Damien his opinion of the testimony by the cult expert, Dale Griffis, Damien calmly observed, "Some of it was okay, but he didn't stop to differentiate between different groups. He just lumped them all together into one big group that he called cults."

The lawyer continued. "As far as several things that Griffis was talking about yesterday—about satanism beliefs—are there any of those things that he was talking about that are your personal beliefs?"

"Not really," Damien replied, though he added that he might share "some" characteristics with what Griffis had described. For example, the defendant said, "Some satanists may be arrogant, conceited, self-important. I might be that, but I'm not a satanist. I don't believe in human sacrifices or anything like that." Asked about the knife that was found in the lake, Damien said, "I had one sort of like that, but mine didn't have a black handle. The handle on mine was camouflaged, and it had the camouflage case and everything. The blade on mine was black. It wasn't silver like that."

Asked how he'd felt during the past year, since being charged with the murders, Damien answered, "Different ways. Sometimes angry, when I see stuff on TV. Sometimes sad. Sometimes scared." Asked about the time when he'd licked his lips at one of the pretrial hearings, he said, "I guess I just lost my temper, because, it was, like, when I went outside, everybody was out there, standing there calling me names, screaming at me, things like that. And I guess it just made me upset when I did that."

"Did you kill any of these three boys?" the lawyer asked.

"No," Damien answered, "I did not."

The front-page headline in the next morning's *Arkansas Democrat-Gazette* announced: ECHOLS DENIES KILLING THREE BOYS. The next line read: ADMITS ON STAND AN INTEREST IN OCCULT. A photograph that ran above the story showed Jason smiling during the trial. The front page of the Jonesboro paper featured a photo of Damien smiling as he was led from the courthouse.

But there was less to smile about the next day, after Davis's cross-examination. The prosecutor handed Damien a sheet of paper with several names written on it in an unusual alphabet. Damien acknowledged that he'd written the names. In response to questions from Davis, he said that one of the names was Aleister Crowley, a well-known writer on witchcraft. Davis identified Crowley as "a noted author in the field of satanic worship" and a writer who "believes in human sacrifice." Damien did not disagree. He said he'd never read any of Crowley's books, though, he added, "I would have read them if I had saw them."

Asking about the incident in Oregon that had resulted in Damien's hospitalization, Prosecutor Davis asked, "Did you threaten to eat your father alive?" Damien said the police were called because he'd been threatening to kill himself. Davis asked him about a reference he had made the day before to a medication he'd been prescribed. "Are you on that today?" Davis asked. Damien said he was—that he had been taking the antidepressant drug Imipramine for the past couple of years, and that it made him sleepy.

"Okay," Davis continued. "Are you a manic-depressive?"

"Yes. I am."

"Okay. Describe for us what happens when you don't take your medication. . . ."

"I cry. I stay by myself most of the time, closed up. If I don't take the medicine, I get headaches. I get nauseous, just generally depressed."

"And when you are in a manic phase . . . is that where you feel nearly invincible?"

"Yes."

Davis started to ask about the incident when Damien threatened to claw the eyes out of Deanna's boyfriend, but Damien's lawyer objected. Davis countered, "Your Honor, they put on evidence yesterday about him being a quiet, passive, peace-loving Wiccan." Davis said he wanted to show that Damien had another side. Burnett sided with Davis, whereupon the prosecutor asked, "Mr. Echols, when you have these mood swings and your medication is out of balance, do you have, do you get violent sometimes?"

"Only toward myself."

Damien would be the only one of the three defendants who would take the stand in his own behalf. Many observers in the courtroom considered his lawyers' decision to let him testify to be an extremely risky one. And now, as Damien stepped down from the stand, most agreed that he had not helped his case—and that he may have seriously harmed it. But Damien did not seem to realize that. As he returned to his seat, he seemed satisfied, as though, in the confrontation with the veteran prosecutor, he felt he'd held his own.

To the reporter for the *Arkansas Times*, it looked like the prosecutors were trying to portray Damien "as a devil-driven monster who was capable of the crime and therefore must have done it."[278] But that was not how Damien appeared to the reporter. "He's sardonic and remorseless," he wrote, "but what he conveys isn't cold-hearted menace; it's a disturbed boy lost in a theatrical posture that he's tried to fashion into an identity. More pitiful than scary."

The Mysterious Christopher Morgan

As the next piece of their defense, Damien's lawyers tried again to question Christopher Morgan, the twenty-year-old from Memphis who'd told police in California that he may have "blacked out" and killed the three boys in West Memphis. Though Morgan had quickly recanted that statement, the defense attorneys wanted the jury to hear Morgan, so that his account might at least raise reasonable doubt. But the prosecutors tried to block the appearance. They told Burnett that he ought to hold another *in camera* session to hear what Morgan had to say before he let Morgan say it in open court. Burnett agreed, and with the jury out of the room, the strangest, most secretive—and perhaps most revealing—part of the trial began obliquely to unfold.

At the start of the *in camera* hearing that followed, Morgan refused to answer questions about anything he'd said to the police. He asked for an attorney. Ignoring his request, Judge Burnett had Morgan sworn in. Morgan answered a few questions, then requested an attorney again. Judge Burnett again refused, and ordered Morgan to respond. Finally, with no attorney, Morgan testified at length under oath. He said he'd once had a job selling ice cream in the victims' neighborhood but that he'd lied when he told police in California that he may have killed them. He said he'd spent the day of the murders either working at a car wash or jumping off sand cliffs into the Mississippi River, and that he'd spent that evening at a Memphis nightclub. Morgan said he'd gone to California a few days after the murders to pick up a car for a friend. He said he went to the police station voluntarily, when he learned he was wanted for questioning, and that he'd confessed in exasperation after seventeen hours of questioning by the Oceanside police. Morgan said he currently faced a federal drug charge in Memphis for possession of LSD.

Judge Burnett asked Morgan about a portion of his statement in which he'd told police that his confession had been false. "From what I recall, I may have told them, 'Are you happy?' They said, 'Is that the truth?' I said, 'No.' " Morgan said that the police had kept him locked in a small room and that he'd finally blurted out the words "Maybe I could have," so that they would leave him alone. Oceanside police did eventually let Morgan go without pressing charges. Fogleman interjected that the West Memphis police had "ruled out" Morgan as a suspect.

Prosecutor Davis then argued that Morgan's testimony was "unreliable." He said defense attorneys wanted "to throw it in a hopper to create a smoke screen," but that the testimony was "absolutely" not relevant. Paul Ford disputed that claim, arguing that police had questioned Jessie under similar circumstances.

"Jessie Misskelley denied that he did it, denied that he did it, admitted that he did it, then denied it and denied it, and he's in prison," Ford said. "This may be the same thing."

At this point, Judge Burnett decided to appoint an attorney for Morgan. The judge ordered Morgan to return to court with his attorney in two days.

"Lost"

Back in open court, the defense lawyers shifted their focus to the quality of the police investigation. With Chief Inspector Gitchell on the stand, Damien's lawyer Scott Davidson asked what kind of manual his police department had that outlined investigative procedures. Gitchell said that no such manual existed. Davidson then asked if the department owned tape recorders and a video camera. Gitchell acknowledged that it did. Davidson asked, "Now, did you ever videotape any interviews with my client, Damien Echols?" Gitchell said that the police had not. Nor had detectives made any audio tape recordings of interviews with their prime suspect.[279]

Damien's lawyer next questioned Gitchell about his department's written procedures for the handling of evidence. Gitchell said none existed. Davidson asked if the blood evidence that was taken from the Bojangles restaurant had been forwarded to the crime lab. Gitchell answered, "No sir. It was, as the term is, lost."

Davidson asked about the recording device that Vicki Hutcheson said police had hooked up under her bed. Gitchell said that Lieutenant Sudbury had handled that attempted surveillance, but that no record of the installation had been kept, and no transcription had been made of the recording because it was inaudible. At this point, Judge Burnett interrupted. "Mr. Davidson," he asked, "are you getting somewhere with something that is relevant?"

Davidson found the comment so objectionable—as a sign of the judge's contempt for the defense—that he immediately called for a mistrial. Turning to Burnett, Davidson said, "We have objected in this case about him losing evidence, about photographic lineups not done properly, and absent records about surveillance. We have never seen the documentation on surveillance. And I think it is certainly relevant to this case."

But the judge would hear none of it. "None of that is relevant now," he said.

"You Did Fine"

On Friday, at the end of the trial's second week, Damien's primary lawyer, Val Price, questioned John Mark Byers about the knife he'd given to the HBO film crew. "Where did y'all keep the knife in your house?" Price asked.

Byers offered the answer that Ridge had earlier suggested. "When I first received the knife," Byers answered slowly, "which was for Christmas, for a few weeks it was in the living room on a little end table by my recliner, and after that it was put in my bedroom on a dresser."

Price grilled Byers about his repeated statements to Gitchell and Ridge that he'd never used the knife. But Byers claimed to only vaguely recall what he'd told the detectives six weeks earlier. He appeared dull on the witness stand, as though he was finding it hard to understand Price's questions. Finally, in exasperation, Price asked Byers if he had ever used the knife on venison. "I did," Byers answered, "and, matter of fact, as I was trying to use the knife in cutting some venison to make beef jerky with it, I cut my thumb with it."

"Oh, you cut your thumb," Price said. "Is it true that you never told Inspector Gitchell on January 26 that you ever cut your thumb with that particular knife?"

It was an imprecise question, to which Byers responded dully, "Yes sir, it seems like during the course of the day I did tell him that."

Asking Byers again and again, "Did you tell Inspector Gitchell . . . ,"
Price made sure that the jury heard how many times Byers had told
Gitchell and Ridge that he had "no idea" how human blood could have
gotten onto his knife. Then the lawyer moved back in time to question
Byers about some statements he'd made to police on May 19, two weeks
after the murders. By asking about that interview, Price got Byers to acknowledge that his last encounter with Christopher had been when
he'd "whipped" the boy with his belt. Byers also acknowledged that
while other searchers were in the woods, he'd gone home to change
clothes, and that even though it was dark when he'd returned to the
woods, he'd gone without a flashlight. But there was no elaboration,
and when Price had concluded his questioning, the prosecutors declined to question Byers and let him be excused. As Byers passed the
prosecutors' table, Fogleman patted him on the back. "Don't worry
about it," Fogleman told him. "You did fine."[280]

Later Fogleman noted that the defense attorneys had not dared to
ask Byers directly if he had killed the boys, and he ridiculed the more
cautious attempt to cast suspicion on Byers by implication. Fogleman
said the move made the defense teams look desperate.

Gag Order

Indeed, as testimony wound toward a close, with only two witnesses remaining, the defense was clearly stymied. Burnett had allowed the highly
disputed weapons—the lake knife and the sticks—to be introduced as evidence. He had allowed the prosecutors to explore Damien's interest in
the occult as a motive for the murders. He had qualified Griffis as a cult
expert and allowed him to testify that the murders showed "trappings" of
satanism. And now, as the trial entered its final week, Burnett issued another ruling, this one affirming the fairness of Jessie Misskelley's trial.
Without comment, Burnett rejected Stidham's argument that Peretti's
change of testimony about the time of death constituted newly discovered evidence that cast additional doubt on the validity of Jessie's confession to the police. The doctor's change of testimony notwithstanding,
Burnett ruled that Jessie would not be granted a new trial.

The ruling did not surprise Damien and Jason's attorneys. It had been hard to imagine that Judge Burnett would have scheduled a retrial for Jessie in the middle of—or even after—the trial of the other two. But the lawyers still had a couple of hopes. One was that the jury would get to hear about Christopher's confession to police in California. But when Morgan showed up with his court-appointed attorney, as Burnett had ordered, the already unusual trial took its most remarkable turn. Until now, all of the *in camera* hearings had been conducted in public; that is, even though the jury had been taken from the courtroom, reporters and other observers had been allowed to stay, since the hearings formed part of the trial. But for reasons that were never stated but that appeared to be related to drugs, Judge Burnett decided that this hearing would be an exception. Judge Burnett barred the media and spectators from the hearing, and he issued a gag order, forbidding the attorneys involved from discussing what transpired. What followed was to become the most secretive part of an already secretive case.

Burnett called Morgan and all the lawyers into his chambers. There, Jason's lawyer Paul Ford gave voice to his exasperation. "Your Honor," Ford protested,

> we would like the record to reflect this is the first *in camera* hearing that has been conducted in this case outside the hearing of the press and public. This court has continually held *in camera* hearings out where everyone can hear, but this is a hearing which has been deliberately orchestrated to be outside the hearing of the public. It is also my understanding that the court is issuing a gag order which prohibits anyone from telling anybody at all that this court will not allow us to call Chris Morgan, and thus, there is no answer to why Chris Morgan was not called, and you are prohibiting us from telling the press that the State of Arkansas objected to this evidence and this witness, and that you would not allow us to question him and you would not allow us to discuss your ruling at all, and this is a public trial, which has been continually played out in front of the press, and at this point in time, when there is evidence that is detrimental to the state, it is being done in private.[281]

Judge Burnett listened without comment. "Anything else?" he asked.

The attorney for Morgan announced that Morgan did not wish to testify. If forced to take the stand, the lawyer said, he intended to exercise his Fifth Amendment rights to avoid self-incrimination. The prosecutors vigorously objected to the prospect of Morgan taking the stand, only to repeatedly invoke the Fifth Amendment. They did not want the jury to get the impression that Morgan might know something that could be self-incriminating about the murders—an impression that would almost certainly arise and divert suspicion from the two defendants.

That, of course, was precisely what the defense wanted. Price cited for Burnett a U.S. Supreme Court ruling that said that witnesses other than the accused had "no right" to refuse to take the stand. Moreover, the opinion read, once reluctant witnesses were on the stand, if they did not wish to testify, they had to invoke their Fifth Amendment rights "to each question" that was asked.[282]

Jason's other lawyer, Robin Wadley, jumped in, arguing that so far, Morgan's lawyer had not shown any reason why he was entitled to claim the Fifth Amendment privilege. "There's been talk from his lawyer about the fact that there's some drug charges in Memphis which this may, in some way, impact," Wadley said, "but there's been no showing as to why or how. Until that's done, I don't believe we can make a determination as to whether or not he is even entitled to make the Fifth Amendment claim."

"Anything else?" Burnett asked.

Morgan's court-appointed lawyer, Scott Emerson, spoke up. In highly veiled language, he noted that the drug charges Morgan faced might somehow relate to the murders, and that they represented part of the reason Morgan did not want to testify. As Emerson cryptically told Burnett:

> There are charges pending against this gentleman in the federal court in the State of Tennessee. I have been on the telephone and I have talked extensively with his attorney from Memphis on the charge, who was shocked and appalled that Mr. Morgan did not have some counsel appointed when he requested an attorney being appointed. . . . I've been advised by my client, and I've been advised by the attorneys that there may be also—in addition to possibly incriminating

himself pertaining to these events—that there are some over-lapping facts regarding the federal court charges.

Jason's lawyer Robin Wadley could hardly contain his frustration. "Judge," he said, "they talk about these federal charges in Memphis. We don't know what the charges are, when the charges were filed, what the allegations in the charges are, when the alleged contact that he has been charged with was contended to have happened."

Then Price spoke up again, citing Arkansas case law, which plainly stated that a trial court "should not accept a witness's blanket assertion of the Fifth Amendment privilege."[283]

"Anything else?" Burnett asked again.

Now it was Fogleman's turn. "Your Honor," the deputy prosecutor said, "what the state objects to is them wanting him to get on the stand in front of the jury and the whole world and exercise his Fifth Amendment rights, which, as the court knows, even though they'll be advised of the privilege, it will appear to the general public and probably to the jurors that that means he must have done something, for him to exercise that Fifth Amendment right, and we object to that being done in the presence of the jury and in the public."

Fogleman also raised another matter rather delicately for Judge Burnett. That was that when Morgan had been questioned during the earlier *in camera* hearing, "he was compelled to be here. He was under subpoena. He was not free once he took the stand to get down and walk off the stand. He was not advised of his rights. He asked for a lawyer during that—"

"He asked for a lawyer when he took the stand," Burnett interjected, "and after about the second or third question. And I directed him to answer the question. It was for that reason I decided he needed to have a lawyer appointed." Burnett then left the issue at hand and lashed out at the defense attorneys. "This has been the most bizarre case I have ever seen in my life," he fumed. "There's every kind of little, incidental matter that's come up throughout it. . . . I'd also want to point out that the defendant's lawyers—Mr. Echols's lawyers—violated one of the rules by disclosing the identity of a confidential source. The court instructed the parties that no mention of—is it Byers?—Mr. Byers's cooperation with the Memphis Police Department, West Memphis Police Department, or the drug task force would be mentioned, and yet it was mentioned. That's just one example of a thousand things. . . ."

The defense attorneys struggled to make sense of what appeared to be Judge Burnett's stream of consciousness. What had begun with Morgan's unwillingness to testify due to unspecified federal drug charges in Memphis had suddenly shifted to confidential sources and from there to "Mr. Byers's cooperation" with drug task forces and police departments on both sides of the Mississippi River. What did any of that have to do, the defense lawyers were left to wonder, with the murder trial at hand? And was Byers's "cooperation" with the police somehow connected to the judge's gag order with regard to this hearing?

Without addressing any of those matters, Burnett settled the immediate question. Noting vaguely that Morgan "seemed to be a young man who admitted that he lied and that those lies could possibly, in some way, incriminate him if he were forced to testify," he ruled that he would not require Morgan to testify.[284] Then, reminding the lawyers of his gag order, Judge Burnett added, "I'm going to make a ruling that anybody that mentions to the press, the jury, or anyone else" what had just transpired "will be held in contempt, and I mean it."

Jason's lawyer Robin Wadley was outraged. "Judge," he said, "so we pick and choose the things we are going to be held in contempt for and not—"

But Burnett cut him off short. "I think I made it real clear," he said. "I haven't put any kind of gag on you on anything at all, but this I'm going to."

As Burnett had demanded, no one who was present in the hearing ever spoke of it. The media never reported a word about the secret discussion of Morgan's quickly retracted confession, or his intention to plead the Fifth Amendment, or the drug charges he faced in Memphis, or Judge Burnett's unexplained reference to John Mark Byers in the midst of a hearing about Christopher Morgan. Nor did the public learn that while Judge Burnett had been disinclined to believe that officers at the West Memphis Police Department had refused the three requests Damien said he'd made for an attorney, Burnett himself had ignored repeated requests in his own court from Christopher Morgan.[285]

"Darker Thoughts and Darker Actions"

Deflated, the defense attorneys returned to the courtroom. As his final witness, Damien's lawyer called Robert Hicks, a police training officer with the Commonwealth of Virginia.[286] The officer said his job there was to "assist law enforcement agencies to develop good, sound written policy and to train and supervise their people accordingly." He testified that he had a master's degree in applied anthropology as it related to law enforcement, and that he had written a book and several articles on "so-called occult or satanic crime and the involvement of law enforcement with that topic."[287]

Price asked Hicks how he had become interested in the unusual field. Hicks explained that, during the 1980s, many law enforcement agencies had become interested, as he put it, "in this broad topic of satanic crime, occult crime, cult related crime." Since part of Hicks's job had been to monitor trends in law enforcement, he'd begun to attend seminars on the subject. "I began to form a suspicion that some of the information presented was not accurate enough for police practice," he said.[288]

Price questioned Hicks about the testimony of Dale Griffis, the cult expert. Price asked Griffis if the date of the murders—near May 1, the pagan feast of Beltane—indicated what Griffis had called "the trappings of occultism." At first, Hicks seemed to be at a loss as to how to respond. He finally said that he'd heard of dates being linked to satanic crimes but that "for Virginia—and at least a few inquiries I've made about this nationally—we see no influence of these dates on the prevalence or absence of violent crime, one way or the other." When Damien's attorney asked about the position of the bodies, which Griffis had said suggested cult involvement, Hicks responded that, "simply finding a body bound in that fashion, in and of itself, is no clue to a religious ideology that I know of."

Price asked if Hicks knew of any empirical data that suggested that sexual mutilation indicated an occult crime. Hicks said he knew of none. And so his testimony went. Point by point, Hicks rebutted the notion that there was any scientific or statistical basis for what Griffis had claimed.

"In your study of this phenomenon," Price asked, "is heavy metal and rock groups, is that something that the cult cops look at when they make their opinion that a particular crime could be a satanic or cult crime?"

"Yes," Hicks replied. "In fact, cult cops, as we have gotten into the habit of using the term, have recommended at seminars to other officers that they find ways to go into rooms in homes where the teenagers live, find out what music they listen to, and see what books they're reading."

"In your studies, are you aware of any particular empirical data or studies that the possession of that type of material leads to some type of criminal activity or satanic crime?"

"This, of course, is much debated," the officer answered, "and there are many people who will attest that these will lead to darker thoughts and darker actions. But . . . where the Metallica music is concerned, we do have empirical evidence to suggest that the music does not cause the kind of harm that is imputed to it, that is, that it will lead people to commit crimes."

Finally, Hicks explained:

> In my opinion, that phrase, "the trappings of the occult" is absolutely meaningless in considering any kind of violent crime. . . . The term "occult" has no fixed meaning, anyway. In most people's minds, it usually refers to certain kinds of practice, certain symbols and signs, that we don't observe and practice, but other people do—people who do nasty things, is usually what that word connotes in the popular mind. To say the word "trappings" again is simply to imbue the whole crime with the tint of something evil. For some police officers, that almost gets into a Christian moral fight. Some officers who teach Griffis's point of view teach that you have to be spiritually armed when you investigate these offenses, which in my view, gets outside of what law enforcement is here to do.

With that, Damien's lawyers rested their case.

"They Came Back and It Was Twenty"

While most of the prosecutors' attention was focused on Damien and his alleged involvement with the occult, the *Arkansas Times* reporter who was covering the trial paid some attention to Jason. "I tried without success to imagine him sucking the blood of dying Chris Byers, as a scruffy cellmate testified that he'd bragged of doing," reporter Bob Lancaster wrote. "No dice," he concluded. To Lancaster, Jason had "the slightly drained look of a kid who's been called to the principal's office and isn't quite sure how serious his situation is."[289]

But the severity of Jason's situation was about to become clear. Jason's lawyers had hurled themselves into efforts to sever the two trials and to keep mention of satanism and the occult from tainting Jason, but now that those efforts had failed and it was time for them to present Jason's defense, they surprised everyone in the court by calling only one witness, an expert in hairs and fibers from a laboratory in Texas.[290] Ford asked the analyst to discuss the single red fiber found with the bodies that analysts from the Arkansas Crime Laboratory had identified as being "microscopically similar" to fibers from a red bathrobe belonging to Jason's mother. The Texas analyst said he disagreed with those findings, noting that his examination of the fiber would "exclude the red robe as being a possible source."[291]

With nothing more than that, Ford announced, "We rest."

Later, Ford explained that he and Robin Wadley, Jason's other lawyer, believed the state's case against Jason was so weak that the assumption of innocence would prevail.[292] "We wanted to just disappear on the radar screen and let Damien be the whole focus," Ford said. "At one point, we went three days of the trial and Jason's name was not mentioned. We were just trying to disappear. We thought that that was a good strategy: to be a nonevent, since there wasn't a lot of evidence to begin with. We thought, if we didn't stir the pot, and they didn't stir the pot, what were they going to convict him on?"[293]

Jason was a bit dismayed, too. He had expected his lawyers to call some of his teachers, to testify about his demeanor in school, including on the day of and the day after the murders. He expected to hear some testimony to support his alibi. In retrospect he thought he would like to have taken the stand himself, if only so that the jury could have heard him say something on his own behalf before they left to consider his fate. As the one witness his lawyers had called stepped down from the stand, Jason later said he felt "lost." He felt young and alone, and he was worried about his family.[294]

Midway through the trial he had made a second crucial decision based on his own ethics and his belief, as he put it, that "the truth was going to come out." It was never reported, but at near the point where Fogleman and Davis decided to play the occult card, they'd approached Jason again, and this time they'd sweetened their offer. Years later, Jason recalled the tenor of that exchange. "Before the trial started, it was forty years," he said, "and then, after the trial got going, they came back and it was twenty." Jason said he was not tempted to accept either time. "It was wrong. It was against everything I was brought up to believe in," he explained. "We weren't rich, moneywise, but my mom instilled good values in us. They were telling me, 'All they really want is Damien. Just testify against Damien. Say he done it. Get up there and lie.' I told him I couldn't help him with anything like that. I told him, 'I couldn't do it even if you said you'd let me go right now.' And I told him, 'I didn't want to hear no more about it.' "

Jason had gone into the trial believing that, as he explained, "I didn't think there was no possible way they could find us guilty when we didn't do it. Not in America. It's not what I was raised up to believe would happen in America." But now, having fended off two deals, while watching the vigor of the prosecution against him, some long-held beliefs were crumbling. He'd seen his lawyers "fighting hard," but now he also saw, as he put it, that "it was hard to fight against Judge Burnett and the prosecutors too." It looked to Jason like "everything we tried to do, Judge Burnett wouldn't allow it. He'd find some reason to turn us down. Even I could see that, and I didn't know anything about it."

Jason said he'd told his attorneys that he wanted to testify. He wanted to tell the jury that he'd been cutting his uncle's grass on the afternoon the boys disappeared, and he wanted them to call his uncle to verify that claim. He wanted to say that he had no recollection of ever seeing Michael Carson at the juvenile detention facility, and that if he had encountered him, he never would have said what the other teenager claimed he did. Mostly, he wanted the jurors to hear him speak in his own behalf, before they adjourned to judge him. But, he would later recall, his lawyers "kept giving me the runaround, telling me I was sixteen and saying, 'You don't need to testify.' They told me, 'Anything you say, the prosecutor is going to twist it and use it against you.'"

Now, Jason reflected, it looked like they'd been right. He felt that any defense was futile and that under Burnett he and his lawyers faced "a no-win situation." "All that mattered," he concluded, "was that Damien was weird and I had black T-shirts."

The three weeks of testimony had produced some remarkable twists and turns. Now, even with the testimony concluded, the trial's peculiarities did not end. Two more oddities developed before the lawyers could make their closing arguments.

Lesser Charges

Ordinarily, when a defendant is tried on a charge of capital murder, he will ask that the jury be instructed to consider lesser charges, such as first- or second-degree murder, since lesser charges carry lighter sentences. Often, though not always, prosecutors oppose that request. In this case, however, the situation was reversed. The prosecutors wanted the jury to be able to consider alternatives to capital murder. After consulting with Damien and Jason in front of Burnett, the defense attorneys announced that their clients were taking an all-or-nothing stance. They wanted the jurors to consider only the most severe charges—or find them innocent.[295] But Burnett decided against them, ruling that the jury would be instructed to consider the range of charges. That was one of what the local paper later described as the day's "startling developments."

The second odd event occurred when Fogleman announced that the West Memphis police had suddenly discovered blood on a necklace they'd taken from Damien. The necklace had been in their possession since the night of the three arrests, ten months before. Upon noticing what appeared to be blood, they'd sent the pendant, which was in the shape of a hatchet, to the state crime lab for analysis. But the amount of blood had been so small that the crime lab had forwarded the pendant to a laboratory in North Carolina for more elaborate tests. As Damien and Jason's trial was drawing to a close, the North Carolina lab had reported finding two types of blood on the pendant. One of these DQ Alpha types, as they were called, was a match for Damien. The other was reported to be consistent with the blood type of Jason Baldwin, Stevie Branch, and approximately 11 percent of what the laboratory identified as "the Caucasian population."²⁹⁶ Despite the ambiguity of the findings, Fogleman wanted to get the necklace before the jury. Although both sides had already formally rested their cases, he took the extraordinary step of asking Burnett to allow the introduction of new evidence.

The effort led to another heated *in camera* session. Again the jury heard nothing of what transpired, as Damien's lawyer reported that the defendants had shared the pendant. "If that is indeed Jason Baldwin's blood on this pendant, and not Stevie Branch's," Val Price said, "then the evidence is of no value at all, and not relevant." Jason's lawyer complained that the attempt to introduce new evidence at this stage of the trial was outrageous. "This is not newly discovered evidence," he said. "They've had it in their possession the entire time. They just didn't do anything with it."

Judge Burnett deemed the situation serious enough that he postponed the trial for a day while he wrestled with the problem. If he granted Fogleman's request, the trial would have to be continued, at the very least. At worst, introduction of the new evidence would result in a mistrial for Jason, who stood to be harmed by evidence for which his lawyers had not been prepared. Finally, Judge Burnett told the prosecutors that if they wanted to introduce the pendant, he would grant Jason's attorneys' repeated requests to sever his trial from Damien's.

Now the prosecutors faced a dilemma. They had fought every effort to prohibit Jason from being tried on his own. Now they were being warned by Judge Burnett that if they kept trying to introduce the blood-specked necklace, a severance would be ordered. Fogleman and Davis backed down. The matter of the pendant was dropped.

The bailiff notified the jurors to return to the courthouse on Thursday, March 17, for the conclusion of the trial. The *Jonesboro Sun* reported "rumors" that the unexplained delay had been caused "by results from DNA testing for traces of blood on Echols' necklace."

CHAPTER TWENTY

The Verdicts

AT LAST, AFTER SEVENTEEN DAYS OF TRIAL, Fogleman rose to face the jury with his closing argument. Ignoring Peretti's testimony, he said the murders had taken place sometime between 9:30 and 10:00 P.M. on the evening of May 5, at the site where the bodies were found. He described as "highly credible" Narlene Hollingsworth's contention that she'd seen Damien on the service road near the Blue Beacon Truck Wash at about that time. As for Hollingsworth's testimony that Damien was with his girlfriend, Domini, and not Jason, Fogleman simply told the jurors to draw their "own conclusions."[297] He cited the two girls at the softball field who'd said they'd heard Damien brag about the murders. "Those were two scared kids up here," he said. "They had no motivation to do anything other than come up here and tell you the truth."

He looked confidingly at the jury.

But you might ask yourself, "Well, now, wait a minute. We've got a crime scene that's clean. The killers were very meticulous about removing any evidence, hiding the bicycles, hiding their clothes, hiding their bodies. Why would he stand out there and tell everybody?" Well, number one, who is he telling? He is telling a group of six or seven of his little groupies that follow him around. Remember, he says he dresses that way and everything to keep people away from him? But everywhere you look, you've got these little groupies hanging around him. Now, then, you say, "Well, still, why would he say that?" Well, remember when Mr. Davis was examining him about this manic-depressive situation? In the manic phase you feel invincible—nobody can touch you.

Fogleman emphasized how the knife had been found in the lake close to Jason's house. He recalled the testimony of Michael Carson, Damien's responses to Detective Ridge's questions, and the fibers found at the scene. "Ask yourself," he said, "if they aren't significant." He acknowledged that all of the evidence in the case had been circumstantial, and that not one piece of it, "in and of itself," pointed to anyone as having been the killer. "But," he advised, "you don't look at it like that." Using the example of a house, he argued, "If you look at one small part and say, 'Well, that's not a house.' The foundation? Is that a house? No. Is the door a house? No. You don't look at it that way. You look at it as a whole. And we submit when you look at all of the evidence as a whole, that you'll find that this circumstantial evidence proves beyond a reasonable doubt that these defendants committed this murder."

Then Fogleman raised the issue he'd introduced midway through the trial. "Now I want to talk to you about motive," he said.

This motive here is something that's inconceivable. And it's, it's something that—it's not something that you anxiously look forward to putting on—that kind of evidence relating to motive—in this particular case, especially. And why is that? This satanic stuff . . . It doesn't matter whether I believe it or the defense attorney believes it, or you even believe in these concepts. The only thing that matters is what these defendants believe. That's the only thing that matters in relation to motive. . . . Look at history. Look at hundreds of years of religious history. There have been hundreds of people killed in the name of religion. It is a motivating force. It gives people who want to do evil, want to commit murders, a reason to do what they're doing. For themselves, it gives them a reason—a justification for what they do.

Then Fogleman read one of Damien's poems to the jury, one that he said described Damien's internal conflict. It was a conflict that Fogleman said was between "Wicca, which is the good, and the upside-down cross, which is satanic." The poem read:

> *I want to be in the middle,*
> *in neither the black nor the white,*
> *in neither the wrong nor the right,*
> *to stand right on the line,*
> *to be able to go to either side with a moment's notice.*
> *I've always been in the black, in the wrong.*
> *I tried to get into the white,*
> *but I almost destroyed it*
> *because the black tried to follow me.*
> *This time I won't let it.*
> *I will be in the middle.*

"That right there," Fogleman proclaimed, "tells you Damien Echols. He don't want to be in the white. He doesn't want to be good. He wants to be both where he can go to the good side or the bad side, however it suits his purpose. If he wants to do bad, let's go to the satanic side. If he wants to be good, then go to the Wiccan side. That poem right there tells you about Damien Echols."

Returning to the circumstantial evidence, Fogleman continued: "No, ladies and gentlemen, each item of this, in and of itself, doesn't mean somebody would be motivated to murder—not in and of itself.[298] But you look at it together, and you get—you begin to see inside Damien Echols. You see inside that person, and you look inside there, and there's not a soul in there. . . . Scary. That's what he is—scary."

The deputy prosecuting attorney mocked the defense attorneys' decision to implicate John Mark Byers "by innuendo." To the charges of police ineptitude, he said, "Were there mistakes made? Sure . . . [But] in the overall scheme of things, it doesn't amount to a hill of beans."

Then Fogleman picked up a grapefruit. "Now, I want to talk to you about these knives," he said. Jason's lawyer jumped up to object. In a discussion in front of Burnett, Ford argued that Fogleman was preparing to perform an unscientific experiment with an item—the grapefruit—which had not been placed into evidence. "I'm just going to show the types of marks that this knife makes and that knife makes," Fogleman countered. "That's all, Your Honor." Burnett told him he could proceed.

Fogleman whacked the grapefruit dramatically with each of the two knives—the one from the lake and the one that had belonged to Byers. Holding the grapefruit up where the jury could see the marks, he said that the pattern left by the lake knife matched the wounds on Christopher Byers. With that knife in one hand, he pointed to the autopsy photo showing the stab wounds to Christopher's groin. "I submit the proof shows this knife caused this," Fogleman said. "Well, true, it could be another knife like this, but I submit to you the proof—the circumstantial evidence—show that this knife, State's exhibit seventy-seven, caused those injuries right there."

Then Fogleman sat down. His closing argument had taken an hour and a half.

Damien's Closing Argument

For the first time since the trial began, Damien's infant son was in the courtroom with Domini, his mother. Val Price, Damien's lead defense lawyer, rose to deliver his closing arguments. He focused on the jurors' responsibility to consider reasonable doubts. Reminding them that "circumstantial evidence must be consistent with the guilt of the defendant and inconsistent with any other reasonable conclusion," he recalled the testimony relating to John Mark Byers. Specifically, he asked them to remember Byers's acknowledgment that he'd beaten Christopher with a belt just before he disappeared; Byers's claim that he went to the woods in the dark, at 8:30 P.M., "still wearing shorts, still wearing flip-flops, still without a flashlight"; Peretti's statement that some of Christopher's injuries "were consistent" with those that might have been caused by the knife Byers had given the film crew; the lab report indicating that DNA found on the knife was "consistent" with that of both Christopher and his stepfather; and the conflicting answers Byers gave when questioned about the blood on the knife. "I think," Price told the jurors, "this evidence—and the possibility of John Mark Byers as a suspect—is certainly an aspect of reasonable doubt."

The lawyer then attacked the police department's handling of the case, as well as the state's theory of the crime. He recalled the man at the Bojangles and the lost evidence. Noting the lack of blood at the site where the bodies were recovered, he asked, "Was there any evidence at this crime scene area that this is where they were beaten, or stabbed or cut? No. There has been no evidence whatsoever." In short, he said, "If something fit in with their theory that Damien was involved, the state investigated that. If it didn't, they chucked it aside. They threw it away. Just like that Bojangles blood."

Then he addressed the state's theory of motive. Noting that most trials hinged on the constitutional guarantees enshrined in the Fifth and Sixth Amendments—guaranteeing the rights to a public trial and to a trial by jury—he argued that this case was unusual because it also raised concerns about the First Amendment, the one guaranteeing freedom of religion. Recalling police detectives' testimony that "Damien wasn't a suspect until he started talking about his Wiccan beliefs," he told the jury that those beliefs should never have been at issue. "Part of being a teenager, when you're growing up in the teen years, is questioning things," he said. "Questioning your religious beliefs. Questioning your parental values. But just because you do, that is not any kind of evidence of murder. . . . It's still all right in America to have weird things in your room. And it doesn't mean you're guilty of murder. And it doesn't give any kind of motivation."

With that, Price took his seat at the defense table beside Damien.

Jason's Closing Argument

Jason's lead attorney, Paul Ford, continued the attack in his closing argument, especially with regard to the police. Recalling a string of gaffes, including the delayed searches of the victims' homes, the sticks Ridge recovered from the woods more than three months after the murders, and the lack of blood at the scene, Ford derided the investigators. "They'll stick to their story," he said, "no matter how preposterous it is to believe."

Ford also asked the jury to question why Inspector Gitchell had scarcely appeared at the trial. "He's in charge," Ford pointed out, "but he was a nonexistent factor in this trial. He didn't tell you anything." And yet, Ford noted, just a week before the arrests, Gitchell had written in his letter to the crime lab that he and his detectives were "blind-folded."

He reminded the jurors of Dr. Peretti's admission that he himself would have found it difficult to perform the castration done on Christopher Byers quickly, in the dark and in water. "And they want you to think a sixteen-year-old boy did it, when their own medical examiner, who is skilled as a physician, would have found it hard." As for Michael Carson's testimony about Jason's alleged jailhouse confession, Ford asked the jurors to remember that at sixteen, Michael already had two felonies. "He's a burglar," Ford argued. "He steals guns. He destroys people's houses that he breaks into—and in the second conversation he's ever had in his life with Jason Baldwin, Jason Baldwin spills his guts."

Turning to the credentials of the state's expert, Dale Griffis, Ford chided,

> He didn't go to college, he went to the post office. And so he's qualified to come in here and tell you things. But despite all of his hyperbole, there's no physical evidence to link Jason. There's no books. There's no pictures. There's no drawings. There's no nothing that linked Jason to these "occult trappings," which the prosecutors say is the reason this crime occurred. If they'd had it, they'd have brought it. . . .
>
> Then they tell you satanic panic. Yeah, that's a scary thing. But it's a scarier thing to convict someone with no evidence. If you can't figure it out, if it doesn't make sense, you call it "occult killing" and find somebody to fit the suit. They're blindfolded. They can't figure it out. Let's call it "occult killing" and find somebody weird. Find somebody who wears black. But they let one thing go by the wayside, and it's that there's nothing that links Jason to these activities. . . .

Ford pointed to Damien. "That's what they want right there; guilty by association. Because he's sitting over there with Damien, they want you to convict him." He ended by pleading with the jurors. "Take the blindfolds off," he said, "and look at it the way it really is. And send Jason Baldwin home."

"Something Strange Going On"

But Prosecutor Davis had the last word. "What I think is a key in this case is not just who killed these boys," he began, "although that's the real issue you all have to decide. But I think also important is what type of person was involved in these murders that could turn these three innocent-looking little eight-year-olds into the mutilated bodies that we've seen in these photographs. Because what type of person could do that is at the very center of this case."

Noting that the defense had made "a big deal" about the absence of blood at the scene, Davis introduced a new scenario—one that had not been mentioned either in any of Jessie's statements or in testimony at either of the trials. "All that had to have been done," he suggested, "was for something to have been laid on the ground when the children were placed there. Whether it was a piece of plastic, a piece of Visqueen, and it's folded up and carried with them when they leave the woods that night. And we don't get them for thirty more days. So, I mean, they can leave the stuff in the drainage ditch on the way home. A big coat spread on the ground could have served the same purpose."

He dismissed the charges of police ineptitude as a standard defense lawyer ploy. "They always get up here and say, 'Well, the police bungled it up, because if they had done a better job, like they do on TV, we'd have all the answers. And so they claim the police messed up.'" Nonetheless, Davis admitted that "there's just a scarcity of evidence." He explained, "Somebody did a good job of cleaning it up. The same person who made sure they punched the clothes down in the mud so they wouldn't float up is the same person that cleaned that area, and they did a dang good job of it, and they removed most of the evidence."

The idea that the defendants had cleaned up the site of a triple murder and castration so well in the dark that police had not been able to find a single definitive clue startled some courtroom observers, as had Davis's mention of Visqueen. But the prosecutor continued, focusing on the theory that Damien's beliefs had given rise to the murders. "The satanic or occult motive thing is kind of a foreign concept to me," he said. "But when you've got people that are doing what was done to these three little boys, I mean, you've got—the normal motives for human conduct don't apply. There's something strange going on that causes people to do this. I mean, you've got some weird people."

Gesturing toward Damien, Davis continued. "Well, I mean, you can judge him from the witness stand. This guy is as cool as a cucumber. He is nearly emotionless, and what he has done in terms of the satanic stuff is a whole lot more than just dabbling or looking into it for purposes of an intellectual exercise. . . . And I put to you, as bizarre as it may seem to you and as unfamiliar as it may seem, this occult set of beliefs and the beliefs that Damien had and that his best friend, Jason, was exposed to all the time, that those were the set of beliefs that were the motive or the basis for causing this bizarre murder."

Then the district's chief prosecutor summed it all up. "We have presented a circumstantial case with circumstantial evidence, and it's good enough for a conviction," he said. "I think Damien is the link with Jason. I think there is a connection between the two that you can consider in determining the guilt of this other defendant. . . . And when you go back there, sort through that evidence. Go through it carefully. Look at this knife. Look at those photos. Look at all the evidence, and piece it together, and when you do, you're going to find that these defendants are guilty beyond a reasonable doubt. And you'll feel—you can feel—good."

March 17, 1994

The jurors left the courtroom at 5 P.M. that night. They deliberated until 9:40 P.M. While they were out, Damien granted a few reporters an informal interview. Ron Lax hung close by to listen. Sounding relaxed, Damien took the opportunity to knock the prosecutors' main witness. If the jury acquitted him, he told the reporters, he planned to pursue a "mail-order Ph.D. and become an expert on cults." He complained that he hadn't been allowed to read books by Stephen King or Anne Rice since his arrest, and that he'd had to resort to Westerns, the only literary fare at the jail.

The next day was Friday, March 18, 1994. The jurors resumed their deliberations at 9:30 A.M. At three-thirty that afternoon, they notified Judge Burnett that they had reached a decision. Damien and Jason were led back into court. Burnett warned against any outbursts. Uniformed police officers filed into position between the spectators and the defendants, forming what one observer called "a human wall."

When all was settled, a hush fell over the courtroom as the bailiff handed the verdict forms to Judge Burnett. "We, the jury, find Damien Echols guilty of capital murder," he read. And then, "We, the jury, find Jason Baldwin guilty of capital murder." The debate about lesser charges had proven unnecessary. The jury found both Damien and Jason guilty of capital murder in the deaths of all three of the children.[299]

"Dark Passages"

"Yes! Yes! Yes!" John Mark Byers exclaimed, despite Burnett's warning. Byers and other family members of the victims began hugging and crying. A reporter noted that "Baldwin appeared to cry as the verdicts were read" but that "Echols did not." A hysterical Domini Teer was led from the courtroom clutching her baby.

As exultation livened some parts of the courtroom, grief subdued others. Judge Burnett told reporters that members of the jury had asked not to be questioned about their decision. The jurors' job was not over. They still had the trial's sentencing phase to go. It would begin in the morning. Burnett warned the courtroom, "I don't want anybody to even attempt to talk to or interfere with any of the jurors whatsoever." Turning to the jury panel, he added, "In fact, I'm going to have an officer escort you to your vehicles." Deputies led Damien and Jason away. Burnett pounded his gavel, adjourning the trial for the day. The spectators rushed from the courtroom.

"Those guys took a life, let them lose a life," Stevie's stepfather, Terry Hobbs, told reporters. Hobbs added that he wished the families could have "ten minutes alone in a room" with the defendants "to do to them what they did to the boys." Stevie's mother, Pam Hobbs, said, "God did get his vengeance. I've got to take a trip to a little boy's grave and tell him, 'We won. Our God didn't let us down.' " Michael's father, Todd Moore, said he was "completely satisfied" with the verdicts, but that they did not relieve his pain. "My son still don't come home," he choked. Melissa Byers called for executions. "If you take a life in a vicious murder—my child was tortured to death," she said, "then I believe they should pay with their lives."

Damien's mother blamed the verdicts on the police investigation. "The lives of three little innocent boys were taken," she said, "and the West Memphis Police Department botched it up, and they had to find somebody. So they take the lives of three more innocent boys." Jason's mother echoed the condemnation, saying her son had been "framed." Noting the lack of evidence, she added, "I don't know how a guilty verdict came about, but I know Jason is innocent." Jason's brother Matt told reporters, "I don't think he's innocent. I *know*. They're not devil worshipers. That's just a bunch of bull they said so they could mess up the jurors' minds." Domini had taken refuge in an old station wagon parked near the courthouse. Passersby saw the seventeen-year-old mother sobbing in the backseat of the car, in the arms of Michelle, Damien's fifteen-year-old sister.

A few minutes later, Damien and Jason were escorted from the courthouse under heavy police guard. They were shackled and wore bulletproof vests. "I love you, son," Jason's mom called out. Jason kept walking but looked at her and quietly said, "I love you too." One of Damien's relatives shouted, "Hold on, there, boy. You'll be getting out." Damien nodded, "I know."

"Where's your God now, Damien?" Pam Hobbs shouted.

"I think you're innocent!" someone else yelled.

"You're going to fry!" another onlooker exulted.

Gary Gitchell watched as police led the convicted teenagers into unmarked cars. "I feel like we've definitely been vindicated in this case," he told reporters. "We knew our case. We felt it was strong." When asked about the absence of evidence, he explained that between the murders and the arrests, the defendants had had time "to get rid of a lot of items." The *Commercial Appeal* reported that "Gitchell's eyes filled with tears as he hugged Detective Bryn Ridge. 'There's a bonding that I can't explain. I can't explain it,' he said, choking back tears."

The *Arkansas Times* reporter covering the trials observed:

> The prosecutors convicted Echols of checking certain
> suspicious books out of the public library, and copying off

dark passages ("full of sound and fury, signifying nothing") from the likes of William Shakespeare. God help him if he'd ever discovered Poe. And yet this vague proposition of the murders as an expression of an ignorant boy's conception of the demands of demonology was the state's entire case. That's all we had. . . . And it proved exactly nothing—except that Damien Echols was being tried, for lack of anything better, for "thoughtcrime." With Jason Baldwin being dragged along as an afterthought.

"A Packet of Information"

Nothing about the trial had proceeded smoothly, nor would the sentencing that began the next day. Before the final phase of the trial began, Burnett—as he had so frequently—asked the jury to step outside while he consulted with the attorneys. When the jurors had left the room, Burnett explained that he had received reports that the jury foreman and his daughter had received death threats from "someone connected to Damien," and that another juror had received what she described as a "crank call." Before asking the jurors to leave the room, Burnett had presented them with a general question, asking whether all still felt that they could be impartial. All the jurors had said yes, and now Burnett was reporting to the lawyers that he was "confident and satisfied" with their responses. But Jason's lawyers worried that the contacts may have tainted the jury. At their request, Burnett called the jury's foreman back into the room and questioned him directly. The foreman acknowledged that in the middle of the trial, a member of his family had received a threat, which he had "discussed indirectly" in the jury room. He said the episode had prompted "probably a ten-second conversation" and that the matter "wasn't brought up again."

Burnett said again that he was satisfied. But the defense attorneys were not. Noting that a threat had been made and that it had been discussed among the jurors, they argued that the possibility of taint on a jury that was weighing life or death was unacceptable. They moved for a mistrial. Judge Burnett denied the motion, telling the lawyers that they could appeal the matter if they chose. In the meantime, he announced, "We're going to proceed."

The trial's sentencing phase was like the guilt-or-innocence phase, but shorter. Here, the prosecutors would present evidence that tended to increase, or aggravate, the crime's enormity, in order to call for the most severe punishment. The defense, on the other hand, would present evidence to lessen, or mitigate, the circumstances, and plead for a merciful sentence. In Damien's case, attorney Scott Davidson would be asking the jury to sentence Damien to life in prison rather than to death. He called a few witnesses to describe difficult circumstances in Damien's childhood, but the defense team expected Dr. James Moneypenny, a psychologist from Little Rock, to be its most important witness.[300] Moneypenny had interviewed and tested Damien, and reviewed many of his records. "I notice that there is a packet of information there in front of you," defense attorney Davidson said. "Are those the records that were compiled in this case?" It was a simple enough question, but Lax, who was sitting in the courtroom, heard it with a sinking heart. He knew what was in those records. And he knew that, now that Damien's own defense team had introduced them into the trial, they were fair game for the prosecutors—if the prosecutors wanted to explore them. "That's right," the psychologist replied.

Davidson proceeded. He asked what the psychologist had concluded from the reports. Moneypenny offered his opinion that Damien suffered from "a severe mental disturbance" that was characterized by depression, and that underlying his depression was "a pretty disordered personality structure." He described Damien as having "a pervasive or all-encompassing sense of alienation between himself and the world," along with "a very painful sensitivity to things like betrayal, hypocrisy, lies—all things that might be hurtful or harmful to a person who's extremely sensitive as a result of what has happened to him." He attributed Damien's "disordered personality structure" to a failure to bond as a child. Moneypenny elaborated.

> What happened with him is he went inward. He withdrew. And as he grew up, he created in his own mind sort of a fantasy world. This withdrawal, I think, was an effort to

pull away from this—what I think he perceived as a—very dangerous, unnurturing, unsupportive world out there. . . . But he was bright enough, and he's very thoughtful, and in his own mind he started answering—or attempting to answer—a lot of the kinds of questions that all children ask. You know: Who am I? Why am I here? What am I going to do? Where are we going? And I think, importantly, asking the kinds of questions such as, you know, why is there unfairness? How come things don't always work the way they're supposed to? How come people get disappointed? And ordinarily, children get what we call corrective messagery. You know, you explain things to your children and you tell them how it can be okay, and you tell them how to survive and get along despite the world's imperfections. I think Damien missed a lot of that kind of thing. . . .

As a result, the psychologist said, Damien had developed some irrational and delusional ideas.

But the doctor predicted that Damien could be "treated successfully" in prison, where "there would be a sense of stability." He explained that he'd once asked Damien what he would teach his son, if he had a chance to raise him. "I would teach him that he was special," Damien had replied, "and I would teach him that he may not be the same, but that don't mean you're wrong." Moneypenny considered that to be "a real reflection" of Damien's needs as well.

When Fogleman rose to cross-examine the psychologist, Lax sank in his seat. His fears had been justified. "In your review of the records," Fogleman began, "did you review his records from the East Arkansas Mental Health Center?" Moneypenny said that he had. Fogleman pointed to the folder in the psychologist's lap. "Could I see that, please?" he asked.

Theoretically, these were confidential records—records that the prosecution should not have seen. "Of course," Fogleman later said, "we didn't know what was in the records." But now that Damien's own defense attorneys had introduced the records, and the prosecutor was free to explore them, Lax expected the worst. He shuddered, wondering only how effectively Fogleman would use the information contained in the files. Fogleman later said that he had never seen the files before, but as the prosecutor flipped through the pages Moneypenny had handed him, it appeared to Lax that the prosecutor knew precisely what he was looking for.

"Are these in chronological order?" Fogleman asked the doctor. Moneypenny said he did not know.

While Fogleman searched, Jason's attorney asked for another consultation with Judge Burnett. He objected on Jason's behalf to what was transpiring. Noting that Damien's medical records had been privileged until "the mental capacity of the defendant was placed at issue" here in the sentencing phase of the trial, Ford argued that the records had the potential to be "extremely prejudicial" to his client. "Jason Baldwin's life is on the line," Ford told Judge Burnett, "and these statements that are going to be brought out may, in fact, take his life without any opportunity whatsoever by counsel for Jason to have ever obtained these records. . . . We are totally and completely handcuffed. . . . We did not know that the psychology of Damien would be placed in issue. We've never had an opportunity to review these records. We are totally and completely helpless, yet his life hangs in the balance."

Ford asked Burnett to instruct the prosecutors "to make no reference to these records," but Burnett declined, though—again—he told Ford that he would instruct the jurors that the records were to apply only to Damien. Again, Ford moved for a severance, and again he was denied.

By now, Fogleman had found what he wanted. Handing the files back to the psychologist, Fogleman asked him to turn to some specific reports; the ones from the county mental health center where Driver had required Damien to go. Moneypenny turned to the pages Fogleman indicated. Fogleman asked him to read from the therapist's notes. The psychologist quoted:

"Reports that he thinks a lot about life after death. Quote—I want to go where the monsters go—end quote. Describes himself as quote—pretty much hate the human race—end quote. Relates that he feels people are in two classes, sheep and wolves. Wolves eat sheep.

"Damien explains he obtains his powers by drinking blood of others. He typically drinks the blood of a sexual partner or of a ruling partner. This is achieved by biting or cutting. He said, quote—it makes me feel like a god—end quote."

On redirect, Damien's lawyers tried to salvage the situation by having the doctor read some of the therapists' more promising entries, with regard to Damien's behavior and prognosis. But the attempt did little good, and Fogleman had the last word. "In your business," he asked the psychologist, "is it not unusual to find people telling you about drinking blood, and that they do it to make them feel like a god?"

"It's highly unusual," Moneypenny said.

"It's what?"

"It's not usual at all," the psychologist repeated. "It is very atypical. I think that represents some of the extremes of his thinking and beliefs and what it has come to for him." With that, the witness was excused.

It was time for Jason's lawyers to present evidence for the jury to consider when sentencing him. The mental health issue that Damien's lawyers had raised was one of several possibilities allowed. While Jason had had no history of psychiatric illness, lawyers who dropped into the courtroom to hear the final arguments expected that Jason's lawyers would present testimony, at least, about his scant juvenile record and his good record at school. But to the amazement of many in the room, Ford called no one—no witnesses at all—to offer mitigating testimony for Jason.

It was time for the trial's final arguments. Fogleman spoke for only a few minutes, then dramatically, he opened the therapist's files again. "Damien reports being told at the hospital that he could be another Charles Manson or Ted Bundy," the prosecutor read. With that statement, he turned to the jury. "We ask for your verdicts," he said.

Having called only one witness during the trial and none in the sentencing phase, Ford now pleaded for Jason's life. He reminded the jury that Jason had no prior criminal record and that he was still just sixteen years old. He concluded, "Your verdict has already decided that Jason Baldwin will die in prison. The question is how will he die. I ask for mercy. Thank you."

Prosecutor Davis wrapped it up for the state. Holding the photographs of Christopher Byers, Michael Moore, and Stevie Branch, he asked the jurors to consider what had been done to the children. He told them that "if ever there was an appropriate circumstance to render the death penalty, this is it." And he asked them to "return a verdict of death."

The jurors filed out of the courtroom at 2:05 P.M. They entered a room where one of them began jotting impressions of the trial on a large easel pad.[301] What followed was a simple, almost simplistic process. Under headings marked "pro" and "con," the jurors assessed the testimony they'd heard during the three-week trial. In the pro column for Detective Mike Allen, they wrote that he seemed to be "good." In the column for cons on Allen's page, someone had written "none." Other assessments were slightly more probing. The jurors wrote that Detective Bryn Ridge appeared to be "honest," but they noted in the con column that he'd "left stick" and "lost blood." Dr. Frank Peretti was judged to be "credible," "impartial," and "professional," though "bad judgment" was listed as a con for him, as was the issue of "time of death." On the page for Dale Griffis, the jurors listed "biased to occult finding," "poor delivery," and "low self-esteem" as cons. On the plus side for Griffis, one of the jurors jotted the words "knowledgeable" and "4,800 books."

Then the jurors applied the same process to Damien and Jason. Under pros for Jason, they wrote "in school," "stuck to story," "exhibited remorse." But the list of cons was longer. On this side of the page someone wrote "Damien's best friend," "jailhouse confession," "low self-esteem," "fiber match," "knife," and "frequented crime scene," though no testimony had been introduced regarding that last point.

Damien's page predicted the outcome. Under pros for him, the jurors listed "intelligent," "manic depressant," "stuck to story," and "loyal family." But the list of cons ran a couple of pages. It included "something to gain," "dishonest," "manipulative," "weird," "Satanic follower," "fiber match," "incriminating testimony—Ridge," "blew kisses to parents," "traveled crime scene 200 times in two years (LIED)," "carried knives," "secondary confession (ballfield girls)," "lied during testimony," "inappropriate thought patterns," "no credible witnesses," "eat father alive." Finally, on one page, in big block letters, a juror wrote emphatically, "YOU ARE WHAT YOU THINK ABOUT!" Within two hours and twenty minutes, the jurors' minds were made up.

Damien had appeared in court throughout the trial wearing long-sleeved tailored shirts, but while the jurors were out of the courtroom deliberating his sentence he changed. When the jurors returned to the room, he sat waiting to hear his fate wearing a black Harley-Davidson T-shirt.

The Sentences

The jury found that all three boys had been murdered in "an especially cruel and depraved manner," a factor that would aggravate, or enhance, the sentence. Taking Jason's youth into consideration, however, plus his lack of a prior criminal record and the jurors' belief that he had acted as an accomplice "under unusual pressure" from Damien, they sentenced him on each of the three counts to life in prison without parole.

They found that although Damien's guilt had been influenced by "extreme mental or emotional disturbance," the cruelty and depravity of the murders outweighed those mitigating factors. They sentenced Damien to death by the method of lethal injection.

Judge Burnett asked the defense lawyers to have their clients stand. "Do either of you have any legal reason to show the court or give the court as to why the sentence should not be imposed? Mr. Echols?"

"No sir."

"Mr. Baldwin?"

"Because I'm innocent."

"Pardon?"

"Because I'm innocent," Jason repeated.

"Well, the jury has heard the evidence and concluded otherwise. Do either of you have anything you want to say?"

"Nope," said Damien.

Jason simply answered, "No."

After reading Jason his sentence, Burnett told the sixteen-year-old, "You will be at this time remanded to the custody of the sheriff for transportation to the Arkansas Department of Correction. . . ."

Then the judge turned to Damien. He informed the convicted killer that he too was now being placed in the custody of a sheriff, who would transport him to the state's prison system. There, Burnett said, "on the fifth day of May, 1994," officials would "cause to be administered a continuous intravenous injection of a lethal quantity of an ultra-short-acting barbiturate in combination with a chemical paralytic agent into your body until you are dead."

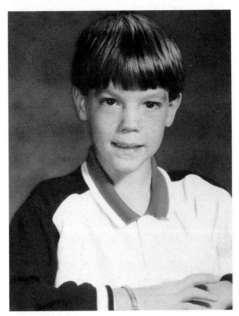

Christopher Byers, age eight.

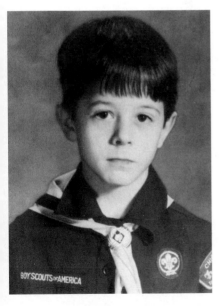

Michael Moore, age eight.

Stevie Branch, age eight.

Detectives stand o[n] pipe across the dit[ch] where the victims['] bodies were foun[d] submerged. The boys' bicycles had also been pulled from the stream.

Detective Byrn Ridge holds one of the sticks that were used to pin the boys' clothes underwater.

Chief Inspector
Gary Gitchell
announces the arrests.
COURTESY OF *THE*
COMMERCIAL APPEAL

John Mark Byers, stepfather of Christopher Byers, sits in Robin Hood
woods, near where Christopher's body was discovered. PHOTO BY JOE
BERLINGER, COURTESY CREATIVE THINKING INTERNATIONAL, LTD.

Police surround Damien Echols, the alleged ringleader, after his arrest.
PHOTO BY STEVE JONES, COURTESY OF *THE COMMERCIAL APPEAL*

Jason Baldwin, at his arraignment, June 5, 1993.
COURTESY OF *THE COMMERCIAL APPEAL*

Jessie Misskelley Jr. is led into court for his 1994 trial. PHOTO BY MORRIS RICHARDSON, COURTESY OF *THE ARKANSAS DEMOCRAT-GAZETTE*

Private investigator Ron Lax.

Dan Stidham,
Jessie's defense attorney.

Prosecutor John Fogleman.

Circuit Judge David Burnett considers an objection by Stidham at Jessie's trial. COURTESY OF *THE ARKANSAS-DEMOCRAT GAZETTE*

Jason smiles briefly during his trial. Damien appears in the foreground, seated across the table from Jason. PHOTO BY DAVID GOTTSCHALK, COURTESY OF *THE ARKANSAS-DEMOCRAT GAZETTE*

Damien remains motionless as he hears himself sentenced to death. PHOTO BY LISA WADDELL, COURTESY OF *THE COMMERCIAL APPEAL*

Defense attorney Edward Mallett talks to reporters following an appeal before the Arkansas Supreme Court. In the foreground, a critic of the trials holds part of a banner urging state officials to "Free the West Memphis Three."

Californians Grove Pashley, Kathy Bakken, and Burk Sauls, founders of a website supporting the West Memphis Three, visit Arkansas in 1997 to meet Damien (shown here separated from them by glass) at the state's Maximum Security Unit.

Filmmakers Bruce Sinofsky (left) and Joe Berlinger (right) visit with Damien in 1999. Photo by Alex Zakrzewski, courtesy of Creative Thinking International, Ltd.

Damien in prison, March 2002.

Jessie in prison, February 2001.

Jason in prison, March 2001.

PART THREE

Revelations

CHAPTER TWENTY-ONE

The Appeals

WHEN JASON HEARD HIS GUILTY VERDICT, he didn't care if his sentence was going to be life or death.[302] Either way was the same to him. He later explained that it wouldn't have mattered if he'd been sentenced to a single day in prison, because "the truth was not found out and proclaimed to everyone." He could not believe the verdict. The word "guilty" rang in his ears.

He'd told himself that the trial would finally bring the truth to light. He believed that God had supreme control, and thus that everything would turn out right. That faith had carried him—and now it was dashed. He recalls that he entered a state of shock and found it difficult to breathe or speak. When Judge Burnett asked if there was any reason the sentence should not be imposed, he had wanted to answer with a scream. Instead, he had felt powerless, crushed, as though a vise was being tightened around him. He'd had to force out his tiny statement: "Because I'm innocent."[303]

Jason: Sixteen and "Tough"

On Monday morning, March 21, 1994, Jason was ordered into a van for the long drive to the penitentiary at Pine Bluff. He carried with him $50—$10 from an ex-inmate who'd visited him in jail and $40 from the jail's warden—and a Bible given to him by his mother. After slipping into a seat by a window, he said,

> I watched as the country went by. I looked at cars and
> their occupants, remembering when my mom, brothers, and

I used to go on trips, and how we would drive way out into the country, in Mississippi, to my aunt Janette's house, and how it would be a long trip, and I would watch the country pass by, just as I was doing now, except that then I was eager for the arrival. This time I wasn't. I was thinking that it would be okay if the destination never arrived, that we could just keep on driving forever and ever, or maybe, the officer driving would take me home and say, "Sorry, Mr. Baldwin. We found out it was a mistake for you to be with us all along. Here, go on home." And I would get out. The cuffs and shackles would be taken off of me. And I would praise God and run into the house.

But the fantasy remained just that. The van turned onto a dusty road that led to the prison department's diagnostic unit, where new inmates spend their first few weeks. His heart beat fast when he saw the guard tower ahead, but everything else seemed to be in slow motion. When the van pulled to a stop, the officer in the tower lowered a milk crate on a rope. The officers from the van placed their guns into the basket and it was hoisted up. Then the bar in front of the van was raised and Jason found himself entering the walled and guarded compound.

He was told to get into a line with other newly arrived inmates who were waiting to be processed. An old inmate inventoried his few possessions and established an account for Jason's money. "My first account," the sixteen-year-old thought ironically. Then he was marched into a room where three men sat behind a table. They ordered him to get naked. Abashed, he removed his orange jumpsuit. "You think you're tough, don't ya?" one of the men said. Jason told himself, "I've got to be tough to survive all this." In that instant he adopted that thought as his prison mantra. "I *am* tough," he told himself. Then he repeated the phrase out loud. The men at the table looked at the 112-pound kid standing naked before them. One of them chuckled, "He won't be tough for long."

In the shower room, where he was led next, the old inmate who'd inventoried Jason's possessions stared hungrily at the boy. Jason told him not to watch. When the inmate continued, Jason stared him in the eyes.

The old man bowed his head and left. It was a small but important victory. For the first time since his arrival at the prison, Jason began to think he might actually survive. But after the shower, the old man was back. He handed Jason some impossibly tight-fitting boxer shorts. Jason told him he'd better get him some that fit. When the man didn't budge, Jason reminded him that he'd been sent to the prison for a triple murder. The man responded that Jason didn't look like a killer. "Did you really murder those kids?" he asked.

"That's what I'm in here for," Jason answered, "so you'd better not mess around with me." The old man left and returned with boxers that fit.[304]

Shortly after Jason's first Christmas in prison, he received a letter from a man who said he'd worked as a counselor at the detention center where Jason and Michael Carson had been held.[305] The letter writer explained that "every word" Michael had said during his testimony against Jason had been based on conversations the counselor had had with him. The counselor explained: "We were discussing the case in a meeting, and I told him what people were saying about the victims and about what was allegedly done to the bodies. This young man then went to the police and stated that you had confessed these details to him while in detention together."

The counselor said that when he "found out what was going on," he was unsure what to do, fearing that he could be sued for revealing confidential information about his discussions with Michael Carson. Finally, however, the counselor had contacted Paul Ford, Jason's attorney, who'd asked him to testify. "I agreed," the counselor wrote, "but later learned that I would not be allowed to tell the Court what had happened. I cannot tell you why because I do not know. They said it had something to do with the fact that the information was privileged." For all of this the counselor expressed profound regret. "I was completely out of line and very stupid for engaging in conversation of that nature," he wrote. "I would give anything in the world if I could take back the comments that I made or change what happened."[306]

By now, only a court ruling could change what had happened. Toward the end of Jason's first year in prison, Paul Ford filed a motion for a new trial. Ford did not cite the counselor's claim; he actually lodged a much more serious charge. In an affidavit accompanying his motion, Ford alleged that at a crucial point in the trial, Judge Burnett had met privately with prosecutors Davis and Fogleman to discuss the prosecutors' trial strategy.[307] Since lawyers for all sides are supposed to be present during any communication with a presiding judge, instances where that does not happen are regarded as improper, ex parte communications.[308] Ford's charge was a serious one. Neither Burnett nor the prosecutors denied that the meeting had taken place. The charge placed Burnett in the position of having to rule on his own conduct as judge. He dismissed Ford's motion for a new trial—and Jason's life in prison wore on.

Jessie: Seventeen and in "The Hole"

Jessie had a harder time adapting. He was disciplined frequently for cussing, refusing to work, fighting, and drinking, because liquor can always be made in a prison. He spent a lot of time in isolation, "the hole," as it's known. He blamed his problems on stress. Years later he would explain, "I get a lot of stuff on my mind. It's hard for me to do anything, thinking about my family, thinking about am I ever going to get out, thinking about what I'm going to do if I ever do get out. It gets me down. It makes me think about stupid stuff, then I try to get into a fight. I try to go to the hole, so that I can be by myself to try to ease my mind. To me, being in the hole ain't so bad. At least you do get a little peace and quiet."[309] Over time, Jessie learned to control his impulse to fight. He was put to work in the kitchen. For fun, he took up dominoes, read wrestling magazines, and slept.

Damien: Nineteen and on "The Row"

Damien's prison experience was markedly different from that of both Jason and Jessie. Damien was driven straight to death row, a cell block in the state's maximum security unit, near Varner, Arkansas. There, he was hustled into a single-man cell, and his antidepressant medication was immediately stopped.[310] During those first few months, the effect of the cold-turkey withdrawal from his medications, on top of the tensions of being placed on death row, was severe. The cell block was constantly noisy. Mentally disturbed inmates ranted. Others shouted angrily from cell to cell. Inmates yelled at guards. Violence occasionally erupted. Guards in riot gear burst into cells. Punishments were meted out. Within a month or two after Damien's arrival, guards came to his cell, searched it, and found a knife. Damien insisted he knew nothing about it, but he was sent to the hole for a month—a month during which, he later claimed, he was denied food and beaten.

In the months that followed, one of the most seasoned criminals in the place took Damien under his wing.[311] Damien would later claim that this inmate had had the knife planted in his cell as a way of demonstrating the level of autonomy he exercised in the prison.[312] After the knife incident, the man offered Damien protection—and introduced him to elements of a plot that had been hatched long before Damien's arrival.[313] As Damien quickly discovered, Arkansas's maximum security unit was at the time a place rife with corruption, and Damien's self-appointed protector was exploiting the situation. Because he and some friends on death row had access to large amounts of money from outside sources, they had been able to bribe guards and certain prison administrators, securing drugs, luxuries, and other contraband items. The ringleader's unique status on death row was evidenced by, among other things, the presence of a recliner in his cell. He also had a Polaroid camera, with which he photographed parties he threw in his cell. The photographs graphically demonstrated the breakdown of security at what was supposed to be the state's most secure prison. By the time Damien arrived there, the inmate and his cadre of friends were using the situation to plan an escape. They had already loosened a window, and they'd removed a cinder block in the wall between the ringleader's cell and the one adjoining it. Shortly after Damien's arrival on death row, he was assigned to that adjoining cell.

The escape plan failed. There was a change in the prison administration, and soon afterward, guards discovered the loosened window and the hole in the wall between the cells, as well as hidden tools and gunpowder. The ringleader was punished severely, his privileges taken away, and when he was finally released from the hole, he wanted to retaliate. He wanted, at the very least, to embarrass prison officials, whom he considered corrupt and equally culpable. Toward that end, he smuggled photographs of his recliner and the parties to a reporter, and they were published in the *Arkansas Times*. Coincidentally or not, at approximately the same time, Damien wrote letters to state officials and to the media, claiming that the veteran inmate had repeatedly raped and beaten him. In the letters, Damien reported that the assaults had begun shortly after he had arrived at the prison, that he'd been photographed in "states of nudity and semi-nudity," and that "several high-ranking officers [at the prison] were already aware of the fact, and would do nothing to prevent it."

The allegation, leveled in March 1995, after Damien had been at the prison for a year, raised the question of how one death row inmate would even have had access to another.[314] In his letter, Damien claimed that "part of the wall was missing . . . so that our cells were joined." The sensational assertion, combined with the photos published by the *Arkansas Times*, called public attention to the breakdown in security at the prison.[315] The Arkansas State Police conducted an investigation, and though investigators said they could not substantiate Damien's claim that he had been raped, three staff members, including an acting warden, were fired as a result.[316]

Jessie's Appeal

As promised, the lawyers for Jessie, Damien, and Jason all filed direct appeals to the Arkansas Supreme Court. Jessie's appeal went to the high court first. In a unanimous opinion handed down on February 19, 1996—two years after his conviction—the seven Supreme Court justices noted that Jessie's statements to police were "virtually the only evidence" offered against him; that they amounted to "a confusing amalgam of times and events"; and that they contained "numerous inconsistencies." Nevertheless, the court found the statements to be sufficient to support the jury's verdict.[317]

Chief Justice Bradley D. Jesson wrote the opinion. In it, he pieced together what he called "the substance" of Jessie's statements to the West Memphis police, laying it out "in such a way as to reveal with clarity." Jessie's description of the crime. Unlike Jessie's statements to the police, the chief justice's summary was presented as a coherent narrative. It noted, for example, that Jessie said he'd been invited to meet Jason and Damien in the woods. "They went to the area, which has a creek, and were in the creek when the victims rode up on their bicycles. Baldwin and Echols called to the boys, who came to the creek. The boys were severely beaten by Baldwin and Echols. At least two of the boys were raped and forced to perform oral sex on Baldwin and Echols." Elsewhere: "The appellant [Jessie] was asked about his involvement in a cult. He said he had been involved for about three months. The participants would typically meet in the woods. They engaged in orgies and, as an initiation rite, killing and eating dogs. . . ."

The Supreme Court recognized that Jessie had gotten some significant details wrong. "The appellant [Jessie] initially stated that the events took place about 9 A.M. on May fifth," Justice Jesson noted. "Later in the statement, he changed that time to noon. . . . [In a later statement], the appellant said he, Echols and Baldwin had come to the Robin Hood area between 5 and 6 P.M. Upon prompting by the officer, he changed that to 7 or 8 P.M. He finally settled on saying that his group arrived at 6 P.M., while the victims arrived near dark." But all seven justices waived off the discrepancies. "When inconsistencies appear in the evidence," they noted, "we defer to the jury's determination of credibility."

Attorney Stidham argued in Jessie's appeal, as he had at Jessie's trial, that the confession had been involuntary. The justices acknowledged that "the age, education and intelligence of the accused" were "factors to be considered" in determining the validity of a confession. They also recognized that a confession made while a subject is in the custody of police "is presumed involuntary" and that "the burden is on the state to show that the confession is voluntarily made." Despite those requirements, however, the chief justice wrote that the entire court had found that Jessie's confession had been voluntary.

Nor was the high court swayed by Stidham's pleas regarding Jessie's age and mental capacity. "Persons younger than he have been held capable of giving voluntary confessions," the chief justice noted. Furthermore, he added, "A low score on an intelligence quotient test does not mean that a suspect is incapable of voluntarily making a confession or waiving his rights."[318]

The high court also agreed with Judge Burnett's decision that the techniques used by Inspector Gitchell and Detective Ridge—the circle diagram, the polygraph, the picture of the victim, and the tape recording of Aaron Hutcheson's voice—had not been overbearing. Though they acknowledged that "the boy's voice gives us pause" and that this type of tactic "comes perilously close to psychological overbearing," the justices concluded that "in this instance, since numerous other factors point to the voluntariness of the confession, we will not invalidate the confession."

But none of those conclusions constituted the most controversial part of the opinion. The part that would reverberate through the Arkansas justice system for years to come centered on Jessie's status as a minor and the fact that detectives had failed to have a parent sign his waiver of rights. The issue was particularly troubling in Jessie's case because, as the high court noted, "At the time the appellant signed his waiver, [Arkansas law] provided that a juvenile's waiver form must be signed by a parent, guardian, or custodian."[319] Despite the law's apparent clarity, the high court nevertheless concluded that it did not apply in Jessie's case. That was, the chief justice wrote, because at the time Jessie was questioned, the State Supreme Court had already ruled "that, when a person under age eighteen *is charged as an adult* in circuit court, failure to obtain a parent's signature on a waiver form does not render a confession inadmissible. . . ." In that opinion, the court ruled that "when a juvenile is charged as an adult, he becomes subject to the procedures applicable to adults. Therefore, the requirement of parental consent is limited to juvenile court proceedings." [320]

To Stidham, the ruling was both maddening and absurd. It meant, he argued, that a minor charged with a relatively light offense, such as throwing a rock through a window, could not sign away his constitutional rights without a parent also signing the form with him—yet a juvenile charged with a serious crime, for which he might receive a sentence of life in prison or even death, did not get that protection.

Stidham continued to attack the validity of Jessie's confession based on the detectives' failure to record his entire confession. But the high court dealt easily with that, noting that "no Arkansas law requires this."[321] Stidham's final points were even more easily dismissed. The high court supported all of Burnett's decisions, including the one to admit into evidence items such as "a picture of Jason Baldwin wearing a black t-shirt with a skull and the name of the group Metallica on it; testimony of a witness that she attended a cult meeting with the appellant and Echols"; and "a book on witchcraft found in Echols's home"—items that Stidham claimed were irrelevant and prejudicial. To the contrary, the high court reasoned, all of the items were relevant because they served to corroborate aspects of Jessie's confession. And, "With the confession being the state's only meaningful evidence against the appellant, any corroboration was highly probative."

Finally, the court addressed Stidham's contention that Jessie should have been granted a new trial when, during Damien and Jason's trial, the associate medical examiner, Dr. Peretti, changed his testimony to a time of death that contradicted Jessie's confession. The high court dismissed this as well, noting that the jury in Jessie's case would probably have found Jessie guilty anyway, even if it had heard Peretti's estimate that the time of death was probably well after midnight.[322]

The Ruling on Damien and Jason

It took the Arkansas Supreme Court a bit longer to address the forty-four points raised by attorneys in Damien's and Jason's direct appeals. The opinion, which the justices handed down two days before Christmas in 1996, was ninety-three pages long, the lengthiest in the court's recent history. And the ruling's effect was equally sweeping. On every point the defense lawyers raised, the justices unanimously found that the trial had been fair and that Judge Burnett had made no errors.[323]

The Supreme Court concluded that although the evidence was circumstantial, it had been sufficient to support the verdicts. In explaining the court's decision, the high court referred frequently to the state's theory that the killings had occurred as part of a satanic ritual. "On cross-examination," the opinion said,

> Echols admitted that he has delved deeply into the occult
> and was familiar with its practices. Various items were found

in his room, including a funeral register upon which he had drawn a pentagram and upside-down crosses and had copied spells. A journal was introduced, and it contained morbid images and references to dead children. Echols testified that he wore a long black trench coat even when it was warm. One witness had seen Echols, Baldwin, and Misskelley together six months before the murders, wearing long black coats and carrying long staffs. Dr. Peretti testified that some of the head wounds to the boys were consistent with the size of the two sticks that were recovered by the police.

Regarding the state's theory of motive, the Supreme Court had this to say:

Dr. Dale Griffis, an expert in occult killings, testified in the state's case-in-chief that the killings had the "trappings of occultism." He testified that the date of the killings, near a pagan holiday, was significant, as well as the fact that there was a full moon. He stated that young children are often sought for sacrifice because "the younger, the more innocent, the better the life force." He testified that there were three victims, and the number three had significance in occultism. Also, the victims were all eight years old, and eight is a witches' number. He testified that sacrifices are often done near water for a baptism-type rite or just to wash the blood away. The fact that the victims were tied ankle to wrist was significant because this was done to display the genitalia, and the removal of Byers's testicles was significant because testicles are removed for the semen. He stated that the absence of blood at the scene could be significant because cult members store blood for future services in which they would drink the blood or bathe in it. He testified that the "overkill" or multiple cuts could reflect occult overtones. Dr. Griffis testified that there was significance in injuries to the left side of the victims as distinguished from the right side: People who practice occultism will use the midline theory, drawing straight down through the body. The right side is related to those things synonymous with Christianity, while the left side is that of the practitioners of the Satanic occult. He testified that the clear place on the bank could be consistent with a ceremony. In sum, Dr. Griffis testified there was significant evidence of Satanic ritual killings.

The high court ruled that all of this constituted "substantial evidence" of Damien's guilt. As for the substantial evidence against Jason, the justices cited only Michael Carson's testimony that Jason told him he had "dismembered the kids." The court labored a bit longer over arguments that the trials should have been severed. But in the end the justices concluded that "almost all of the factors" they considered "clearly" weighed in favor of a joint trial.[324] Similarly, the court had little trouble approving the extraordinary nighttime search; the fact that the West Memphis magistrate who'd issued the search warrants had also instructed police in how to prepare the affidavit; and the vagueness of warrants authorizing police to search for "blue, green, red, black, and purple fibers" and "cult or Satanic materials." The high court did deal at some length with arguments concerning the admission of evidence regarding the occult. But ultimately, all of those arguments were rejected as well. Relying heavily on the testimony of Griffis, the high court ruled that Judge Burnett's decision to qualify Griffis as an expert had not been error; that allowing Griffis to testify had not been error; that Judge Burnett's ruling admitting the dog's skull, heavy metal music posters, and books Damien had read into evidence had not been error; and that there was no problem with Judge Burnett's ruling allowing Jerry Driver to testify that he'd seen Damien, Jason, and Jessie walking together six months before the murders, carrying "long sticks or staffs."[325]

The Supreme Court also rejected arguments that Judge Burnett should have required Christopher Morgan to take the stand, even if he had invoked the Fifth Amendment for every question he was asked. The justices ruled that the trial judge had the discretion to decide whether Morgan should testify or not. Since they found no "manifest abuse" of that discretion, they declined to second-guess Burnett's decision.

And so it went. The high court approved of Burnett's decisions to admit as evidence the sticks found in the woods months after the killings and the knife taken from the lake, based on Dr. Peretti's testimony that wounds to the victims "were consistent" with injuries that might have been caused by such objects. Similarly, the high court supported Fogleman's demonstration in front of the jury with the knives cutting the grapefruit. And it found no problem with the fact that, even now, two years after the trials, none of the court-appointed defense lawyers had been paid.[326]

Though the opinion was exceptionally long, its bottom line was simple: the convictions would stand. The only avenue of appeal left to the defendants now, in the state of Arkansas, was for them to claim that their lawyers had been grossly inadequate. But no court would appoint someone to do that, and all three of the inmates were indigent.

Paradise Lost

At a point when it appeared that Damien, Jason, and Jessie might slip into obscurity, Sinofsky and Berlinger, the filmmakers who'd recorded the trials, released their documentary. *Paradise Lost: The Child Murders at Robin Hood Hills* premiered in 1996 and created an immediate sensation. Against a sound track by Metallica, the documentary showed gritty scenes of West Memphis and the families involved in the case, on the sides of both the victims and the defendants. Images of poverty, grief, and anger played against the formality of courtroom proceedings. Interviews with Damien, Jason, and Jessie in jail were interlaced with comments from the victims' families, and long segments in which John Mark Byers railed against the accused. The film aired on HBO. Its directors never offered a conclusion, beyond the actuality of the convictions, but thousands of viewers—and most reviewers—found the film and its contents shocking.[327]

Many viewers in Arkansas were dismayed by the image of their state presented in the film—and by the way reviewers focused on the small-town mentality that they generally assumed had given rise to the verdicts. Michael Atkinson wrote in *Spin* magazine that West Memphis was "the kind of dreary hellhole that America is sick in the blood with."

Robin Dougherty observed in the *Miami Herald* that Damien's "wardrobe and his page-boy-gone-bad haircut wouldn't get a second look at South Beach." Roger Ebert focused on the prosecutors' explanation of motive. "Oh, it's a great film," Ebert said, "and one of the things it points out is the need, the real need to create the idea of Satanic rituals in order to explain crimes, because it's not enough that there could be a sick deviate out there who would kill these boys. . . . But everybody in the town and in the courtroom and on the jury are all blinded by their fantasies about Satanic cults, and they can't listen to reason."

wm3.org

Many filmgoers assumed that since release of the documentary, all three defendants had appealed, and that if the problems revealed in the film were real, they were now being corrected and the teenagers would soon walk free. But three friends in Los Angeles—writer Burk Sauls, graphic artist Kathy Bakken, and photographer Grove Pashley—were not content to assume. They wanted to know more about what had happened in the case, but found it hard to get information. Sauls later explained that after seeing the documentary, "I felt like I'd missed that part where they show why they thought these teenagers were responsible for the murders." Bakken was equally perplexed. "I felt like I was hanging," she said. "It was a horrible feeling. I hoped that something was going on, but just to make sure, I wrote to the lawyers and what I found out was that the guys were still languishing in prison."

In October 1996, the three traveled to Arkansas, trekked through the woods where the bodies were found, drove to three different prisons, and met with Damien, Jason, and Jessie. They also met with Jessie's lawyer Dan Stidham, the only one of the defense attorneys still committed to proving his client's innocence. As they later recalled, they found "not a single thing" that supported the idea that the three teenagers had committed the murders. Equally troubling was the sense that "no one was out there helping them, and they had just been abandoned."

The three began to view what happened in West Memphis as a modern-day version of the infamous Salem witch trials, in which rumors and hysteria had supplanted reason, and resulted in executions. As they often later explained, they also became convinced that just as an uncritical media had promulgated the view of the defendants as evil, a forum for a more rational discussion of what had actually taken place might introduce some of the objectivity that only the passage of time had been able to bring to Salem—in that case, many years too late for the unjustly convicted.[328]

As the three Californians obtained answers to their questions and dug up supporting material, they decided to publish their findings on the Internet. The Web site they founded, wm3.org, quickly became a clearinghouse for information and opinion on the case.[329] A synergy developed between the documentary film and the Web site, as film viewers, intrigued by the same questions that had bothered the Web site's founders, searched the Internet, found wm3.org, and in surprising numbers responded to its calls for action.

The Web site founders produced T-shirts featuring pictures of the three Arkansas inmates and the rallying cry "Free the West Memphis Three." They urged supporters to write to Arkansas's governor, Mike Huckabee, asking that he press for a reexamination of the case. A support fund was established to offset costs of maintaining the site.[330] The site tried to personalize the inmates by publishing current photographs and offering glimpses into their lives in prison. In a neatly formatted 1996 "one-minute interview" with Damien, for instance, he responded to the question of what he'd like to do if he were released. "I would love to eventually own a secondhand bookstore," he said. "I love to read, and it would be pretty peaceful." Jason was reported to be working as an office clerk at his unit, while Jessie, like the majority of Arkansas inmates, worked outdoors on his unit's hoe squad.

By 1997, the site reported that although the inmates' direct appeals had failed, all three still had postconviction petitions pending before the Arkansas Supreme Court. As the Web site became increasingly sophisticated and its founders' understanding of the legal processes deepened, documents from the case were posted, links to relevant Arkansas Supreme Court's rulings were established, different discussion boards flourished (one for newcomers seeking information and another where the converted could discuss strategies), and an archive was developed.[331]

While officials in West Memphis dismissed both the documentary and the Web site as the work of misguided and misinformed would-be do-gooders from out of state—people who didn't know what had *really* happened—the movement to "free the West Memphis Three" had struck an unusual chord in America. It hummed with reminiscences of ostracism, with passion for recognizable justices, and with a commitment to freedom of expression—whether it be artistic, intellectual, or religious.[332]

As *Paradise Lost* aired again on HBO, continued to play at small theaters, and moved to video, the interaction between viewers and the Web site expanded. In Arkansas, the public effect was muted, but personal responses were often intense. One video rental store in Little Rock allowed the film to be checked out for free, because the store's owners believed Arkansans should see it.[333] Almost the entire audience stayed for two hours after *Paradise Lost* was shown at the annual documentary film festival in Hot Springs, Arkansas, for a discussion with the producers and some of the lawyers who'd represented the West Memphis teens. In 1998, a woman from Jonesboro who'd attended part of the second trial said that after she'd seen the film she'd gone straight to her computer. "I did a search," she said. "I typed in a name and *bam*, there was the site. And I thought, 'Damn, I didn't think anybody would give a rip. And it amazed me no end that anybody besides myself would care.' "[334]

Fame in Prison

The three inmates at the heart of the mounting attention were not allowed to see *Paradise Lost*. E-mails flew back and forth about them, but they could not send or receive them. The case was discussed in newspapers, but the major media in Arkansas, and across the river in Memphis, paid it scant attention. For Damien, Jason, and Jessie, prison still consisted, day after day, of bad food, iron bars, and boredom. Still, the documentary and the Web site would affect their lives. For one thing, mail began to pour in.[335] Among the letters sent to Jason was one from a seventeen-year-old high school student in Little Rock. Sara Cadwallader later recalled, "I saw the documentary on HBO and knew I wanted to write to them. I guess I picked Jason because he was the youngest one."

In an interview in 1996, Damien reported that among hundreds of other letters, he'd received one from Sister Helen Prejean, the author of *Dead Man Walking*. He recalled later that the letter said, " 'Choose life,' whatever that means." By then, Damien had come to see life—and especially his own—differently than he had before. "I came in here as a child," he explained, "and a few years have passed, and in this type of environment, I think you might age a little more rapidly."[336] Damien's world widened through contacts from people who'd seen the film and visited the Web site. Many sent him books, which he read voraciously. His reading tastes expanded to include major works of literature. And he too began a serious correspondence with a woman who'd seen the film and made the effort to contact him. Lorri Davis, a New York architect and film buff, had seen *Paradise Lost* when it premiered at the Metropolitan Museum of Art. She began sending Damien books, and when phone calls were allowed from death row, most of his were placed to her. He'd been off his antidepressant medication since his arrival on death row, and by the end of 1996, he acknowledged that "unfortunately" he'd grown "quite a bit more cheerful"—"unfortunately" because, as he put it, "I always feel like an idiot when I'm cheerful."

CHAPTER TWENTY-TWO

The Drug Informant

LIFE AFTER THE TRIALS remained hard for the families of the victims, including little Aaron Hutcheson. Though he was not a direct victim, in that he had not been killed, his involvement in the investigation had certainly exposed him to the crime's horrors. Even after the trials, his mother's interest in the case continued, and thus so, to an extent, did his own.

After the trials concluded and the defendants had been locked away, Vicki Hutcheson contacted Ron Lax, the Memphis private investigator, several times to report that she was "bothered" about parts of the investigation. In April 1994, a few weeks after Damien and Jason were taken to prison, Lax paid a call on Hutcheson in the apartment where she now lived. During the visit, Lax later wrote in his notes, "Vicki turned to me and asked who had received the reward money. I told her I did not think anyone had and she stated she felt she should have since her son's voice is what 'broke the case.' She then went on to tell me the police had interviewed Aaron on numerous occasions without her being present and that they had no right to do that and she intended to sue the city because their actions had caused Aaron severe mental problems."

But those were not her only concerns. According to Lax's notes, Hutcheson also "stated she had never signed a release to have the tape recorder installed in her trailer and that Gitchell was lying on the stand when he said there was a release"; she reported "that Bryn Ridge told her they would take care of the hot checks in return for her testimony, but Ridge cautioned her not to tell anyone about that"; and when Lax told her that Damien did not drive, she said, "Well, maybe I dreamed that."

Three months later, in July 1994, Hutcheson called Lax to ask if anything new had developed. "When I told her we were still working on

Damien's appeal," Lax wrote, "she began telling me of her experience in New York on *The Maury Povich Show*. According to Vicki, the Hobbses were present, as were Mark and Melissa Byers and Mr. Hicks, Pam Hobbs's father. Vicki stated Mark Byers was out of control and the full tape of his comments and actions should be viewed."[337]

In the following month, Hutcheson called Lax's office four more times. The first time, Lax was unavailable, and she asked to speak to Glori Shettles. Shettles later wrote, "I asked Vicki what her three biggest concerns and issues were presently, to which she responded: One, why is Mark Byers on the street? Two, why is most of the West Memphis Police Department quitting? And three, why are three boys behind bars when police had much more evidence on Mark Byers than the three?" Hutcheson called Shettles again the next day, and again two days later. "She stated she was thinking of calling Channel 13 News in Memphis to advise she had, in fact, perjured herself," Shettles wrote after the second conversation. "She went on to say she did not lie, but she wanted to 'get out of it.' " Four days after that, she called and had another rambling conversation with Shettles. After this one Shettles wrote, "Needless to say, Vicki is experiencing many pressures and frustrations. She desperately wants to 'know the truth' and realizes she cannot trust the police."

In light of the calls, Lax arranged for Hutcheson to come to his office in Memphis, so that he and Jessie's attorney, Dan Stidham, could formally interview her. She agreed, and on August 17, 1994, the investigator and the attorney tape-recorded a session with Hutcheson. It lasted for five and a half hours. Lax and Stidham were particularly interested in the part of the interview where Hutcheson discussed the esbat. Lax wrote in his summary:

> Vicki feels that she went, but she was drunk and is not sure with whom she went. She had broken up with her boyfriend that day at around 2 or 3 P.M. and went to the liquor store and bought two fifths of Wild Turkey. She drank one bottle by herself and then went to this meeting in the area around Turrell, Arkansas. She still recalls what the area looked like, but cannot recall if Damien and Jessie went with

her or not. When we tried to get her to recall how arrangements were made for her to go to this meeting, she was at a loss to do so. She recalled seeing the people painted black and realized they were undressing and stated she had to get out of there and someone took her away; however, she does not remember anything afterward and woke up the next morning, lying on the ground in her front yard with a whiskey bottle. She was alone at this time and she has no recollection of anything else.

Hutcheson's account of her role in the case would remain ambiguous. In the late 1990s, writer Burk Sauls posted on the wm3.org Web site the transcipt of an interview he'd conducted with her. It remained on the site until Hutcheson, citing fears of her safety, asked the site's managers to take it off. In the interview she's described Jessie Misskelley as having been "like a little brother" to her. "What is you story about that time?" Sauls had asked Hutcheson. "Well," she'd replied, "I'm really concerned about legal issues right now with it. But basically I said what the West Memphis police wanted me to say. And that was that I went to the meeting. The esbat meeting. It was all their stories." She characterized the police investigation as having been "just an overreaction." At one point she told Sauls, "You know what I want to say more than anything? I want to say that I'm sorry. I just want to tell Jessie and Jason and Damien that I'm sorry."

A Knife Fight and a Restraining Order

Shortly after the trials, during about the same period that Vicki Hutcheson was calling Lax and Shettles, the investigators were also receiving calls from Ricky Murray, Christopher Byers's biological father. Shettles wrote for the agency's files that Murray "had been very disturbed recently, while watching *The Maury Povich Show*, as Mark Byers had stated that on the date of the murders, he picked up his wife from work and had an airtight alibi. Rick had spoken with Mark Byers at Chris Byers's funeral. At that time, Mark did not say he had picked up Melissa at work, only that he had been at court that day." Lax noted that Murray also stated that "Melissa Byers has been a heroin addict since age twelve. She was using heroin before she smoked marijuana." Finally, Shettles noted that Murray "also stated he never gave up parental rights and that Chris had not been adopted by Mark Byers."

But by then, calls from Melissa's ex-husband to the Memphis private investigators were the least of the Byerses' problems. After the trials, they had moved away from West Memphis, leaving a string of hot checks behind, and settled into a house in Cherokee Village, a planned community in north-central Arkansas near the Missouri line. Though they told their new neighbors that they wanted to live quietly and be granted privacy in their grief, they quickly attracted police attention. In September 1994, both Mark and Melissa were jailed by officials in Sharp County, after investigators concluded that they were responsible for the theft of antiques worth more than $20,000 from a residence near their new home.[338] Police charged Mark and Melissa Byers with residential burglary and theft of property. They posted bond of $5,000 each to be released from jail. If convicted, a judge told them at their arraignment, they faced sentences of three to ten years in prison and fines of up to $10,000 each. They both pleaded not guilty.[339]

Within two weeks, Mark Byers was arrested again. This time he was charged with contributing to the delinquency of a minor, a misdemeanor. The charged stemmed from an incident the previous July in which a teenager had been seriously injured in a knife fight that Byers had instigated, encouraged, and supervised.[340] The police chief who arrested Byers recalled, "He kept asking me, 'What is your opinion?' He said, 'I think they ought to have fought it out, don't you?' I said, 'No, I don't. That's one of the reasons I'm arresting you.' "

By the end of October 1994, seven months after Damien and Jason's trial, the area's newspaper was reporting that the Byerses faced "criminal charges, restraining orders, and a feud" that involved the Byerses' next-door neighbors. Police were called to settle differences between the two couples eight times in one month. Mark Byers told a reporter for the local paper that his relationship with his neighbors had turned sour when he had swatted their five-year-old son with a flyswatter. The neighbors complained that the swatting had been hard enough to leave bruises. In another incident, the neighbors told police that Melissa had stood in the road outside their house and yelled that if she and Mark were sent to prison, it would be the neighbors' fault.[341]

When a local reporter went to interview the two couples, she noted that the Byerses, who were living on Mark's disability income, had "no phone, no gas for hot water, and little, if any, cash on hand." Seated at the family's kitchen table, Mark Byers told her that he and his wife were being persecuted because of accusations that had been made against him at the trials. "We are the victims turned into villains," he told the reporter. But before long, yet another incident brought the Byerses into the news again. A motor home belonging to the woman whose house they'd been charged with burglarizing mysteriously exploded and burned in her driveway. The woman, who was out of town at the time, told authorities that the vehicle's propane tanks had been empty.

Spurred by the stories about the Byerses' latest troubles, a reporter for the *Arkansas Times* decided to look into John Mark Byers's background. She contacted a retired deputy sheriff from Marked Tree, the town in eastern Arkansas where Byers had grown up. The former deputy recalled that in 1973, when Byers was just sixteen, his parents had called police to their house, claiming that their son was threatening them with a butcher knife.[342] The *Times* reporter also learned about a more recent, though less violent, incident in Jonesboro. The owners of a jewelry store there said that Mark and Melissa had worked for them briefly in October 1990, during which time jewelry valued at $65,000 had been stolen from the store. When the police failed to make an arrest, the owners filed a civil lawsuit against the Byerses and another couple. The case, which was heard in a Jonesboro court in April 1991, resulted in the Byerses' two codefendants being ordered to return the items. The attorney who represented the Byerses' two codefendants in that case was Val Price, the Jonesboro lawyer who was later appointed to defend Damien.[343]

By the end of 1994, the year of the murder trials, the Byerses faced twelve misdemeanor charges in West Memphis for more than $600 worth of hot checks; their neighbors had a restraining order against them; they faced charges for residential burglary; Mark faced charges of contributing to the delinquency of a minor; he and Melissa both were suspects in the explosion of the motor home; and Melissa faced charges of aggravated assault, stemming from an incident in which she'd held a gun on a carpet installer who'd refused to work in her house until the floors were cleaned.

In January 1995, the local municipal judge found Mark Byers guilty on the charge relating to the boys' fight.[344] The judge ordered Byers to pay half of the injured boy's medical expenses, a sum of $2,000. (The offending teenager was ordered to pay the other half.) The judge also sentenced Byers to one year in jail, but Byers posted an appeal bond of $1,000, which allowed him to remain free. How Byers secured the money for the appeal bond, when it was known that he faced hot-check charges and that as recently as three months earlier, he and his family had been living without a telephone, heat, or hot water, apparently did not concern the court.

The couple kept a low profile for the next several months. The other charges against them were still pending, and the third anniversary of Christopher's murder was drawing near, when police were again called to investigate a tragedy involving the Byerses. This time, however, the call came not from neighbors but from the local hospital, where doctors had just pronounced Melissa Byers dead.

Melissa's Unexplained Death

The date was March 29, 1996. The hospital staff told the sheriff that an ambulance had been called to the Byerses' house at 5:20 P.M. Melissa was unconscious when the medics arrived.[345] She was pronounced dead at the hospital an hour and ten minutes later. But the doctors were perplexed. They told the sheriff that they could find no evidence of trauma on her body, and could not readily determine what had led to her sudden death. In contrast to Inspector Gitchell's decision after discovery of the eight-year-olds' murders, the sheriff immediately called for help from the Arkansas State Police. Within two hours of the call for an ambulance, a team of state police investigators had gathered at the hospital. The state police investigated the death as a "possible homicide."[346]

Observing Melissa's nude body, investigators noted the presence of "IV puncture marks on the top of both her feet, on the inside of her right wrist, and on her upper right thoracic area." The right thoracic puncture mark and the right wrist puncture mark were both covered by

Band-Aids, suggesting that they might have resulted from efforts to revive Melissa at the hospital. But other puncture marks were not bandaged. The investigators took fourteen photographs of the body, which they identified by number in their report. The report itself was three pages long, but even in that short amount of space it conveyed more information than was recorded in any report by the West Memphis police after the discovery of the murdered boys' bodies. The investigator noted that the county coroner had arrived "at approximately 8:10 P.M. to obtain possession of the body for the state medical examiner's office."

By that time, however, the investigators were already interviewing a witness who'd called police after hearing the news of Melissa's death. As the lead investigator later wrote in his notes, the witness reported that "Melissa and Mark were having family troubles lately, and that Mark had a girlfriend by the name of Mandy. . . . She also said that she believes that Melissa has been taking Dilaudids [*sic*] and Zanex [*sic*]."

At 9:40 P.M., a team of local and state investigators began a search of the Byerses' house. While the search was being conducted, Byers stood outside the house with a woman who was identified in the state police reports as Mandy Beasley. One investigator videotaped the interior of the house while another took still photographs. The lead investigator dictated a careful description of the single-story wood-frame house, paying special attention to the bedroom where the ambulance workers had found Melissa. A third state police investigator prepared a diagram of the "crime scene." In the bedroom, they seized as evidence three towels and a shirt, all found on the bed; "suspected marijuana and paraphernalia"; a couple of glasses, one of which was believed to contain peach schnapps; and "seven different types of prescription medication prescribed for Melissa Byers," all of which the investigators listed.[347]

At midnight, the lead investigator was still at work, interviewing the neighbor who had called the ambulance.[348] The neighbor told the investigator that Byers had called him a little after 5 P.M. The neighbor said Byers "advised him that he could not wake up Melissa and asked him to come over and see if she had a pulse." The neighbor said he asked Byers "why he didn't call an ambulance" but that Byers had dismissed the question, insisting that he "come over—come through the kitchen door."

According to the investigator's report, the neighbor said that "he went immediately to the bedroom and saw that Melissa was totally naked, lying on the far side of the bed on her back. He advised her mouth was wide open, her eyes were closed, she was totally limp, and her arms were down by her side. [He] advised he checked for a pulse, lifted her eyelids, and looked at her eyes. He advised that he told John Mark to do CPR on her and he started it. He advised that she gurgled up some fluids, and he told Mark he was going to call EMS [emergency medical service]." After the neighbor placed the call, he saw that Mark and his stepson Ryan Clark, now sixteen, were trying to put pants on Melissa. The neighbor reported that when he asked Mark if Melissa was dead, Mark told him no, but that as Mark made the pronouncement, "Ryan had a funny, eerie look on his face."

The neighbor also advised the officer "that Mark was not totally hysterical, but he was worried and concerned. He advised when the EMTs got to the residence, Mark kept telling them, 'They've got to bring her back.'" Ryan, meanwhile, "kept mumbling something, and he did not seem coherent." Ryan left the house before the ambulance arrived. The neighbor reported "that when he left, he almost flipped the car over, he left so fast, spinning gravel. . . ."

The neighbor told the investigator for the state police that he followed the ambulance to the hospital, where he met with John Mark Byers. "He advised that at the hospital, Mark told him he was afraid Melissa had overdosed on a drug that is in the streets in Memphis." The neighbor said "that Byers told him it could be bought for fifty dollars on the street. He told him the name of the drug. He could not remember it, but thought it started with the letter 'D.' [The neighbor] advised that John Mark Byers also told him he thought her death was a drug overdose and that they were going to accuse him of smothering her. He advised that Byers did not clarify who 'they' were."

That same night, the state police investigator also had Byers outline in writing his activities in the hours preceding Melissa's death. The statement was slim on detail. Byers said principally that he and his wife had taken a nap, and that when he'd gotten up, he'd found he could not wake her.[349]

Banished

The focus of the investigation into Melissa's "possible homicide" shifted to the Arkansas Medical Examiner's Office, where, it was hoped, an autopsy would explain the mysterious death. But just as Inspector Gitchell in West Memphis had spent weeks in frustration waiting for autopsy results, the state police investigator and the sheriff now waited for the medical examiner's findings on Melissa. When five months had passed with no word from the state crime lab, the state police investigator called to inquire.[350] The investigator finally received the autopsy report on September 30, 1996—a full six months after Melissa's death.

But the report was of little help. And its conclusion—or more precisely, its failure to arrive at one—was unusual. Despite the fact that Melissa's body had been taken to the crime lab immediately, the Arkansas medical examiner reported that his office had been unable to determine either the physical cause of her death or the legal manner of her death; that is, whether it had resulted from natural causes, or been an accident, a suicide, or a homicide. The sheriff issued a press release explaining that though drugs had been found in Melissa's body, there were "not enough to be lethal." Still, the sheriff said, the case would remain open—and the autopsy report would be sealed.

The investigation into Melissa's death was not the only matter relating to Byers and the law that was taking some unusual turns. On August 28, 1996, five months after Melissa's death and a month before the medical examiner released her autopsy report, John Mark Byers appeared in court to face the residential burglary charge. He pleaded no contest to the charge, whereupon the prosecutor agreed to a deal that would allow Byers to stay out of prison.[351] Byers still had no visible means of support beyond his meager disability income. Nonetheless, the prosecutor announced that he had agreed not to send Byers to prison if he met two conditions: (1) that Byers pay $20,000 in restitution to the woman whose house he'd burgled, and (2) that Byers would leave town and never return. Specifically, Byers was ordered "not to remain, reside, or enter" any of the five counties that comprised the north Arkansas judicial district. Byers assured the judge that he would be moving, and the judge, in turn, warned Byers that his no-contest plea would be immediately changed to guilty if he ever returned to the district or was arrested again, in which case he could be charged as a habitual offender.[352]

The decision to banish Byers marked another odd episode in his highly atypical history with courts and prosecutors. The condition of banishment, or exile, is almost never imposed because the Arkansas constitution forbids it.[353]

"A Deep Story"

In December 1997, a year after Byers left the judicial district, a reporter for the *Arkansas Times* looked further into his wife's unexplained death. The investigation into it had stalled, though the case remained open. Although the medical examiner's office and the local prosecutor refused to allow either the reporter or Jessie's lawyer to see the autopsy report, the reporter obtained a copy from the state police. It noted that Melissa weighed 211 pounds at her death; that she had "Christopher" tattooed on her right upper back; and that, in addition to the puncture marks investigators noticed, both of her wrists bore "multiple, well-healed scars." The toxicology lab reported finding no alcohol in her system and no opiates in her blood, though traces of some of her prescribed medications were detected. The report said her urine tested positive for marijuana and hydromorphone, the synthetic narcotic commonly known as Dilaudid. (Dilaudid is highly prized on the black market, and its street price at the time of Melissa's death was about $50 per tablet.) Melissa did not have a prescription for Dilaudid.

The reporter noted with some surprise that in the autopsy report's section for the examiner's opinion, hydromorphone was not mentioned. Rather, the conclusions repeatedly identified a different drug, hydrocodone, as the one that was found in the urine. When contacted about the discrepancy, the state crime lab's director blamed it on a typographical error.[354] When questioned about the numerous puncture wounds on Melissa's body, he said that they might have resulted from medical intervention after the ambulance was called. According to the director, there was "not any way to tell if the wounds were two hours or six hours old" and the pathologist who'd performed the autopsy believed that "all those wounds were probably done at the hospital."[355]

Interest in Melissa's death rekindled briefly in late 1997, when state police investigators interviewed three people, all of whom had reported suspicions relating to John Mark Byers.[356] But little was heard from him. When the *Arkansas Times* reporter contacted him in Jonesboro, where he had moved after his extraordinary (and apparently illegal) banishment from north-central Arkansas, he professed never to have known about Melissa "injecting any drugs." He said she had died of "a broken heart," and that "after Christopher passed away, she gave up her will to live."

When asked about himself, Byers said that a brain tumor had left him "100 percent disabled" and that he suffered "terrible migraine headaches" because of it. At times, he said, his head "felt like a medicine ball, like there are sirens going off in my ears, and like a camera's going off in my face." He said he was "living below the poverty level" and that, because of his financial condition, he hadn't had to pay the woman who'd been burglarized. "I'm judgment-proof," he said. "I'm indigent."

John Mark Byers derided his former neighbors in the mountainous north Arkansas region, calling them "backward," "narrow-minded," and "banjo-picking hillbillies." He said, "I was railroaded up there." But mostly Byers bemoaned the loss of his wife and child and the good life he said he'd once had. "This is a deep story," he said. "I was a thirty-second-degree Mason. I went from my big fine home and being a respectable citizen to feeling like I'm just an outcast thrown to the bottom of a pit." More than once he reminded the reporter, "I am the victim here. Let's not forget that." As for the murders of Christopher, Michael, and Stevie, Byers had this to say: "Anyone that takes anyone's life has got to be someone that's very depraved and very twisted. Not retarded sick, mean sick. They must have some type of problem that's deeper than I can imagine."

Wrong Number

Byers's tale of woe soon grew longer, however. Just as trouble followed him from West Memphis to Cherokee Village, it followed him to Jonesboro. There, in June 1998, in the same courthouse where Judge Burnett had sentenced Damien and Jason, another judge convicted Byers on a misdemeanor hot-check charge. But again, no punishment ensued. According to court records, Byers received only a twelve-month suspended sentence, despite the assurance he'd been given upon his banishment from the adjoining district that he'd face prosecution as a habitual offender if he committed another crime.

It appeared that Byers was not only "judgment-proof," as he claimed, but incarceration-proof as well. But then, on April 19, 1999, Byers dialed a wrong number.

At about 9:20 P.M., an Arkansas State Police trooper was standing beside a car he'd stopped, issuing a citation, when his personal cell phone rang. He didn't recognize the caller's voice, but he became intrigued when the caller invited him to "come by his house and buy some more stuff." The trooper later said he thought it was one of his buddies "messing" with him, but he was cautious enough to ask, "What kind of stuff?"

"Pot," the caller replied. "Good stuff." Now the trooper was certain that the caller had no idea whose number he had dialed. But by the same token, the trooper had no idea who the caller was. According to the trooper's report, he was able to find out the caller's address by claiming that he was "busy with a girl" at the moment and couldn't come himself; he asked if he could send a friend, a guy by the name of Jeff. The caller chuckled and agreed. Then, feigning a bad memory, the trooper said he couldn't remember the name of the streets that led to the caller's house, which he'd need to give Jeff directions. The caller helpfully outlined the route to his door. The trooper said Jeff would be right over. He hung up, then contacted undercover narcotics officers working in Jonesboro. A few minutes later, they showed up at the address. Byers was waiting outside. One of the officers, who introduced himself as Jeff, later reported that he'd "made a purchase of narcotics from the subject," after which Byers was promptly arrested. The trooper said that after hustling Byers to the police station, the officer called him back. The trooper laughed. "He said, 'You should have seen the look on his face when we told him who he'd called.'"[357]

Byers was charged with selling Xanax, a controlled prescription drug. He appeared again in circuit court, where, once again, he was convicted. This time he was sentenced to five years in prison. But as usual, he was not sent to prison. According to the circuit clerk's records, the judge[358] suspended the five-year sentence. Byers was placed on twenty months probation, and ordered to pay a fine.

It looked like Byers was going to avoid prison again. But this time, the prosecutor[359] who'd accepted the banishment deal decided that something had to be done. Upon learning of the Jonesboro drug conviction, he made good on the promise to change Byers's plea of no contest in the residential burglary case to a plea of guilty. On May 26, 1999—five weeks after his misplaced phone call—sheriff's deputies drove Byers to the state prison unit at Pine Bluff, to begin serving an eight-year sentence.

For the first time in his criminal career—a career that included a conviction for felony terroristic threatening, admitted guilt in the $20,000 Rolex fraud, drug and weapons arrests, hot-check convictions, and a conviction for contributing to the delinquency of a minor—Byers was behind bars. But though a drug conviction had precipitated Byers's trip to prison, no reference to that conviction would appear in his prison records. Instead, records at the Arkansas Department of Correction would indicate that Byers was serving time only on his burglary and theft convictions from the judicial district where he'd been living with Melissa before she died. Byers still had not served a day in prison for any crime from prosecutor Brent Davis's district—or for any crime relating to drugs.[360]

The "Story" About the "Dream"

While he was in prison, Byers was never housed at a unit where Damien, Jason, or Jessie was being held.[361] But Byers took the opportunity to berate them during a prison interview by a reporter in June 2000. In a small conference room at the minimum security unit in south Arkansas where he was held, Byers, now wearing his own prison whites, referred to the three as "the sorry bastards" who'd murdered his "son," and he gloated that while he would soon be walking free, they were "going to die in prison."

His biggest complaint about prison life was that cigarettes had recently been banned. Interrupting himself occasionally to express a wish for one, he talked willingly about his life. His account, while very specific on some details, was vague and contradictory on others. Some episodes, such as illegal activity in West Memphis, were entirely omitted. Rather, Byers claimed that he'd had "a spotless record" until his recent troubles. He expressed bewilderment that police in northern Arkansas had made such a big deal of his involvement in the teenagers' "little" fight. He said he was innocent of the burglary and blamed his no-contest plea on "bad advice" from his lawyer. He never acknowledged that he'd sold drugs, but he did admit to having abused them, though only *after* Melissa's death. He called his decision to turn to drugs a "mistake" brought on by "self-pity" in the wake of Melissa's death, and he lauded his incarceration as "probably the best thing that ever happened" to him because it had snapped him out of a downward spiral.

Though Byers vowed that he would never "say anything bad" about his late wife, he noted that she'd begun abusing drugs long before they'd met. She'd had a heroin and Dilaudid habit, he said, which he'd tried to help her break. In fact, Byers said, his first call to the West Memphis police—the one that led to their use of him as a confidential drug informant—had been to report some of Melissa's suppliers. But Byers's account of events shifted during the four-hour interview. At another point, when his status as an informant was mentioned, he downplayed this and offered a different version of his initial contact with the police. "I saw someone dealing in an area close to where I lived," he said. "I saw an individual on the street corner making transactions to school students that, in my opinion, appeared to be selling drugs. I called Crime Stoppers. They used my house for an observation. The West Memphis police filmed some transactions from my home. As far as I know, there weren't but, like, two arrests ever made. And that is the alpha and the omega of my drug informant status. John Gotti I am not."

Asked about his arrest in Memphis a year before the murders, when he was booked on drugs and weapons charges, Byers looked blank, as though trying without success to remember such an incident. He suggested that the John Mark Byers who was taken out of the Memphis jail and released to the custody of U.S. marshals must have been someone else, and he emphasized that until his recent troubles, he'd had "*no, no* criminal record; no felony arrests—no trouble with the police."[362]

In fact, Byers said, he'd been "pretty much an all-American" boy.

He'd been "a pretty well-rounded teenager," he said, "an average student" who'd enjoyed "a very happy childhood" with the "greatest parents who ever lived." When asked about the incident he'd described to the filmmakers, in which he said that once, when he was a teenager, he himself had been sexually attacked and left in a ditch, Byers launched into a convoluted explanation. "That was a dream," he said, "a dream that I was telling Melissa. It was fiction, not fact."[363] Byers characterized his decision to cooperate with the filmmakers as having been motivated solely by public service. He said he'd wanted people to know that "there are such sick individuals out there in the world that will sodomize and kill your children."

After the murders of Christopher and his friends, Byers said, he recalled "sitting in the office with Gary Gitchell" as Gitchell related the news that one of the boys' testicles had been removed. "We asked which child it was," Byers said. "He told us Michael Moore. Then two or three days later, Gitchell came by our house and said it was Christopher." In the months that followed, Byers said he knew that some people suspected him of having committed the murders—a situation that had caused him "pain on top of pain." But he said he didn't worry about the rumors because "my timeline on May 5 makes O. J. Simpson's look like Swiss cheese. From seven o'clock that morning of May 5 and for the next three days, almost every minute of my time was documented."

Just as he had complained about the failure of police in West Memphis to search for the boys on the night they disappeared, he complained about the treatment Melissa had received at the hands of medics on the afternoon she died. "They only did the paddles and shocked her once," he said. "They did not try to save her life."

As for his own health, Byers raised a hand to his forehead and pointed to a spot above his right eye. That's where his brain tumor was, he said, "right here, in the front lobe." As he described it, the tumor distorted his depth perception, weakened "the grip and feeling" in his left hand, blurred the vision in his left eye, and partially deafened his left ear. He said seizures could be triggered by overexertion, "or if I get real angry, real mad, that will cause me to have one—or if I get real anxious. Sometimes I will wake up on the floor retching. I lose bowel control. There's gritting of teeth. Then, for three or four days, all my muscles will hurt from cramping."[364] To control the seizures, Byers said that he'd been prescribed Dilantin and Tegretol, and that one of the medications had caused deterioration of his gums, or periodontal disease. In April 1997, he said, the gum disease had prompted him to have all of his teeth removed by a dentist in Shreveport, Louisiana. But as with other topics, his story of what happened to his teeth was not clear. At another point in the interview, he explained his decision to have his teeth pulled without mentioning his gums. "I had several fillings that had come out, several teeth that had been chipped and broken from accidents," he said. "My teeth were just giving me a whole lot of trouble. They had been for years."

Only when he spoke of the three convicted killers did Byers's congenial demeanor change. "I don't think they were born rotten," he said. "But they are the guilty three. They were found guilty because of what they did. And they did what they did, in my opinion, because of the things they were reading and putting into their minds. It's like people get into that game, Dungeons and Dragons. Only they took their fantasy to the ultimate level, the level of human sacrifice.

"You reap what you sow," he added sternly. "If you dwell on good thoughts, you're going to be a pretty good person. If you put poison into your system, you're going to be poisoned."

He blamed Damien, Jason, and Jessie not only for the murders, but for most of the grief in his life. "They killed my son. They contributed to the loss of my business. They were a factor in my wife's death. And I believe they were a contributing factor to my being in the penitentiary. I have been searching my mind and heart to try to find a way to forgive them. However, to this day and time, I have not achieved that. I feel like I could come closer to forgiving them for their actions if they could ever be man enough to stand up and admit what they did. But it appears they can't do that, and I really can't have sympathy for a coward."

He added, as the interview concluded, "If I had one hope, it would be that Echols, Baldwin, and Misskelley would be man enough to stand up and say, 'Yes, I did that. I wasn't in my right mind. I'm sorry that I did that. Could those families ever forgive me?'" Then, as though realizing what he'd described was impossible, he added, "But there's a slim chance of that. They probably don't have the intestinal fortitude."

Melissa's Parents

The only point on which Byers expressed regret during the interview while he was in prison concerned his relationship with his other stepson. Sixteen-year-old Ryan Clark left home on the afternoon his mother died, and Byers said he had not heard from him for years. "I acknowledge that I was not a perfect father," he said, wiping away a few tears. "There are no perfect fathers. Even my dad had a few shortcomings. But I still love Ryan and I want nothing but good for him. I can only say that I hope he's done well."

Ryan was more reserved. When contacted in 2001, he was twenty-two—and reluctant to speak about the deaths of his brother and mother.[365] He said that he believes they are both "in heaven," that talking will not bring them back, and that he would like to be left alone. He asked that he be left alone to "be just another person in the world."

Melissa's parents were not as reticent.[366] Interviewed at their home in Memphis, they spoke freely about the anguish that followed the deaths of first Christopher and then Melissa. They reminisced about their love for Christopher, whom they'd helped to raise before Melissa's marriage to John Mark. They denied any knowledge of Melissa's involvement with drugs, voiced confidence that the three convicted West Memphis teenagers were in fact guilty of their grandson's murder, and said they didn't see much point in reexamining either the boy's death or that of their daughter. "It ain't going to help," her father said.

Nonetheless, they did speak, and much of what they had to say centered on their former son-in-law John Mark Byers. "He was a good jeweler, but he was lazy," Melissa's father said. Her mother interjected that "he was supposed to have a brain tumor." But Melissa's father stuck to his harsher view. "He's sick," he said, "and a liar." Byers "beat Melissa up more than once; he blackened her eye," the father said, adding that whenever something like that happened, Byers would "blame everybody but himself."

Seated in their living room, surrounded by family pictures, Melissa's parents said that the West Memphis police had never questioned them after Christopher's murder. They still knew very little about the investigation. But if detectives had questioned the pair, they would have heard a disconcerting vignette—one that might have raised questions about the period of time just after Christopher had gotten out of school on the day he disappeared. While Byers had told police that he'd gone to a clinic in Memphis that day and had not been able to find Christopher when he'd returned home at around 3:10 P.M., Melissa's father recalled a markedly different version of the afternoon's events.

He said that Melissa had arranged with him to come to the house and stay with Christopher after school, in case Mark wasn't back from the clinic. The child's grandfather said that he had driven to West Memphis as planned, but when he got there—shortly before Christopher was to get out of school—Mark was already home. "I was on my way up to the schoolhouse," Melissa's father said, "which was right near their house, you know, when Mark saw me and told me he was going to pick up Chris by himself. He told me not to get him. He said he'd take care of it. So I just went on my way. I've thought about it a hundred times. I wish I'd went ahead and got Chris. They called me that night and told me he was missing."

Melissa's father told the story, apparently unaware of the light it cast on Byers's account. He and his wife knew little more than the general public about the investigation into the children's murders. And they had not attended the trials. "Melissa told us not to," her mother explained. "She said it would only upset us." Once the trials concluded, they believed, along with most of the public, that justice had been done. After all, they asked, echoing a widespread opinion, who would confess to a crime like that if he didn't commit it? "Misskelley may be retarded," Melissa's father said, "but he ain't that retarded."

Their grief was compounded in the months after the trials by concerns about Melissa and Ryan, who were now living farther away, in north-central Arkansas. Melissa's parents said they'd given Mark and Melissa money to put down on a house because they knew that, now that Melissa was no longer working, the family was subsisting entirely on Mark's disability check. But the money seemed to disappear. They said Ryan would call and report that he was having to take cold showers before school, and come home to an unheated house where there often was not enough food.[367]

But the couple's concerns had intensified in the days just before

Melissa's death. "She'd called up and said, 'Daddy, I need $200. I'm broke.' I sent her the money," the father said. "I sent her $200 on Monday and she died on Friday. They said she had $3 in her purse." But the couple said Melissa was also worried about more than money that week. They said her marriage to Mark was on the verge of collapse. "We knew he was shenaniganin'," her mother said. "He was foolin' with a woman up there. Melissa said she was going to divorce him. She told him she was going to leave him. But he said he wasn't going to divorce another woman."

Melissa's parents said that shortly before Melissa died, she'd told them that she was coming home to stay with them for a couple of days. They expected her on Friday. When she hadn't arrived by midafternoon, "We called the house to see if she was coming, and Mark said, 'No, she's not feeling good and she's asleep.' Later on that night the phone rang. Mark just laid it out: 'Melissa's dead.' That's all he said."

Her mom, who'd answered, remembers stammering, "Melissa's what?"

"We wanted to go up there," Melissa's father recalled. "But Mark said there wasn't no need because the police had seized her body."

As after Christopher's murder, the couple said they were not contacted by police after Melissa's unusual death, either. But this time, they said, doubts about the circumstances surrounding Melissa's death caused them to sever their relationship with Byers.[368]

The couple's other former son-in-law, Christopher's biological father, held a different opinion of the case. In a letter posted on the wm3.org Web site, he proclaimed his belief that the teenagers convicted of killing Christopher, Michael, and Stevie had not committed the crime.[369] "I want to know who murdered my son," he wrote, "and I want to know that they will be caught and punished for what they did. I don't want three innocent people to suffer for something they didn't do."

On August 29, 2000, Byers was released from the Arkansas Department of Correction. Having served fifteen months of his eight-year sentence, he was placed on parole until May 2007.[370]

CHAPTER TWENTY-THREE

The Public

IN 1997, PAM HOBBS, the mother of Stevie Branch, filed a $10 million lawsuit against the documentary filmmakers, alleging that they had breached an agreement not to show graphic material in the film.[371] The lawsuit was decided in favor of the filmmakers. Two years later, in September 2000, Hobbs again protested the commercial use of images from the police file, this time after someone offered crime scene and autopsy photos for sale on the Internet auction site eBay.[372]

One young supporter e-mailed Arkansas's governor, Mike Huckabee, who is a Republican and a Baptist minister. An aide who identified herself as the governor's "criminal justice liaison" replied. After noting that the governor could not reopen a case or have any investigation done, the aide continued: "I do want to assure you that DNA testing was done, and that a match was found among the men convicted." The statement was flagrantly misleading. It could only have referred to the DNA test conducted on blood found on Damien's pendant necklace, the rough results of which suggested that the blood could have come from Jason Baldwin, Stevie Branch, or 11 percent of the Caucasian population, and it had never been introduced into evidence. Moreover, the aide wrote that the documentary about the case had been a "fictionalized" account and not a documentary. She referred the letter writer to the prosecuting attorney who had handled the case.[373]

A Forensic Analyst

The conduct of the West Memphis police during the murder investigation had raised enough questions for one of the Web site's founders that she enrolled in a course in evidence analysis taught by a criminal profiler.[374] The instructor, Brent Turvey, became intrigued when told about the West Memphis case, and his interest was heightened when he was shown photos and other evidence pertaining to the victims' autopsies. In 1997 the profiler prepared a report, outlining his own assessment of the case. It raised a number of new questions. He noted in photos of Michael Moore what he called a "directional pattern abrasion" just below the boy's right shoulder. He wrote that the abrasion did not correspond with any of the evidence collected at the site where the bodies were found, and that it was "inconsistent with any of the naturally occurring elements that exist in that environment." In one of the photos taken in the woods, he also noted what he believed was a "piece of cloth" in Michael's right hand. "This is a very critical piece of physical evidence," he wrote, and he urged that it be found and "fully examined."

The profiler's analysis of photos of Stevie Branch was even more disturbing. He noted "the existence of patterned injuries all over this victim's face that could be bite marks." He wrote, "Bite mark evidence is very important in a criminal case because it demonstrates behavior and lends itself to individuation. It can reveal to an examiner who committed the act, because bite marks can be as unique as fingerprints." He recommended that a forensic odontologist, or dentist, review the photographs.

With regard to Christopher Byers, the profiler noted, "The general constellation of wounds to this victim is more advanced, more extensive, more overtly sexually oriented, and includes the use of a knife." After describing the wounds created by the removal of the boy's penis, scrotal sac, and testes, he observed, "The nature of this emasculation, as indicated by these wounds, is neither skilled nor practiced. It was a rageful, careless, but purposeful act carried out in anger." The profiler also looked for evidence of the whipping John Mark Byers said he'd given Christopher before the boy disappeared. He identified three sets of injuries on the body's buttocks, two of which he concluded were "inconsistent" with marks from a belt. The third set, described in the autopsy report as "five superficial cutting wounds on the left buttock," were "actually lacerations" that were roughly parallel, and Turvey concluded that they were "most consistent" with a whipping by a belt. He added, "It is further the opinion of this examiner that after having received this set of injuries, which tore open the skin and would have resulted in some severe bleeding, the victim would have been unable to walk or ride a bicycle without incredible pain and discomfort."

The profiler also offered his assessment of the site where the bodies were found. He concluded that this was not where the boys were murdered, and that "at least four crime scenes" were involved. He identified these as what he called "the abduction site," where the boys were apprehended; "the attack site," a nearby structure or residence where they were killed; "the dump site," the ditch where the bodies were found; and "the vehicle" that was used to transport the bodies from the attack site to where they were dumped. He cited three reasons for his conclusions. One: "The nature and extent of the wounds inflicted upon these victims, especially the emasculation of Chris Byers, required light, required time, and required uninterrupted privacy. As it was dark in those woods, and as search parties were traveling in and out of the area all evening, this dictates a secluded structure of some kind away from the area of immediate attention." Two: "The nature and extent of the wounds inflicted upon these victims, especially the emasculation of Chris Byers, would have resulted in a tremendous amount of blood loss. Very little blood was found at this scene on the banks of the drainage ditch." And three: "The stabbing injuries and emasculation injuries inflicted upon Chris Byers alone, because Chris was conscious during at least part of the assault [as indicated by evidence of struggle during the attack on his penis], would have resulted in a great deal of screaming." Of all the sounds reported that evening by searchers and local residents, screaming was not among them. The fact that the three boys were apprehended together and that their wounds showed they put up "limited resistance" suggested to the criminal profiler that they had been approached by "someone that the victims knew and trusted."[375]

The Sequel

Filmmakers Berlinger and Sinofsky were now also looking at the case from a different point of view. They'd won prizes and accolades for their documentary *Paradise Lost: The Child Murders at Robin Hood Hills*, but their pride had been accompanied by disappointment that discussion of the film had never, as they put it, gotten "off the entertainment page." While most viewers were appalled by what they saw in the film, a sizable number—the filmmakers estimated 20 percent—saw the documentary as proof that the three who were convicted were guilty.[376] Berlinger and Sinofsky decided to make a sequel. Where the first film had been "more artistic," this one would "be stronger, more of an advocacy film." "Our attraction to the second story was much more that we wanted to help," Berlinger later explained. "The first film never got the social attention it deserved. With this one, we wanted it to be discussed, not just on the entertainment pages, but on the editorial pages. We wanted people of power to rally."

Footage from the trials had formed and informed the first film, but the filmmakers decided to base the sequel on creation of the Web site and the activism it had spawned. Another challenge was that many of the people who'd appeared in the first documentary didn't want to be interviewed again. "Most people in Arkansas were pissed off at us," Berlinger recalled. "The Moores would have nothing to do with us. Pam Hobbs had tried to sue us. Brent Davis wouldn't talk to us. That left pretty much John Mark Byers. He was more than willing to appear on camera, and we put him front and center."

Most of the filming took place in 1998—after Melissa's death and after Byers's banishment from the judicial district where they had been living when she died, but before the drug arrest that had led to his stint in prison. As in the first film, Byers expounded at length for the cameras, only now the pitch of his orations was more hateful and more histrionic. The film, *Paradise Lost 2: Revelations*, premiered on HBO in March 2000. Byers was more than "front and center." He was the film's target.

If the producers had understated their belief in the first film that the defendants were innocent, they made it clear in the second film that they believed Byers should be viewed as a prime suspect. Even with the cameras rolling, Byers did little to divert suspicion. Having agreed, for instance, to submit to a polygraph exam for the film, he unself-consciously referred at one point to his wife, Melissa's, "murder." After the polygraph examiner questioned Byers about the murder of the eight-year-olds and Byers replied he had nothing to do with them, the examiner pronounced his finding that Byers was telling the truth "as far as [he] could see them." This finding was offset, however, by the information that before taking the exam, Byers had acknowledged that he was on several prescription drugs—medications that, the viewer was left to conclude, could have distorted the examiner's readings. Nonetheless, Byers was thrilled with the examiner's report. "Yes!" he exclaimed, slapping the examiner a big high-five. "I knew I was innocent!"

Reviews of the second film were favorable, though less enthusiastic than for the first.[377] As before, the region where the documentaries were set came under fire. A reviewer for New Jersey's *Newark Star-Ledger* described West Memphis as "a bastion of Judeo-Christian righteousness threatened by the dark allure of secular America," noting that "this theological landscape" probably explained "why the police would stick to their story and much of the town would support them."[378] In a similar vein, film critic Roger Ebert called for the facts of the case to be reexamined in "a neutral setting" because it was clear, as he put it, "that the local people involved have a vested interest in being right about this, no matter whether they're right or wrong."

Not surprisingly, reaction in Arkansas was different. When the second documentary was released, two reporters for the *Arkansas Democrat-Gazette* interviewed several people involved in "the bizarre case."[379] They reported that Todd Moore had been "outraged" by suggestions that Byers had been involved in the murders. "Even though I did not like him as a neighbor, nor a friend, he is not a murderer," he told the paper. Prosecutor Brent Davis said he was disgusted by the way the films were "slanted toward the defense," and detective Mike Allen, who was now a lieutenant, agreed. "If I lived in California and saw that movie and didn't know the facts, I'd be appalled they charged those boys with the murders," the paper quoted Allen as saying. "I can understand someone living in New York City or Los Angeles getting fired up after listening to all this garbage." On the other hand, Allen claimed, "If HBO would run the entire trial without editing it, and then ask viewers if he's [Damien's] guilty, I bet there'd be a different response." But the foreman of the jury that convicted Damien and Jason said that he had seen the first documentary and found its coverage of the trial to be fair, just as he believed the verdict was. "If I was back in that courtroom now," the foreman told the paper, "I'd vote 'guilty' again."

When the second documentary aired on HBO, thousands of viewers went immediately to the Web site. The site's organizers reported that from March 13, when the show first aired, to the end of that month, the site had received approximately 133,000 hits. The site urged visitors to send in a postcard from their state, with a message to "Free the West Memphis Three." Organizers advised that the postcards would be assembled into a long banner, which would be taken to Arkansas as evidence of the national interest in the legal future of the men in prison. One of the site's founders said that after the second film aired on HBO, the address they'd posted on the Web site began to receive up to sixty postcards a day.

That gratified the filmmakers. But they still hoped for a more dramatic result, such as had been achieved by *The Thin Blue Line*, the classic 1988 documentary that had led to the exoneration of a Texas man who'd been held for years on that state's death row. In that case, questions raised by the film had prompted Texas officials to reopen the investigation. The filmmakers believed that someone in power could initiate a similar review of the case in Arkansas. They focused on getting the films to the former Arkansas governor who was now the president of the United States.

Berlinger, who was now working on another film, said he asked everyone he knew in Hollywood who socialized with President Bill Clinton to send him copies of the documentaries, but that most had demurred. Given his conviction that the inmates were innocent, and that one could be put to death, he found their reticence frustrating.[380]

Berlinger finally e-mailed Roger Ebert, who'd praised *Paradise Lost*, both one and two. He asked Ebert if he would mind sending the films to the president (as Clinton had been on Ebert's show), and to Berlinger's delight, Ebert agreed. "Two months later," Berlinger said, "I get a letter from Bill Clinton. It's on official White House stationery, and it comes in protective cardboard, as if I'm going to frame it. It said, 'Dear Joe, I found both of the films fascinating and disturbing, but please be aware. . . .' He said that as president he had no influence on the court system in Arkansas. It was a total cop-out."

More Artists Sign On

If the president of the United States felt powerless with regard to the case, a growing number of musicians, oddly, did not. The group Metallica had been the first to express support for a new look at the case when it donated its music for the sound track of the first documentary. As the realization spread that prosecutors had linked Damien and Jason's tastes in music to the satanism the state claimed had been the motive for the murders, other musicians saw the tactic as an assault—one that they felt threatened both their form of artistic expression and, potentially, anyone who listened to it. Where the filmmakers had been from New York and the founders of the Web site from Los Angeles, the musicians who stepped most energetically into the case hailed from Seattle.

In March 2000, the manager of a Seattle-based band announced a project that would pull together several groups in support of the three Arkansas convicts now known as the West Memphis Three. Danny Bland, manager of the Supersuckers, a Seattle band, explained the project's genesis in an opinion piece published in one of the city's entertainment newspapers.[381] Bland described his encounter with the case through the HBO documentary, his further explorations at the Web site and letters to the three young inmates. "Something about this story filled me with great sympathy for these guys and great anger for the justice system in Arkansas," he wrote. "I gathered up the troops—Supersucker Eddie Spaghetti [lead singer Eddie Daly], his wife, Jessika, and [record promoter] Scott Parker—and headed down to Arkansas to visit Damien and Jason." The visit with Damien lasted three hours, during which the visitors explained their idea.

We told him about the benefit CD we're putting together to raise awareness about their case, and how bands like

Rocket from the Crypt and L7, as well as solo artists Tom
Waits and Mark Lanegan, were stepping up to the plate with
their time and music. Damien admits he doesn't know much
about these groups; after all, he's been in prison for seven
years, and before that he lived in West Memphis. Kelley
Deal (of the Breeders) said that along with the song she's
contributing, she wants to send a picture of herself wearing a
Black Sabbath shirt, black lipstick and fingernail polish for
the artwork. When I told Damien this he smiled and said,
"Oh, good. Now she can have the cell next to mine."

It was not easy to pull together dozens of musicians, most of whom
needed permission from their own recording studios to participate in the
project. But, seven months after the Seattle group's visit to Arkansas, the
CD *Free the West Memphis Three* was ready for release. Some of the more
famous names on the liner notes were Tom Waits, singing his own song
"Rain on Me"; Steve Earle, doing "The Truth," which he'd written; and
Eddie Vedder, the lead singer of Pearl Jam, singing "Poor Girl," by John
Doe and Exen Cervenka, in a performance with the Supersuckers.[382] The
front of the CD case featured a gritty collage of shackles, prison bars,
and images of the three Arkansas inmates. On the back was a photo of
the guard towers outside Damien's prison.[383]

Just before the CD's release, Pearl Jam appeared in concert in Memphis, a city where one radio DJ routinely mocked West Memphis Three
supporters and where TV reporters received castigating calls from
viewers if they aired news of the growing movement. At the end of
Pearl Jam's performance before a crowd of about ten thousand fans in
Memphis's Pyramid Arena, the band played two encores. Then Eddie
Vedder, Pearl Jam's lead singer, returned to the stage a third time. "This
last song is for a friend I haven't met yet," he announced. "He's from
West Memphis. I'm going to meet him tomorrow." With that, the band
launched into a biting rendition of the Who's "Teenage Wasteland."
The crowd roared, though few in the audience could have known to
whom Vedder was referring. The next day, Vedder rode in a limousine
across the Mississippi River into mid-Arkansas, to the state's maximum
security unit, where he visited with Damien. Later, Vedder told a re-

porter, "I went and visited Damien in this little God-forsaken place, this prison—he's on death row—and everyone was treated like dirt there."[384]

Soon after the CD's release, however, Music City Record Distributors of Nashville, Tennessee, announced that it was removing the compilation from the shelves of its Cat's Music stores.[385] In a letter sent to its stores, the company reported that the Pop Tunes and Best Buy chains had reached a similar decision. But in other parts of the country, reaction to the disk was different. The *Village Voice* called it "a weird and exciting little collection."[386] The writer for the *Village Voice* articulated an issue that burned both at the heart of the West Memphis case and in the motives of many of the inmates' musical supporters. That was the amalgam of hope, confusion, sexual energy, and rebellion that pounded through rock and roll and through the lives of many teenagers who found themselves drawn to the music. Since its origins, in the same Mississippi delta that gave birth to the blues, rock and roll had been embraced and denounced as "bad." Memphis's historic Beale Street had become a tourist attraction, but in its heyday, the street was a string of riverfront dives where some of the country's greatest musicians played—against a backdrop of scorn and condemnation from the city's churchgoing elite. It was the same with Elvis Presley. His name graces nearly everything in Memphis today. But, in the early sixties, when he burst onto the scene, he outraged the city's defenders of decency—and many continued to view him as bad until they realized he was good for the economy. Rock and roll plays with big taboos: sex, drugs, and—worst of all—subliminal notions of evil.[387] It's risky. It blurs reality with theatricality. It expresses dangerous emotions—a quality that fans find liberating but that others find terrifying. What did the music of Metallica, Megadeth, and Slayer say about Damien and Jason? Did it represent, as Prosecutor Fogleman suggested, parts of a mosaic that pointed to satanism and murder? Or did it say, as the producers of the benefit CD believed, that the two were searching for music that gave voice to the fears and forces at the heart of their own lives? In an interview accompanying the disk's release, Eddie Spaghetti of the Supersuckers said that his commitment to the project arose in part out of a sense of obligation to the "kids" who listened to the music he played—and apparently risked, in some cases, having that used against them in court.[388] As the publisher of a Little Rock weekly wrote, "What seems to frighten Spaghetti and similar musicians who explore the 'dark side' of music, is that anyone who buys his record and T-shirts could be considered a devil worshiper and become a scapegoat in a legal system that fears the unknown vistas of 'dark music.' "[389]

When the CD was released, some supporters worried that support from rock musicians who made their livings being "bad" might muddy the Web site's more mainstream efforts on the inmates' behalf. Those concerns were underlined when Trey Parker, cocreator of *South Park*, one of television's most irreverent shows, joined the list of celebrities supporting the West Memphis Three. "Bad publicity," fretted one supporter, "is what got them locked up in the first place." But the storm of concern blew over—partly, no doubt, because it's hard to harm the image of someone who's already on death row—and the movement for the West Memphis Three widened.

"Back Channel Conversations"

But a columnist for the state's main daily paper, the *Arkansas Democrat-Gazette*, was not troubled by such concerns. In a column published in February 2001, Philip Martin, the paper's chief writer on cultural affairs, noted the support that was building nationally for the three Arkansas inmates, including that from musicians and certain "Hollywood types." Martin wrote that he realized that many of the West Memphis Three's supporters were "well-meaning and sincere," and that "reasonable, decent people can disagree." That said, Martin informed his readers that he believed that Damien, Jason, and Jessie were the killers.

For several reasons, Martin's opinion piece was an important comment on the case, in that it reflected attitudes prevalent in Arkansas six years after the trials. The piece acknowledged a litany of "questions" about the case—questions that Martin said he found "troubling." At the same time, it echoed the confidence that Martin, like many Arkansans, maintained: that justice had been served.

Martin went to lengths to acknowledge the supporters' concerns. He admitted that, like them, he had not been convinced of the defendants' guilt "beyond a reasonable doubt." He said he initially had had "some misgivings about the way the police identified the suspects," and that he had been "troubled by the Satanist hysteria surrounding the case." He said he knew that the Arkansas judicial system was "capable of atrocity," that it was "probably capable of convicting and even executing the wrong person," and that the West Memphis case had been "messy" and "largely circumstantial." He said he realized that "confessions can be false," that Jessie's confession was "hardly convincing evidence," and that the teenager probably had "some sort of cognitive disorder in addition to an extremely low IQ." Martin admitted that he disliked "the state's insistence on dragging a self-styled expert on Satanic rituals" into Damien and Jason's trial, and that "it probably would have been better to try those two separately." He wrote that he understood that "police routinely cut corners," that "there are innocent (or at least 'not guilty') people in our prisons," and that "if you are poor and friendless you are treated differently than if you are wealthy and well connected."

Nevertheless, Martin wrote, two juries had found the defendants guilty and he had seen no convincing evidence that their verdicts were wrong. "It makes a good story—," he wrote, "yokel cops crucify the misfit. It could sell some books. But it ignores the facts." Martin did not cite what "facts" he believed had been ignored. Rather, he explained that his own doubts about the case had been laid to rest by "a couple of back channel conversations" with people whom he trusted. Without divulging what in those conversations he had found so persuasive, Martin wrote, "Their word was good enough for me. The cops had the right guys."[390]

Then Martin sounded the deepest theme of the case, though he did it superficially, as though it were all the explanation needed. While granting that he "wouldn't mind too much" if Damien, Jason, and Jessie "somehow" managed to get new trials, Martin wrote that he didn't "much care" if their case was never reviewed. "While I'm opposed to capital punishment," he wrote, "I don't think Damien Echols is a particularly good argument against it. I could be wrong, but he seems thoroughly calculating and cynical about all this, he seems to be enjoying the attention. He seems evil. Which, I imagine some of his supporters would argue, is what got him into all this trouble in the first place— Echols *seems* evil."

CHAPTER TWENTY-FOUR

A Decade Behind Bars

THE HORROR THAT UNFOLDED ON MAY 5, 1993, ended life forever for Christopher, Michael, and Stevie. The trials ended life in the free world for Damien, Jason, and Jessie—and put Damien on a list of men awaiting execution. But outside the stillness of the cemeteries and beyond the walls of prisons, participants in the drama surrounding the murders carried on with their lives.

Within weeks of his dual victories in the sensational West Memphis trials, deputy prosecuting attorney John Fogleman was running hard for circuit judge. Though some voters considered his campaign ad—on a billboard near the Blue Beacon—tasteless, Fogleman's claim on it, that he could "make tough decisions in tough cases," proved powerful at the polls. As the three convicted teenagers were being introduced to prison life, John Fogleman was stepping up to the bench, where he'd serve with Judge David Burnett.

During the next several years, Judge Fogleman had little to say publicly about the most sensational trial of his career. But in 2001, when contacted for this book, he hesitantly agreed to discuss it.[391] Seated in his plain and sparsely furnished office in Marion, around the corner from the Crittenden County Courthouse, Fogleman said he was concerned that his statements "might be taken out of context." The interviewer observed that if Jessie Misskelley had been a bit more wary, he might have harbored similar qualms when he was questioned by the police, but the remark elicited no comment. The former prosecutor addressed most questions, however, with an air of polite, if formal, cooperation.

John Fogleman

He said that though he and Inspector Gary Gitchell were "good friends," he'd "cringed" when Gitchell bragged that on a scale of one to ten, the department's case against the accused was an eleven. He acknowledged that at the time of the arrests, "basically, the only thing we had was Jessie's statement," which was why the police investigation had continued almost until the start of the trials. Fogleman noted that elements of the case, such as the detectives' failure to investigate the bloody man at Bojangles, "could have been handled better, much better," and that their loss of the blood evidence taken from the restaurant was "very unfortunate." He also acknowledged that he had not been "comfortable" with the roles Vicki Hutcheson and her son Aaron had played. Those considerations aside, however, Fogleman expressed confidence in the conclusions, reached by the police and two juries, that the three accused teens had been guilty.[392]

He cited his reasons for believing that the children had been murdered where they were found: chiefly, police reports that no sign of vehicle tracks or a bloody trail had been found leading into the woods. That, coupled with police observations "that one bank had that unnatural appearance," had convinced him, Fogleman said, "that the murders had to have happened there." He felt equally sure that the killer had not been the man who'd cleaned up in the Bojangles rest room. "Keeping in mind that whoever did this crime took the time to hide every piece of evidence, put the bicycles in the water, the bodies in the water, the clothes all crammed down in the mud . . . to take that same person and say that immediately after he'd done all this, he goes into a public place all covered in blood and leaves blood laying around—to me that's a complete absurdity."

Fogleman said that he and the police had tried to consider "every possibility" they could think of—and that included the possibility that John Mark Byers was the killer. Recalling the terroristic threatening charge brought by Byers's first wife, which Fogleman had handled as a young prosecutor for the city of Marion, he said, "Quite frankly, as soon as I'd heard who one of the [murdered] kids was, I called the police and told them they ought to consider him." He said his concern was based on the tape recording Byers's first wife had made of the attack, which she'd played for Fogleman. "Because of the way he [Byers] sounded on the tape, I just thought he was somebody they [the police] should consider. Not that I thought he did it. It's hard to consider parents or stepparents as suspects in a child's murder. But the tape sounded bizarre enough—the nature of his voice and the way he sounded—that I thought he should be considered, and he was."

Fogleman described Byers as "a guy who's not an upstanding citizen of the community." But when asked about Byers's record, the judge was vague. He said Byers's terroristic threatening conviction had been expunged after he "completed his probation" but seemed unaware that Byers had not met the terms of that probation; he expressed surprise at hearing that Byers was not prosecuted in the Rolex watch scam ("I thought he was. Was he not?"), and he spoke vaguely about what he and the West Memphis police had known about Byers's involvement with drugs. "I don't know if my memory is correct," he said, "but I do know that we weren't able to confirm what his status was, one way or another. . . . I do seem to recall that the police talked to somebody, either with the Shelby County Drug Task Force [in Memphis] or the U.S. attorney's office, or the DEA or FBI over there, and that they confirmed he was working with them." But he said no actual information developed. And when asked if police in Memphis and West Memphis did not cooperate, Fogleman replied obliquely, "I would say metro narcotics in Tennessee were coordinated pretty well with here, but maybe not as well as you might think."

Fogleman's recollections about the three defendants were more clear. He cited the fibers found with the bodies ("They're little bitty but they're important"), the knife taken from the lake ("I still believe it's more significant than even Dr. Peretti would say"), and particularly Jessie's confession. Fogleman said he'd been uncomfortable about the discrepancies in Jessie's various statements. As to why Jessie had given so many different accounts of what he said had happened, Fogleman seemed mystified. Pointing out that Jessie at one point said he'd been drinking, he observed, "If you want to look at it from a prosecutor's perspective, you could say that that clouded his judgment and that's why he got all these details wrong." But when pressed as to why he thought

Jessie had offered so many differing accounts, Fogleman said, "I don't know. I don't know. They were generally consistent, but specifically they weren't. I don't know."

He then added, "You've got the situation where there are a couple of things—the time involvement and also the thing about how the boys were tied—that were obviously wrong. But at the same time, you've got him telling things that only somebody would know who was there." These included, he said, "the injuries to the left side of one of the boys' face, the mutilation of the Byers boy, and [Jessie's] picking out photographs of which one had which injuries. The way I looked at it—and I even asked the officers to make sure that they hadn't somehow leaked that information to him, and they assured me that nothing like that had happened—the way I looked at it, these were things only someone who'd been there could know."

At another point, he said, "If you look at each individual piece of evidence throughout the case, no matter which one it is, you'd say, 'I won't convict on that.' But when you put everything in combination, that's the way you have to look at circumstantial evidence. It's like looking at the spokes of a wheel, and pulling out a spoke and saying, 'Well, that's not a wheel,' but you put it all together and it is a wheel."

Motive is an important part of the wheel that explains a crime. But motive had been elusive in this case. None of the usual motives for murder—anger, revenge, robbery—had seemed to fit the defendants. Beyond little Aaron's wild statements and the alleged photographs that Jessie reported having seen in the alleged briefcase at the alleged esbat—none of which had been produced at the trials—there was nothing to indicate that the defendants had ever laid eyes on the victims. Davis and Fogleman had waited until midway through Damien and Jason's trial to even suggest a motive. On the day before the prosecutors called their expert, Dale Griffis, the Jonesboro paper quoted Fogleman's announcement that he and Davis planned "to show that the motive was cult related."

Now, six years later, Fogleman shied away from questions about why he'd pursued the occult theory of motive. Rather than showing motive, Fogleman now said, the testimony of Dale Griffis had been introduced to explain Damien's state of mind. Noting that some of the writers Damien "admired" had "advocated human sacrifice and that kind of thing,"

Fogleman said he'd introduced the evidence of Damien's interest in the occult simply to show the jury that Damien was not a "typical teenager."

Nonetheless, Judge Burnett had ruled that he would allow introduction of testimony pertaining to the occult only if it "went to motive," and the prosecutors, in announcing their decision to introduce it, had told the judge that it did. Now Fogleman sought to distance himself from that decision. He explained that at Damien and Jason's trial, he, Davis, and Griffis had avoided using the term "satanic ritual." What they had argued, he said, was simply that the crime had born "the trappings of occultism," a term that Fogleman now said "was relevant to show the mind-set, particularly of Damien." Despite his latter-day squeamishness on the subject of motive, Fogleman remained confident that Damien was the killer.[393]

For Fogleman, the case was history. "Obviously," he said, "if I prosecuted somebody who got the death penalty, and I was wrong, I would feel bad about it. Very bad. I'd feel terrible. If that's the case I hope new evidence comes forward." But now that he was a judge, Fogleman was no longer legally involved. The same was not true for Brent Davis. He remained the district's chief prosecuting attorney, and was still in a position to oppose all challenges to the verdicts.

Defense Lawyers

By the late 1990s, those challenges were coming from several directions. And with the exception of Stidham, who was still defending Jessie, the new efforts were being led by lawyers with no ties to the judicial district. Spurred by publicity and calls from supporters, some of the nation's most prominent defense attorneys—lawyers from outside Arkansas—had taken an interest in the case.

But it was growing late in the game. Damien, Jason, and Jessie's appeals to the state Supreme Court had failed. The avenues of appeal left in the state were growing narrower. The main one still available was called, in Arkansas, a Rule 37 petition: a procedure that allowed convicted persons to argue that their trials had been unfair. A Rule 37 petition is not heard by the state Supreme Court but by the same judge who tried the case. Not surprisingly, judges do not frequently find fault with their own rulings, so most are summarily denied. But in cases where an inmate has been sentenced to death, the judge is held to stricter standards than for other denials. When a judge denies a Rule 37 petition from someone on death row, he must carefully state his legal reasoning for every point raised by the defense. An inmate can make several claims to attack his trial's unfairness, but the most common one is that the lawyer who represented him outrageously botched the job; that is, in legal terms, that he received "ineffective assistance of counsel." The question facing Damien and his codefendants now was how they would find lawyers to file their Rule 37 petitions, considering that they remained just as poor as they'd been at the time of their trials.[394]

Unbeknownst to them, the lay interest that had been building in support of their claim of innocence sparked the interest of some leading criminal defense attorneys. One of those was Barry Scheck, a lawyer noted for his work on the O. J. Simpson case and his expertise in the burgeoning field of DNA evidence. Another was Edward Mallett, a trial lawyer from Houston, Texas. In 1997, Mallett informed Damien he would work on Damien's Rule 37 petition for free, and that Scheck had signed on to help.[395] Mallett visited Arkansas and met with Val Price, the lawyer who, Mallett would be arguing, had failed in his representation of Damien. Mallett said he found Price to be "very, very nice, not the kind of person you'd like to take on as a professional enemy." Nonetheless, he pressed Price to explain why, at such a crucial time, he had participated in the making of a film and to allow Damien to participate as well. That was when Price explained the role money had played in the case.

Price explained that the filmmakers had offered Damien $7,500 for three interviews. Damien was indigent, and this was money the attorney thought could be used toward his defense. Even though Damien's lawyers had been appointed by the court and would be paid through public funds, they said they wanted to use funds from the film to hire expert witnesses. Mallett was astounded. He asked, wouldn't the court provide money for such necessary expenses? Price said he didn't believe Judge Burnett would have authorized that much.

Price then offered some financial background on the case, to wit, that the lawyers themselves had not been paid until years after the trials' conclusions. They had had to cover their own expenses before and during the trials. After the trials were over, Judge Burnett had ruled that the six court-appointed defense lawyers who represented the three defendants would be paid a total of $142,000, plus an additional $1,000 for out-of-pocket expenses.[396] They said the amount was already out of proportion with the amount of time they'd spent on the case, but as it turned out, collecting it would prove even more difficult. Because the West Memphis case had unfolded at a time when responsibility for paying court-appointed attorneys was being transferred from the state to the counties, a dispute arose over who would pay the bill—the state of Arkansas or Crittenden County. The issue was fought all the way to the Arkansas Supreme Court, and while it was being fought, the attorneys continued to go unpaid.

In the midst of the dispute, Jason's lawyer Paul Ford complained, "Judge Burnett got paid for what he did; the prosecutors got paid; the state witnesses got paid; everyone involved got paid, except for the defense attorneys. There's unfairness there. The state can get what they need for a trial and get paid for it, but the defense attorneys must subsidize the costs themselves." Jessie's lawyer Dan Stidham said his law firm had had to take out bank loans to cover expenses incurred during Jessie's trial. "The prosecutor has a staff of expert witnesses at his disposal and dozens of investigators," Stidham said. "But this sends the message that if you're indigent, you don't have a chance." Damien's lawyer Val Price was equally put out—and outspoken. "If the state is going to have people prosecuted and ask for the death penalty, then it should be willing to pay for a vigorous and zealous defense for the defendants. The state has the FBI, crime labs, and various other agencies at its disposal, but we don't have the same access and must pay for our research." A year and a half after the trials, the Arkansas Supreme Court ordered the state to pay the six attorneys. The county was ordered to pay Ron Lax and a few expert witnesses.[397]

That was the climate, Mallett learned, in which the lawyers for the West Memphis defendants had opted to get funding where they could. The appearance of the filmmakers had seemed an opportunity. The lawyers representing Jason and Jessie had arrived at the same conclusion: that the money was critically needed. Upon the advice of their defense lawyers, the defendants had signed contracts with the filmmakers, agreeing to three interviews apiece; for which they were to be paid $7,500 each. The payments were to be held in trust. Damien's and Jason's lawyers signed on as trustees for their clients' trusts. Stidham, however, regarded that role as a conflict of interest. He referred Jessie Misskelley Sr. to another attorney, who advised the Misskelleys on the contract and served as trustee for Jessie's account.

Despite his personal regard for Price, Mallett left Arkansas appalled. The circumstances he'd heard described provided an astonishing backdrop, he reflected, for a case that already seemed to hold more than its share of peculiarities.[398]

The Yearlong Hearing

By the end of March 1997, three years after their convictions, all three of the West Memphis inmates had petitioned Judge Burnett under Arkansas's Rule 37.[399] As expected, Mallett argued that because Damien's counsel "was being unfairly deprived of funds for experts and adequate and timely recompense for their own services," they had entered into an agreement with the filmmakers, which had "created an unwaivable and actual conflict of interest between themselves and Echols." Prosecutor Davis disagreed. Judge Burnett agreed to hear arguments from both sides. He scheduled a hearing for May 5, 1998, the fifth anniversary of the murders.

As Mallett prepared for the hearing date, the gossip at the Crittenden County Courthouse centered on a motion that he had filed to have a dentist obtain bite mark impressions from Damien, Jessie, and Jason.[400] The criminal profiler in California had raised the possibility—which had not been presented at either of the trials—that the unusual marks on Stevie Branch's face had been inflicted by a human. Mallett said that if the marks had indeed been made by human teeth, and if the bite impressions could be identified, they might point to another assailant.

Mallett arrived in Arkansas for the start of the hearing aware, as he later observed, that "in Arkansas, these things are typically handled in an hour or two." But nothing about the West Memphis case had, so far, been typical.[401] When arguments were not completed by the end of the day, Burnett ordered the hearing continued to the next date it could be worked into his schedule. This happened two more times, resulting in a hearing on Damien's Rule 37 petition that lasted for eight days, spread over four sessions, in two different courthouses, over a period of ten months.[402]

The oft-continued hearing brought Burnett and Damien back into the courtroom together often between May 1998 and March 1999. Many of the participants from the original trials were there as well. Prosecutor Brent Davis, Detective Allen, Damien's defense attorneys, Dr. Peretti, Ron Lax, and family members of the victims all filed into the courtroom, as either witnesses or spectators. But now the atmosphere in the courtroom was very different from the atmosphere during the trials. Damien was different, for one thing. Gone was the funky haircut, the distracted air of self-absorption, the adolescent haughtiness that had so offended onlookers at his trial. Now the death row inmate appeared composed and almost studious. He wore glasses and subdued street clothes. His dark hair was trimmed short. He sat quietly near Mallett, seldom looking around the room.

Another change was the absence of cameras. Since release of the first documentary, Burnett had publicly expressed his regret at having allowed the trials to be filmed, and he'd said he would not be repeating that "mistake." A third difference was in the public who'd come to observe the hearing. Having been notified of upcoming hearing dates via the Web site, supporters of the West Memphis Three from up to a dozen states traveled to northeast Arkansas simply to be present in the courtroom each time Damien's petition was argued. They wanted, along with the Web site's founders, for "the state of Arkansas to know that the world is watching."[403]

Outside the courtroom, Judge Burnett made it clear, in banter with the supporters, that he was not impressed by their presence. Inside, he allowed Damien's new lawyer broad latitude in calling and questioning witnesses. "I give Judge Burnett credit," Mallett later said. "He heard us out. I have no quarrel with his willingness to sit and listen."

Sit and listen Burnett did, through days of often surprising testimony—none of which proved as sensational as that about the alleged bite marks. First the California criminal profiler, who had called attention to the marks on Stevie's face, explained how he'd arrived at his opinion that the marks that were described as "bell-shaped" in the autopsy report might have been made by human teeth. That view was supported by Mallett's next witness, a specialist in forensic dentistry. In a dramatic display, the dentist held up dental molds taken of Damien, Jason, and Jessie. None of them, he said, would have left the patterns seen on Stevie's face.

THE BITE MARKS DON'T MATCH! the Web site proclaimed that night. But the next day in court, it was the prosecutor's turn. Davis called another forensic dentist, and this one testified that in his opinion, the marks visible in the photos were not from a human bite at all.[404] Davis then called Dr. Peretti. The associate medical examiner told the court something he had never said before, nor noted in his autopsy report: that while the boys' bodies were at the crime lab, "just to be overly cautious," he had asked a forensic dentist to come in and examine them. Next, Davis called the dentist who Peretti said had examined the bodies. The dentist insisted that he had indeed been called to look at the marks, that he'd paid particular attention to the ones on Stevie's face, and that he had concluded that none of the marks had resulted from human bites. Under questioning by Mallett, however, the dentist acknowledged that he had not made notes of his examination, had not written a report, nor billed the crime lab for his time.[405]

For the supporters, it was an indecisive and unsettling outcome, especially since, outside the courthouse, John Mark Byers was once again talking into the cameras, this time about how the medication he'd been taking for his brain tumor had caused him to lose all of his teeth.

Mallett's Attack

On June 4, 1999, six years and a day after the arrests, Mallett handed Burnett his written arguments. Omitting the entire subject of teeth, he focused instead on the conflicts of interest he said were imbedded in the way attorneys Price and Davidson had conducted Damien's defense. Mallett excoriated the attorneys' decision to seek funds for experts from the filmmakers, rather than from the court. "Based only on their belief about what the court would pay," he wrote, "without actually making an inquiry, trial counsel failed to request funds from the court, then made inadequate expenditures to defend their client." Moreover, he charged, Price and Davidson had "appropriated" money from the film contract "for themselves as 'reimbursement,' contrary to the trust agreement and without [Damien's] consent. They were in Jonesboro, while he was on death row, thinking the money was being held in trust for the benefit of his child."[406] In fact, the fund had been emptied.

On yet another point, Mallett attacked Damien's lawyer for not disclosing that he had represented two people accused with John Mark Byers in the Jonesboro jewelry store incident.[407] Similarly, Mallett noted that Price had never told Damien that "he had served as counsel for the witness, Michael Carson, who testified that co-defendant Baldwin had made a jailhouse confession." In both situations, Mallett contended, "there was a conflict of interest which adversely affected counsels' performance."

But the most scathing part of Mallet's argument concerned Price's questioning of the psychologist during the sentencing phase of Damien's trial. "No one watching the movie, trial, or reviewing the transcript will ever forget," Mallett wrote, "the devastating cross-examination Dr. James Moneypenny presented as a defense witness. Moneypenny told the jury the records showed that unnamed persons told the defendant he could be compared with serial killers Ted Bundy and Charles Manson." Noting that Price had not jumped up to offer a legitimate objection, Mallett continued, "the image of Mr. Echols as a calculating serial killer was thus introduced through double hearsay from an unnamed source by a witness produced by the defense." For these and other reasons, Mallett argued, Damien had been denied his constitutional right to a fair trial.[408]

In Davis's brief to Judge Burnett opposing Damien's petition, the prosecutor argued that though Mallett had placed Price on trial, the Houston lawyer had failed in his efforts at "character assassination." Judge Burnett agreed. In a perfunctory ruling handed down on June 17, 1999, the judge denied Damien's Rule 37 petition for a new trial.

Stidham and DNA

Burnett's ruling brought Damien closer to the end of his Arkansas appeals—and closer to execution. But Mallett was not through. Stidham was still in the fight for Jessie. And now, as a result of widening interest in the case, additional legal help was gathering in the wings. Quietly, legal support for the three inmates was building. Mallett and Stidham began receiving help from legal experts whose roles in the case would not be known for years. The result in Arkansas was that despite Burnett's terse denial, efforts on behalf of the inmates intensified. Mallett appealed Burnett's denial of Damien's Rule 37 petition to the Arkansas Supreme Court. And in addition, the fight was expanded to two new fronts.

The first of those was also before the Arkansas Supreme Court. In February 2001, Mallett filed a rarely used writ of error *coram nobis*. The title refers to an error so grave that it has affected the very core, or heart, of the trial. In the writ, Mallett argued that Damien never should have been placed on trial at all because of his mental condition at the time. As it was, Mallett argued, Damien had been mentally incompetent—basically, insane—when he was tried and sentenced to death, and a trial under such conditions violated the U.S. Constitution. It was a stunning claim, but Mallett provided extensive documentation to support it. He submitted notes from the jail where Damien was held, documenting his attempted suicide. He supplied the notes Glori Shettles and Ron Lax had made after their visits to Damien, in which they described his hallucinations and paranoid delusions. Mallett also provided records showing that three times in the year before his arrest, Damien had been committed to psychiatric hospitals by a juvenile court in the same district where he'd later been tried.

Mallett also produced important evidence that had not come to light before: records showing that at the time of Damien's arrest and trial, he had already been declared "one hundred percent mentally disabled by the federal Social Security Administration" and was receiving payments for that disability. Courts generally accord substantial weight to Social Security designations of disability, since they tend not to be granted lightly. But Damien's mental status had not been explored, except in the sentencing phase of his trial. Neither Damien nor anyone in his family had mentioned the Social Security designation to his attorneys, and though Glori Shettles had requested Damien's Social Security records, they had not arrived by the start of the trial.[409] In an affidavit submitted with the writ, Val Price acknowledged that, had he been aware of Damien's Social Security disability, he "would have dramatically altered the manner in which we conducted investigation, preparation and presentation of evidence on his behalf. . . . Every aspect of my representation of Mr. Echols would have been affected."

Stidham launched the other assault, this one before Judge Burnett. In November 2000, he and an evidence analyst paid a visit to the West Memphis Police Department. There, for a couple of days, the two pored over the hundreds of items still in storage from the case. They concluded that there was a reasonable chance that some of the items they examined might yield new information. Nearly eight years had passed since the murder investigations. Those years had seen profound advances in the science of DNA testing. Smaller samples could now be analyzed, yielding more precise results. Across the country, guilty verdicts were being overturned on the basis of DNA evidence, some of which had been stored for years. Though many prosecutors resisted defense efforts to have DNA evidence retested, legislators in many states, including Arkansas, were passing laws that recognized the potential the science offered to correct errors and injustices.[410]

After reviewing the evidence at the police department, Stidham promptly filed a motion with Judge Burnett. The lawyer said that he wanted to retest several items, including the knife with blood in its fold that had belonged to John Mark Byers. "Additional testing with newer, more sensitive, and more discriminating tests," Stidham wrote, "may help resolve previously inconclusive test results. . . ."

When Prosecutor Davis objected to having the evidence retested, Stidham wrote to Burnett again. Reminding Burnett of the new state law that allowed inmates to seek retesting of evidence that might exonerate them, Stidham asked for a hearing on his motion. Burnett did not respond.

Arguments at the Supreme Court

Nearly two years after Judge Burnett's denial of Damien's Rule 37 petition, the Arkansas Supreme Court scheduled a hearing on Mallett's appeal. The Web site buzzed: Mallett had requested and the high court had agreed to hear oral arguments. They would be held on March 15, 2001, at the Arkansas Justice Building, on the grounds of the state capitol in Little Rock. Many supporters saw the event as an opportunity to again display their concerns about the case in the state where it had unfolded. Dozens of "WM3" supporters made plans to attend.

The day dawned cold and overcast. The chamber was packed to standing room only as Mallett and a lawyer for the Arkansas attorney general's office made their brief presentations.[411] Standing before the seven robed justices, Mallett reiterated many of the points he'd argued in his petition to Judge Burnett. Again, he stressed the conflict of interest he asserted Damien's lawyers had created by involving Damien in the documentary. Then Mallett added another complaint, this one aimed specifically at Judge Burnett. Mallett told the justices that in Judge Burnett's cursory ruling denying Damien's petition, he had failed to address each point the defense attorneys had raised, and so he had not offered his "findings of fact and conclusions of law" as Arkansas's Rule 37 required. Instead, Burnett had addressed only a few of the defense lawyer's points. He had ignored others entirely. And the rest he had simply dismissed with a few broad strokes. An attorney for the state argued that Burnett's responses were sufficient and that to now send the issue back to the judge for a more detailed order would do "gross injustice to the issue of finality."

It was over in less than an hour. Outside, as reporters gathered around Mallett, the West Memphis Three supporters began to unfurl a banner across the front of the Justice Building. While television cameras panned the colorful 160-foot display, one of the Web site's founders explained that it had been created from some three thousand postcards sent by the inmates' supporters from around the world.

Reporters asked what the supporters thought they could accomplish with their demonstration. Did they expect to influence the justices? An answer appeared that night on the Web site. "Instead of becoming discouraged, and feeling powerless against the justice system," the site's cofounder wrote, "it seems that a good number of people are still hopeful enough to believe that their support and their efforts can really bring about a change for the better." Mallett offered a more lawyerly reaction. "A naivete runs through American culture that assumes 'if I make a lot of noise, judicial behavior will be affected,' " he later told a reporter.[412] However, he added, "I don't think judges are favorably affected by young people's groups and websites."

A month after the oral arguments, the justices of the Arkansas Supreme Court issued their ruling. Without addressing most of Mallett's arguments, they agreed with him on one: that Judge Burnett's broad-brush denial of Damien's Rule 37 petition had not met the requirements of law, particularly as it concerned an inmate who'd been sentenced to death.[413] The justices sent the petition back to Burnett, ordering him to specifically address each issue Damien's lawyers had raised.

The high court's ruling merely tossed the case back to Burnett. Still, Mallett noted, it did mark the first time in the history of the trials that the appellate court had found even the slightest error. No one expected that when Burnett reissued his order addressing the defense lawyer's points, the ruling's effect would be any different. And a few months later, when Burnett finally issued his revised response, that assumption was proven correct. Even so, Mallett and the other lawyers were astounded when they read the new document. Instead of delineating his findings of fact and conclusions of law, as the court had demanded, Burnett had, on point after point, simply copied the attorney general's brief verbatim and issued that as his ruling.

"This is very unusual in a criminal case," Mallett complained. "The court didn't make independent findings. We think this violates the principle of an independent review of the evidence."[414] Again, Damien's lawyers appealed to the Arkansas Supreme Court to consider for itself whether or not Damien's representation at trial had met the standards required by law.[415]

Request for a New Judge

While Damien's lawyers focused on the issues before the state Supreme Court, Stidham found himself stymied with regard to his motion to retest certain physical evidence for DNA. In May 2001, Stidham reminded Judge Burnett of the motion he had filed six months earlier. "Your Honor," Stidham wrote in a letter, "we still have no hearing date on our motion to retest the physical evidence in this matter." Stidham pointed out that Jessie's Rule 37 petition had been pending for nearly four years and that Jessie was "eager" to have the new tests conducted.

But eight more months passed without a response from Judge Burnett. In February 2002, Stidham wrote again: "Dear Judge Burnett: It has been almost a year since I requested that my Motion to Preserve and Retest Evidence in this case be set for a hearing. . . . May I request that it be set in front of a different judge?" Stidham added, "This case is almost nine years old and I would really like to move it along." For Stidham, who was now a municipal judge in his hometown of Paragould, Arkansas, the fight had been a long one—and promised to be longer still. "There's been times when I've wished they were guilty, so I could get on with it and put this to bed," he said. "But they're not." Burnett finally responded. A tentative hearing date on the DNA evidence was set for November 2002.

After nearly nine years, frustration with the legal processes was demoralizing almost everyone involved with the inmates' appeal. Since their convictions, the hopes of all three had hung largely on the outcome of Damien's appeals, since a new trial for him, if one were granted, would indirectly impact the appeals of the other two as well. But by the spring of 2002, with the ninth anniversary of the murders approaching, Damien's Rule 37 appeal and his petition for a writ of *error coram nobis* still awaited rulings from the Arkansas Supreme Court.[416] "We're going to try to win the case in state court," Mallett said. Somewhat wearily, he added, "There is a federal process available, if we do not succeed."[417]

The Detectives

Chief Inspector Gary Gitchell resigned from the West Memphis Police Department two months after Damien and Jason's convictions. The forty-one-year-old detective announced that he was moving across the river to Memphis, to work for Pinkerton Investigation Services.[418] In August 2000, he told a reporter for the Internet magazine Salon.com, that he still "adamantly" believed in the guilt of the three accused killers. "You've got a lot of circumstantial evidence is what you've got," Salon quoted Gitchell as saying. "There's no smoking gun. This is not a smoking-gun-type case."[419]

Detective Allen was eventually promoted to captain. In one of his rare public comments, he told a reporter for the *Atlanta Journal-Constitution*, "If I just watched those documentaries and knew nothing else about the case, I would have questions too. I would say to myself, 'Those boys might not have done it. There are a thousand and one questions. This is a crying shame.' But the reality is HBO did a one-sided, biased job. They did the case a real injustice. If this country gets to the point where, instead of a trial, we say, 'Let's have HBO do what they do and have people e-mail the courts, well . . ." At that point, the article noted, Allen's voiced trailed off. Then, it said, he added, "As I know the case, I can sleep at night in peace, knowing who killed those kids."[420]

Bryn Ridge also remained with the West Memphis police. Like Allen, he criticized the documentary and the "stupidity" of the people who were supporting Damien, Jason, and Jessie. "I looked at the entire case," he said in 2002, "and I am convinced that those are the three." But Ridge, like the other investigators, was short on specifics as to why. "I'm not going to talk about that," he said.

Detective Don Bray, of the Marion Police Department, who'd introduced Vicki Hutcheson and her son Aaron into the investigation, suffered a debilitating stroke shortly after the trials.

Steve Jones, the juvenile officer who'd made the first crucial find in the case—the child's tennis shoe floating in the water—resigned as a juvenile officer a year after the trials. He moved away from West Memphis.

Jones's boss, Jerry Driver, who'd been the first to suggest that Damien, Jason, and Jessie should all be considered suspects, was placed on administrative leave in February 1997, after an audit of his department found a shortage of nearly $30,000. He resigned from the Crittenden County Juvenile Probation Office the following month.[421] Three years later, on January 21, 2000, Driver appeared in court before Judge Burnett to face a charge of theft. When Driver pleaded no contest, Burnett placed him on probation for ten years and ordered him to repay the missing funds at a rate of $241 per month.[422]

Lieutenant James Sudbury, like Gitchell, Allen, and Ridge, had little to say about the case in the decade after the trials, though he made his

opinions clear. When a reporter visited the department in 2001 to examine evidence held in storage, Sudbury escorted her to the vault,
where he told the officer in charge, "She wants to see the garbage."[423]

But Sudbury's career was clouded. When the three eight-year-olds
were found murdered, Sudbury and other West Memphis narcotics detectives were under investigation by the Arkansas State Police. Soon after the murders, that investigation was quietly set aside. During the
investigation and trials that followed, few people knew anything about
the investigation of the police. But word of them did leak out, and by
the end of the trials, a Memphis reporter had begun making inquiries
into the results of that state police investigation of the narcotics unit
that Sudbury headed.

Ron Lax had no idea that some of the officers involved in the murder
investigation had been under investigation themselves until two months
after the trials, when he spoke with the reporter. "These officers worked
with the drug enforcement division of the West Memphis Police Department," Lax noted after that conversation, "and there were allegations that they had appropriated drugs and/or stolen merchandise for
their own use. The only name [the reporter] mentioned was that of Detective James Sudbury. What was truly amazing was the fact that [Prose-
cutor] Brent Davis signed a consent order to terminate this investigation
sometime during mid- to late June 1993." Lax did not know it at the
time, but Sudbury had been the highest-ranking officer implicated in the
corrupt enterprise. At the time of the murders, state police investigators
were still looking into allegations that, as one state police report noted,
Sudbury was "leading a higher than normal lifestyle" on his police salary.

The state police reported to Prosecutor Brent Davis that in interviews just two months before the murders, Sudbury had admitted that
he'd taken guns and other items from the evidence locker and that he'd
lied when investigators had first questioned him. But Sudbury was not
placed on administrative leave. He was active in the murder investigation. And after Damien, Jason, and Jessie were arrested, Davis declined
to prosecute him.

Sudbury remained a narcotics detective for the next several years,
but his job security ended abruptly when a new chief of police fired him
in 2001. "We were dealing with police corruption, is what it amounts

to," the new chief of police said.[424] At a press conference called to announce the dismissal of Sudbury and two other narcotics officers, the chief reported that the FBI had been investigating "indiscretions" within the department, some of which he said traced back "as far as ten years."[425]

Jessie, Damien, and Jason

"It's crooked," twenty-five-year-old Jessie Misskelley said, offering his opinion of Crittenden County. By the spring of 2001, Jessie had spent a third of his life in prison. He had seventeen tattoos, including one with his nickname, Midget Biker. He said he was thinking of getting another one. "I want to get a tattoo on my head," he said. "I want a brain. I want a brain tattoo on the top of my head. Because I ain't never seen no one that has one." He described himself as hopeful—and a bit smarter than when he'd been arrested. Now, he realized, "If you didn't do it, don't ever admit that you did."

Damien's interest in metaphysics—which had so colored his trial—continued on death row.[426] He'd read books on Buddhism and come to embrace that philosophy. As a result, many Arkansans were doubly surprised when they read, in December 1999, not only that Damien had married but that the ceremony had been a Buddhist one performed at the prison.[427] The woman marrying him was Lorri Davis, the architect from New York with whom he'd been corresponding since the release of the first documentary.[428]

Captain Allen said he was "stunned and dismayed" to learn that Damien had wed. "I thought to myself, 'What's this old world coming to?'" he told the *Arkansas Democrat-Gazette*. "I know it's federally mandated, but unless [a prisoner] is getting married to a cellmate, they really need to revamp the system." Brent Davis said he thought it was "strange" that Damien had so many supporters, and that one would even marry him. "We made him what he was," the prosecutor said. "We elevated Echols from a psychotic-fringe to being admired by thousands."[429]

As the ninth anniversary of the murders approached, Jason was living a life as close to a middle-class life as he could manage inside a prison. Because he was quick to learn computers and maintained an impeccable prison record, he'd been assigned to a series of white-collar jobs in various clerical positions. He'd joined the prison Jaycees and begun to study investments. "I don't want to get out and be that sixteen-year-old kid I once was," he said. "I want to keep up."[430]

He'd taken college courses in subjects like anthropology, accounting, and American politics—"because I want to see what our government's built on"—and dreamed of attending law school. And he had a sweetheart. The correspondence that he'd begun in 1997 with young Sara Cadwallader had grown into a serious romance. She was in high school when they'd met. Now Sara had graduated from college and had herself been accepted into law school. Jason credited Sara, his faith in God, and the support of friends, many of them "total strangers," for his emotional stability—for his ongoing belief "that right will prevail."

"I have grown up in prison," he wrote at the end of 2001. "Even with all that I have suffered, I have not allowed myself to become hateful, spiteful or resentful of either those who put me here unjustly, or of those who allowed it to happen. I know you've got to love life, enjoy it, embrace it while you've got it. I love this country we have. I love America and her people. And I hope that someday I will be able to live here as a free man again, with my reputation intact."

Jessie, Damien, and Jason all had different visions of what life would be like if they were freed. Jessie dreamed of a "big party." Damien said he wanted to "disappear" with his wife. Jason foresaw a life of activism relating somehow to law.

"Being in here has made me stronger," he said. "It's made me more reflective on things I should be proud of and enjoy, things like freedom. I don't take things for granted. And I'm not as naive as I was. The reason I'm here—the real reason—is that someone had to pay the price." Jason said that the police and prosecutors had been "content just to say we did it" and that that had been "enough" for the public. But he added that he understood the public reaction. "I used to think that way too," he said. "To me, a suspect meant, 'That's who done it.' But I didn't do it, and that's the main matter."

EPILOGUE

THIS STORY IS A CHILDREN'S TRAGEDY. The victims—and there were many—were all minors.

The lives of Michael Moore, Stevie Branch, and Christopher Byers ended not just too soon, but in horror. We know that hours before Christopher suffered the savage attack on his genitals, he was beaten with a belt—a not uncommon punishment dealt to far too many children. As a teenager, Christopher's brother, Ryan, had to cope not only with Christopher's murder but with his mother's unexplained death less than three years later.

The witnesses were all children, and they were victims as well, especially young Aaron Hutcheson. Encouraged to tell and retell his story, with no guidance or restraint from adults, he embellished his account from a man with yellow teeth to scenes of orgies in the woods, and finally to lurid visions of buckets of blood. The teenagers who testified at the trials were but bit players in a drama that could not have unfolded without the exploited utterings of children. Other teenagers recanted their accusations, admitting later that they'd said only what they believed police wanted to hear.

Jessie himself had begun by saying he knew nothing about the crime. Told he'd failed a polygraph, he also tried to accommodate the police— only Jessie was so unwitting that he also implicated himself.

When he, Damien, and Jason were arrested, none of them was old enough to buy a beer, a cigarette, or a *Playboy* magazine, much less execute a contract. Nevertheless, all three could be interrogated repeatedly and for hours by armed police officers, with neither parent nor lawyer present, and all three could be charged as adults and face possible execution.

Children don't write their own tragedies. That is the work of adults. The vulnerabilities of children in this story were evident before the murders occurred. Poverty and instability weakened homes; intolerance, violence, and official corruption weakened the community. The serious mental health problems that some of this story's children exhibited—Christopher, Jessie, and Damien, in particular—were tragedies in the making.

Sentimental nostrums about "babies" and "little lambs" could not muffle the harshness that cracked through this story like a belt. Who was protecting Aaron Hutcheson from his galloping fantasies—or from the effect that the detectives' voracious attention would have on him in later years? Who was looking out for Ryan? What kind of concern for children allowed police to question them without even a parent around? If the tactics that led to Jessie's confession were acceptable, as the state Supreme Court ruled, whose interests were being protected? Certainly not Jessie's. *Not any child's.*

A terrible disingenuousness wields the corrective belt. This is for the child's good. This is to send a message. This is for society. This is to teach respect. This is for law and order.

"I think it's important that we all be held accountable," Judge John Fogleman told me in an interview eight years after the murders, "whether it be me or the police officers or the people who commit crimes." But police officers in this story were not sanctioned after they stole from their evidence locker, and John Mark Byers committed multiple crimes without being "held accountable." Judge Burnett committed a serious error when he ordered a witness to testify under oath without an attorney, although the witness had twice requested one. Burnett then avoided accountability by imposing a gag order on everyone who'd witnessed his action. Holding people accountable—or not—is the privilege of those in authority.

So the question becomes: how should children deal with that authority?

I asked Fogleman if he would feel comfortable if one of his own children was questioned by police without him or another lawyer present. His immediate response was, "Well, I wouldn't be comfortable myself being questioned without a lawyer." Then he added, more deliberately, "But this was not Jessie's first exposure to being questioned and to being advised of his rights. And really, comfort's not really an issue."

"What would you advise your children to do if they were brought in by police for questioning?" I pressed.

Again, Fogleman evaded. "In a vacuum," he said, "it would be, 'You be extremely polite to the police and answer whatever questions they've got. Be truthful.' That's in a vacuum. But I don't expect my kids to be in that kind of trouble."

But children do get picked up and questioned by police, I said. And the world is not a vacuum. "So if you were speaking to the Rotarians, and someone asked you what they should tell their kids, what would your answer be?"

"I honestly don't know," the judge said. "I don't know."

If John Fogleman doesn't know, who does? If even a judge cannot advise parents on how to advise their children, how in heaven's name are children who are suddenly picked up for questioning by police supposed to figure out for themselves what to do? Fogleman, who'd had years as a prosecutor and judge, could not come up with an answer, yet high school dropout Jessie Misskelley was expected to understand because, after all, his interrogation by Gitchell and Ridge hadn't been his "first exposure" to being questioned by police.

But the tragedy plummets deeper. The cornerstone of justice in the United States of America is that persons accused of crimes are presumed innocent until proven guilty. Children, supposedly, are presumed to be even more innocent. But here, all of that was swept aside. There were no special protections. There were no juvenile courts. There was not even a basic presumption of innocence. Damien, Jason, and Jessie were not proven guilty. They were presumed guilty. And that, as Jason noted, was "enough."

AFTERWORD

Since this book's publication, I have been asked about its title.

In the early stages of writing the book, I focused on knots that bound the victims. Those knots were some of the few clear signs the killer or killers left behind. I wanted never to forget Christopher Byers, Michael Moore, and Stevie Branch, or the vision of their naked bodies being bound with their own shoelaces. Even as I tried to view their tragedy with overdue rationality, I could not ignore my own human cry that what was done to them was diabolical. As I wrote, I wanted to keep the knots front-and-center: Who wrapped those loops and figure-eights around the boys' thin wrists and ankles? Whose hands yanked the square knots? Who tied the cruel half-hitches?

As my work progressed, a different kind of knot emerged. I saw it forming in the investigation and trials. This time, it was three teenagers who were being bound. Like the little boys, Damien Echols, Jason Baldwin, and Jessie Misskelley had been caught by something bigger, more powerful than they—something intent on ending their lives. Over time, the twists and turns of the proceedings against the West Memphis Three would form an ugly new set of knots: strange legal bindings that hold them to this day.

Lacking rope, whoever tied the children made do with the boys' own shoelaces. What the prosecutors of the West Memphis Three lacked was evidence. They had three bloody, muddy murders and three young defendants, but not a scrap of physical evidence linking the accused to the crime. So they made do. They tied Jessie with his raggedy confession.

Lacking a confession–or anything else—for the other two, they resorted to triangulation. By linking the crime to the words "the occult," then linking Damien and Jason to those words, they indirectly linked them to the crime. The judge allowed the tactic and—voilà! That easily—and that insubstantially—the bedeviling absence of evidence was overcome.

Since the book's release, I have begun to view its title more broadly.

After the attacks on September 11, 2001, the United States witnessed a swift erosion of freedoms that citizens once took for granted. Protections once required by law were abandoned, in the name of defending the country against terrorism. The parallels to what happened in West Memphis—the horror, the panic, the rush, and the willingness to set aside standard legal procedures—are obvious. And so are the attendant risks.

Imagine now that the vague word "terrorism" is substituted for the vague word "occult." Imagine a violent crime, hastily-rounded-up suspects, a similar dearth of evidence. Imagine witnesses coming forward to say that the crime bore the "trappings" of terrorism. Imagine evidence acquired under the so-called USA PATRIOT Act that the suspects had checked out a library book on Islam, had written e-mails critical of U.S. policy, or had owned a CD with lyrics about violence. Imagine that just that easily and indirectly the accused are linked to the crime.

It's another devil's knot. Add the strangling element of panic, and any of us could be snared.

—Mara Leveritt, March 2003

NOTES

1. Unless otherwise noted, accounts of the search for the missing boys cited in this chapter were drawn from police logs and other records of the West Memphis Police Department.

2. The officer was Regenia Meek. The subdivision where Byers lived was known as Holiday Garden.

3. The manager's name was Marty King.

4. In some written reports, Dana Moore, as she was usually called, is identified as Diana. In later statements, Moore said that she reported her son, Michael, missing while Meek was at the Byerses' house, but apparently Meek did not fill out a written report on Michael at that time. According to Meek's records, she responded to the call at Bojangles, then returned to the Moores' residence at 9:25 P.M., at which time she filled out the report that Michael was missing.

5. These were the Mayfair Apartments.

6. Climatological data for Memphis in May 1993 from the National Climatic Data Center.

7. The West Memphis Police Department claimed in a summary of the night's events that "the victims were reported missing by their parents at approximately 8:10 P.M. 05-05-93, at which time a search was initiated," but the department's logbook for that date contains no mention of a search other than the walk through the woods by Officer Moore, from 9:42 to 10:10 P.M.

8. Gitchell credited Sergeant Allen with making the crucial discovery, but subsequent testimony revealed that Jerry Driver's assistant, Steve Jones, of the county juvenile office, was the first to report the sighting.

9. According to police accounts, Allen slipped on the muddy bank while trying to retrieve the shoe with a stick, and ended up waist deep in the water. However, Gitchell told the local paper, the West Memphis Evening Times, that Allen's plunge had been deliberate. "Being inquisitive," Gitchell told a reporter, "he jumped in the water and started feeling around."

10. From a six-page unsigned police report dated May 6, 1993, labeled only "Crime Scene Notes."

11. There is some disagreement about the location of the bodies. The unsigned "Crime Scene Notes" indicate that the first and third bodies were found thirty feet apart. However, the West Memphis Evening Times reported that Gitchell said the bodies were found "about ten feet apart." An undated police summary of the recovery effort said that all three of the bodies were found within five feet of one another.

12. Crittenden County's coroner was Kent Hale, the manager of a funeral home.

Under Arkansas's system, each county has a coroner. Coroners are not required to be medically trained. There is one medical examiner for the state. The medical examiner and his assistants are required to be pathologists.

13. The paper quoted the report as saying: "This department has a case of three male juveniles being abducted. They were found with their hands tied behind their backs and their genitals had been removed with a sharp instrument. Their bodies had been dropped in a remote area. Any department with a case similar to this, please advise this department, attention Inspector Gitchell. All information appreciated."

14. The boys attended Weaver Elementary School, whose playgrounds bordered on the lot where Michael Moore and his family lived.

15. Some state police investigators said privately that they found Gitchell's position surprising, especially in light of the pressure that Gitchell was under to solve the crime. It had attracted national attention; there were apparently no clear suspects; and the help of trained investigators, especially in the first several days, seemed only to make sense. But others in the police community sympathized with Gitchell's position. They noted that detectives pride themselves on being able to solve crimes in their own jurisdictions, and that what made even more sense was Gitchell's official explanation, that "we've got fifteen people on this now, and if we get too many, we'll be tripping over each other."

16. On January 15, 1993, relatives of Deputy Clark White, an undercover member of the county's drug task force, found him dead in his trailer home. The county's sheriff, Richard Busby, contacted the state police. Investigators found the deputy's partially decomposed body lying on a couch in the living room. In the kitchen, they found a package of liquid poison. An autopsy report concluded that White had died from drinking the poison. White's parents, who lived nearby, reported that shortly after White was last seen alive, they had seen two men driving White's black Pontiac Firebird without White in the car. The Firebird was registered to the sheriff's office, which used it in undercover narcotics work. Four days after the discovery of White's body, police across the river in Memphis located the Firebird, and a few hours after that, they also located a person who witnesses said had been driving it. Law enforcement from both sides of the Mississippi River swarmed on the neighborhood. A few hours later, officers of the Memphis Police Department's Organized Crime Unit captured two suspects, both of whom were arraigned in Clark White's murder. The two suspects told police that White had hocked many items, including various guns and his service revolver, to purchase drugs. A few days before White's death, they said, he had offered the Firebird as collateral to a drug dealer in Memphis for an advance of $300 worth of crack. One of the suspects was subsequently tried and found guilty of the deputy's murder.

17. Ironically, just as that investigation was beginning, the U.S. Department of Justice named the West Memphis–Crittenden County Drug Task Force the best in Arkansas, and one of the top rural drug task forces in the nation. The honor was awarded, in part, because of where West Memphis was located—at the juncture of Interstates 40 and 55. With a level of truck traffic at least twice that of its nearest competitor, West Memphis liked to boast of being the truck stop capital of the world. For the police that offered the opportunities—for both enforcement and corruption—of a huge flow of drugs through the county. The location of Memphis, the eighteenth largest city in the United States, directly across the river, con-

tributed to the illegal milieu. With the federal Drug Enforcement Administration estimating that one in every eighty-five vehicles on the interstates carried illegal drugs or drug money, property seized from vehicles had become a major source of income for rural Crittenden County. In 1992, the county drug task force seized, in addition to a wealth of drugs, more than a million dollars in cash, seventy-four vehicles, thirty-seven guns, and assorted other property. The seizures bulged the coffers—as well as the evidence locker—of a county with just fifty thousand residents, one-fourth of whom lived at or below the federal poverty level.

18. Details of the drug task force investigation from Arkansas State Police files.

19. While information about the state police investigation of the Crittenden County Drug Task Force did not make it into the West Memphis paper, the *Evening News* that spring did report information from another state agency that the rate of child abuse in the county was one of the highest in the state.

20. Byers's first wife's name was Sandra; their children were John Andrew and Natalie Jane.

21. Accounts of the arrest and conviction for terroristic threatening were found in the records of the Crittenden County clerk's office that were apparently overlooked when Byers's conviction was expunged.

22. Records of the request for a restraining order are from Crittenden County Court. In an author interview in April 2001, Fogleman acknowledged that he'd heard the tape but said he did not know where it ended up.

23. Author interview with Melissa's parents, Dorris and Kilburn DeFir, April 2001.

24. In an author interview in 2001, Byers said he'd volunteered to work as a drug informant out of a sense of "a civic responsibility." He said, "I did what America needs a lot of citizens to do." But if he was reporting on drug activity strictly for altruistic reasons, he was an exception to the rule. Most drug informants agree to assume that dangerous role only after having been arrested, in a plea bargain arranged with prosecutors.

25. Usually, records are expunged for people who were young at the time of their offenses. Byers was thirty when he was charged and convicted, and thirty-five when the record was expunged.

26. The arrest was made and recorded by the Shelby County Sheriff's Office.

27. For example, detectives said they placed the clothes taken from the water into paper grocery sacks, and the clothes were brought back to the police station to dry. These items were then said to have been repackaged—reportedly in the original sacks—and sent to the state crime lab. But the sacks received by the crime lab showed no water marks or other signs of having been wet. Other concerns focused on the quality and completeness of the investigative record. Later reviews of the file would show that officers took notes but left many undated and unsigned. In some instances they added names and addresses to the case file without indicating the significance of the names or why they had been filed. They filed copies of fingerprints, sometimes without attaching a name. They conducted interviews in a variety of fashions with no apparent policy or consistency of approach. Notes were taken of some interviews and not of others; some interviews were tape-recorded, some were videotaped, and others were recorded only in part. Officers

showed people photo lineups in their search for suspects but failed to record whose photographs were shown and which, if any, had been recognized.

28. The summary read like a press release, but since much of the information it contained was being guarded, it may have been prepared for dissemination to other law enforcement agencies. The West Memphis police would not elaborate on the summary's purpose. When asked for interviews during preparation of this book, detectives Gitchell, Sudbury, Ridge, and Allen all refused comment.

29. Later tests of Aaron's vision, conducted by a private investigator, would indicate he was color-blind.

30. Ridge noted that blood found on the side of one bank "may have been the result of the perpetrator standing in the area with an amount of blood on him or one of the bodies may have been placed there prior to being placed in the water." He surmised that other spatters "may have been the result of blood transfer from the crime scene either on the feet or clothing of someone leaving the area." This could have been the killer or killers. Or it could have been the police.

31. This was especially true in light of the victims' ages. By 1993, law enforcement agencies in the United States were becoming increasingly aware of the grim statistical link between child abuse and child homicide. By then, murder had been identified as the third leading cause of death of children between the ages of five and fourteen. Police departments dealing with child murders were advised to respect the grief of parents but also to weigh the possibility that a family member may have been the killer. Because children usually stay close to home and are taught to be wary of strangers, police agencies around the country were being advised to look carefully at the people around them.

32. Dawn's friend, Kim Williams, was a fourth-grader who lived near the woods.

33. No records indicate that Gitchell ever sought court records to confirm whether or not Christopher had been adopted, and the matter apparently went unquestioned throughout the investigation. Byers told the author in an interview that a local attorney named Jan Thomas had handled the adoption. But when Thomas was asked how Byers had been allowed to adopt the child while he was on probation for a felony, was not complying with the terms of that probation, and claimed to be unable to pay child support for his two biological children, Thomas said he was unaware of the felony conviction and no longer had records of the adoption. Adoption records in Arkansas are confidential; but R. L. Murray, Christopher's biological father, said he never relinquished his parental rights, which would have been necessary for Byers to have adopted Christopher.

34. Melissa Byers worked at Fargenstein's Jewelry Store, at Poplar and Highland streets in Memphis. At rush hour, a round trip from municipal court in West Memphis, across the Mississippi River, to the store in the heart of Memphis, and back again to the Byerses' house would have taken at least an hour.

35. The detectives who interviewed Taylor were Diane Hester and Mary Margaret Kesterson.

36. Ryan had been called to testify in a reckless driving case.

37. Patrol Officer John Moore reported to his dispatcher that he was searching the woods between 9:42 and 10:10 P.M.

38. The following day, May 20, Sergeant Allen and another detective did interview Ryan again, but the question of what happened at midnight was not brought up. Still, in this interview, another statement Ryan made disagreed with that of his stepfather. Ryan told the detectives that until the day or two before the murders, he had never seen Christopher play with Stevie Branch. Moreover, Ryan reported some disturbing aspects of his brother's friendship with Michael. Once, near the beginning of the school year, Ryan said, he had caught Christopher and Michael playing "nasty" behind the school. "They had poo-pooed in the field," Ryan said, "and were throwing it at each other." More recently, he said, "Chris has not played with Michael a lot since they got in trouble for breaking into Weaver school."

39. Byers said he threw the party for Dallas Brogdon, sheriff of St. Francis County, which adjoins Crittenden County on the west. The occasion was reportedly Brogdon's fiftieth birthday.

40. Without suggesting a link to violence, detectives did ask Byers about the brain tumor he was reported to have. Byers told them he'd been aware of it for the past two years. "I've been having blackouts," he explained, "and even though it's cool in here, at times, I just break out in a sweat. A bad migraine headache starts. I start getting like, tunnel vision, and then it's like somebody flashes a camera in front of you, and it's just like spots in front of me." At first, he said, "They thought I had epilepsy and then they thought maybe I had a brain aneurism. They found out at one time that I had meningitis, and they thought maybe that's what caused it." He said doctors had put him on Dilantin, "but it causes your gums to bleed, and it's real bad on your teeth," so he'd been unable to take it. Doctors then prescribed Tegretol instead. Byers said he had been hospitalized five times in one year because of the tumor, and that the problem had caused the loss of the jewelry store.

41. Christopher's life had been hard from the start. He'd weighed less than four pounds at his birth, which was premature, and had had to undergo immediate abdominal surgery.

42. The neurologist, Dr. Donald J. Eastmead, reported that Christopher had "a great many problems. . . . He overreacts and has temper tantrums at home. He is aggressive on occasion with little remorse. Bedtime, morning, mealtime, riding in the car and various other social situations are a problem. He frequently interrupts." The doctor prescribed Tofranil for Christopher's hyperactivity. But on a visit three months later, he was dismayed to see that Christopher seemed to have regressed. Eastmead noted that the child seemed to be suffering from paranoia, complaining about "something being in his hair." The doctor kept him on the Tofranil and prescribed, in addition, five milligrams of Ritalin twice a day. By the time Christopher was seven, the Tofranil had been stopped and the dosage of Ritalin quadrupled. But the boy's problems did not abate.

43. During the visit shortly before Christopher's death, Eastmead noted that he showed signs of "extreme impulsivity, destructiveness, opposition, defiance, hyperactivity, extremely low frustration tolerance and refusal to follow commands." Eastmead reported: "I am in a quandary as to the reason. He has been on Ritalin 20 mg twice a day, which has improved his hyperactivity and inattention but has made no appreciable change in his poor social skills, including such things as play-

ing with his feces and poor judgment in terms of self-care and self-help. . . . This is
certainly a difficult child who may require in-hospital treatment to gain control of
his behavior. I am increasing the medication and changing it to Dexedrine 5 to 10
mg morning and noon, 5 in the afternoon, as well as adding Tegretol."

44. The case was handled by state police Investigator Steve Dozier. The ring that
had been part of the shipment was apparently never recovered.

45. Gitchell to Kermit Channel, Arkansas crime lab, May 26, 1993.

46. Gitchell to deputy prosecuting attorney John Fogleman, May 28, 1993.

47. The deputy prosecutor who accompanied Fogleman to the crime lab was James
"Jimbo" Hale.

48. When interviewed in April 2001, Fogleman said that he did not often take such
measures but that he and Hale visited the crime lab in this instance "because it was
a very difficult case."

49. From *Darkfall* by Dean Koontz.

50. General offense report, Marion Police Department, March 6, 1992.

51. Personal information about Jerry Driver in this chapter was drawn from an author interview with him conducted by phone on November 1, 2000.

52. General offense report, Marion Police Department, May 13, 1992.

53. Record of arrest, Crittenden County Sheriff's Office, May 19, 1992.

54. Petition and detention order in the Juvenile Division of Chancery Court, Crittenden County, May 19, 1992.

55. "I found several instances of animal sacrifices," Driver later explained. "They
were mostly small animals. The largest was a dog. We could tell they had been
mutilated. The dogs would be skinned, with the entrails out of them. We found
some in an old school building in West Memphis that had a pentagram on the wall
and 666. I found, like, a little altar made with sticks and stones. And there was a
lot of bird bones there, and a cat that had been skinned."

56. In the late 1980s and early 1990s, alarm was spreading throughout the
United States about crimes that had reportedly been committed as part of cult-
related rituals. Concern first arose in the mid-1980s, when a few psychothera-
pists began to report that a startling number of their clients had described,
while under hypnosis, vivid "recovered memories" of ritual abuse they claimed
to have suffered in childhood. Many "survivors" of ritual abuse, as they came to
be called, reported having been raped; some reported witnessing murders. Interest in the reports spread from the mental health profession to other fields,
including religion and law enforcement. Groups were formed to help victims
of ritual abuse and to identify likely offenders. A task force formed to address
the problem in Los Angeles noted that "ritual abuse does not necessarily mean
Satanic. However, most survivors state that they were ritually abused as part of
Satanic worship."

57. "A Law-Enforcement Perspective on Allegations of Ritual Abuse," Kenneth V.
Lanning, supervisory special agent, Federal Bureau of Investigation.

58. The consultant was Steve Nawojczyk, a former coroner in Little Rock. According to his press releases, Nawojczyk consulted with law enforcement officials nationally on gang activity, as well as on "cults and occultic groups."

59. Driver also kept in touch with other cult watchers scattered around the country. He and a police officer in New York exchanged faxes in order to compare graffiti. They concluded that some of the graffiti Driver was seeing in Crittenden County resembled graffiti that police in New York had discovered as part of the infamous Son of Sam murder case. As Driver later explained, "There was an abandoned school, and when you went down a long hall and into this room, it looked sort of cavelike. The whole scene looked very similar—eerily similar, I'd say—to a picture that was published in a book about Son of Sam."

60. Records supplied to Jerry Driver by Charter Hospital of Little Rock.

61. According to family members, Damien had suffered from intense motion sickness since childhood. Even when he turned sixteen, he showed no interest in learning to drive. He'd seemed content to walk, and drivers in Marion and West Memphis had grown accustomed to seeing Damien, often wearing a long black trench coat, walking along the roads.

62. Report of Calvin L. Downey, juvenile department counselor, Washington County, Oregon; August 14, 1992.

63. Damien was taken to St. Vincent Hospital and Medical Center.

64. Affidavit to the Juvenile Division of Chancery Court of Crittenden County, Arkansas, sworn and filed on September 9, 1992.

65. Petition filed in the Juvenile Division of Chancery Court, September 9, 1992.

66. Notarized document authorizing change of guardianship signed by Pamela Joyce Echols in Oregon on September 11, 1992. The Arkansas court order changing custody and the order adjudicating Echols a delinquent were entered three days later, on September 14.

67. Undated report of Joyce Cureton, director of the Craighead County Juvenile Detention Center.

68. Charter Hospital physician's discharge summary, September 28, 1992.

69. Damien was seen by Sherry Dockins, LMSW, a clinical social worker at the East Arkansas Regional Mental Health Center. He told Dockins that he often slept during the day, that he usually visited Domini at night, and that he liked to "trance out" when he was alone, because it took him away from "what's going on." He acknowledged having used alcohol, cocaine, acid, and marijuana in the past, but said he had never been a major drug user and had used no drugs for several months. Dockins also noted that Damien told her that he had a history of self-mutilation; that he usually felt "neutral or nothing"; that "he feels people are in two classes— sheep and wolves. (Wolves eat the sheep.)"; that he revealed "a history of abuse as he talked of how he was treated as a child [but] denies that this has influenced him, stating, 'I just put it all inside' "; that he "describes this as more than just anger— like rage. Sometimes he does 'blow-up.' Relates that when this happens the only solution is to 'hurt someone' "; and that "when questioned on his feelings, he states, 'I know I'm going to influence the world. People will remember me.' "

70. According to a 1998 Southern Focus poll conducted by the *Atlanta Journal-Constitution* and the University of North Carolina, more than 60 percent of Southerners polled—and almost three-quarters of all churchgoers—said they believed that humans are sometimes possessed by the devil.

71. Martin B. Bradley et al., *Churches and Church Membership in the United States* (Atlanta: Glenmary Research Center, 1990). Nationally, Southern Baptists accounted for about 8 percent of the population.

72. In November 2001, the Arkansas Baptist State Convention passed a resolution to "firmly denounce" J. K. Rowling's best-selling series of books about the boy wizard Harry Potter. The resolution was intended to alert merchants—particularly booksellers—to the Baptists' concern that the series was "inconsistent with biblical morality," sounded an "anti-Christian theme," and "promoted pagan beliefs and practices."

73. Driver was an Episcopalian. His wife, a Roman Catholic, attended St. Michael's Church in West Memphis—the same church that Damien Echols had attended for a time. Driver knew that before his hospitalizations, Damien had taken an interest in Catholicism. He knew that the teenager had completed a course for converts and that he had been baptized into the Catholic faith. Damien had told Driver the same thing that he had told officials in Oregon, that he had changed his first name from Michael to Damien when he was adopted by Jack Echols, and that he had chosen Damien in honor of a famous Catholic priest by that name who'd cared for the lepers of Hawaii. But Driver doubted the story. He knew that a century ago, there was a Father Damien who'd cared for Hawaii's outcasts. But Driver also knew that Damien was the name of the demon child in the 1976 movie *The Omen*, and he suspected that, if any identification was being made, it was with that character.

74. Author interview with Driver, November 2000.

75. Baldwin's account of his early life, as presented in this chapter, is drawn from interviews by and correspondence with the author while he was at the Grimes Unit of the Arkansas Department of Correction, during 2000 and 2001.

76. Jason's favorite band since first grade was Metallica. He liked the way the group could "build with music, the way they build all these different harmonies and melodies with their single instruments, and yet the music that they build independently becomes an instrument in itself, to make the overall song." By the time Driver had focused his attention on Damien—and secondarily on Jason—Jason's favorite song was Metallica's "Nothing Else Matters." He loved the music as well as the lyrics. Music played a big role in the boys' lives, partly because there was so little else. Jason would recall, "Damien listened to different music for the same reasons."

77. The friends had much in common—and many differences. "People thought we did drugs because we looked wild," Jason would recall, "but we didn't. We didn't need them. Damien smoked cigarettes. I never have. He was smoking cigarettes before we ever met. If he wasn't smoking when we met, he would never have started that bad habit. Most of the people we knew smoked, and a lot of people did drugs, like smoking marijuana. We couldn't have afforded to buy drugs, anyway. We just never had any money to do anything wild or adventurous. We lived on a lake, so that was cool. I liked to fish, but Damien didn't. But that was okay. He could sit on the dock, feed the ducks, and watch me fish. We also had a Super Nin-

tendo, with the coolest game at the time, which was Street Fighter II. I know it's a violent game, but it was fun! We would spend time at my house playing Super Nintendo and listening to the stereo."

78. Jason said he'd often been told that he was going to hell because he liked a type of music that some local ministers denounced. By sticking together, he and Damien were able to absorb the barbs. "After a while," Jason said, "it was water off a duck's back." He dismissed their critics. "You know how kids are," he'd say. "They probably got it from their families and their church."

79. After that incident, Jason said, "Steve Jones would hound me for wearing rock and roll T-shirts and the like. He was always around messing with me. But I didn't care. It wasn't until he started hounding Damien that I began to care. He absolutely hated Damien. He told all the kids in the neighborhood that Damien was a Satan-worshiping faggot. That caused all types of trouble for Damien. Someone always wanted to kick him down, but he was smarter than that. He thought it was humorous, all the rumors about him. He didn't realize how a lot of people took what was said, along with his name and how he looked, serious."

80. Jason did not like Deanna. He said, "When her parents forbade her to see Damien, it was her idea for them to run away to California. As I look back on it now, I should have been a better friend and talked him out of it. I tried, but not as hard as I could have. He wanted me to go with him, but I couldn't. I had responsibilities to my family. I told him that I did not want him to go, but she put herself on him and got her way. I wished him the best and we collected money up for his trip. I don't remember how much he ended up with, but it wasn't much. That was a sad dark day. Especially when the police picked him up. After that, the police had a 'legitimate' reason to keep Damien out of Marion. Because of his love for Deanna, Damien went to juvenile hall and afterward lived in Portland for a while. He tried coming back to Marion a couple of times and even tried to return to Marion High School. The police escorted him out. All because of a girl who really did not care for him, who was just rebelling from her parents and looking for the first person she could manipulate into taking her away."

81. Interview notes of Don Bray taken by investigator Ron Lax, October 7, 1993.

82. The pastor was Dennis Ingall, of Lakeshore Baptist Church.

83. When Lax interviewed Bray in October 1993, the police officer still carried the piece of paper in his shirt pocket. Lax wrote in his notes of that interview, "I asked if he knew Damien Echols personally and he admitted he had never met him, nor had he ever had any connection with him. He stated there was a case in Marion in which a teenage girl was raped and he felt Damien Echols was involved; however, under further questioning, he stated a young man had been arrested for the rape and Echols had never been charged or questioned."

84. Pam Echols later recalled the interview as having taken place on May 6. Damien said he remembered a helicopter circling the city while he was being questioned.

85. Handwritten notes of Detective Bill Durham.

86. This appears to be a reference to the interview on Friday, May 7, when Sudbury and Jones questioned Echols.

87. On matters relating to the occult, however, Ridge's report was extensive. "When asked if the water had any type of meaning in the Wicca or black magic, Damien stated that water was a demon type symbolism and that all people have a demonic force," Ridge wrote. "He further stated that people have control over the demonic force in them. . . . Damien went further to explain that in his Wicca religion, he knew that evil done comes back three times. He stated that meant that any evil done by a person would be rewarded by the person doing the deed having three times the evil done to him in revenge. Damien stated that his favorite book of the Bible was that of Revelations because of the stories in it about what was being done by the devil and the suffering done by people at the hands of the devil. . . . Damien stated that he likes books written by Anton LaVey, which would be Satanic in nature. He also likes Steven [*sic*] King type books. . . . It was noted that Damien had the tattoo of 'E,' 'V,' 'I,' and 'L' across his left knuckles, and he stated that Jason Baldwin had the same tattoo on his knuckles."

88. From a sermon by the Reverend Fred Tinsley, the rector of Holy Cross Episcopal Church, where the Moores attended.

89. The same day that officers questioned Deanna Holcomb, they received a call from Memphis police about an inmate in the jail there. The officer in Memphis said the man had been heard discussing devil worship and human sacrifice with two other men in the jail. Memphis police sent records on all three to police in West Memphis, and these were placed in the murder case file, but there was no record of any follow-up, no indication that West Memphis detectives ever crossed the river to question any of the men.

90. She identified the friends as Randy and Susan Sanders.

91. The West Memphis police were receiving a lot of encouragement to consider the satanic theory. At the end of the first week of investigation, a patrol officer who identified himself as "the official cult and occult expert for the New York City Police Department" contacted them to offer his opinion that the murders might be "occultic in nature." The New York patrolman volunteered that missing body parts were a key sign that the murders were "occultic." He advised the police in West Memphis to look for signs such as a circle, candle wax, an inverted cross, a pentagram, the numerals 666, or an altar where the bodies were found. But the site where the bodies were found had already been scoured, and police had not found one of those signs. The same day, a local teenager told police that he'd heard that members being initiated into an area cult were required to do something "real bad," such as drilling three holes into the heads of their victims and draining out the blood. Also that day, a Texas woman sent Gitchell a book about how cults that engaged in murder were proliferating in America. And two girls telephoned *America's Most Wanted* to report that two teenagers they knew in West Memphis—neither of whom was named Damien—were "into devil worship." The girls said that one of the boys had told "one of the caller's boyfriend's best friends" that he had committed the murder. Another man told police that he knew nothing about the crime, but that a friend of his felt certain that Damien was the killer.

92. Statements attributed to Bray in this chapter were drawn from an undated three-page typewritten report about his conversations with Vicki and Aaron Hutcheson that Bray provided to the West Memphis police.

93. Statements of Vicki and Aaron in this chapter were compiled from police notes and transcriptions of interviews that were conducted with the pair on May 27 and 28 and June 2, 8, and 9, 1993.

94. Statements attributed to Jessie are drawn from an author interview, conducted February 2, 2001.

95. On October 25, 1983, Jessie was administered the Wechsler Intelligence Scale for Children—Revised; the Peabody Picture Vocabulary; and the Bender Gestalt Test.

96. James Fitzgerald, a clinical social worker at East Arkansas Regional Mental Health Center, recorded that Jessie was seen at the center, along with his father and stepmother, Shelbia Misskelley, in the spring of 1983.

97. Quotations are from the notes of Dr. Terry B. Davis.

98. Psychological assessment by Terry B. Davis, Ph.D., March 25, 1983.

99. Assessment by Dr. Davis, October 23, 1985.

100. Psychoeducational evaluation conducted at Marion High School, April 14, 1992.

101. Jessie said, however, that he and Jason had never been close friends. Jason's recollection was that he and Damien had "hung around" with Jessie for a couple of years, beginning in about the sixth grade, a time "when there wasn't too many people who would associate with me." But over time, the boys had parted ways. "Damien didn't like Jessie," Jason said, "and Jessie didn't like him. I hung around with both of them until the eighth grade. Then me and Jessie fell out over a girl."

102. After reading about the case in the papers, Hutcheson explained, she "just thought how they were killed was odd, like, you know, maybe it was like a devil worshiping thing." She said, "Jessie had told me that Damien hung out at Lakeshore, and so I went out of my way to try to go around Lakeshore. And, you know . . . I told Jessie I had seen Damien . . . and he said, 'Well, you know, he's kinda weird.' I said, 'No, I think he's hot. I really want to go out with him. Can you fix me up with him?' And you know, he was real surprised, but he said, 'Yeah, if you want to go out with him, I'll fix you up with him,' and he did."

103. As Hutcheson described the meeting to the police, she had first sent her children to visit their father in western Arkansas, then she'd removed their photos from her home so that Damien would not see them. She'd then placed "some Satanic books and witchcraft books" strategically around her trailer, which had the effect of prompting Damien to reveal a lot about himself. Among the startling information she reported, as a result, to Bray was that Damien's cult was called the Dragons and one of its rituals involved the sacrifice of animal genitals.

104. The word "esbat" is not found in the *Oxford English Dictionary*, which is considered the most exhaustive lexicon of the English language.

105. While overlooking some questions that countered the satanic theory, the police sharpened their focus on reports that supported their growing suspicions. The day after Hutcheson's alleged visit to the esbat, officers questioned two children of Narlene Hollingsworth, the woman who said she'd seen Damien and Domini on the service road near the Blue Beacon on the night the boys disappeared.

Hollingsworth's children said they'd been with their mother and confirmed her account in every detail. They said they'd clearly seen Damien and Domini—both dressed in black and both muddy.

106. No one discussed Aaron's initial statement, about the tall black man with yellow teeth driving the maroon car who'd picked up Michael Moore after school, nor was that initial report questioned in subsequent interviews, in which Aaron gave sharply different accounts of what happened that afternoon.

107. When the West Memphis detectives questioned Aaron that day in Bray's office, the boy told them that on at least five occasions, he and his friends had witnessed, from a distance of about five feet, five men with black-painted faces. He said the men had chanted in Spanish around a fire, smoked strange cigarettes, killed animals, talked about "bad stuff," and done "nasty stuff." The detectives pressed for details, but Aaron was vague. Ridge asked, at one point, "What kind of bad stuff were they talking about?" "Um, Jesus and God," Aaron said. "I mean, the devil and God." Aaron added, "They said they like the devil and they hate God."

108. Misskelley's statements drawn from an author's interview with him, February 2, 2001, at the Varner Unit of the Arkansas Department of Correction.

109. Jessie's friend Kevin Johnson had helped in the search.

110. Statements by Bray in this chapter are from an undated three-page typewritten report prepared by Bray for the West Memphis police.

111. Jessie had known Allen for most of his life, just as he had known Gary Gitchell. As Jessie later explained, "They knew me since 1980, when I was five years old, 'cause that's when I first started getting in trouble with the police. I got in trouble for stealing and fighting. That's it: stealing and fighting. I stole toys, bicycles, flags. And I got into fights. When I got older, I'd fight anything; walls, mailboxes, bottles, stop signs, window—anything. Whenever I got mad, I hit something. If it was a person, I hit them." Since Jessie hadn't hit anyone lately, he said, he wasn't worried about this visit. (The times noted in this paragraph are from a report of Misskelley's questioning written by Detective Bryn Ridge.)

112. Most of the questions put to Jessie before the polygraph focused on Damien. According to notes Allen wrote at eleven that morning, Jessie stated that he had known Damien for about a year; that Damien was "sick"; that once, when Jason had gotten a bloody nose, "Damien stuck his finger in the blood and licked it." Jessie also reported that he'd met Hutcheson after the murders occurred; that she had, in fact, asked him about Damien; and that he had never been in Robin Hood. Ridge also jotted a report. He noted that Jessie had been picked up in the first place because "it had been previously discovered that Jessie, Damien and Jason were members of a cult-like group of youngsters who had previously had meetings in various locations in the state." Ridge added that when he entered the room while Allen was questioning Jessie, the boy had appeared "nervous and failed to look at me in the eyes, and had the gestures that he was being deceptive." Contrary to anything that either detective wrote in their early notes, Ridge later wrote in his typed report that, "Jessie stated that he thought that Damien had committed the murders with a friend of his being a partner in the murders. Again he was nervous throughout the interview from this point, and he appeared to be with-

holding information." It was after this, Ridge reported, that he asked if Jessie would be willing to submit to a polygraph examination.

113. There is a discrepancy regarding time between Ridge's typewritten report and the forms signifying waiver of rights. Ridge reported that Durham began the polygraph exam "at about 10:30 A.M.," but the time on the waiver of rights form that Durham gave Jessie prior to the exam lists the time as eleven-thirty.

114. For Ridge, Jessie's response to the child's voice on the tape recording marked the turning point in the case. Here is how Ridge described the moment in his report: "Jessie told of one occasion he had gone to the scene of the murders and sat down on the ground and cried about what had happened to the boys. He had tears in his eyes at the time, telling of the incident. I felt that this was a remorseful response about the occurrence and that he had more information than what he had revealed. At about 2:20 P.M., Jessie told Inspector Gitchell that he was present at the time of the murders and began crying about what had happened. Jessie seemed to be sorry for what had happened and told that he had been there when the boys were first coming into the woods and were called by Damien to come over to where they were. At this time, myself and Inspector Gitchell gave Jessie some time to compose himself and for me to compose myself, due to the emotional situation that had just began. We then prepared for the interrogation to be taped, due to this being the first indication that Jessie had actually taken a part in the murders and was present in the woods at the time."

115. While no law requires that police interviews with citizens be recorded, police organizations in Arkansas won passage of legislation requiring that if an officer is questioned by police, that interview or interrogation must be recorded in its entirety.

116. Under the heading "Neck Injuries," the medical examiner reported: "Situated on the left side of the neck were a few scattered abrasions. Subsequent autopsy of the neck showed no hemorrhage in the strap muscles of the neck. The hyoid bone and larynx were intact. No petechial hemorrhages were noted. No fractures were noted."

117. After the tape recorder was shut off, according to an unsigned, undated chart in the files of the West Memphis police, "Work was started in reference to obtaining search warrants and arrest warrants."

118. After the time chart was typed, someone wrote "incorrect" across an entry that claimed that the second recorded interview began at 3:45 P.M. (The Arkansas Supreme Court later concluded that Jessie had been questioned "off and on" for more than seven hours.) A typed transcript of the second recorded interview did not mention the word "discrepancies." It was simply titled "Second interview conducted to clarify previous statements."

119. Misskelley's strange way of referring to Christopher Byers and Stevie Branch may have reflected both his confusion (calling Byers "Myers") and a mangled version of the manner of speech he had been hearing from detectives, some of whom referred to the victims as "the Byers boy" or "the Branch boy."

120. During the pretrial testimony of Detective Bryn Ridge, Paul Ford asked, "Judge Rainey was assisting in preparing the search warrant affidavit. Is that what you're telling me?" Ridge said, "Yes sir." Ford asked how Rainey had assisted. "He

was informing us as to the elements that needed to go in this affidavit in order for it to be a legal document," Ridge replied. Ford asked, "So he told you what you needed to get and you went out and came back and met with Judge Rainey?" Ridge said that that was correct. "Who was present?" Ford asked. Ridge answered, "Myself, John Fogleman, Gary Gitchell, [James] Jimbo Hale, and the court clerk."

121. Jason's brothers, Matt and Terry, were fourteen and ten years old.

122. Long after his arrest, Baldwin would have time to reflect on the circumstances that had brought it about. "The way I figured," he said, "the police had been accusing me and Damien of satanism for the longest. They'd spread the rumor that the motive for the murder was satanism. At that time, they were picking up a lot of people and talking to them. And one they talked to was Jessie. Now, Jessie's got some hate and vengeance in his heart for me because of the girl thing. And maybe he thinks, 'I'll get a whole bunch of money.' Maybe they came and talked to him and he had a spur-of-the-moment idea, and went along with it, and got his foot in his mouth. He didn't understand the seriousness."

123. He said that all that registered was that he was being led in handcuffs out of Damien's house. "They took me to the police station," he later recalled. "We went through all kinds of rooms, and ended up upstairs, in a room with blue walls, and pictures and certificates on them, and a ball bat in the corner. They handcuffed me to a straight-back chair. Ridge and Allen were there, and a uniformed officer. They came in and tried to get me to admit to murder. They had this statement already typed up and told me to sign it, but I wouldn't sign. They told me there was no way out of it. I might as well admit to it. I was trying to tell them where I was at that day, but they said, 'No, that's a lie. We know different. Somebody's already ratted on you. You committed the murders. We want you to admit it.' Somehow, I fell out of the chair. I fell backwards. I think Allen pulled it out with his foot. He said, 'You ain't nothing but white trash.' Later on, Ridge was in the room with me by himself. He said, 'Nobody knows you're here. We could throw you into the Mississippi River and write you off as a runaway; nobody would know the difference.' "

124. After he'd come home from school, Jason said, "Damien and Domini were already at my house waiting for me. They didn't go to school. We went in and played Super Nintendo. I got something to eat. Then Dennis, my mom's boyfriend, said I had a phone call. It was my uncle Herbert. He said, 'You forgot something.' I was supposed to mow his yard. I was supposed to have done it earlier, but I had an art exhibit at school, so I'd put it off. My friend Ken and Damien said, 'We'll go over there with you.' I cut my uncle's yard. And while I was there, Damien had to call his mom, and tell her to pick him up at my uncle's house instead of at my house. He and Domini went to the Laundromat to call, and his mom picked them up there. It took an hour to finish the lawn. My uncle paid me $10. Me and Ken went to Wal-Mart. Then we went to Sam's and bought ten-cent Sam's sodas. We played Street Fighter for a quarter. Then we went back to my house. Ken left to go home, and then I went over to my friend Adam's house. It was dark by then. He had this Iron Maiden tape I'd been wanting. I went over there to try to buy it. He sold it to me for $4. I had a necklace of a dragon with a silver ball that this girl had given me at the skating rink. He wanted me to sell it to him. By then it was getting close to ten or ten-thirty. I wanted to get back before curfew started, so I went back home. Matt and Terry and

Dennis [Jason's stepfather] were there." Jason said he told the police all this the night of his arrest. "I told them I didn't do it. But they didn't want to listen."

125. Officers who booked Jason noted that he did have a tattoo, but not the *E-V-I-L* that Vicki Hutcheson claimed to have seen. According to a police intake form, he had small ankh, the Egyptian symbol of life, in the web between the thumb and index finger of his right hand.

126. Author interview with Fogleman, April 2001.

127. One of the young people who'd accused Damien was William Winfred Jones, a teenager who lived in the Lakeshore trailer park near Jason. As was common in the investigation, Ridge had questioned William, then questioned him again on tape. In the portion of the interview that was taped, William stated that he and Damien had been friends for the past five years. He said that Damien had not been "weird" at first, but that he'd started acting strange after he'd gotten into "that satanic cult stuff." William said that one night when Damien was drunk, he'd asked Damien if he'd murdered the boys. William said Damien admitted that he had. William told Ridge that Damien loudly proclaimed that he'd had sex with the boys, and then killed them with a "little," eight-to-ten-inch knife. William added that "everyone" in the Lakeshore trailer park had heard the drunken claim. However, when Ridge asked William for the names of others who'd heard the alleged confession, William modified his statement. On second thought, he said, only he, Damien, and Domini had been present.

128. Ridge listened as Gail Grinnell recited some of what she'd heard. She told him of one instance when some girls had told a neighbor "that the police had been telling them to stay away from that boy named Damien—that he was a member of a gang." But Ridge was not interested in hearing complaints about police conduct. Without addressing her remarks, he told Grinnell, "It's really not complicated— the position we're in and the position that Jason is in. If he'll tell us a story, if he'll tell us where he was that day, what time he got places, and we'll check with those people that say he went to those places. If we prove that his story is true and correct, then Jason is a free person. But we can't even start until Jason tells us what happened and where he was. . . . If we can prove that that's where he was, I'm more than willing to see him be a free man. I mean, that's the truth. But I can't even start until Jason tells me something."

129. Normally, arrest and search warrants, along with the affidavits submitted to support them, are open to public review. The practice, which has existed for centuries, is intended to safeguard citizens against unfounded arrests. But now Rainey was announcing that that normal level of openness would not be allowed in this case. He justified his order to seal the records, saying that the "high level of publicity" the case had attracted threatened "the defendants' right to a fair trial."

130. Bruce Whittaeker, of WMC-TV, channel 5, in Memphis, said he had turned down the offer because "we don't buy news."

131. This article was written by Bartholomew Sullivan, the *Commercial Appeal*'s lead reporter on the case. Another of the paper's reporters who wrote extensively about the case was Marc Perrusquia. Sullivan and Perrusquia teamed up with Guy Reel to write a book about the case, *The Blood of Innocents*, which was published by Pinnacle Books in 1995.

132. When Gitchell was asked if parents in West Memphis could now allow their kids to "go out and play normally," he answered obliquely. "I think all parents need to always know where their children are at," he said. He added that "kids should stay away from" Robin Hood, which he described as "dangerous."

133. An editorial in the *West Memphis Evening Times* noted that ever since the murders, "the rumor mill in Crittenden County has been grinding on overtime. The level of supposition reached wildfire proportions after the three teens were arrested last week, and community comment linked them with Satanism. Public curiosity being what it is, in the absence of any hard, cold facts other than the names, ages and addresses of the suspects, speculation is bound to continue." The editorial advised that "giving the public a bare framework of facts surrounding these murders would have gone a long way toward suppressing the rumor and supposition. It seems to us that's much more dangerous to these defendants' eventual fair trial than the truth would be. But beyond that, the failure of the courts to allow the public even a limited knowledge of the facts in this case means Crittenden Countians have no choice but to take on faith the word of the police and prosecutors that this crime has been solved and that the community can breathe a sigh of relief. . . . While this community has no particular reason to distrust its law enforcement officials, a little reassurance wouldn't hurt. But the case remains shrouded in secrecy, and the public's questions remain unanswered. We hope, above all else, that our faith in the law enforcement and judicial system is justified. We just wish we knew for sure."

134. Rainey's order sealing the normally public records was affirmed by circuit judge Ralph Wilson Jr.

135. Reporters did ask a few questions about the variations in Jessie's confession. One reporter for the *West Memphis Evening Times* asked Fogleman about the part in which Jessie had said that the boys were murdered at around noon, when it was known that they were in school. Fogleman's answer was terse: "Obviously, the time is wrong." The *Commercial Appeal* also took note of Jessie's apparent "confusion about the issue." The principal of Weaver Elementary School confirmed that the victims were in school all day, but the principal of Marion High, where Jason attended, refused to release attendance records that would have supported his claim that he had been in class there all day. In another article, the paper noted that the transcript of Jessie's statement "places commas in unusual places." For example, it reported that at one point the transcript quoted Jessie as saying, "Well after, all this stuff happened that night, that they done it, I went home about noon, then they called me at nine o'clock that night, they called me."

136. The Reverend Rick McKinney warned, "Satanism is out there. Parents and young people need to be aware of its reality." He advised that "a fascination with horoscopes is an early sign. If you go to the library and look for information on horoscopes, they will send you to the occult section." And he added, "There is definitely a connection between hard metal music and Satanism." The Reverend Tommy Stacy, another Baptist, said the situation in West Memphis called for "spiritual warfare." But it was warfare, he advised, that was best left "in the hands of the Lord and law enforcement." Yet another Baptist minister, the Reverend Tommy Cunningham, began a series of sermons on satanism. He told an overflowing crowd, "Satan wants us to believe he is a nonreality. If he convinces us of that, then his work is carried out best."

137. The psychologist, Dr. Paul King, was identified by the paper as the author of *Sex, Drugs and Rock and Roll: Dealing with Today's Troubled Youth.*

138. Quotes about cults ran the gamut. "Cult experts gave warning in 1992," a front-page Sunday headline in the *Commercial Appeal* read. John Mark Byers told the *Commercial Appeal* that even after the arrests, he and Melissa remained afraid that members of a satanic cult might be free in the community. The paper reported that Byers believed "that others may have seen the three defendants 'all bloody and muddy and wet' after the murders"—others who "knew that these three little boys were going to be sacrificed." "My wife and I are scared," Byers told the paper. "The devil is at work, and recently, Satan and his demons have been at work in West Memphis." Crittenden County librarian Nelda Antonetti told the *Commercial Appeal* that "she was alarmed by a sharp increase a few years back in students checking out books on Satanism, the occult and magic." In an article by Marc Perrusquia, on June 13, 1993, the paper went so far as to note that "one book inspected recently by a reporter had a dog-eared page that listed human fat in a recipe for a potion enabling witches to fly, and also mentioned the heart of an unbaptized baby as a delicacy following a black mass."

139. Bray acknowledged this in an undated three-page typed report that he gave to the West Memphis police.

140. At one point, in the interview on June 8, 1993, Bray asked Aaron if he'd seen any of the assailants "abusing" Michael Moore. Aaron answered, "I didn't know he was abusing him." Bray then asked, "Well, you told me they raped him at one point. Is that what they did? Who raped him?" Aaron responded that Jessie did.

141. Author interview with Lax, May 2001.

142. Eight years later, Jason recalled: "I was there for two weeks before I could talk to my mom. They put me in an orange jumpsuit that said 'Craighead County' on it. But I didn't know where that was at. I didn't know where I was. My mom didn't know where I was, either. For two weeks, she visited jails—two whole weeks. Once she came to the jail where I was at and they told her I wasn't there. Sometimes, in the middle of the night, guards would come around and wake me up, to show me off to other police. They'd point and say, 'Yep, that's him.'"

143. When assigned to write about who he'd be if he could be someone else, Jason had reflected: "I am satisfied with being who I am. I admit I have certain flaws I wish I didn't have, but that's life. Everyone has at least one thing about them that makes them special. My special quality is art. I have always been able to entrance people with my artwork, and I like that. It is the one thing that I can do that mostly no one else can do. So I am happy with being myself." Another assignment called for him to contemplate his future. Jason had reflected: "Well, in my immediate future, I plan to graduate high school and go to some art college, and major in commercial art. Within the next ten years, I plan to be doing art for MTV on their videos and stuff, or doing album covers, T-shirts, etc. Within the next thirty years, I'll probably be mellowed down and be reduced to doing wildlife paintings at home and selling them. Or I may have my own tattoo business somewhere. Well, I guess that's just basically it with my career." Asked to describe his musical tastes, he'd written: "The kind of music I like mostly is heavy metal. But I listen to all kinds of music. My favorite groups are Metallica, Megadeth, Iron Maiden, Tes-

tament, Slayer, and Ozzy Osbourne. But I also like Guns n' Roses, Pink Floyd, Nirvana, Red Hot Chili Peppers, Pigface, Alice in Chains, and Pearl Jam. The reason I like this music is that it sounds good. Most of them make a point or statement in their lyrics, and I like that."

144. The three defendants had been taken to jails in different towns, and though families were told where they were being held, authorities refused to make the locations public, claiming that the secrecy was for the defendants' protection.

145. As reported in the *Commercial Appeal*, June 9, 1993.

146. The drug Echols took was amitriptyline, an antidepressant sedative that must be prescribed by a physician. Overdoses can cause an erratic heartbeat or coma. The 1993 *Physicians' Desk Reference* stated that "potentially suicidal patients should not have access to large quantities of this drug." Arkansas law requires that prisoners be seen by a physician, who must approve any prescription medications, but in this case that precaution was not taken.

147. Lax and Shettles soon learned that the information they'd been given about Damien's name was incorrect. But since Damien didn't care which name they used, and since they'd already gotten to know him as Michael, that was the name that stuck. After one interview, Shettles wrote, "He stated he asked to be named Damien as, at one time, he thought about becoming a Catholic priest and knew that father Damien was a person who was kind and helped lepers." She found the story poignant; Michael, the social leper, taking the name of a priest who'd cared for suffering outcasts.

148. Shettles learned from her research that Damien had, in fact, attended nine schools in five states before the age of ten. Damien entered kindergarten in West Memphis in 1980. He attended first grade in schools in Tupelo, Mississippi; Walker, Louisiana; and back in West Memphis. Second grade was divided between Wichita Falls, Texas; and a school in West Memphis. He attended third grade in West Memphis; in Columbus, Mississippi; and in Frederick, Maryland.

149. Shettles wrote: "Michael stated he had ideas the world was to be destroyed as if in a nuclear war due to his mother talking about the world being destroyed as in the Book of Revelations. Michael told me he liked very scary movies and was a fan of Stephen King books. He described his favorite Stephen King book as being 'The Children of the Corn.' . . . Michael states he became involved in Wicca, which is white witchcraft, through his relationship with Deanna. . . . Michael stated his main source of information regarding Wicca was 'Buckland's Complete Book on Witchcraft.' He stated Wicca does not practice animal sacrifices or blood rituals in any way. He further stated participants do not engage in orgies and said he has never practiced bestiality or homosexuality. Michael described his talents as being a poet and a skateboarder."

150. Driver and Jones had questioned Damien and Jason several times: when an abandoned school burned and dead cats and birds were found inside; when graves in a Marion cemetery were desecrated; and when Driver had found some dead animals at the abandoned cotton gin. Damien said he'd had nothing to do with the incidents but that, in light of the police attention, he had not been surprised when officers showed up at his door the day after the murders.

151. The autopsy reports on each of the boys specifically stated, "No adhesions or abnormal collections of fluid were present in any of the body cavities."

152. After an interview with Damien's mother, Shettles wrote: "Pam stated Michael and Jason would talk on the phone after they had been questioned by the police and would jokingly say, as an example, 'This is Suspect Number One calling Suspect Number Two.' "

153. As information on the case was slowly being released to the defense attorneys, other information continued to be leaked to the media. Despite Gitchell's stout refusal to speak with reporters, and the judges' seal on the records, a reporter for the *Commercial Appeal* learned about a burglary in the neighborhood where the victims lived that had occurred a year before the murders. Word reached the paper that reports of the burglary had been included in the murder case file, and someone had even provided details. The burglar had reportedly stomped the family's Yorkshire terrier to death and left it dead in the master bedroom. But when reporters asked to see police records on the incident, they were told that since the records were now part of the murder investigation, they fell under Judge Rainey's seal. "This whole case is just so huge," Gitchell told the paper. "Anything to do with it, be it significant or insignificant, we followed up on." While defense lawyers worried about leaks they could not combat, neither the judges nor Fogleman complained. When asked about the murdered dog, Fogleman replied obliquely, "I'm not saying any crime is related. I'm saying it's part of the investigative file." In its report on the incident, the *Commercial Appeal* pointed out that Driver had noted "an increase in Satanic-related graffiti and reports of animal sacrifice." In July, elements of Aaron Hutcheson's statements to police were leaked. A Memphis television station reported that, at times before the murders, the victims and "a fourth eight-year-old child" had visited a tree house of sorts, which they had called "the clubhouse." The boys had reportedly witnessed "wild, ritualistic orgies, possibly cult-related," while hiding in the tree house. Gitchell would not comment.

154. Lax described one report, for example, dated a week before the arrests, as "a handwritten investigative report by Bill Durham regarding a search of the crime scene area for a tree with a tree house, as had been described by 'a witness interviewed on May 27, 1993.' " Lax noted that "the correct tree was found, but there was no indication there had ever been a tree house in that particular tree." Since the interviews with Vicki Hutcheson and her son Aaron had not yet been released, Lax and the lawyers were left to wonder why, so late in the investigation, police had returned to the woods to look for a tree house they might have missed. The media were also trying to piece together the puzzle of what had led to the arrests, but with even fewer clues.

155. Author interview, May 2001.

156. Emotions surrounding the case were inflamed in early August when the owner of a book store in Jonesboro, the city where Jason was being held, announced plans to lead a march on behalf of witches and pagans, in support of religious freedom. The event drew loud opposition. Steve Branch, Stevie's biological father, condemned it in the press. "I'm telling everybody, if they believe in God and Christianity—even if they don't go to church—to be out there," he told the Memphis paper. Stevie's grandmother Marie Hicks said she would not attend the march, because if she did, "I'd take a bunch of grenades with me." The local chief

of police said he was "preparing for the worst." In August 1993, the high priestess for a Memphis group of Wiccans told the *Commercial Appeal* that "Wiccan do not acknowledge the existence of Satan, so it is hardly likely that we could worship this entity." She added, "We look forward to the day when Christians, Wiccan, Jews, Buddhists, Muslims, Hindus and all other practitioners of loving faiths can coexist in harmony." But the march of about seventy Wiccan was not harmonious. The *Commercial Appeal* reported: "With rows of pedestrians and dozens of police looking on, the two groups passed within inches in a bizarre Main Street meeting as Christian hymns and bellowed prayers competed with pagan songs and chants in a loud, confusing cacophony." One man reportedly shouted, "I don't know what's wrong with you people. Don't you care about the youngsters in this community? You know this is wrong!" A woman told the paper, "I just wanted to let my kids see there are bad people in this world . . . . There are evil people who do evil things." On the other hand, one man told a reporter that he had driven to Jonesboro from Little Rock because he supported freedom of religion. He said, "I believe in speaking out against religious persecution of any type." But his was the minority view. After the march a group of local ministers, led by Bob Wirtmiller, pastor of the Woodsprings Church of the Nazarene, vowed to see that the bookstore whose owner had organized the march was closed. Referring to the West Memphis murders, they issued a statement saying, "We want our children protected against any possible recurrence due to occult activity of any kind."

157. "Initially, I thought Michael was voluntarily participating in church services," Shettles wrote; "however, I was somewhat shocked to learn these ministers come into their cells with or without the inmates' permission. Michael stated these ministers were preaching directly at him and telling him he needed to turn his soul over to Jesus or he would not be allowed into heaven." Shettles wrote that when she mentioned the trial ahead, Damien "laughed and stated he definitely did not want any priests on the jury. He also kidded and stated, if he had a choice, he would not have any males, females, whites or blacks on the jury, either."

158. Berlinger and Sinofsky had gained prominence in the world of documentary filmmaking in 1992, with release of *Brother's Keeper*, their look into the life of a dairy farmer who was accused of suffocating his brother. The following June, when the *New York Times* carried a brief report about the arrests in the West Memphis case, a producer at Home Box Office called it to Berlinger and Sinofsky's attention. "By all accounts," they later explained, "it seemed to be an open and shut case: three blood-drinking, Satan-worshiping teens had committed a horrifying act of violence. We were intrigued, so we went down to Arkansas to do some initial research." The more the pair looked into the case, the more intrigued they became. They decided to film the unfolding events as their next documentary project, to be pursued in conjunction with Home Box Office, a division of Time Warner Entertainment Co. Inc. When Lax learned of the filmmakers' interest, he called to speak with them. Lax noted afterward that Sinofsky "continually assured me he wanted to present an objective film, based on the human element and not so much on the guilt/innocence issues. . . . Bruce said he is interested in portraying the defendants' families and their pain, as well as that of the victims' families. . . . I expressed my concerns regarding this as being two-fold. First, we have no way of knowing what the family members will say. . . . Second, even if the state does not subpoena the interviews and film (and I cannot believe they would not do so), and the production company does not release the film

until six months after the trial, which Bruce indicated they would do, we are faced with the potential harm the film could do to our defense during the appeals and post-conviction stages." Lax concluded his memo with the note: "I have spoken with Scott Davidson [who, with Price, was representing Damien], and he and I agree it would be better to politely decline to allow this filming and interviewing of family members until an indefinite time in the future."

159. The girls were Holly George and Jennifer Bearden, both of Bartlett, Tennessee.

160. Lax wanted to examine the photographs that one of the police reports indicated detectives had shown to little Aaron. If one of the photos shown to Aaron had been of Damien, and if Aaron had not identified him as one of the killers, that information might be important, particularly if Fogleman were to call Aaron to testify. Gitchell and Ridge "initially attempted to inform me they had not shown any photographs to Aaron," Lax wrote in his notes. "However, when I provided them a copy of the statement, they conferred and stated they did recall pulling photographs from various files and showing them on a board to Aaron. . . . Both Inspector Gitchell and Detective Ridge informed me Aaron Hutcheson did not identify any of the individuals in any of the photographs they provided. When I asked if they had those photographs available, they stated they did not and they had not made a record of which photographs were shown to Aaron." The officers then put forth the names of several people, including Damien Echols (but not Jason or Jessie), whose photos, they acknowledged, might have been on the board.

161. Less than a year and a half before this hearing, Burnett had issued the order expunging John Mark Byers's conviction for having threatened to kill his ex-wife.

162. Not long after Burnett became a judge, Burnett presided at the trial of fifteen-year-old Ronald Ward, who was convicted of another triple murder, this one also in West Memphis. For a time, Ward was the youngest person on death row anywhere in the United States, but then the Arkansas Supreme Court ruled that Burnett had erred in allowing Ward, who was black, to be tried by an all-white jury. When Ward was tried a second time, again in Burnett's court, before a jury that was racially mixed, he was sentenced to life in prison.

163. Mike Trimble in the *Arkansas Democrat-Gazette*, February 22, 1994.

164. As reported by Bartholomew Sullivan, January 16, 1994.

165. The decision was based on a 1968 U.S. Supreme Court ruling based on the Sixth Amendment to the U.S. Constitution. The court ruled that if a confessing defendant is tried jointly with defendants he has implicated and does not testify, the nonconfessing defendants are denied their constitutional rights to confront and cross-examine their accuser. Since Misskelley had retracted his confession and, presumably, would not be testifying against his codefendants, his trial had to be severed from theirs.

166. In Arkansas, the actual legal term is "not guilty by reason of mental disease or defect."

167. Until just a few months before the murders, fees for Arkansas lawyers who represented indigent clients, even in cases where the clients faced death, were capped at $1,000. That policy had been challenged in Judge Burnett's own court by a

lawyer who'd refused to represent an indigent woman for the state-mandated fee. Burnett had ordered the lawyer to accept the assignment. But the lawyer had appealed to the Arkansas Supreme Court. There, the justices—citing the Eighth Amendment to the U.S. Constitution, which forbids involuntary servitude—ruled that the lawyer had a right to refuse. In early 1993, the legislature had been forced to amend the state's law regarding payment of court-appointed lawyers, and at the time of these pretrial hearings, the new law had just taken effect. But how it would be implemented was still uncertain. Crittenden County officials wanted the bill for the boys' defense to go to the state, which was the responsible party when the lawyers were appointed. The Arkansas attorney general's office, on the other hand, contended that the state was responsible for the legal bill only from the time of the lawyers' appointment in early June until July 1, when the new law took effect.

168. According to Stidham, Burnett promised that the lawyers would receive $60 an hour for in-court time and $40 an hour for their work on the case out of court.

169. From Shettles's interview notes, October 25, 1993.

170. The samples collected on the night of the arrests had been obtained illegally. Though Ford had fought a state's motion seeking to obtain new samples, Burnett had approved the state's request.

171. Lax, who by now had worked more capital cases than any of the lawyers, told them he'd never seen anything like it. By August, they'd received some thirteen thousand documents from the monthlong police investigation, but they had no indication which of those pertained to the arrests and which had been discounted.

172. Ford argued, "I feel that he's going to know within reasonable certainty which of those pages he's going to use, and he's going to know that the great majority of it he has no intention to introduce. If that is the case, then we shouldn't have to be spending all our time and effort reviewing all those documents for the conceivable possibility they may be introduced into evidence."

173. "When you arrived at the residence of Mr. Baldwin," Ford said, "basically what you were doing was going from one room to the other, one drawer to the next, one closet to the next, looking for something in that color range or fiber type, the right type of material, the right color of material, that might match what you had obtained in your lab at Little Rock. Is that correct?" Sakevicius answered, "That's correct."

174. Author interview with Fogleman, April 2001.

175. Gerald Coleman was appointed to represent the Echols family after they were subpoenaed by Fogleman.

176. The Eighth Amendment to the U.S. Constitution forbids "cruel and unusual punishment."

177. Death-qualified juries are those from which anyone harboring reservations about imposing the death penalty is excluded.

178. After a hiatus of fourteen years, during which the death penalty was deemed unconstitutional, executions in Arkansas had resumed in 1990. Between then and the time of these pretrial hearings, the state had executed four men, one by electrocution and three by lethal injection.

179. Wilkins testified at a pretrial hearing in November 1993 that he held a Ph.D. in psychology from Cornell University and that he was a member of the American Congress of Forensic Psychology.

180. The speedy trial rule requires the state to bring a criminal defendant to trial within twelve months, unless his attorneys request a delay.

181. Crow told Burnett, "We were constantly confronted with people stating, 'They can't get a fair trial, but I'm not going to sign for them because I want the blankety-blank to fry.' That's the kind of attitude we have in this district, Your Honor."

182. Author interview, April 2001.

183. The diver, who did not testify at trial, was identified by Sergeant Allen as Joel Mullens, of the Arkansas State Police.

184. Author interview, April 2001.

185. The article, published on November 18, 1993, was written by Kathleen Burt. Burt also took the photo.

186. Seth was born on September 9, 1993.

187. Frances Goza Haynes had lived with Pam and her children for all of Damien's life.

188. Shettles wrote, "Michael does not know what causes him to shake," and at times, "his arm jerks uncontrollably." She showed him some of the police investigative reports. While Damien was reading one, she wrote, he "asked about the significance of a notation that the full moon was at 7:41 P.M. I told him I could only assume perhaps the full moon had significance if the murders were cult related." Damien then told Shettles that a new Baptist minister had recently visited him and asked to pray with him. Because the man was polite, rather than imposing as the others had been, Damien had agreed. Shettles recounted: "The minister asked if he could touch Michael, placing his hand on Michael's shoulder. Again Michael agreed and the minister asked him to repeat after him that Michael renounced cult activity, demon worship, and would accept Jesus as his savior. Michael repeated the words and the minister asked if he felt different. Michael told him he did not. The minister left after giving a brief sermon and thanked the men in the cellblock for not killing him."

189. At another point, Driver described a conversation he said he'd had with the pastor of Saint Michael's Catholic Church, where Damien had studied to become a Catholic. Driver told Durham that someone had broken into the sacristy, and that the priest had suspected Damien, though the culprit was never found. "Of course," Driver continued, "that's one of the things that those guys do—that kind of modus operandi. They go to the Catholic church and find out as much as they can, break into the sacristy, steal the host and the lunette, and that's how some of them operate. That's not to say he did that, but that would not be out of character with the things that they do." But when Shettles contacted Father Greg Hart, the church's former pastor, in February 1994, she wrote, "Father Hart stated he never had a conversation with Jerry Driver about a break-in. The sacristy had never been broken into."

190. The boy's name was Buddy Sidney Lucas. During the interview, Lax asked Lucas if the statement he'd given to Ridge and Durham had been the truth. Lucas

answered, "I told them the truth, the first one I gave them. But they—but Durham—he screamed at me, yelled at me, like I was lying."

Lax: "Did he tell you you were lying?"

Lucas: "Yes sir. He called me a liar."

Lax: "Did he tell you what to say then?"

Lucas: "No sir. He didn't tell me what to say, but I told him what I felt like he wanted to hear, and he was grinning."

Lax: "He was grinning? And did you then give another statement on video camera?"

Lucas: "Yes sir."

Lax: "Saying what you thought he wanted you to say?"

Lucas: "Yes sir."

Lax: "And when you said what he wanted you to say, or at least what you thought he wanted you to say, did he scream and yell at you then?"

Lucas: "No sir."

Lucas said he'd tried to satisfy Durham so that he "wouldn't get into trouble." He explained, "I mean, I didn't know what to do. I mean, I don't have no problems with the police. I ain't never had to go and see the police. I mean, I ain't never did nothing. I didn't know what to do."

191. According to Lax's notes, the teenager, Christopher Littrell, said he felt that "Durham and Gitchell were trying to 'good-guy/bad-guy' him. He stated he was not scared or intimidated at all. He said he knew his rights and felt he could get up and walk out at any time."

192. Lax tape-recorded the interviews with Stephanie Dollar, Linda Sides, Marine Collins, Jennifer Roberts, and Rhonda Dedman on January 11, 1994.

193. Lax noted that one woman told him, "She was talking about Aaron had seen this colored guy carrying knives and ropes." Another reported that soon after the murders, she'd heard Aaron say "that he had been out in the woods with those other three boys before, and this black guy had chased them." A third, Stephanie Dollar, reported that sometime after that, Aaron told her that the police had questioned him. Dollar recalled, "I said, 'Really? What did you tell them?' And he said, 'I just told them that I seen a black man down there. He was either drinking whiskey or beer or something in a paper sack.'" Lax asked Dollar, "Did he seem upset at that time?" Dollar reportedly answered, "No. He was playing Nintendo with my little boy." Another woman, Rhonda Lea Dedman, told Lax that she and Hutcheson had been "best friends." Dedman said that on May 7, the day after the bodies were found, she had accompanied Hutcheson when she'd taken Aaron to the school counselor. Lax asked, "Did Aaron tell the counselor that he was present on the date that the little boys were murdered?" Dedman reportedly answered, "No sir." Lax asked, "Or that he had had to fight any of the people off. . . . Or that he had been tied up? . . . Or if he [had given] her any indication that there was anything to it other than the fact that he had been with the little boys playing in that area in the past?" To each of those questions, Lax wrote, Dedman had answered, "No sir." According to Lax's notes, Jennifer Roberts, the seventeen-year-old niece of one of the women, said that on the afternoon the bodies were found, after her meeting with Bray, Hutcheson already had information that was not being reported by the media. "She said that they were mutilated and castrated and tied up."

194. After reviewing the proposed agreement, Lax had cautioned, "Although I have no experience in the entertainment field, it seems as if Damien would be giving these individuals carte blanche to do as they like with whatever film they acquire." He added, "I think we are all aware if Damien is found guilty of this crime and is sentenced to death, his appeals will continue, and believe the potential damage far outweighs any monetary remuneration he might receive."

195. Concern was warranted. When word that Jason had been filmed reached Fogleman, the prosecutor subpoenaed the footage. A lawyer for HBO wrote to Ford and Wadley, assuring them that, "HBO will take all lawful steps . . . to vigorously resist turning over any footage." In the end, Burnett denied the subpoena and that legal fight was averted.

196. At times, Byers ranted about, rather than to, the accused. In part of his tirade, he said: "Good Lord said Lucifer and a third of the angels were cast out of heaven. He didn't need them. He took their minds and he manipulated them, and they prayed to Satan and they prayed to the devil and they had their satanic worship services out here, and they had all types of wild, homosexual orgies, I've been told. Crazy things. To me, this place, as I stand, is like hell on earth, because I know that three babies were killed right out here where I stand. I know my son was castrated and possibly lay right there on that bank and bled to death. I know that he was choked. I know one boy's head was beat in beyond recognition. I know one little boy was skinned almost like a animal, cut, had to shave his head, had all types of injuries to the head where they just kept beating and pounding on them and killing them and killing them. It's like they enjoyed it. They killed them two and three times."

197. Byers's speech while he shot at the pumpkins was chilling. "You know, Todd," he said, raising his gun and taking aim, "I could save the state a lot of money if they'd just let me line the sons of a guns up. I'd say, 'This one's for you, Jessie. I'm going to go for the jug of water. [Firing.] Oh, Jessie, I just blowed you half in two, son. Now this one's for you, Damien. You're that black circle, right in the middle. [Firing.] Oh, you got hurt. [Taking aim again.] Hey, Jason, I want you to smile and blow me a kiss for this one.' [Firing.] All right, let's go back to Jessie. I just wounded him. I want him to bleed a little bit, like he made my baby bleed. [Firing.] 'Oh, Jessie.' You know that breaks my heart, thinking about that scum, because this right here is all that need to be done to 'im; be shot slowly, with a real nice firearm. And it ain't got no consideration or feeling about who it's aiming at, just like they didn't care about killing my baby. I wouldn't mind lining 'em up. I wouldn't have no problem with it. [Taking aim again.] I think ol' Jessie's still kicking a little. We'll put him out of his misery."

198. *Commercial Appeal*, January 16, 1994.

199. From "A Conversation with Joe Berlinger and Bruce Sinofsky," in a press release prepared by the producers, issued in 1996.

200. This from a handwritten statement and three pages of handwritten notes compiled by the West Memphis police on January 24, 1994, in the midst of Misskelley's trial. These notes were not turned over to the defense teams until February 15, a week before the scheduled start of Echols and Baldwin's trial. The member of the film crew who'd been given the knife was reported to have been Doug Cooper, a cinematographer.

201. These statements were also dated January 24 and not released until February 15.

202. The laboratory's name was Genetic Design.

203. Author interview, May 2001.

204. Byers's mother- and father-in-law, Kilburn and Dorris DeFir, also recalled the transfer of the knife as having been in November. Specifically, they said that Byers presented the knife to the member of the film crew at a Thanksgiving dinner given at the Byerses' house, which the DeFirs and the film crew attended. In an interview at the DeFirs' home in Memphis in April 2001, Kilburn DeFir said, "We were there. I saw Mark hand him the knife."

205. Byers's statements were clear and unequivocal. "No one" had been cut with the knife, and he himself had "never used it." But at this point, Ridge proposed a possibility. "Is there a period of time," Ridge asked, "that this knife may have been kept in the den by your chair?" Byers answered, "It seems like when I first got it, I trimmed on my fingernails some with it, right there under the lamp."

Ridge: "Now, you say 'when you first got it.' Is that just that particular day it may have been there, or could it have been there for a period of time?"

Byers: "Possibly a day or two . . ."

Ridge: "Were you there with that knife that entire time? Was there ever a time that anybody, or a youngster, could have gotten to that knife without your knowing about it?"

Byers: "Well, I guess that I could have been to the bathroom or something, and I wasn't in the room. It's possible. But I never saw any evidence or signs that they had, and there was never any signs that they cut theirself with it . . ."

206. According to Lax's notes, he spoke with Jonathan Karpa and Charlene Blum at the National Center for Forensic Science, which was a division of Maryland Medical Laboratory, Inc., located in Baltimore.

207. It was notable that no mention of Byers's conviction for terroristic threatening had been placed into the murder file. Though the record had recently been expunged, the attack had taken place in nearby Marion; Fogleman, obviously, had been aware of it; and many police reports had been placed in the file relating to possible suspects with far less connection to the murders. It was, perhaps, even more odd that reports from the state police about their investigation of Byers with regard to the Rolex scam were not included in the file. This was particularly true since word had leaked that records of the police investigation into the burglary a year before the murders, in which the dog was stomped to death, had been included in the murder file. When asked why reports of that incident had been included in the file, Gitchell had explained, "This whole case is just so huge. Anything to do with [it], be it significant or insignificant, we followed up on."

208. Davis had also opted not to prosecute Lieutenant Sudbury and the other investigators on the local drug task force after a state police investigation turned up evidence that they had been taking for personal use guns and other evidence seized in the line of duty.

209. The memo cited an interview that state police investigator Steve Dozier conducted on June 24, 1993, with Tom Larson of Dallas, Texas. In his final report on

the Rolex fraud, Dozier wrote, "This case has been reviewed by the prosecutor, who declines to prosecute the suspect, Mark Byers, at this time."

210. Description by Bob Lancaster in the *Arkansas Times*, April 7, 1994, after the conclusion of both of the trials.

211. Melissa also testified that a few weeks before his death, Christopher had told her about a man with dark hair who wore black pants, a black shirt, and a black coat, who'd driven a green car into the driveway and taken pictures of him. Stidham objected that the testimony was hearsay, but Burnett allowed the testimony.

212. When Byers was interviewed by Ridge and Sudbury on May 19, 1993, he said he'd begun looking in the woods at about 8:30 P.M. "It had got dark," he said. "I had on a pair of shorts and a pair of flip-flops, so I run back to the house and changed clothes and put me on some coveralls and boots that I had on probably for the next two or three days."

213. Author interview, May 2001.

214. Early reports from the state crime lab to the West Memphis police had suggested that the boys were sodomized. Not having received the autopsy reports, detectives still believed that to be the case when they questioned Misskelley.

215. "The atmosphere was very laid-back and of a subdued nature," Gitchell said. "We treated him with kid gloves, as if we were talking to one of our own children."

216. At one point, under cross-examination, Gitchell said he believed that Jessie had gotten confused about the boys having skipped school, "and meant Baldwin was to have skipped school that day." However, as the police knew, Jason had attended school.

217. Hearings held in camera—literally, in the judge's chambers—are not necessarily held outside of the courtroom. The intent is that the jury not be privy to what is said, though reporters may attend, and the hearings are part of the trial record. Some judges order the jurors to be removed from the courtroom when they hold in camera hearings, as Burnett often did in this case. But it is also common in Arkansas for judges to hold brief in camera hearings quietly at the bench, without dismissing the jurors, who have been instructed not to listen. This practice, which Burnett also employed at times, results in quicker trials. Arkansas's average trial length is one of the shortest in the country.

218. Later in the trial, Stidham attempted to discredit Hutcheson's statement that she'd never been interested in the reward by calling to the stand one of her former neighbors, who'd been interviewed by Lax. Stidham said that the woman was prepared to testify that Hutcheson had spoken repeatedly about her plans for the reward money. But Judge Burnett would not allow the woman's testimony. He claimed that he did not recall that Hutcheson had ever said she was not motivated by the reward.

219. Author interview, April 2001.

220. Lax file notes, January 30, 1994.

221. Stidham and Crow considered calling Buddy Lucas to testify about his treatment by the police, as evidence of the coercive tactics they said police had used on Misskelley. In what Stidham described as "a very difficult decision," they opted

not to use the boy. Like Misskelley, they said, he was low-functioning, and had been in special education at school. He was also very nervous and the attorneys thought he would not have made a good witness. Finally, as Stidham later explained, the lawyers considered that "the jury might have believed Buddy's statement to police, which the prosecution surely would have used to impeach him."

222. Author interview, May 2001.

223. Before the trial, Wilkins reported to Stidham that Jessie could count from three to thirty by threes only if he used his fingers; that when asked the meaning of the maxim "Don't cry over spilt milk," Jessie said he didn't know, but added, "People say that all the time, though"; that when asked about the proverb "The grass is greener on the other side of the fence," Jessie responded, "I guess it's greener on the other side of the fence"; and that when Wilkins asked, "What would you do if you were walking down the street and found an envelope which was already stamped, addressed, and sealed?" Jessie answered, "I'd just leave it," then, after a pause, he'd added, "Maybe I'd pick it up and see whose name was on it. If it was somebody that I didn't know, I'd probably just leave it there." Wilkins wrote that "in the strictest interpretation of the legal statute, Jessie appears to be able to distinguish right and wrong." However, he noted that the boy "clearly demonstrates a significant deficit in his ability to do abstract reasoning. . . . That is, we see Jessie is still doing problem solving and making moral decisions on a level comparable to a five-to-eight year old. . . . For Jessie, decisions about right and wrong are made on the basis of the consequence of the action, not in terms of any kind of intent."

224. From Stidham's 1994 "Synopsis of the Case," published at wm3.org.

225. Holmes added that peak attention tests are the only kind of tests run by police in Israel and Japan, because authorities there believe they have the highest degree of validity.

226. Author interview, July 2001.

227. In 1979, Ofshe had been part of a team that won a Pulitzer Prize for reporting on the murderous California cult known as Synanon.

228. Stidham believed it would be a conflict of interest for him to be involved in disbursal of the funds, so another lawyer was brought in to handle the negotiations with HBO. The lawyers for Damien and Jason had no such misgivings and handled the HBO negotiations on behalf of their criminal clients.

229. Judge Burnett's position with regard to Ofshe's testimony demonstrated the legal conundrum facing Jessie's lawyers on an issue central to Jessie's defense: if a judge determines that a confession was voluntary and would not let that determination be "second-guessed" in court, how could a defendant ever present evidence to a jury that his confession had been coerced?

230. Elements of this explanation by Ofshe were spliced together, to make a more concise statement, in the film *Paradise Lost*, later released by HBO.

231. Arkansas was one of five states at the time that held such bifurcated, or two-phased, trials, in which juries decide both guilt and sentencing.

232. *Memphis Commercial Appeal*, March 17, 1994.

233. As reported by the *Memphis Commercial Appeal*, February 5, 1994.

234. As recorded in the film *Paradise Lost*.

235. For reasons that were never addressed, Domini Teer was never treated as a suspect in the crime, even though her name appeared on Driver's list and the Hollingsworths' testimony placed her near the scene with Damien.

236. The writer of the report was Deputy Jon Moody.

237. This was the second time attorneys had tried to subpoena portions of the HBO film. In the first instance, Davis and Fogleman tried to see an interview that had been filmed with Jason. Burnett had also rejected that request.

238. The deputy prosecuting attorney in this part of the district was C. Joseph Calvin.

239. Elements of this series of events are drawn from a motion filed by Stidham in the Circuit Court of Clay County, Arkansas, Western District, Criminal Division, on February 22, 1994.

240. Davis asked Jessie to describe "what you saw Jason do." Jessie responded: "First, he cut one of 'em on a face, on his left side, just a little bit, like a scratch. Then, he went to the other one and got on top of him, started hitting him and then pulled one of 'em's pants down and get on top of 'm and cut 'm." Although, during his trial, Jessie had listened to extensive testimony about the injuries each of the victims received, in this statement to the prosecutors, he did not mention any names. Davis asked, "Were the three little boys, were they saying anything, doing anything during this?" Jessie answered, "They were saying, 'Stop. Stop.' " Davis: "And what about the boy that you were hitting? Was he saying that?" Jessie: "Yeah, he was telling me to stop, and then I stopped. And Damien told me, 'No. No, don't stop.' And I got on 'm again." Jessie said he saw Jason "swinging" a knife at one of the boys, sending blood flying into the weeds. In the first part of the statement Jessie said he never saw any of the boys unconscious. But when Davis asked what happened to the boy whom Jessie was beating, Jessie replied, "He's unconscious." Davis wanted to know when the boys were tied. Jessie said one boy had been castrated and another was unconscious, when "we tied 'em up."

241. At the end of the interview, before the tape recorder was turned off, Jessie's attorneys inserted a statement of their own. They pronounced their "strong" belief that Jessie had perjured himself.

242. Stidham also complained that despite his notification to prosecutors that Jessie would not testify, Judge Burnett had ordered the boy brought from prison to the judicial district. "While it is not uncommon for state prisoners to be moved to a county jail to testify," Stidham argued, "it is quite uncommon for them to be moved this far in advance. This 'advance time' gave the prosecution an opportunity to work on Jessie." Stidham cited Davis's and Fogleman's meetings with Jessie in the three days leading up to the trial, all without Stidham's knowledge, as a "gross instance of misconduct." He charged that "nothing" in the prosecutors' conduct in the events had been "fair or honorable." Damien's and Jason's lawyers were also indignant. They handed Burnett a brief of their own, charging that the prosecutors had "made a mockery of the law." Damien's attorney Val Price wrote, "The defendants anticipate that the prosecution will argue that they did not violate Jessie Lloyd

Miskelley, Jr.'s Fifth Amendment rights because they granted him 'use immunity' before taking a statement from him, and therefore nothing he says can be used against him." But, Price argued, "the court should analyze how this grant of immunity was effectuated. The grant of immunity was obtained by prosecutorial misconduct. . . . Had the prosecutor acted properly, he would have never been in a position to even offer the immunity. . . . The prosecution should not be allowed, and the court should not condone, the violation of one co-defendant's rights to the extreme detriment of the other co-defendants." Price added that the prosecutors had "improperly drawn attention to Jessie Lloyd Misskelley, Jr.'s alleged confession, which he [Jessie] submitted throughout the course of his trial was coerced," and that the effect of this "grandstand play" on the pool of potential jurors had "seriously undermined and impaired" the defendants' right to a fair trial.

243. Burnett told Jessie's lawyers that the whole issue had apparently arisen because they had sent "mixed signals" to the prosecuting attorneys. The judge said he was appointing another attorney, Phillip Wells of Jonesboro, to meet with Jessie to ascertain the boy's true wishes.

244. Stidham, who recalled having seen the tip in police documents he'd been supplied, brought it to Lax's attention. Lax, who was unaware of the report, could not find it in a search of the documents that had been supplied to Price and Davidson.

245. Lax wrote in a memo in February 1994 that Sandra Slone had been "quite candid in informing me she was afraid of her ex-husband, Mark Byers." Lax noted that Slone "stated she met Mark in church in 1977, and they married in 1978. Byers had had a drug problem and his mother informed Ms. Slone his problem began when he was in Texas [a jewelry school]. According to Ms. Slone, Byers was supposed to be 'cleaned up' at the time she met him and promised her he would never become involved in drugs again; however he continued to do so. Ms. Slone informed me that while they were living in Jackson, [Mississippi], Byers worked for Gordon Jewelers and had a good job, but began staying out late and it was her opinion he was using drugs then. They left Jackson abruptly and she was never able to determine the reasons. . . . After leaving Jackson, they moved to Mobile, Alabama, where he again worked with Gordon Jewelers and was on the road a great deal of time. He had been out of town for approximately two weeks on one occasion and returned and informed her they were moving and he was quitting his job. Again, they moved quickly (within two days) and she never was informed of the reasons. She was surprised he would give up the good job he had with Gordon Jewelers. Leaving Mobile in 1982, they moved to Memphis, where Byers obtained employment with two jewelers, both located in Germantown, [Tennessee], and he worked for himself as well. They remained in the Memphis area until 1985, when they moved to Marion, Arkansas. She divorced Byers in 1986. Ms. Slone informed me Byers had some problems with the police or authorities in Germantown, [Tennesse], but it was apparently handled and she never knew exactly what had occurred. Ms. Slone stated it always seemed as though Byers had connections with someone, because he became involved in drugs and illegal activities, but never was arrested." Lax added to his report, "We have since researched criminal records on file in Germantown, Tennessee, and have found no records relating to John Mark Byers."

246. The boy was Kenneth Clyde Watkins. His mother's name was Shirley Greenwood.

247. From a video-and audiotaped statement taken February 12, 1994.

248. Lax noted: "Ridge admitted there were no items found laid out in any type of pattern. There was no pattern to the placement of the bodies. There was no slab or log found to be in the area [that might have been used as a sacrificial table]. Ridge stated there had been no reports that revealed any new or unusual activities prior to the homicide, but that a friend of the victims stated that he was being recruited to be in some type of club and he would have to kill someone to get in the club."

249. The information about the police decision to search the library records proved almost too much for Lax. The usually restrained investigator looked up Cotton Mather in an encyclopedia and dictated a lengthy memo. He noted that Mather, who had lived in Boston from 1663 to 1728, was a highly respected writer who had fanned the popular belief in witchcraft. He was the son of Increase Mather, who had served as pastor of Boston's North Church and president of Harvard University. "Also, in this same encyclopedia I found the discussion of witchcraft quite interesting," Lax wrote in the memo. "It is as follows: 'Witch'craft: A supernatural influence, once thought to be acquired by certain persons by reason of some league with Satan or other evil spirits. Until the Sixteenth Century, belief in witch craft was universal, and the law of all Christian countries recognized it as a crime. Roger Bacon, Sir Matthew Hale, Blackstone, Richard Baxter, and John Wesley believed in witches. Though this old delusion was beginning to wane at the opening of the Eighteenth Century, a local frenzy broke out in New England just about that time. It began and endured mainly about Salem Village and, fanned by the utterances of Cotton Mather, it caused a special court to be constituted to try those suspected of witchery, of whom there were over one hundred in jail at one time. This court, in 1692, caused the death of twenty victims. With the tragedy, reaction set in, and over one hundred fifty persons charged with the same crime were delivered from prison the following year.' "

250. Bob Lancaster, in the *Arkansas Times*, April 7, 1994.

251. Stidham said Jessie had reached the decision the night before, after meeting with his father and stepmother, his attorneys, and Phillip Wells, the lawyer appointed by Burnett to ascertain Jessie's true wishes. When reporters checked with Wells, he reported that the prosecutors had offered Jessie a deal, though he did not divulge its terms.

252. In a memo dated February 23, 1994, Ron Lax wrote that Jessie's stepmother had described the meeting to him. She said Jessie had told her and his father that he was not present at the time of the murders and that he knew nothing about them. He said he'd admitted to the crimes a second time, after his conviction, because he was afraid of the "men with guns" and of what would happen to him at prison. Lax noted that Mrs. Misskelley also said that "Jessie was laboring under the impression the prosecution would reduce his time significantly. Jessie stated he realized now none of this was true and said he would not testify."

253. Author interview with Stidham and Misskelley, February 2001.

254. During that same interview, Stidham recalled the moment, right before Damien and Jason's trial began, when he advised the prosecution, for the last time, to leave his client alone and that Jessie would not testify against his codefendants. "I said, 'If you bother my client one more time, I'm going to hold a press conference, and I'll tell the world what you have been doing to my client, how the pros-

ecutors in this district met with my client without me ever knowing about it, about the promises to bring Susie to him for sex, and that someone brought him beer.' I said I'd tell how they put him through an interrogation once, and then they put him through it all again—because they were afraid they couldn't make their case if they didn't have him."

255. "Voir dire" means "to speak the truth." It refers to the legal process by which lawyers question potential jurors to determine their suitability to serve in a particular trial.

256. "I remember the news conference that the West Memphis police detective held," one excused juror said upon leaving the courthouse, "and the statement that Jessie Misskelley made has been well rooted in my memory." Another noted only that he had formed a "strong opinion" about the case. A third admitted, "The way they were talking about the evidence, I just didn't want to see it." Two women who were excused said that even being questioned for the jury had been emotionally taxing. "I have small children," one said. Another reported having been "close to tears" during the questioning. Another prospective juror was excused because she could not impose a death sentence. "I would have trouble with it," Kathy Cravens of Jonesboro told a reporter. "I think because of their age, I would have a problem with it."

257. *Commercial Appeal*, February 26, 1994.

258. "Simply put, jury selection is part of the trial proceeding, and must be held in the open," a lawyer for the paper argued. The paper's managing editor, Henry Stokes, said, "We believe that an open judicial process is the fairest for everyone. The *Commercial Appeal* has asked for no more than Arkansas law already demands: that jury selection takes place behind no shadow."

259. Burnett said the matter fell to the discretion of the trial judge and that he would continue to conduct the voir dire in his chambers. "To ask laypeople to come in from their work, their homes, their normal pursuits and to be bombarded by very sensitive questions, to where they have to verbalize their innermost feelings in front of a few hundred people, the eyes of the cameras, the eyes of the world—to me that's unreasonable," he said.

260. "Was the court's order excluding the public and press from the voir dire valid?" the high court asked rhetorically at the end of its opinion. "It is clear by what has been said that we have answered with an emphatic 'No!' " The court offered no opinion, however, as to how—or even if—the invalid process should be corrected.

261. Report of Jonesboro patrol officer C. Gellert.

262. Despite the lurid opening, reporter Marc Perrusquia's piece took an unusual turn for reporting at the time, in that it also offered less sensational descriptions of the defendants. It quoted Dian Teer, Domini's mother, as saying, "He liked vampire movies and vampire books, but I do too—so what? What really scares me is the one who really [killed the boys] is still out there, and the cops are sitting there, patting themselves on the back." Similarly, Perrusquia portrayed Jason as a boy who was "largely known as a polite and courteous youngster." Speaking of Jason, one neighbor said, "He never struck me to be no mean kind of kid."

263. Fogleman never did directly explain why the state had had to rely on "negative evidence" in the case, other than to suggest that almost all other evidence that might have existed, including fingerprints, blood, and possible DNA, had been washed away by the water.

264. "Two of them were pushing bikes, one was carrying a skateboard, and one was just walking," witness Bryan Woody said. When one of the defense lawyers asked Woody if the West Memphis police had ever shown him pictures of other children, or asked him to help identify the fourth boy, Woody said that they had not.

265. Reporters also noted the significance of the move to call Bryan Woody, who testified that he saw four boys enter the woods. "If Woody's testimony is accurate," the *Jonesboro Sun* explained, "it would support a statement that Aaron Hutcheson . . . gave to West Memphis police. . . . While attorneys in the case refuse to discuss Hutcheson's claim, speculation has grown that the child could be an eyewitness to the crime." The paper noted that Aaron had not testified at Jessie's trial, and citing unattributed "reports," it added that it was "unclear" whether he would take the stand in the current trial "because of his mental state from recurring nightmares about the boys' murders."

266. Price told Burnett, "It's our position, Judge, that within two or three days after the murders, the West Memphis Police Department was alleging that this is a cult-related killing. That is the reason they went after my client, Damien Echols. They're trying to link him in what they thought was a cult-related killing."

267. Peretti's reference to Christopher's "neck injuries" in the same breath as his mention of the horrendous injuries Christopher had suffered to his head and genital area appeared to exaggerate the findings Peretti had noted in his own autopsy report, which had listed "no fractures" and "no hemorrhages" and only "a few scattered abrasions" on the left side of his neck. The reference may have carried weight with the jury, however, in light of Jessie's statement that the children had been strangled.

268. Author interview, April 2001.

269. Jason's attorney Paul Ford confirmed that the offers were made, though he said he could not remember the exact terms. "I know they [the prosecutors] made some offers," Ford said. "And I know they got better. My most specific recollection is that Jason wasn't interested."

270. The attorney was state senator Mike Everett of Marked Tree, Arkansas.

271. Author interview, April 2001.

272. Jason's lawyer raised yet another issue, regarding the prior juvenile history of the prosecution witness Michael Carson, which Burnett had ruled inadmissible and which the jury did not get to hear. "It is the opinion of Jason Baldwin that if they are going to be able to use the juvenile file of Damien Echols to show that he had a belief and that he acted in conformity with that belief," Ford said, "we should have been able to inquire as to the LSD dependence of Michael Carson, which is contained in his juvenile file, to question his credibility because he has a drug dependence on a hallucinogenic."

273. The prosecutors' decision to introduce books, fashions, and beliefs into the proceedings provoked a smattering of opposition. The *Jonesboro Sun* also reported

that "a group of teenagers" had shown up at the trial "wearing mostly black," and that "one of the males wore a necklace with a pentagram attached to it."

274. This witness was Christy Van Vickle.

275. This witness was Jody Medford.

276. Bob Lancaster of the *Arkansas Times.*

277. The quotation, while from Shakespeare, is in fact from *Macbeth.*

278. Bob Lancaster.

279. Gitchell explained that his detectives had "talked with several hundred people in regards to this investigation" and that "it was not possible to do a recording of everyone." Gitchell acknowledged that detectives' notes were the only record police produced from their interviews with Damien—even though they had video and tape-recorded interviews with many other subjects, and despite the fact that Damien had been a prime suspect from the start.

280. As reported by Stan Mitchell in the *Jonesboro Sun*, March 12, 1994.

281. Because the public and the press were barred from this unusual hearing *in camera*, and Judge Burnett placed a gag order on the participants, what transpired was never reported. It was not carried by newspapers or television news and the jury did not get to hear about it.

282. From the 1923 decision in *U.S. v. Murdock.*

283. From the 1920 case of *Locking v. State*, 145 Arkansas 415, 224 Southwest 952.

284. Burnett told the lawyers that any probative value Morgan's testimony might have in the case was "substantially outweighed by the danger of unfair prejudice and by confusion of the issues."

285. Record of this argument and ruling exists only in the trial transcript, pages 2286–302.

286. Hicks said he was being paid $500, the cost of his expenses for coming to Arkansas to testify.

287. Hicks said his degree was from the University of Arizona. He testified that his book was titled *In Pursuit of Satan: The Police and the Occult.* At one point, Price asked Hicks to read a quotation he had included at the end of his book. It was attributed to Kenneth Lanning, an FBI agent who had researched alleged connections between crime and the occult. Hicks read: "Bizarre crime and evil can occur without organized Satanic activity. The law enforcement perspective requires that we distinguish between what we know and what we are not sure of." Looking up from the book, Hicks volunteered, "I agree."

288. Hicks said he grew particularly skeptical about the ideas, promulgated at many of the seminars, "that a belief in satanism or certain occult subjects was indicative of criminal behavior" and "that people found to be practicing these other religious behaviors might also be engaged in crime." Price at first tried to question Hicks about documents prepared by the West Memphis Police Department that referred to satanism and the occult. But the prosecutors objected to the prospect of jurors hearing Hicks testify about "policies and procedures of the West Mem-

phis Police Department," and Burnett agreed that they shouldn't. The judge ruled, "It doesn't matter what policies, if any, they had."

289. Jason appeared to some observers to sit through the trial with a somewhat dazed look on his face. That might have been because the boy was seriously near-sighted. Jason said that when Paul Ford found out how weak Jason's vision was, and that he could not see clearly more than three feet in front of him, Ford had promised that as soon as the trial was over, he'd get Jason fitted for glasses.

290. Charles Linch identified himself as a trace evidence analyst from the South-western Institute of Forensic Sciences in Dallas.

291. Six years after the trial, in May 2000, the *Dallas Morning News* reported that Linch, a trace evidence analyst at Southwestern Institute of Forensic Sciences in Dallas, had been released from the psychiatric unit of that city's Doctors Hospital, where he was a patient, in order to testify. In a copyrighted article, Holly Becka and Howard Swindle reported: "Declared a danger to himself or others and pre-scribed powerful anti-depressive drugs, he had been temporarily released to testify in two of the southwest's most infamous capital murder trials. Notwithstanding cir-cumstance, he was an expert witness." The paper reported that Linch acknowl-edged that he had been depressed and "drinking too much," and that his commitment to the hospital had been involuntary. The paper quoted Paul Ford as saying he had no idea the forensic scientist had been hospitalized for psychiatric treatment, and that it "bothered" him that neither Linch nor his supervisors at SIFS reported that he would have to be released from a psychiatric hospital to testify.

292. Author interview, November 2001.

293. Author interview, November 2001.

294. Jason's mother, Gail Grinnell, had lost her job over the trial. She'd asked her boss for time off to attend it, and he had refused. Rather than leave Jason alone while he was on trial for his life, she'd quit the job in order to be at the courthouse. However, because she had been listed as a potential witness, Grin-nell was not allowed into the courtroom. When it became clear that she was not going to be called, Jason realized how much had been lost. His mother had given up her job to spend the entire three weeks waiting, sitting in a lobby out-side the courtroom, where she could not even see, let alone try to encourage, her son.

295. Ford told Burnett, "Your Honor, we would like to be able to argue to the jury that the state of Arkansas does not even believe it has proven the charges of capital murder because they are requesting that you consider first-degree murder, which places less burden on them."

296. The North Carolina lab, Genetic Design, identified the DQ Alpha type as "1.2,4." The lab reportedly tried unsuccessfully to amplify the results.

297. Fogleman told the jury that because Jason had long hair, Hollingsworth had probably mistaken him for her niece.

298. Arkansas law requires that for circumstantial evidence to be deemed sub-stantial enough to support a conviction it must "exclude all other reasonable hypotheses."

299. After the verdicts were read, Burnett asked the clerk to poll the jurors, but foreman Kent Arnold interrupted. "Judge," he asked, "do you have to use names?" So far, the identity of the jurors had not been made public, and Burnett had further instructed that they not be photographed. He now consented to allow the jurors to be polled by number. All affirmed that they had voted for the convictions. In addition to Arnold, the jurors were Peggy Roebuck, Joan Sprinkle, Vicki Stoll, Barbara White, Sharon French, Peggy Van Hoozer, Howard McNatt, William Billingsly, John Throgmorton, Jennifer Dacus, and Oma Dooley.

300. Jack Echols, Damien's adoptive father, recalled how kids in the schools Damien had attended were always "picking on him, hitting on him, fighting him on the bus." Joe Hutchison, Damien's biological father, told the court, "I didn't do what I should have done, and as far as his raising goes, if anybody's to blame for that, it's me."

301. The pages are stored, along with items of evidence and artifacts from the investigation, at the West Memphis Police Department.

302. Descriptions of Jason's first year in prison are drawn from a letter written by him to the author, dated December 10, 2001.

303. Back in the jail, he said, he "cried it all out" and then he made up his mind "to never cry again." He prayed "for all things to come out good"; that his mother and brothers "would hold up"; and that the God he felt had deserted him would, indeed, "bring the truth to light." The warden at the jail where he was being held, along with other female staffers, joined him to pray that he would be protected in prison. One of the jailers tried to help the new convict by bringing a former prison inmate to visit. "He told me what to expect," Jason later recalled, "and how I should not trust anyone there, no matter how friendly they acted toward me. He informed me that prison is a violent place, full of hateful people, and that I, especially being as young and small as I was, would always have to be on guard. 'Great,' I thought. He then told me that I would be okay, and he gave me $10 out of his own pocket to carry with me." When Jason's family came for their last visit with him before his removal to the penitentiary, Jason did his best to act unafraid. He told his mother and two younger brothers not to worry about him, that they were to stick together as a family, and that they should never lose hope. "Our love will get us through," he said. But privately, he worried about what lay ahead for them. Rough as the future might be for him, he knew that he would be locked away in a cell, but they would have to "live out there" amid "all the lies and rumors."

304. Jason was placed on a sixty-day suicide watch, but he never thought of taking his life. To the contrary, he worked at adapting to the prison routine. He played basketball with the chaplain, studied Bible booklets, which were plentiful in the prison, and forced himself to eat food that he thought his mother wouldn't have served to their dog and cat at home. When officials moved him to the nearby unit at Varner, Arkansas, Jason told a few inmates that he was innocent, but he soon gave that up, as hardly anyone believed him. He worked long days in the Arkansas sun on one of the infamous prison hoe squads. As the months passed, he got used to just about everything except the occasional visits from his mother. Her sorrow and his inability to help her he found nearly impossible to bear.

305. The letter writer was Danny Williams.

306. From a letter from Williams to Jason dated January 7, 1995.

307. Ford argued that on the last day of the trial, after Fogleman sought to introduce Damien's blood-speckled pendant after the state had already rested its case, Burnett met privately with Davis and Fogleman to discuss the unusual request. Ford claimed that during a recess called by Burnett, the judge and the prosecutors "convened in the office of Judge Templeton, at which time an *ex parte* conversation occurred." In a sworn affidavit, Ford stated his beliefs "that during said *ex parte* conversation, the court [Burnett] advised the prosecuting attorneys that in the event they proceeded to offer the evidence of the test results on the necklace . . . that the court would have no alternative but to grant a severance and/or mistrial to . . . Baldwin" and "that based upon said information . . . , the prosecuting attorneys elected not to offer the evidence . . . and thus avoided having the court grant a severance and/or mistrial to the defendant, Charles Jason Baldwin."

308. Ex parte communications are those that involve one side only.

309. From author interview in February 2001.

310. Damien would later maintain that getting off the antidepressant drugs was the best thing that happened to him during his first year at the prison. He said later that once he had gotten over the shock of withdrawal, he had been able to think more clearly.

311. The inmate, Mark Edward Gardner, had been sentenced to death for the murder of three members of a family in Fort Smith, Arkansas.

312. Gardner also told the author that he was responsible for planting the knife. One time when she visited him, he demonstrated a similar access to drugs by having a guard deliver to her, on the other side of the glass that divided them, a handmade greeting card, which bulged where a joint of marijuana had been (not very well) hidden. The episode illustrated both the availability of marijuana at the state's maximum security unit and the willingness of certain officials to participate in what was obviously a suspicious transaction.

313. Damien's friends on death row came to include Frankie Parker, Gene Perry, Mark Gardner, Don Davis, and Daryl Hill. During the period when Damien arrived on death row, this author was reporting on prison conditions for the weekly *Arkansas Times.* She corresponded with Gardner and spoke with him frequently. Elements of the plot reported here are based on statements made by Gardner and information provided by Department of Correction officials. By the time this book was written, Parker, Perry, and Gardner had been executed.

314. In another expression of distress, Damien notified the Arkansas Supreme Court on June 27, 1995, that he wanted to waive all challenges to his death sentence and to concentrate only on efforts to overturn the guilty verdict. If that could not be done, he said he was willing to die. The state Supreme Court sent the issue back to Judge Burnett, asking that he make the determination whether Damien had "the capacity to understand the choice of life or death and to knowingly and intelligently waive any and all rights to appeal the death sentence." Before the matter had to be resolved by Judge Burnett, however, Damien's lawyers prevailed on him to pursue all avenues of appeal.

315. Though prison officials later confirmed that a block in the wall between the

cells had been removed, serious questions were raised about whether the opening was large enough for Damien or Gardner to have passed through. A state police report concluded that, though items could have been passed between cells, the opening was not large enough for a man.

316. In addition to publicizing his situation, Damien filed a $1.5 million lawsuit against prison officials, alleging emotional, mental, and physical torment. A hearing was held at the prison, during which Damien told a U.S. magistrate, "The reason for this lawsuit, basically, is that I just want to be left alone. I was sent here to die. I would just like to be left alone until that time comes." In 1996, a settlement was reached in the lawsuit. Its terms assured Damien that he would not be punished for calling attention to conditions in the prison and that he would be treated like any other inmate. Damien had appeals of his death sentence pending at the time this book was written. Upon the advice of his attorneys, he declined to discuss this and other aspects of his life in prison. Gardner was executed by lethal injection in 1999. He maintained to the end that he had concocted the rape allegation, that Damien had cooperated in it, and that he and Damien remained friends.

317. The opinion, No. CR94-848, was written by Chief Justice Bradley D. Jesson. It was delivered on February 19, 1996.

318. The opinion cited an earlier case in which it had held that "a fifteen-year-old with an IQ of 74 and a second-grade reading level was capable of comprehending his Miranda rights and of waiving those rights." Justice Jesson wrote, "The appellant's situation is similar. In fact, he was two years older than [the other boy] and had a slightly higher reading level."

319. The Arkansas legislature eliminated that requirement the following year.

320. Stidham knew of the earlier decision. He'd argued that it was absurd to require parental involvement when a juvenile was charged with a minor crime, but not when a juvenile was charged as an adult, with a crime that might result in a sentence of life in prison or even the death penalty. The court recognized the problem, but ruled against the juveniles, in favor of the state. "The appellant urges us to overrule [that earlier decision] and its progeny," the opinion in Jessie's case noted, "but it would be the height of unfairness for us to tell the prosecutors and law enforcement officials of this state that a parental signature was not necessary, then declare nearly three years later that lack of such a signature was fatal to an accused's confession. . . . We therefore decline the invitation to overrule this line of cases."

321. While Arkansas law requires that interrogations of police officers must be taped in their entirety, the state has no law affording that special protection to children—or to adults who are not police officers.

322. "The question regarding Dr. Peretti's opinion is whether it would have impacted the outcome of the trial," the justices wrote. "We think it would not have." As Justice Jesson wrote, "The appellant's statements were already filled with mistakes, inconsistencies and gross inaccuracies regarding the time that the murders took place. It is obvious that the jury disregarded the appellant's time estimates, as it was their right to do. Dr. Peretti's opinion could only have served to reinforce what the jury already knew: the appellant was either mistaken or not telling the truth regarding the timing of events on May fifth."

323. This opinion was written by Associate Justice Robert H. Dudley.

324. The only argument that the court deemed significant with regard to severance concerned the different ways that Damien's and Jason's lawyers wanted to treat allegations relating to the occult. "Echols contends that his strategy would have been to openly admit all evidence of Satanic worship in order to show its absurdity," Dudley noted, "while Baldwin contends that he wanted to exclude all of the evidence." Despite the diametric opposition of those positions, the court found that "the jury obviously did not think the proof of occultism was absurd, and it is doubtful that Echols would have freely admitted Satanic worship as a matter of strategy, even if he had a real choice in the matter."

325. Specifically, the court wrote that "Dr. Griffis had much more than ordinary knowledge of nontraditional groups, the occult and Satanism"; that testimony about the "trappings of occultism" was proper because it "admitted the evidence as proof of the motive for committing the murders"; that the dog's skull, posters, and books had been "relevant to show motive"; and that Driver's testimony was relevant because "the trial court ruled that the murders could have been committed with staffs and that they could have been occult murders."

326. The justices explained that the lawyers had not demonstrated in their appeals that the defendants had been "prejudiced in any matter by the state's failure to pay."

327. Janet Maslin wrote in the *New York Times* that the filmmakers captured "the orgy of emotion and prejudice" the case stirred in West Memphis, and the town's "tattered social fabric." A reviewer for *Entertainment Weekly* noted that the case's "shivery ambiguities" inspired "a gripping sense of moral vertigo." Gene Siskel described *Paradise Lost* as "an aching portrait of a small town with small minds and broken hearts." Other reviewers thought the film portrayed mass hysteria or "satanic panic." In a review in the *Los Angeles Times*, writer Howard Rosenberg quoted Berlinger's recollection of his first sight of the defendants. "The portrait of them was so black, so monstrous, that we bought into the stereotype," Berlinger told the reviewer. "And when we first saw Damien turn to us and the rest of the press in the courtroom, there was a chill, as if he was Hannibal Lecter. While we were down there, there was never a voice in the dark saying these kids didn't do it." Rosenberg said the film explored "the impact of deadly stereotypes." By the end of 1997, *Paradise Lost* had won a dozen awards, including an Emmy, a Best Documentary award from the National Board of Review of Motion Pictures, and a Silver Gavel Certificate of Merit from the American Bar Association.

328. Lisa Fancher, one of the Web site's early supporters, said she hated the documentary. "I can almost demarcate my life into "before PL" and "after PL," she wrote. "Before, I had my eyes closed, and I guess I was happy that way." She considered the film's account of the trials to be "the most sickening, outrageous, scurrilous, cruel thing ever to be perpetrated on three goofy teens." Like hundreds of others who contacted the site, she said she wanted to right the wrong.

329. Max Schaefer, a college student who had also become intrigued by the case, designed and maintained the site in its early days.

330. "We're not about raising money," Pashley said in a 1998 interview that was published on the site. "We're about raising awareness. But it takes money to raise awareness."

331. By 1998, that archive had become the most extensive resource of its kind on the Internet relating to a single case. It was all the more unique for having been created and funded entirely through the efforts of lay volunteers. Visitors were advised that the site was maintained by three individuals who had "no involvement with law enforcement or the justice system." Sauls, Bakken, and Pashley asked readers to regard it as "a storage space" for information and opinions. Never claiming that the site was neutral, they announced their belief that the three young men in prison were innocent and their purpose of mobilizing whatever public action might lead to them being freed. They declared, "Our primary goal is justice, and our method of reaching this goal is publicity. We want the state of Arkansas to know that the world is watching." Visitors to the site could read large chunks of the trial transcripts. They could peruse a lengthy examination of the Arkansas Medical Examiner's Office, which, at the time of the West Memphis investigation, had lost its accreditation by the National Association of Medical Examiners. There was a site in German. A calendar announced legal activities in Arkansas and fund-raisers throughout the country. Links offered connections to a wide range of materials including numerous police interviews, partial transcripts of court testimony, a poem written by Pam Hobbs, essays from a Canadian group on religious toleration, an apology from Geraldo Rivera for his exaggerated reporting about alleged satanic crimes, information about the Innocence Project founded by Barry Scheck and other attorneys, and a report by two Web site supporters who'd examined boxes of evidence held in storage by the West Memphis police. The site became a vehicle by which visitors could scrutinize the case. For example, one overview of the case reported: "A scrap of what appears to be dark cloth is seen in the photographs taken at the site where the bodies were found, held tightly in the hand of one of the young victims. This scrap does not appear in later photographs. We can only guess what happened to it." By 1999, the Web site reported averaging 150 hits a day.

332. In chat rooms, many supporters recalled their own isolation and even persecution as teenagers; painful experiences with exclusion that were based on nothing more than unconventionality. For some, the exclusion was based on poverty or their religious beliefs. For others, it was some physical or social distinction. Others recalled being shunned simply for harboring nonconformist tastes in clothes, literature, music, or art. Site cofounder Sauls said his own nephew had suffered harassment from "moral crusaders" in Florida, "who were simply punishing him for being different." He said his response to the events in West Memphis almost certainly had been in reaction to the tragedy his own family suffered when his nephew had committed suicide at seventeen. Other supporters felt they too could have been blamed for crimes they did not commit, just because they did not adhere to local religious norms. "My background pretty much mirrors Damien's," one said. "I didn't buy everything the religious people where I lived believed." He said he'd been told he was going to hell. Others voiced concerns that money—or the defendants' lack of it—had played a role in the verdicts; they said they'd joined the fight for the West Memphis Three because they saw the case as a symbol of poverty's impact on justice. "This wouldn't have happened if their parents were rich," was an oft-repeated refrain. A similar one cited regionalism, the fear that, if justice in America related to money, it also might relate to place. Supporters new to the Web site often commented that "this would not have happened in" New York, Seattle, or any large city, rather than a rural community.

333. RAO Video on Main Street in Little Rock, Arkansas.

334. Comments from the founders of the Web site and its supporters quoted here are drawn from author interviews conducted between 1998 and 2001.

335. Issues surrounding the inmates' mail would become a serious grievance for many supporters who tried to contact them. Letters to Damien, in particular, were frequently not delivered by staff at the maximum security unit. The problem, which cropped up repeatedly, was often temporarily solved only after the senders contacted United States postal officials.

336. In that 1996 interview with the author, Damien also said, "I've always had this extremely self-destructive streak, which coming here has somehow made me overcome." He recognized that his behavior during the police investigation and at his trial was "stupid" and a form of "extreme vanity." Asked why he had not moderated his behavior by, for instance, refusing to talk to the police, he answered, "I guess for the same reason that people dodge trains. It's something to break the mundanity of their lives, something to give them some distraction."

337. The episode of *The Maury Povich Show* was titled "Murder in a Small Town." It aired in West Memphis and east Arkansas on August 2, 1994. By then, Pamela Hobbs, the mother of Stevie Branch, and her husband, Terry, had moved to Memphis. On November 6, 1994, eight months after deputies drove Damien and Jason to prison, police in Memphis received a report of a shooting at the Hobbs residence. A Memphis police officer later offered the following account: Pam Hobbs told investigators that Terry had beaten her with his fists earlier in the day. The officers noted having observed injuries to her face and the back of her head. Hobbs said that after the beating, she'd called a relative in Blytheville, Arkansas, to report that she believed Terry had broken her jaw. Hobbs had then gone to a hospital. While she was there, a group of her Arkansas relatives gathered and drove to Memphis, where they confronted Terry about the assault. According to the Memphis police, Terry Hobbs left the house when they arrived, went to a truck outside, and returned with a .357 Magnum pistol in his pocket. At that point, Pam's brother, Jackie Hicks, confronted Terry again. An investigating officer said it appeared that "Hicks passed the first lick," and a fight ensued. Hicks reportedly had wrestled Terry Hobbs to the ground, when Hobbs reached into his pocket, pulled out the gun, and shot Hicks in the abdomen. Police said Hobbs then rose and pointed the gun at the other relatives, threatening to shoot them too. Police took Terry Hobbs into custody and charged him with assault on his wife and aggravated assault on his brother-in-law. Hicks survived, though he was hospitalized in critical condition. Tragedy also followed the parents of Michael Moore. In June 1995, eight months after the Hobbses' altercation, Dana Moore struck and killed a pedestrian while driving on a rural road in Crittenden County, Arkansas. Newspapers quoted police as saying that Moore was charged with driving while intoxicated. Through her lawyer, Moore negotiated a plea of guilty. She was sentenced to sixty months probation, fined $250, and ordered to pay "restitution" of $2,500, an outcome that offended members of the dead woman's family. The Moores, who of all the families had had the least contact with the media during the trials, grew even more private after them. Their main contact with the public was through a Web site, midsouthjustice.org, that had been created by a friend. The site contained a memorial for Michael, Christopher, and Stevie, which it called "the real West Memphis Three." It expressed confidence in the police work that had been done and in the juries' verdicts, and criticized those who were calling for a review of the case.

338. Acting on a tip, police had obtained permission to search the Byerses' house. There they found three Oriental rugs, which were among the items that had been reported stolen. An officer noted that "Mrs. Byers told us that she had purchased them from a flea market, but she couldn't remember when, where or produce any receipts." Other items stolen from the house were recovered from pawnshops in the area.

339. Accepting the plea was Sharp County circuit judge Harold Erwin. After the hearing, the Byerses' attorney, Larry Kissee, told reporters that he would be filing a civil suit on their behalf against the West Memphis Police Department, for the department's failure to launch a search for the missing boys until the morning after they disappeared. The lawsuit was not filed.

340. The incident occurred in the town of Hardy, Arkansas. Hardy police chief Ernie Rose reported that Byers had goaded a boy who had been riding with him in his car to fight another boy, who had reportedly hollered a taunt at Byers's passenger. According to other teenagers who witnessed the fight, Byers had stopped his car, gotten out, and advised his rider, "Take it over in the shade and settle it like a man." Byers reportedly told Hardy's police chief, Ernie Rose, that as the fight ensued, he'd stood by his car with a .22 bolt-action rifle pointed at the ground in order to assure that the fight was "fair." Byers acknowledged that he'd also instructed his passenger to get a pocketknife out of his car and fight with it, holding it closed in his fist. The boy reported to Chief Rose that, when he'd closed his hand around the knife, Byers had told him, "That's the way to do it." Witnesses said they wanted to stop the fight, but that anytime they moved to do so, Byers had warned them to "stay put." A highway department employee working nearby did rush to intervene. He told Rose that by the time he arrived at the site, the fight was over and Byers and his friend were leaving. The highway worker said Byers had told him, "Some smart-ass kid got his ass kicked. He got what he deserved." When Rose arrived at the scene, he found one boy who needed to be taken to a hospital. The remaining boys offered a description of the man who'd insisted on the fight. They described him as "dirty, with a blond beard and sunglasses, 230 to 250 pounds, wearing 'like a flag shirt' with blue jeans, thirty-five to forty years old, with brownish black hair." Rose later recalled that when he telephoned police in Cherokee Village and read them the description, "they told me who I was looking for."

341. According to an affidavit filed by the neighbors, John and Donna Kingsbury, Melissa Byers said "that we had put them in a hole and they would put us in a hole we wouldn't get out of." The statement said that the Kingsburys' children were afraid of the Byerses and that Melissa had warned the parents, "You can't watch your family twenty-four hours a day." Much of the reporting about the Byerses' troubles in Cherokee Village was done by Angelia Roberts, of the local paper, the *News*. John Kingsbury told Roberts that there were bullet holes in the side of his house. "I cannot prove how they got there," he said, "but they are there." Donna Kingsbury added, "They say they are victims, but we are victims too. No friends of our children are allowed to come to our house because of all the trouble we've had."

342. Byers grew up in the town of Marked Tree, Arkansas. The *Arkansas Times* reporter who uncovered the story of the early knife attack was this author. Her source was former Poinsett County sheriff's deputy C. L. Carter. When questioned about the attack on Byers's parents, Carter recalled, "Mark had a knife after

them. He wanted them to give him money to buy dope with." The former deputy said he cornered Mark in a closet and ordered him to throw down the knife. Carter said he vividly recalled that, as he was putting handcuffs on Byers, the teenager looked at him and vowed, "I'll cut your throat."

343. Val Price declined to be interviewed for this book, citing Damien's pending appeals.

344. "The court feels in this society that a dispute under the shade tree is not necessary," Judge Kevin King told Byers, "and that, as an adult, you could have stopped the altercation instead of encouraging it."

345. Melissa was taken to Eastern Ozarks Regional Hospital. When staff there saw her condition they notified Sonny Powell, the sheriff of Sharp County.

346. Arkansas State Police investigator Stan Witt headed the investigation.

347. The list included alprazolam, 1 mg.; lithium capsules, 300 mg.; Paxil tablets, 30 mg.; Lithonate capsules, 300 mg.; Desyrel, 150 mg.; and Paxil, 20 mg., plus Midol and other nonprescription medications.

348. Police reports identified the neighbor as Norm Metz.

349. Angelia Roberts, the reporter from the local *News*, who'd interviewed the Byerses about their problems, eulogized Melissa, after a fashion. "When I first heard that Melissa Byers was dead," she wrote, "sadly, I was not surprised. From my first encounter with John Mark and Melissa Byers, it seemed that trouble wasn't even their middle name, but came first, with a capital T." She noted that Christopher was dead, that now Melissa was dead, and that "for John Mark Byers, there will always be a perpetual dark cloud hanging over his head because, for many, there are still too many unanswered questions that began during the investigation of the West Memphis killings."

350. Investigator Stan Witt reported being advised "that the autopsy report could not be completed until the toxicology results were completed, and the case was still in toxicology." Witt then asked to be transferred to the toxicology section. "Personnel in toxicology advised this investigator that the case was not in toxicology," he wrote, "and their tests had been completed for quite some time. They advised they didn't know where the case was at this time, and redirected this investigator back to the medical examiner's section. . . . Personnel in the medical examiner's section . . . advised they didn't know what the status of the case was, but they would research it." About thirty minutes later, Witt wrote, "personnel advised this investigator that the case was currently in the trace evidence section, where tests were being performed for arsenic and other types of poisoning."

351. The plea agreement was approved by Stewart Lambert, deputy prosecuting attorney for Arkansas's Third Judicial District. Officiating in the case was circuit judge Harold Erwin.

352. The deputy prosecutor was Stewart Lambert; the venue, Sharp County Circuit Court.

353. Article 2, Section 21 of the state constitution is titled "Life, liberty and property—Banishment prohibited." In comments made to the author in December 1997, Stewart Lambert, the deputy prosecutor who arranged the deal, said, "Our

understanding on that type of condition is that if it's by agreement with counsel and the defendant, a condition like that is legal. We don't have a right just to tell someone to leave the county, but if it's agreed upon, we understand it's okay. We didn't just get together at a corner of the courthouse and say, 'Get out of town.' " Two years later, however, the Arkansas Supreme Court issued a ruling reiterating the constitutional ban on exile under any terms (*Reeves v. State*, #CR98-872).

354. The crime lab's director was Jim Clark.

355. Stephen A. Erickson, M.D., an associate medical examiner, was the pathologist of record.

356. A prison inmate serving time for drugs told investigators in a written statement that he had known the Byerses. "I can remember Mark giving her pills and other drugs on more than one occasion," he wrote. A seventeen-year-old from Cherokee Village told Witt that, on the day Melissa died, he had been "partying" with the Byerses at their residence, "drinking Crown Royal and taking Valium and Xanax, and that he saw Mark Byers with a sandwich baggie of K-4 Dilaudid." The third person interviewed was Mandy Beasley, the woman who'd been at the Byerses' house when Witt and other officers conducted their search. In December 1997, Beasley told Witt that on that night, "Byers told her that he had three syringes in the bottom drawer of the chef robe [*sic*] dresser in their bedroom that he hoped the police didn't find. She advised that Byers did not tell her whether or not the syringes had anything in them, and that police did not find the syringes, and later on that night Byers threw them away." Beasley also told Witt that she lived with Byers for two months following Melissa's death. She said that during that time, "he threatened her life if she ever told anyone about the syringes." Attorney Dan Stidham later interviewed Beasley, as did this author. Beasley told both that she had been having an affair with Byers, that Melissa had found out, and that on the day she died, Melissa had told Mark she was going to divorce him.

357. In an author interview in January 2002, former Arkansas State Police trooper Brant Tosh reported that he was a bit surprised when he learned that his caller was John Mark Byers. Tosh had been a deputy sheriff in Craighead County when the West Memphis murders occurred, and in the months after the arrests, he'd encountered all three of the defendants. "I transported Damien Echols to Tucker Max twice," he recalled. "And I had to baby-sit Jason Baldwin there in the detention center after his conviction. I also drove Jessie Misskelley to a meeting in Clay County one night." Asked about that trip, which led to Jessie's controversial interrogation by prosecutor Davis, Tosh reflected, "I was a young officer back then. I just remember that he talked all the way. It just seemed he had the mind of a seven-year-old. It struck me that he seemed very childish, like way behind his age."

358. Circuit judge Ralph Wilson.

359. Deputy prosecutor Stewart Lambert.

360. Arkansas State Police officer Brant Tosh testified at the hearing in which Byers's probation was revoked. But when he later checked on the disposition of those cases he was surprised. Looking them up on the computer, he said, "This is not the typical disposition." Tosh reported that Byers had been sentenced to sixty months for the residential burglary and sixty months for theft of property, plus twelve months on the charge of contributing to the delinquency of a minor. To-

gether, the sentences totaled 132 months, or eleven years—three years more than the eight years he was ultimately ordered to serve in prison. Prosecutor Brent Davis, citing pending appeals in the West Memphis murder case, declined to be interviewed for this book.

361. For most of his incarceration, Byers was held at the Delta Regional Unit, in Dermott, Arkansas.

362. Byers spoke about his first marriage but made no mention of his conviction for having threatened his first wife's life. He said that after jewelry school, he'd risen quickly through the ranks of Gordon Jewelers, until 1981, when the chain's management wanted him to move to Houston "to be a home-office supervisor over 168 stores." He claimed his wife didn't want to move to Houston, "and so being the good, Southern Baptist family man that I was raised up to be, I chose my family and resigned." Byers said he'd "felt used" after that marriage failed, but insisted that he had "never hit a woman." To the contrary, he insisted, "It takes a very small man to strike a woman."

363. He said he'd described the dream in the presence of the filmmakers after Melissa had mentioned that she'd been raped. "She used that rape as part of her reason for why she did drugs," he said. "I was telling her the story about the dream to help her see that that didn't make sense. I told her, 'If this had happened to me, like I had dreamed, would that give me an excuse to do drugs?' But the filmmakers, they edited where I said this was a story. They left out that it was a dream."

364. Byers quickly added, however, that he's "never had a bad temper" and that he was, in fact, "a very mild-mannered person." Nevertheless, he said, he'd taken a course in anger management in prison. He said that while some inmates were required to take the course, he had volunteered.

365. Author interview, November 2001.

366. Melissa's parents were Dorris and Kilburn "Dee" DeFir.

367. "When they moved up there," Dee DeFir said, "we paid for gas to heat the house and so Ryan could have hot water. They didn't have a telephone, so I had a phone put in and the bill sent to me, just so Melissa and Ryan could call us. I paid the telephone bill and the gas bill. We brought groceries up there to them at least once a month."

368. "Mark might have had something to do with it," Dorris DeFir said. Her husband agreed, "We don't want nothing to do with him." Yet they express no interest—and see little point—in any future legal inquiry. "If he killed her and got away with it," they say, "he'll pay for it in the long run."

369. Rick Murray was now living in Tennessee. In his letter to the Web site, which was posted in May 2000, he wrote: "I know the people who are close to this thing, and I know that people were mad about it, and they were wanting it to be solved quick. It got to the point where they weren't thinking about the truth, they were only listening to what the police and the reporters were telling them." He continued, "There was no evidence to convict the three who are in prison and everybody knows this. They just don't want to see it this way because it's easier to believe that the police got the right people." In a subsequent interview, Murray said he had never signed papers to allow Byers to adopt Christopher and that Byers's claims

that the adoption had taken place were false. Murray is entitled to see Arkansas records pertaining to the reported adoption, if they exist, but as of this writing, he had not pursued that option. If his statement is correct, and Christopher never was adopted, his burial under the name of Byers would constitute an early and significant legal error.

370. Information about Byers's location while on parole was not part of the public record. However, sources reported that after his release from prison, he was granted permission to move to eastern Tennessee.

371. In fact, the documentary opened with scenes from the video footage shot by the police during the recovery of the three victims' bodies. Hobbs had signed a release and accepted payment for her participation in the film, but she claimed in her lawsuit that she'd been extremely upset at the time and not competent to enter into a contract.

372. She claimed that the availability of the photos on the site had caused her great emotional distress. This time she prevailed. As a result of her complaint, eBay announced that it would modify its policy and no longer allow the sale of morgue and crime scene photos. Rob Chestnut, an attorney for eBay, pointed out, however, that the issue was not a simple one. "The people who monitor our site really focus on the illegal items," he said, "and there is nothing illegal about crime scene photos." Reported by the Associated Press, September 25, 2000.

373. When word of the exchange was passed to members of the Arkansas media, a reporter called the governor's office to clarify the matter but the aide would not return her calls. Prosecutor Brent Davis would not comment either, saying that the matter should be decided in the courts. "I regret my involvement that led to the documentary," he said. "In hindsight, I think it was poor judgment and I don't think I'm going to make the same mistake twice." The supporter who wrote to the governor's office asking that he "look into this case and see if there is something you may be able to do," was Johnny Bratton Jr., of Cabot, Arkansas. The governor's aide who responded on March 23, 2000, was Teena L. Watkins.

374. Web site cofounder Kathy Bakken signed up for the course taught by Brent E. Turvey, a self-employed criminal profiler based in San Leandro, California. Turvey lists among his credentials a master's degree in forensic science from the University of New Haven, located in West Haven, Connecticut. He was a partner in Knowledge Solutions LLC, a company that specialized in criminal profiling.

375. In November 2001, Turvey wrote a similar analysis of information from Arkansas State Police files about the death of Melissa Byers. That "equivocal death analysis" concluded, "This examiner's review of the autopsy report would suggest that this death was not likely consistent with natural causes, given the victim's history, and given that no natural causes were found. It would also suggest that this death was not likely consistent with suicide, given the nature of the needle marks, abrasions and contusion that could suggest the involvement of a second individual. It would also suggest that this death was not likely consistent with accidental causes."

376. "Personally, we felt they were innocent and that they deserved a new trial because there were so many questions," Berlinger said, "but we weren't making an advocacy film. To me, it was clearly a film about injustice, and it showed the trial to be a mockery, but we weren't trying to shove that down peoples' throats. The

majority of people saw it the way we saw it. But to my surprise and dismay, that 20 percent confused our desire to present a full portrait and our lack of narration with the idea that the film was saying, 'Those fucking kids got what they deserved.' " Berlinger said that members of that latter group cited clips of Damien in the courtroom as evidence of his guilt. "Damien was a young, narcissistic kid, and his behavior was apparently part of the reason people thought he must be guilty. We felt we had to include scenes like the one of him combing his hair in the courtroom, and talking about being remembered as 'the West Memphis bogeyman,' because those are what make a full portrait. They said, 'This is what Damien was like when he was put on trial. This is what he was like on the stand, being questioned about Aleister Crowley.' It's not there to say he's guilty, but to say that somebody with this kind of personality and this kind of intelligence in this part of the world, in this kind of case can be found guilty for being this way."

377. A headline in the *Wall Street Journal* noted: "Documentary Raises Questions About Teens' Guilt but Strays Into Support-Group Babble." But most critics seemed most taken up by the extensive footage of Byers. One wrote that Byers's numerous orations left the impression "of a very bad actor imitating grief." Others called him "strange" and "obsessed." Another wrote that Byers seemed "to be playacting, as if dramatizing his psychic turmoil will make it more real to the public (and to him)." Still another reflected, "He's starring in his own horror movie, and not only does he understand this fact, he seems to thrive on it." Howard Rosenberg, of the *Los Angeles Times*, took a more cautious view. In a review published in March 2000, Rosenberg noted that Byers was paid an "honorarium" for participating in *Revelations*—a fact that the writer said made him, in effect, "a paid performer" and tainted the film's credibility.

378. Matt Zoller Seitz, March 12, 2000.

379. From an article headlined "Sequel Rekindles Doubts in Triple Murder Case" by Cathy Frye and Kenneth Heard, February 20, 2000.

380. "So one day," Berlinger recalled, "I was sitting in my underwear after a very long day and I flipped on the television. It was January 2000, and Roger Ebert was doing his annual show at the end of the year, where he sat down with Bill Clinton, and Clinton was saying that his top pick of the year was *The Hurricane* [Norman Jewison's 1999 film starring Denzel Washington about the controversial murder conviction of prizefighter Rubin 'Hurricane' Carter]. Clinton was saying all these things about what a great film it was, and I was flabbergasted. I kept thinking, 'Hey, fella, you should see a film about what's gone on in your own state.' "

381. Bland's piece appeared in an issue of the *Rocket*, one of many publications catering to Seattle's vibrant music scene.

382. Also featured were the Clash's Joe Strummer with the Long Beach Dub All-stars, the John Doe Thing, L7, Murder City Devils, Tony Scalzo of Fastball, Nashville Pussy, former Breeders singer Kelley Deal, Rocket from the Crypt, Mark Lanegan, Zeke and Killing Joke—who had reunited specifically for the cause. Portions of Jello Biafra's performance "The Murder of Mumia Abu Jamal," were also used on the CD. In interviews that accompanied the CD's release, the Supersuckers' lead singer, Eddie Spaghetti, explained, "I guess the thing that touches me about those guys is the fact that it could be any one of us." Doe said, "The world is unfair, damn it, and we're here to keep it a little more fair in any

small way we can" (*Arkansas Times*, April 21, 2000). Earle, who'd spent a year in prison himself on a drug charge, said his opposition was to the death penalty, period. Bland told a reporter for the *Willamette Week* (October 10, 2000), "The best we can do in this situation is just make sure that the authorities in Arkansas don't get away with anything, that whatever happens is publicized, that people know about it." He added, "Tom Waits said something about this case. He said, 'The worst two things you can be in our justice system are poor and different, and these guys were both.' "

383. The notes were written by Burk Sauls, who warned that a CD such as this could, in some jurisdictions, send a person possessing it "on a horrible descent through the criminal justice system, and eventually into a lifetime in a maximum security prison." Sauls wrote that the inmates for whom it was made "liked the kind of music that's on this CD. They wrote poetry and read Stephen King and Shakespeare and wore black concert T-shirts. That was enough for the judge and jury." The notes referred listeners to the www.wm3.org Web site, and to the Justice Project's Campaign Against Wrongful Executions at TheJusticeProject.org.

384. From an article titled "Death Penalty Ignites a Musical Coalition," by Ann Powers, in the *New York Times*, June 27, 2001.

385. A letter to Todd and Dana Moore from Bruce Carlock, owner of Music City Record Distributors, and Scott "Perk" Perkins, vice president of retail, was posted on the MidSouthJustice.com Web site. In the letter the chain's owner explained, "After speaking with the mother of one of the murdered victims and the chief investigating officer in the case, we have made the decision to support the victims' families by not carrying this release. The case has gone through multiple reviews and appeals, all the way up to the Arkansas Supreme Court, and the judgment of each appeal confirmed the guilt of the accused."

386. Robert Christgau's review in the *Village Voice* was published in November 8, 2000.

387. One of the Supersuckers' own CDs was titled *The Evil Powers of Rock and Roll*.

388. The reviewer for the *Village Voice* understood the phenomenon. "These three unjustly convicted outcasts may have identified with big shots like Megadeth on their black T-shirts," Christgau wrote, "but in fact they were scuzzballs like Zeke. As young bands turn into old road warriors like L7 and Rocket From the Crypt, they meet many fellow scuzzballs along the way, and this piece of outreach puts that connection into musical practice."

389. Dotty Oliver's article "Hurricane in Arkansas" appeared in the March 21, 2001, issue of the *Little Rock Free Press*.

390. Similarly, Martin assured readers that the documentaries had "omitted much of the less sensational yet damning evidence." But again, he said nothing about what that "damning evidence" was.

391. Author interview, April 2001.

392. "There's been a lot of suggestion about the murders happening somewhere else," Fogleman said. "And we seriously considered that. But [since] they were last seen in that general area about six o'clock the night before, what you would have

to conclude, if they were killed somewhere else, is that they were abducted in that general area, taken somewhere else and murdered, and then taken back to the place—where people would have been searching—to dispose of the bodies. Criminals aren't smart, but I think they're smarter than that."

393. Fogleman said he had been convinced of Damien's guilt in part by some of the books he'd read, "some songs, and some of his own writings that were kind of bizarre; they dealt with death and blood and stuff like that, and his apparent obsession with black, which kind of fit the mold of some of these people who believe in animal sacrifice and all that." Then too, there'd been Fogleman's own earlier experience, meeting Damien in juvenile court, which Fogleman had found "unnerving." Recalling when Damien was brought into court after he'd attempted to run away with Deanna, Fogleman said, "I remember the way he just turned and looked at me. And it wasn't evil. It wasn't laughing. It wasn't sad. It was just blank. There wasn't anything there. I commented to somebody at the time, the way his eyes were, and how empty they seemed. At that point, I just thought it was odd."

394. The Arkansas Supreme Court has ruled that inmates have no constitutional right to have a court-appointed lawyer for their postconviction appeals. Whether to appoint one or not is left to the discretion of the trial court.

395. Mallett, who was in line at the time to become president of the National Association of Criminal Defense Lawyers (NACDL), said that each year hundreds of criminal defense lawyers agree to work on difficult cases pro bono, or for free. He explained that he became involved in the West Memphis case while attending an annual meeting of the NACDL. Mallett said he was standing in the back of a conference room, talking to a friend, Robert Fogelnest of New York, when the organization's staff person for indigent defense matters walked to the podium. Fogelnest, a past president of the organization, motioned for Mallett to be quiet. "He said, 'Be quiet. I want to hear this,' " Mallett recalled. "'It's about a guy from Arkansas.' " Mallett didn't hear the particulars of the case, but he understood that a group was forming to help with the Arkansas death row inmate's postconviction appeals. Fogelnest told him that he and Scheck had agreed to help. "I said, 'Sure, sign me up,' " Mallett recalled. "At that time I didn't even know the name of the defendant. It was probably a couple of hours later, when we were out of the meeting, that I asked what the case was about." Fogelnest explained that he and Scheck had been asked to review the movie *Paradise Lost*, in hopes that their approval might be used to help in the film's promotion. "But, in fact," Mallett said, "after seeing it, they were shocked, dismayed, and offended by the conduct of the defense attorneys." Mallett said that the two New York attorneys had found it incredible that the lawyers representing the teenagers had agreed to let them participate in the film, both before and during their trials. Scheck and Fogelnest reportedly felt that at the very least, that decision had created a distraction, taking the attorneys' focus away from their clients' defense. "I agreed with that," Mallett said. He, Scheck, and Fogelnest discussed the case after the meeting and concluded that the Arkansas attorneys' decisions with regard to the film provided a strong starting point for a Rule 37 petition.

396. The payment was to be broken down as follows: Price, $30,500; Davidson, $25,000; Stidham and Crow were to split $40,000; and Ford and Wadley would split $46,500.

397. For their services, Lax was paid $7,000 plus interest, Warren Holmes was paid $1,216 plus interest, and Dr. Richard Ofshe was paid $1,500 plus interest.

398. When the filmmakers learned that Damien's new lawyer from Houston was intending to use their film as proof of Damien's ineffective assistance of counsel, they were astonished. In an interview in February 2002, Sinofsky commented, "I think it's got to be one of the most ridiculous defenses in the world." Far from working against Damien, he said, the film had focused attention on the case and had helped attract the new lawyers to it. Despite the filmmakers' chagrin, they agreed to work with Mallett. "We said, 'Fine, do what you have to do,' " Sinofsky recalled, " 'but we don't think we did anything wrong.' We felt that, if the defense worked, and the Rule 37 hearings brought about justice, we wouldn't care what was said about us."

399. Jessie and Jason filed their petitions *pro se*, meaning that they did not have the official help of a lawyer in drafting them. Both, however, are professionally written. Stidham said "a little bird" helped write Jessie's. The "little bird" was necessary, in part, because one of Jessie's claims was that his lawyer had been ineffective in several respects. The petition noted that one of Jessie's "principal lawyers at trial, Dan Stidham, had never tried a murder case as lead counsel. Many of the issues encountered and raised during the course of this case were issues with which neither attorney Stidham nor his co-counsel Mr. Crow were familiar." In addition to Jessie's Rule 37 petition, Stidham also filed a petition with the state Supreme Court for a rehearing of his case. In Jessie's petition for a rehearing, filed March 6, 1996, Stidham argued that police had withheld pertinent evidence when Officer Allen and other detectives "somehow forgot to turn over to the defense the tape recording of the little boy's voice which was used during the interrogation. This tape recording, which this court said gave it 'pause' . . . [and] came 'perilously close to psychological overbearing,' was not even disclosed to the defense until the suppression hearing itself." Jason raised seven issues in his petition, the most striking of which was his charge that the prosecutors and Judge Burnett had engaged in official misconduct when they met after discovery of Damien's blood-specked pendant, without the defense lawyers present.

400. Mallett was joined in his work on Damien's Rule 37 petition by Arkansas attorney Alvin Schay.

401. At the end of the second trial, Judge Burnett told a reporter for the *Memphis Commercial Appeal*, "You kept expecting it to reach that level, what I described as the ordinary criminal trial, where there are no more surprises, where it just goes from this point to the end. And it never happened in either of those trials."

402. The hearing began on May 5, 1998. It was continued to June 9–10, 1998; October 26–28, 1998; and March 18–19, 1999. They were also divided between the courthouses in Jonesboro and Marion.

403. The Web site founders' growing familiarity with the case affected them in ways they had not expected. "I've learned so much," Sauls said in an interview in 2001. "It's a paradox. I respect some aspects of the criminal justice system, and I have complete mistrust in others. It's owned, operated, and run by human beings. That's its strength and that's its weakness." Bakken said that before her involvement, she'd lived in "an idealistic bubble." "I believed I was being protected by the

forces of justice and the police. Now, all that has been stripped away." She added, "But at the same time, it's like, wow, people can make a difference. I've become more cynical and more hopeful all at the same time." Pashley said that before he heard of West Memphis, he "wasn't sure" about the death penalty, but that now he is "definitely" against it. "I came into this being an idealist," he said, "thinking that our justice system was the best in the world. And it is. But it's got so many flaws that now I know that even if I get pulled over for a little traffic offense, I'm going to get a lawyer before I answer questions from the police."

404. Dr. Thomas J. David, a forensic odontologist and consultant to the Georgia medical examiner's office, agreed with the view that at least one set of marks in the photos of Stevie Branch appeared to have been made by a human bite. Dr. Harry Mincer, a consultant in forensic odontology to the medical examiner of Shelby County, Tennessee, testified that he did not believe the marks were from a human bite.

405. The forensic dentist who testified he was called to the crime lab to examine the bodies was Dr. Kevin Dugan of North Little Rock, Arkansas.

406. Damien and Jason both claim that they did not authorize their attorneys to use the money in their trust funds. Damien expected the money to go to his infant son, Seth. And Jason wanted his fund to go to his mother. Nevertheless, defense counsel emptied the trusts.

407. "Again," Mallett wrote, "there is the appearance here of a conflict of interest. Counsel didn't question Byers about the allegation that he had committed a burglary of a jewelry store and the taking of property, which would have been a serious felony if prosecuted."

408. Not stopping with the attorneys, Mallett also criticized Judge Burnett for not having stepped aside to allow a different judge to hear the Rule 37 petition. Mallett pointed out that the judge himself had been a witness to the trial, as when he'd noted from the bench that he'd always allotted money for expert witnesses in the past. "Because of the inherent conflict between the court's role as an elected judge and the court's role as witness," he wrote, "these proceedings have been, and remain, fundamentally unfair." This issue has been raised before the Arkansas Supreme Court many times, and the court has repeatedly ruled that "the allegation is insufficient to overcome the presumption that the trial judge is impartial."

409. According to affidavit of Glori Shettles, December 27, 2000.

410. In January 2001, the Arkansas legislature passed Act 1780. It allowed persons convicted of a crime to seek retesting of DNA evidence that might demonstrate their "actual innocence."

411. Mallett was assisted in his presentation by Rob Owen, an attorney from Austin, Texas. Senior assistant attorney general David Raupp argued the case for the state.

412. As quoted by reporter Drew Jubera in the *Atlanta Journal-Constitution*, February 22, 2002.

413. Burnett had been wrong, Associate Justice Donald L. Corbin wrote, "to deny review of issues raised in death cases on a purely procedural basis, without first exercising great care to assure that the denial rests on solid footing."

414. In its ruling remanding the petition to Burnett, the state Supreme Court had rejected Mallett's contention that the judge should have recused himself from the Rule 37 proceedings. The court ruled that Mallett's argument that there was an inherent conflict in asking a judge to rule on the fairness of a trial over which he himself had presided was "insufficient to overcome the presumption that the trial judge is impartial."

415. Ironically, at the same time the high court was being asked to evaluate the performance of Damien's original lawyers, it was quietly taking action to disbar one of the lawyers who had represented Jason. On June 21, 2001, the Arkansas Supreme Court, citing "serious professional misconduct," issued an order barring George Robin Wadley from the practice of law. The court cited Wadley for accepting payment for legal work he never performed and for lying to the court and to his clients. None of the complaints for which Wadley was censured, however, involved his work on Jason's case. The following year, the Arkansas Public Defender Commission fired Damien's lead lawyer, Val Price. In April 2002, the commission accused Price of using office funds to pay for personal items, such as Christmas cards and trips to Arkansas Razorback football games. According to a letter made public by the commisison's executive director, Price admitted to the allegations.

416. In March 2002, the Arkansas Supreme Court did, however, designate Judge Burnett as chair of its Committee on Criminal Practice.

417. "When I started on this," Mallett reflected, "I thought, 'I have a child who someday will be eight years old.' Now, I have a child and he was eight years old. He's ten. And these boys are still in jail. And those eight-year-olds who were killed don't get any older."

418. Mayor Keith Ingram, announcing that Gitchell would be missed "by all but the criminal element he dealt with," proclaimed May 19, 1994, as "Gary Gitchell Day."

419. "The Fight to Free the West Memphis 3," by Stephen Lemons, August 10, 2000.

420. "Did Arkansas Town Go on a Witch Hunt, or Are Activists Playing the 'Redneck' Card?" by Drew Jubera, February 11, 2002.

421. The total found to be missing was $28,757.19. Driver was chief custodian of the fund, which was set up to hold fees paid by juvenile probationers. The audit covered a three-year period that had begun in September 1993, three months after Damien, Jason, and Jessie were arrested. State auditors reported that during those three years, sixty-eight unauthorized checks had been written to or endorsed by Driver, while two other unauthorized checks had gone to Steve Jones, Driver's assistant.

422. In an interview in November 2000, Driver, who was then living in Michigan, said he remained convinced that Damien, Jason, and Jessie had killed the eight-year-olds. When asked why he thought they'd done it, Driver said, "I think it was probably a cross between what they thought was a ritual and a spur-of-the-moment thing." Driver dismissed the convicts' supporters as ill-informed "hangers-on" who'd been influenced by documentaries that were "weighted heavily toward the defendants." Driver was less willing to discuss his own legal troubles. His explanation was simply this: "The politics of Crittenden County are very

convoluted, and evidently, I got on the wrong side of them." "I pled nolo contendere" Driver stressed. "I didn't plead guilty." He described the audit and the resulting charges as "a long, involved situation," adding that he felt he was "kind of a political target," but he declined to elaborate. However, he said, "I will tell you this. I did not have enough money to fight this."

423. The officer now responsible for the evidence locker was Reginia Meek, who had taken the missing-person reports for Christopher and Michael on the night they disappeared. Meek had also taken the call to the Bojangles restaurant, where she'd questioned the manager about the bloody man from her car at the drive-through window.

424. Chief Bob Paudert came to the West Memphis department from a small police force in Missouri. Before that, he had served as a narcotics detective in Memphis. In an author interview in January 2002, Paudert said that, upon his hiring, the mayor of West Memphis told him, "You've got a department that needs help." Soon after his arrival, he said, members of the department reported that certain officers were helping themselves to money and other evidence that was seized during arrests and taking kickbacks from prostitutes and their pimps. Much of the alleged malfeasance centered on the interstate highways, roads that Paudert called "hot corridors" for contraband. According to official records, in the twelve months before the firings, city and county narcotics officers had seized an average of $5,000 a day in drug-related traffic stops on I-40 and I-55. Paudert said that not all of that money, however, was showing up on the books. To address the problems, Paudert said, he had created an internal affairs office—a first for the department—and drafted a procedures manual, which was another first.

425. In the interview in January 2002, Paudert said that none of the allegations of misconduct that had been reported to him related to the department's investigation of the 1993 murders. Sergeant Lawrence Vaughn, head of the department's new internal affairs office, agreed. Vaughn said that he had been working as a uniformed patrol officer in 1993 and had participated in the search for the children. "I was there on the scene at the discovery," he said. "I was there when they were bringing the bodies out of the woods. There were so many people there, we had to set up a perimeter. We were sitting by the hearse. We assisted in putting the bodies into the vehicle." (Inspector Gary Gitchell had begged the crime lab for information about the "Negroid hair" found in the sheet around Christopher's body, but no explanation had surfaced. Yet, during the trials, when defense attorneys had asked the crime lab's trace evidence expert, Lisa Sakevicius, if she had ever received "any Negro type hairs from any West Memphis police officers to compare with the questioned hair," Sakevicius testified that she had not.) Vaughn also reported that Sudbury's role in the murder investigation had been unique within the department. According to Vaughn, after the boys' bodies were found, Gitchell had assigned all of his regular criminal detectives to work the murder investigation, and he'd temporarily reassigned the department's narcotics unit, where Sudbury was second in command, ordering them take over the regular detectives' duties. Vaughn said that Sudbury—who'd been the first West Memphis detective to question Damien, the first to report Jerry Driver's suspicions, and present during key interviews with John Mark Byers and Vicki Hutcheson—was the only narcotics detective whom Gitchell had allowed to participate in the murder investigation. Sudbury, Vaughn recalled, "was the only one who worked both."

426. Damien's son, Seth, born six months before his father's trial, turned eight in 2001. Seth and his mother, Domini, had left Arkansas after the trials, and their contact with Damien in the years that followed had been slim.

427. The wedding, which was approved by Warden Greg Harmon, took place on December 6, 1999.

428. She'd moved to Little Rock, and two years later the couple asked the warden for permission to marry. The wedding ceremony, held in a visitation room at the maximum security unit, began and ended with the sound of a bell. Damien wore his white prison uniform and shackles. His head was shaved in the manner of a Buddhist monk. A Buddhist priest from Little Rock, who also worked as a volunteer chaplain at the prison, performed the ceremony, which was attended by a half dozen of the couple's friends, including some of the supporters from California. Officials at the prison stressed that while inmates generally had a right to marry, they do not have a right to sexual contact. "There was no reception, no honeymoon, no overnight stay in Branson," a prison spokesman said, referring to a popular vacation spot in southern Missouri.

429. "Death Row's Echols Ties the Knot in Prison Fete," by Cathy Frye, December 7, 1999.

430. Though the handling of money was illegal in prison, and Jason had never had much of it to begin with, he was trying to understand finance. "I know to stay away from credit cards," he said. "I know that mutual funds are a safer investment and offer a higher yield, but that right now is the best time to buy stocks. I wish I could get out right now and just buy a bunch of stocks while it's low, and just keep buying stocks every month, every month. . . . I just don't want my kids to live in a trailer park."

Index

Ex parte communications, 282
Expert witness
  cult expert, 210, 231, 232, 236–38, 243–44, 249, 288–89, 328
  funds for, 330, 334–35
  Jessie's trial, 175–76
  payment to, 331, 332

FBI, 44, 204, 343
Fibers, 127, 128, 149, 289, 327
  evidence, 195, 231, 261
  microscopically similar, 120, 136, 166–68, 208–9, 228, 256
Fifth Amendment privilege, 251–52, 253, 264, 289
Filmmakers, 199
  paid defendants for interviews, 330, 331–32, 335
  see also Documentary
Fingerprints, 24, 30, 118, 119, 215
First Amendment, 238, 264
Fogleman, John, 20–21, 35, 39, 45, 49, 56, 90, 92, 95, 96, 126, 132, 135–36, 139, 152, 204, 322, 346–47
  case against J. M. Byers, 154
  circuit judge, 325
  circumstantial evidence, 120
  Damien and Jason's trial, 212, 215, 219, 220–21, 227, 231, 330, 233, 235, 237–38, 239, 247, 249, 252, 259
  Damien and Jason's trial: closing argument, 260–63
  Damien and Jason's trial: knives, 290
  Damien and Jason's trial: meeting with judge, 282
  Damien and Jason's trial: new evidence, 258–59
  Damien and Jason's trial: sentencing phase, 272–73, 274
  and Damien's writings, 210
  evidence, 195–96
  filed charges against Damien, 43
  finding knife, 136–37, 150, 153, 201, 209, 229
  finding whiskey bottle, 197, 198
  and Jessie's confession, 186
  and Jessie's statement, 101, 172–74
  Jessie's trial, 156, 158–60, 161–63, 164–65, 166, 167–71, 175–76, 185

Jessie's trial: closing argument, 189, 190
  offered Jason deal, 257
  possibility of Jessie testifying against Damien and Jason, 192–93, 194–95, 196, 199, 202, 204
  prosecutor's subpoenas, 129–30, 134, 135
  pretrial motions, 128–29, 130–31, 133, 135
  releasing files, 116, 118, 126–27, 138, 140, 146, 149
  on the trial, 326–29
  witnesses, 141, 206, 207
Ford, Paul, 106–7, 125–26, 214
  Damien and Jason's trial, 215–16, 219, 224–25, 226, 231–32, 233, 238, 247, 250, 256, 262–63
  Damien and Jason's trial: closing argument, 264–65
  Damien and Jason's trial: sentencing phase, 274
  motion for new trial, 281–82
  on payment, 331
Forensic analyst, 315–16
Forensic dentists, 334
"Free the West Memphis Three," 1, 2, 292, 293, 319
Free the West Memphis Three (CD), 321–23
Full moon, 5, 39, 236, 238, 239, 241, 289

Gang or cult suggestion, 14–15, 23, 25, 40, 51
Gitchell, Gary W., 9, 10, 19, 35, 72, 74, 102, 107, 112, 130, 137, 142, 155, 166, 170, 198, 204, 207, 216, 218, 248–49, 295, 300, 303, 309, 326, 347
  absence from trial, 264–65
  and accuracy of Jessie's statements, 90–91
  attempt to depose, 134–35
  and blood-stained knife, 147, 149–50
  control of information, 16, 25
  focus on cult activity, 219
  Ford's letter to, 125–26